THE ANNUAL OF THE AMERICAN SCHOOLS OF ORIENTAL RESEARCH

Volumes 47–48

Edited by
Joseph A. Callaway

Vol. 47: THE EXCAVATIONS AT ARAQ EL-EMIR, Vol. 1

Nancy L. Lapp, Editor

Vol. 48: THE AMMAN AIRPORT EXCAVATIONS, 1976

Larry G. Herr, Editor

Published by the
AMERICAN SCHOOLS OF ORIENTAL RESEARCH
1983

THE EXCAVATIONS AT ARAQ EL-EMIR

Volume I

THE ANNUAL OF THE AMERICAN SCHOOLS OF ORIENTAL RESEARCH

Volume 47

Edited by
Joseph A. Callaway

The Excavations at Araq el-Emir

Volume I

by
Nancy L. Lapp

with contributions by

Robin Brown, Jennifer Groot, Michael Toplyn, Gary Cooke, David McCreery, J.-M. Dentzer,
F. Villeneuve, F. Larché, Ernest Will, and Frank M. Cross

Published by the
American Schools of Oriental Research

Distributed by

Eisenbrauns
P.O.B. 275
Winona Lake, IN 46590

Size 2.
DS
153.3
.L3
1983

Library of Congress Cataloging in Publication Data

Lapp, Nancy L., 1930–
    The excavations at Araq el-Emir.

    (The Annual of the American Schools of Oriental
Research ; v. 47)
    Includes bibliographies.
    1. Araq el-Emir Site (Jordan) I. Brown, Robin,
1952–   . II. American Schools of Oriental Research.
III. Title. IV. Series.
DS101.A45 vol. 47, etc. [DS154.9.A7] 930s [933] 83-11819
ISBN 0-89757-047-2

Printed in the United States of America
1   2   3   4   5

Table of Contents

LIST OF CONTRIBUTORS

Robin Brown	State University of New York, Binghamton
Frank M. Cross	Harvard University
Gary A. Cooke	Gulf Research & Development Company, Pittsburgh
J.-M. Dentzer	Institut français d'archéologie du Proche-Orient
Jennifer Groot	Fennville, Michigan
François Larché	Institut français d'archéologie du Proche-Orient
Nancy L. Lapp	Pittsburgh Theological Seminary
David McCreery	University of Montana
Michael Toplyn	Harvard University
François Villeneuve	Institut français d'archéologie du Proche-Orient
Ernest Will	University of Paris, Sorbonne

ABBREVIATIONS USED IN TABLES AND DESCRIPTIONS

sf.; surf.	surface	frag.	fragment
unstr.	unstratified	incl.	inclusions
intru.	intrusive	ext.	exterior
m	medium	int.	interior
l	large	prov.	provenience
s	small	reg.	registration
dia.	diameter	str.	stratum

For abbreviations used in ch. 9 (Skeletal Remains) see Key for the tables, p. 93.
Ware descriptions are given according to Munsell Soil Color Chart, Munsell Color Company 1971.

When provenience identifications are given in the form II.11.26, the first Roman numeral refers to the Field, the second number refers to the area, and the third, to the sherd basket number. Locus numbers are always identified specifically, preceeded by the word 'locus".

CREDITS

Photographs: Dept. of Antiquities of Jordan, figs. 9, 10, 13, 14, 16, 50, 51, 53; James Walther, Jr., figs. 15, 36, 38; Gulf Research (G. Cooke), fig. 17; P. W. Lapp, figs. 2-5, 7, 8, 25-28, 33-36, 41-43; N. L. Lapp, figs. 45, 49; Photography by Dereich, figs. 7-10, and special thanks for custom developing.

Plans and Drawings: M. Brett, plans 1-5, figs. 6, 29, 44; F. Larché, figs. 60-63, 66; J. Muhawi, figs. 46, 48, 52; W. Fulco, figs 9, 10; F. Cross, fig. 12; J. Loynd, fig. 16; B. Zogbi, figs. 19-24; N. Lapp, figs. 30-32; B. R. Gould, figs. 37, 39, 40; A. Yousef, figs. 54-56; with assistance from draftsmen: G. Hall, D. Stilson, J. Loynd, and A. Yousef.

LIST OF FIGURES

LIST OF TABLES

LIST OF PLANS

Introduction

NANCY L. LAPP

Today Araq el-Emir is approached by a paved road from the village of Wadi Sir, now almost a suburb of Amman. For the 1961 and 1962 excavations a roadbed had to be cleared, "bridges" constructed over the wadi, and only with a Landrover would one attempt the trip. Today the excavators and architects commute from Amman; in the '60s the excavators made the trip in on Sunday evening, hopefully before dark, and except for village messengers, police, or occasional adventurous visitors they were isolated from the world until they returned to Jerusalem at the end of the week. Tales can be told of adventures in road-building, lost wheels, and hikes when cars had to be abandoned. Those staff members returning to the site today are amazed at the window-paned stone houses, native-owned cars, and the general prosperity a paved road has brought to the valley.

Just a few years before we began the excavations, C. C. McCown gave directions to the site either by horseback, from near Tell Nimrin west of the site, or by footpath, from Wadi Sir, or from near a bridge over the Wadi Sha'ib to the north (McCown 1957: 3). The early explorers rode horseback for their expeditions in Transjordan.

Situated 17 kilometers west and slightly south of Amman, one approaches Araq el-Emir today from the north, winding around near the wadi floor where a spring, the Ain Deir, supports a number of agricultural villages. One passes flourishing fields and farming homes from which products are trucked to the nearby cities of Amman, Salt, and Zerka. Modern roadways may have changed the way of life and lessened the visitor's sense of adventure, but it has brought prosperity to the inhabitants, and it is a great sight to see the green fields and orchards, even in the middle of a hot dry summer.

As one nears the site of Araq el-Emir the Wadi Sir cleft is on the left, and as one turns to the west the steep cliffs are on the right (figs. 1, 2). Turning again toward the south into the broadening valley (fig. 3) the road leads past the North Gate right up to the Qasr, where one sees the imposing feline fountain, which was uncovered in the 1962 excavations (fig. 4), in the east wall of the monumental building. Still somewhat out of the way for the ordinary foreign tourist, the area attracts the more serious visitor and scores of local Jordanians for whom the flourishing Wadi Sir has become a favorite picnic spot.

The dominant ruin from antiquity is the Qasr el-Abd, situated in a natural depression shielded by hills on the north, northwest, and west. On the east is the Wadi Sir which continues southward beyond Araq el-Emir, dropping sharply into the Wadi Kefrein, which eventually flows into the Jordan River. The Qasr itself sits upon an earthen fill platform surrounded by a rectangular retaining wall. Traces of a dam remain to the south for the retention of water which would have otherwise run off into the steeply plunging wadi bed (see below fig. 57). An ancient aqueduct follows the wadi and then skirts the ancient cliffs. It is in these cliffs that the ancient name *Tobiah* is carved in well-formed Aramaic letters over openings into two of the caves. The ancient village lies on a plateau to the west of the wadi about 300 meters northeast of the Qasr, approximately the site of the small modern settlement (fig. 5).[1] Remains of ancient terraces still surround the village and spread out around the Qasr. Other ancient remains include the "Square Building" north of the Qasr, the Monumental Gate not far from its northeast corner, and evidence of quarrying and worked stones in the area.

Josephus describes the building operations of Hyrcanus, the youngest son of Joseph, a son of Tobiah, during his short control of the area (*Ant.* 12.4.11 §229-236):

Hyrcanus, therefore, gave up his intention of returning to Jerusalem, and settled in the country across the Jordan, where he continually warred on the Arabs until he killed many of them and took many captive. And he built a strong fortress, which was constructed entirely of

[1]For a full description of the village site, see Lapp 1962: 18-19. Descriptions of the caves and Qasr with surroundings can be found in Butler, Conder, and De Saulcy, among others.

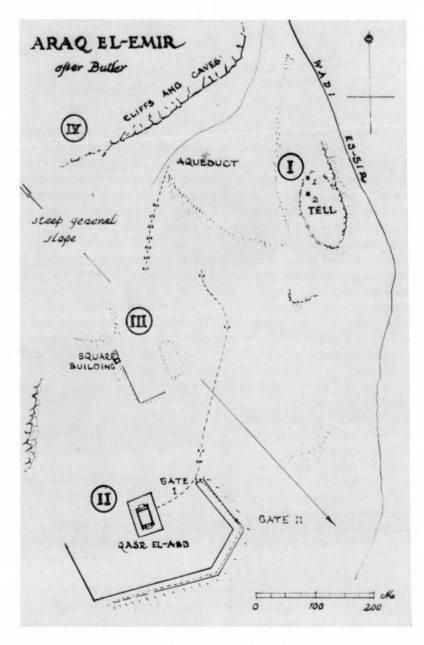

1. Plan of Araq el-Emir environs showing excavation fields.

white marble up to the very roof, and had beasts of gigantic size carved on it, and he enclosed it with a wide and deep moat. He also cut through the projecting rock opposite the mountain, and made caves many stades in length; then he made chambers in it, some for banqueting and others for sleeping and living, and he let into it an abundance of running water, which was both a delight and an ornament to his country-estate. The entrances of the caves, however, he made narrower, so that only one person and no more could enter at one time; and this arrangement he made deliberately for the sake of safety, in order to avoid the danger of being besieged and taken by his brothers. In addition he also built enclosures remarkable for their size, and adorned them with vast parks. And when he had completed the place in this manner, he named it Tyre. This place is between Arabia and Judaea, across the Jordan, not far from Essebonitis [Heshbon]. And he ruled over those parts for seven years, during all the time that Seleucus reigned over Asia. Now when this king died, his brother

2. Looking north toward the caves with the Tobiah inscriptions, excavation camp below.

Antiochus, surnamed Epiphanes, occupied the throne after him. . . . As for Hyrcanus, seeing how great was the power which Antiochus had, and fearing that he might be captured by him and punished for what he had done to the Arabs, he ended his life by his own hand. And all his property was seized by Antiochus.

It was Irby and Mangles who visited Araq el-emir in 1817 and first recognized the site as the location of Tyre of Hyrcanus as described by Josephus (Irby and Mangles 1886: 146). Later travelers left plans of the ruins and accounts of their journeys: de Vogüé (1864), de Saulcy (1865 and 1867) and Conder (1889 and 1892). Conder included in his publications brief discussion of the paleography of the Tobiah inscriptions (1889: 76-77), a description of the etymological relationship between the present Arabic name Wadi Sir and the Greek name of Tyre or Tyros (1892: 170), and an account and interpretation of the local legends concerning the origins of the Qasr el-Abd (1889:

78-79 and 1892: 363-64). More extensive investigation was undertaken by Howard Crosby Butler in 1904 when the Princeton Expedition spent six days at the site. His study resulted in plans and concise descriptions of the ruins, detailed drawings of capitals and other decorative elements from the Qasr el-Abd, and reconstructions which attempted to illustrate the original façades of the collapsed Qasr (Butler 1919).

Historians and epigraphers have also long been interested in Araq el-Emir for its significance concerning the Hellenistic Tobiads. Historical references to the Tobiads are known from several sources including Josephus (Ant. xii.iv.2-v.1), the Old Testament (Ezra 2:60; Nehemiah 2-4, 6-8; 2 Chr 17:8; Zech 6:8-15), and Babylonian documents (Mazar 1957: 231). Although the problematic genealogy of the Tobiads received a resurgence of attention subsequent to the discovery of the Zenon papyri (McCown 1957; Mazar 1957;

3. Looking into the broad valley at the Qasr with the caves above to the northeast.

Tcherikover 1961; 96-105), the correlation of the literature with the various ruins at Araq el-Emir has not yet been conclusively demonstrated.

The knowledge of the site from the brief investigations of de Vogüé, de Saulcy, Conder, and Butler was necessarily limited, and the hope for more extensive investigations had long been expressed (Butler 1919: 2, McCown 1957: 74). It is not surprising that excavators of the 1960's and 1970's should be attracted to Araq el-Emir. Paul W. Lapp undertook his first soundings at Araq el-Emir in 1961 in an attempt to determine the stratigraphical history of the site and to date the construction and subsequent history of the monumental building, the Qasr el-Abd (Lapp 1962: 16). In the second and third campaigns of 1962 more extensive areas were uncovered to clarify the stratigraphical history and gain an understanding of the structures in the Village. The origins of the Qasr still needed confirmation, and an effort was made to obtain evidence for its reconstruction (Lapp 1963: 8, 20).

It is with these excavations of Paul Lapp that this volume is mainly concerned. Lapp had hoped to return to Araq el-Emir for another series of excavations after an interlude for some salvage work and the publication of the early campaigns. He would have liked to investigate the caves and the monumental buildings in the Village, as well as work with an architect for the reconstruction of the Qasr (Lapp 1963: 39; letter of 1 July 1966 to R. Diplock). His untimely death made this impossible.

The Jordan Department of Antiquities took up renewed interest in the site in the mid-1970's, especially in an effort to make Jordan's antiquities attractive for tourism. Efforts were joined with the Institut français d'archéologie du Proche Orient, and a thorough study of the architectural remains was undertaken by E. Will, with the assistance of F. Marché.[2] Partial reconstruction of the Qasr is

[2]See E. Will, 1977, 1979, and ch. 13 below; the final report is now in preparation.

4. The feline fountain discovered in 1962 in the east wall of the Qasr.

now underway (see below fig. 65). In the process of examining and studying the architecture limited excavation and stratigraphical study has taken place. A few reports from the work of the 1970's are in Part II of this volume.

The 1961 and 1962 Excavations

Paul W. Lapp's excavations consisted of three campaigns: a sounding in the spring of 1961 (the "first campaign"), and full campaigns in the fall of 1961 and the spring of 1962.

The first campaign, from April 10-May 6, 1961, was carried out with fifteen full- and part-time staff members, through funds from the 1960-1961 archaeological budget of the Jerusalem School allocated by the Director, and a substantial contribution from the Graduate School of Concordia

Seminary (Lapp 1962: 16).[3] Two areas were opened in the northwest quarter of the Village (Field I), designated Areas I.1 and I.2, in order to test the depth of debris and span of occupation. Four strata were delineated, Nos. I-III of the Hellenistic-Roman period, and No. IV of Iron Age I. Further

[3] Thanks are especially due Professor Oleg Grabar, Director of the School 1960-61, and Professor A. von Rohr Sauer of Concordia Seminary for monetary contributions, as well as all members of the staff: field supervisors and assistants Herbert Huffmon, James Zink, Dean G. McKee, A. von Rohr Sauer, Norman W. Paullin, John D. Zimmerman, Alfred J. Hoerth; Mrs. Herbert Huffmon, registrar, assisted by Mrs. James Zink; James Sauer, pottery recording; G. R. H. Wright, architect; Ahmed Abdullah Hassan, representative from the Department of Antiquities; Muhammed Adawi, cook; Mustafa Tawfiq, foreman.

5. Looking southeast over the excavation camp toward the modern village of Araq el-Emir situated over and around the ancient remains. In the northwest corner of the Village are the Field I excavations.

excavation was needed to refine the later strata and to investigate the extent of the Iron I constructions. The previously unknown Iron I occupation suggested the identification of Araq el-Emir as Ramath-Mizbeh of Joshua 13:24-28 (Lapp 1962: 24). At the Qasr (Field II) three areas were laid out from the center of the Qasr westward across the west Qasr wall (Areas II.1-3), and three were placed against the outside face of the east Qasr wall, Area II.11 at the north and Areas II.12 and 13 at the southeast corner (plan 1). Three periods of occupation were disclosed, two of the Byzantine period and one of the Hellenistic. The Hellenistic evidence was very limited, but seemed to point to the early second century B.C. as the earliest occupation in the area during Hellenistic times (Lapp 1962: 33-34). No evidence regarding the function of the building was forthcoming, and full excavation was planned.

The second campaign lasted from September 4 to October 20, 1961, and the third from Septem-

ber 10 to October 12, 1962. The staffs consisted substantially of members and residents of the Jerusalem School, and both campaigns were supported by the regular archaeological budget of the Jerusalem School. In the second campaign a substantial grant was secured from Iliff School of Theology and a contribution was obtained from Bethany Biblical Seminary. A substantial grant for the third campaign was made by Princeton University, and a contribution toward the cost of labor was made by the Jordan Department of Antiquities (Lapp 1963: 8).[4]

[4]Special thanks are due Walter Williams of the Iliff School of Theology, David Wieand of Bethany Biblical Seminary, R. B. Y. Scott of Princeton University, and Awni Dajani of the Jordan Department of Antiquities for the contributions they obtained on behalf of their institutions. Staff members of the second campaign included Field Supervisors Dorothea Harvey, Murray Nicol, Walter Williams, David Wieand, John Zimmerman, James Jones; Mrs. Murray Nicol and Mrs. Walter

In the Village (Field I) during the second campaign the area between the original two squares was cleared to obtain a section and to discover the natures of structures which might be excavated completely (Areas I.1-12). In the third campaign the area within the two major walls, N-1 and W-1 (plans 2, 3) was cleared as completely as possible and the area west of W-1 was investigated for what was at first thought might be an Iron I fortress. The basic stratigraphy remained the same, though an earlier Hellenistic phase was defined (becoming Stratum IV) and Early Bronze surfaces appeared in limited areas which were designated Stratum VI (see below). The western extension uncovered what became known as the "Plaster Building" (Areas I.14, 16, 21, 23; plan 4); belonging to Stratum IV, it can be associated with the extensive building operations of Hyrcanus described by Josephus. Lapp concluded that this is very likely one of the *aulē* Josephus referred to in his account when he describes "enclosures remarkable for their size" (Ant. 12.233).[5]

At the Qasr (Field II) more information was sought concerning the origins of the Qasr, and sections were obtained north-south through the center of the Qasr (Areas II.6-10), from the center westward past the west retaining wall (Areas II.1-5), and south from the southeast corner of the building (Areas II.12-14). In the third campaign special effort was put forth to unearth evidence for the architect's reconstruction of the building (Areas II.15-22). The most spectacular find was the feline fountain sculptured in high relief near the northeast corner of the east Qasr wall (below fig. 25). More second century B.C. pottery was found, but only detailed study of the finds and the stratification brought forth the archaeological evidence for the date of the construction of the Qasr (see below

and ch. 7). The stratified Byzantine pottery groups provide important normative material for the mid-forth and the late fifth centuries A.D.

The Square Building (Field III, plan 5), which had visible evidence of a similar history to that of the Qasr, was excavated in the fall of 1961 in hopes that it may provide indirect evidence for dating the construction of the Qasr. The layers excavated did correspond to those at the Qasr. The "Square Building" itself was of Byzantine construction, Stratum II, while the small monumental building with affinities to the Qasr belonged to Stratum III. Beneath was an earlier layer from the Early Bronze horizon, designated Stratum IV.

Preliminary reports of the three campaigns were published soon after the excavations (Lapp 1962, 1963), D. Hill (1963) published a study of the feline fountain, and M. Brett, architect for the third campaign, published a proposed reconstruction of the Qasr (1963). P. W. Lapp did some preliminary studies on the pottery, glass, and the history of the site, but it was the late 70's before definitive work was undertaken for the final publication.

The Name of the Site

Considerable confusion has surrounded the transliteration of the name of the site, Araq el-Emir. Early transliterations included ꞌArâk el-Emīr (Conder 1889) and Aâraq el-Emyr (de Saulcy 1867). Today Jordanians as well as other scholars prefer the dialectic form ꞇIraq el-Emir (cf. Brown 1979, Lapp 1976), while the French seem to prefer a classical spelling, ꞇIraq al-Amir (Will 1979). It has been decided to continue in this publication the principle form for the name of the site during the period of modern investigation, following that used by W. F. Albright and P. W. Lapp. Frank Cross writes in a letter to the author:

> I should avoid classical notation as WFA and Paul always did (not ꞌal-ꞌAmīr), but use modern: ꞌel-ꞌEmīr. For the first element, I think I should follow WFA and PL with ꞇArâq. Such a form exists dialectically. However, I suspect the Jordanian form is ꞇIrâq.

Unfortunately, due to necessary accomodation to printing costs, it is impossible to supply the diacritical marks throughout the volume.

An ꞇarâq has been variously translated "cave," "cavern," or "cliff." The term can also mean "rock-veins" or "mountain road." Cross writes that "veined cliff" is probably close to its meaning, that is a mountain side or cliff with crevices or caves.

Williams, recorders; Peter Parr, W. Lankester, J. Kikuchi, architect and assistants. For the third campaign field supervisors were Alexander DiLella, Dorothy Hill, George Landes, John Zimmerman, William Casey, Sten Lundgren, and Carney Gavin; Michael Brett was architect, and R. B. Y. Scott was Associate Director and recorder. For both campaigns Ahmed Hassan represented the Jordan Department of Antiquities, Mrs. Paul Lapp was business manager, Mustafa Tawfiq was foreman, and Muhammed Adawi was cook. Paul W. Lapp was Director and photographer for the second and third campaign as well as the first.

[5]That is *aulas tō (i) megethei diapherousas*. As Lapp notes (1963: 20), *aulē* could well be a court or quadrangle "round which the house itself was built, having a corridor all around," according to Liddell and Scott.

ᵓ*Emīr* is of course "prince," and the name of the site means "cave of the prince." The *Qaṣr el-ᶜAbd* means "castle of the slave," and Conder tells about the local legends which gave rise to this name (1889: 78-79 and 1892: 363-64).

Stratification of the Qasr and the Square Building (Fields II and III)

The various investigators and excavators of the Qasr at Araq el-Emir during the nineteenth and twentieth centuries have sought to delineate its history and relation to the surrounding ruins. The Qasr has long been considered a Hellenistic building, and it was described in detail by Josephus as part of the building operations of Hyrcanus (see above). Archaeological collaboration of this information was hoped to be forthcoming in the excavations undertaken in 1961 and 1962. When the evidence after the first campaign proved inconclusive, excavation was undertaken in the spring of 1962 at the Square Building where visible architectural fragments indicated construction contemporary with the Qasr. It was hoped that indirect evidence from the Square Building might date the Qasr.

Occupation and stratification were indeed similar; the same pottery horizons and periods of occupation were present at both the megalithic and the smaller monumental buildings (Fields II and III). Details supplement one another, so the stratification of the Qasr and Square Building, Strata I-IV, can be presented together.[6]

Stratum IV

In the massive fills which form the platform for the Qasr small quantities of Early Bronze I A and Early Bronze IV pottery were consistently present. No floor levels or constructions witnessed to occupation in this area, so the evidence was either disturbed or in the fills imported for the building of the Qasr. At the Square Building only EB sherds were found in the layer of green clay on bedrock, an occupational layer laid by EB occupants. Stratum IV then represents the earliest occupation in the area of the monumental buildings, dating to the Early Bronze I A and the Early Bronze IV periods.

[6]For P. W. Lapp's discussion of the stratification see his preliminary reports, especially 1962: 29, 32-34; 1963: 32-38.

Stratum III

The determinations after the 1961 and 1962 campaigns that the Qasr was of Hellenistic construction was due to its architectural style, the historical references, and the scattered Hellenistic sherds rather than decisive stratigraphical evidence. Detailed study of the pottery has shown that layers associated with the Qasr's construction consisted of fills which contained a few Hellenistic as well as EB sherds (Lapp 1963: 22, n. 25, and see Hellenistic pottery discussion below, ch. 7). Pottery evidence and the stratigraphy thus corroborate the laying of the Qasr foundations in the early second century B.C. At the Square Building, Stratum III represents the small monumental building with affinities to the Qasr. Inside the later "square" building well-finished slabs below the Byzantine floors may have served as part of a Stratum III floor. Outside the building a sandy layer separated later remains from a system of terrace walls (see plan 5 and section, fig. 6) associated with the Stratum III construction.

Stratum III thus represents the monumental building operations of Hyrancus in the first quarter of the second century B.C.

Stratum II

Following the construction of the Qasr, left unfinished by the Hellenistic builders, the monumental buildings were not used for sedentary occupation until early in the Byzantine period. Stratum II represents reoccupation by the Byzantines when they made use of the internal Qasr wall foundations, added walls to support their roofs especially outside the east and west Qasr walls, and laid soil and plaster floors. Two floors of Stratum II were distinguished at a number of places at the Qasr, with the earliest at the level of the Hellenistic pavement either replacing the Hellenistic pavement or providing one where the early builders had never done so. Stratum II at the Square Building is the period of the construction of the "square" building which was the distinguishing feature before the 1962 excavations took place. One floor of Stratum II was delineated there.

Fourth century A.D. pottery is characteristic of Stratum II both at the Qasr and in the Square Building. At the Qasr the tumbled megaliths of the wall onto the Stratum II floors separate Stratum II from the one above. A Theodosius I coin dating to A.D. 393-395 (reg. no. 51) from the fill for the

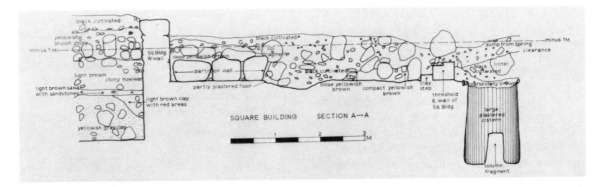

6. Square Building section A-A.

second floor above the destruction debris provides a *terminus ante quem* for the catastrophic event, probably an earthquake. A major earthquake is known to have taken place in Transjordan in A.D. 365 (Kallner-Amiran 1950-51: 225). At the Square Building a Constantine II coin, dated A.D. 335-337 (reg. no. 180) was found in the Stratum II floor east of the building so a *terminus post quem* is provided. The dates, A.D. 335-365, Early Byzantine I (according to Sauer's terminology, 1973: 4), may tentatively be assigned Stratum II, though a detailed study of the pottery may refine these dates.

Stratum I

Following the earthquake at the Qasr a leveling off, which in some areas meant the importation of a massive fill, was necessary to cover the earthquake debris. The main line of the Stratum III Qasr walls continued to be followed with only slight deviations. Two floors were distinguished inside some rooms of the Qasr and outside on the west. On the porches fallen debris precluded occupation. At the Square Building almost a meter of debris and three floors were associated with Stratum I, but no earthquake destruction separated Stratum I from Stratum II. The floors were distinguished both inside and outside the Square Building and some of the Stratum II building features were reused.

The Byzantine pottery of Stratum I is typologically later than that of Stratum II, and more absolute dates can be assigned the stratum by some coins. The Theodosius I coin (A.D. 393-395) was in the fill for the I A floor, that is the second floor above the earthquake debris. Thus a period of time, perhaps about thirty years, can be allowed

for the first phase of occupation in Stratum I. At the Square Building a coin of Arcadius, dated A.D. 383-408 (reg. no. 179), was found laying on the earliest Stratum I floor. In the fill above the latest floor inside the Qasr was a coin of Zeno, A.D. 476-491 (reg. no. 24), suggesting occupation to the end of the fifth century, and the pottery indicates heavy occupation in the latter half. Stratum I can tentatively be dated A.D. 365-500, Early Byzantine II-IV (according to Sauer's terminology, 1973: 4).

To summarize, the strata at the monumental buildings are:

Stratum IV	Early Bronze	
Stratum III	Hellenistic	1st quarter of the 2nd cen. B.C.
Stratum II	Early Byzantine	ca. A.D. 335-365
Stratum I	Early Byzantine	ca. A.D. 365-500

Stratification of the Village (Field I)

Detailed publication of the Village excavations is not presented in this volume, but since some of the included reports consider material and artifacts from the Village a brief summary of its stratification is given below.[7] When the pottery is studied in more detail, some of the dates may have to be adjusted.

Stratum VI

Near the center of the Village excavations, where there was considerable depth of debris, about a meter of loose brown earth served as the make-up for a packed floor (cf. Lapp 1963: fig. 2, sec. F-F; Area I.7). The ceramic evidence indicated this was

[7]This summary is based on P. Lapp's preliminary reports, see especially 1962: 22, 23; 1963: 10-17.

an EB I A surface. A fairly large quantity of EB pottery appeared throughout the excavated areas, but this is the only clear Stratum VI surface.

Stratum V

An elaborate system of Stratum V wall foundations were uncovered on the western side of the Village excavations (cf. plan 2). However, Stratum IV floors lay directly on scraped off Statum V fill and clear occupational evidence appeared in only a few places (Areas I.9, I.12, I.1). Two walls were wide enough to suggest a fortification (NW-1 and NW-2), but a clear relationship could not be established between them and their associated smaller walls. The preliminary study of the pottery with these constructions dated them to the eleventh century B.C.

Stratum IV

The whole area had been leveled off, including scraping away Stratum V debris and chipping off bedrock in some areas, for the thick plaster floor of Stratum IV. The floor originally extended beyond the north and west Stratum IIIb walls which bordered the excavations. A drain (Plan 2:10, Area I.10) and remnants of a few other Stratum IV remains were oriented differently than earlier or later installations. Except for the bare surface, however, there were only a few vestiges of the Stratum IV occupation.

When the excavations were extended to the west, the Plaster Building (plan 4) was revealed. The building consisted of an area 19 × 22 meters. Its outer wall was plastered on the interior and a second wall placed concentrically in this area was plastered on its outer surface. The corridor between the walls was 2.5-3 meters wide and had a hard-packed floor. The inner wall had several doorways to a courtyard which had a hard-packed floor of poorer quality. Pottery evidence beneath the court floor and near foundations date the building's construction to the early second century B.C. Three stamped Rhodian handles came from the Plaster Building excavation, but two of them were illegible (reg. nos. 293 and 294). The other (reg. no. 292), from the Stratum III B leveling off operations over the area, can be dated between 280 and 220 B.C. (see ch. 2 below).

An illegible stamped Rhodian handle (reg. no. 158) came from Stratum IV in the Village (Area I.1), and another (reg. no. 173), dated to 220-180 B.C., was found in Stratum I debris. Two Antiochus III coins (reg. nos. 29, 72) and a Seleucus IV coin (reg. no. 177), although also from later strata, witness to early second century occupation. Early second century pottery associated with Stratum IV features was plentiful.

Stratum III

To Stratum IIIb belong the construction of the walls which form the wide corridor with partitions on the east and north side of the excavations (plan 2 and see Lapp 1963: 10 for details). A plaster floor of poorer quality was laid against walls N-1 and W-1 and in most cases the other walls were laid on top of this Stratum IIIb floor.

The Stratum IIIa occupants reused the IIIb walls with few alterations. They cleared out earlier domestic installations and artifacts. In some places they laid forty cm of brown fill on the IIIb plaster floor, but in most other areas they reused the IIIb floor.

The pottery of Stratum III indicates construction of the walls about 100 B.C. Whether occupation was continuous through the first half of the first century A.D. until the phase IIIa alterations of about A.D. 50, or if there was a short period of abandonment is impossible to say. Several coins of the first century B.C. and especially the first half of the first century A.D. (reg. nos. 257, 175, 217, 243, 176, and 242) were found in later debris.

Stratum II

The Stratum II occupants continued to use the main walls of Stratum III, adding a parallel north-south wall in the corridor and partition walls to make smaller rooms (plan 3). The west end of a new building extended into the open courtyard and new rooms were added to the south corridor. Remnants of Stratum II plaster floors were partially preserved inside the rooms and a disturbed hard surface spread over the remaining open courtyard. Threshholds, ovens, water channels, and some large homogenous ceramic groups preserved in ash deposits represent the finds of Stratum II.

Pottery dates the Stratum II operations about A.D. 100, continuing half a century or so. Two coins from Stratum II contribute to absolute dating, one of Domitian, A.D. 81-96 (reg. no. 181), and one of Trajan A.D. 103-112 (reg. no. 256).

Stratum I

Stratum II walls were reused in Stratum I with minor alterations. Evidence for Stratum I floors was confined to a broken plaster floor, several threshholds, and remains of ovens. Typological considerations of the pottery date the final reconstructions of the ancient village to about A.D. 200.

In summary, tentative stratification in the Village (Field I) is as follows:

Stratum VI   Early Bronze I A
Stratum V   11th century B.C.
Stratum IV   ca. 200-175 B.C. (= Stratum III at the Qasr)
Stratum IIIb ca. 100 B.C.-A.D. 50 (with gap?)
Stratum IIIa ca. A.D. 50
Stratum II   ca. A.D. 100
Stratum I   ca. A.D. 200

BIBLIOGRAPHY

Ant.
    Josephus. *Jewish Antiquities*. Trans. Ralph Marcus from Greek, Loeb Classical Library. London: Heinemann and Cambridge, MA: Harvard University, 1943.

Brett, M. J. B.
    1963   The Qaṣr el-ᶜAbd: A Proposed Reconstruction. *Bulletin of the American Schools of Oriental Research* 171: 39-45.

Brown, R. M.
    1979   Excavations at ᶜIraq el-Emir. *Annual of the Department of Antiquities of Jordan* 23: 17-30.

Butler, H. C.
    1919   *Syria*, Division II, Section A. Publications of the Princeton University Archaeological Expeditions to Syria in 1904-5 and 1909. Leiden: Brill.

Conder, C. R.
    1885   *Heth and Moab*. London: Bentley.
    1889   *The Survey of Eastern Palestine*. London: Palestine Exploration Fund.

Hill, D. K.
    1963   The Animal Fountain of ᶜArâq el-Emîr. *Bulletin of the American Schools of Oriental Research* 171: 45-55.

Irby, C. L., and Mangles, J.
    1868   *Travels in Egypt and Nubia, Syria, and the Holy Land*. London: Murray.

Kallner-Amiran, D. H.
    1950-   A Revised Earthquake-Catalogue of Palestine.
    51   *Israel Exploration Journal* 1: 223-46.

Lapp, P. W.
    1962   Soundings at ᶜArâq el-Emîr (Jordan). *Bulletin of the American Schools of Oriental Research* 165: 16-34.
    1963   The Second and Third Campaigns at ᶜArâq el-Emîr. *Bulletin of the American Schools of Oriental Research* 171: 8-39.

    1976   ᶜIraq el-Emir. Pp. 527-31 in vol. 2 of *Encyclopedia of Archaeological Excavations in the Holy Land*, ed. M. Avi-Yonah. Jerusalem: Israel Exploration Society.

Mazar, B.
    1957   The Tobiads. *Israel Exploration Journal* 7: 137-45, 229-38.

McCown, C. C.
    1957   The Araq el-Emir and the Tobiads. *Biblical Archaeologist* 20: 63-80.

Rostovtzeff, M.
    1959   *Social and Economic History of the Hellenistic World*, I. Oxford: Clarendon.

de Saulcy, L. F.
    1865   *Voyage in Terre Sainte*. Paris: Didier.
    1867   Mémoire sur les Monuments D'Aâraq el-Emyr. *Mémoires de Academie des Inscriptions et Belles-Lettres*, 26, Part 1: 83-115.

Sauer, J. A.
    1973   *Heshbon Pottery 1971*. Berrien Springs, MI: Andrews University.

Tcherikover, V.
    1972   Hellenistic Palestine, Part 2 in *The Hellenistic Age*, ed. Abraham Schalit, *The World History of the Jewish People*, vol. 6. New Brunswick: Rutgers.

Vincent, L.-H.
    1923   La date des épigraphes d'"Arâq el-Émîr. *Journal of the Palestine Oriental Society* 3: 67-68.

de Vogüé, C. J. M.
    1864   Ruines d'Araq el-Emir. *Revue Archeologique* 10: 52-62.

Will, E.
    1977   L'Édifice dit Qasr el Abd à Araq al Amir (Jordanie). *Comptes rendus de l'Académie des Inscriptions & Belles-Lettres* 1977: 69-85.
    1979   Recherches au Qasr el 'Abd à 'Iraq al-Amir. *Annual of the Department of Antiquities of Jordan* 23: 139-49.

Part I
Finds of the 1961 and 1962 Campaigns

Chapter 1
Coins

NANCY L. LAPP

Thirteen coins could be identified from the Village excavations (fig. 7), in addition to a few Early Byzantine and Arabic coins. Their dates range from the third century B.C. until the early second century A.D., thus approximately the dates of Village Strata IV to II. Most were dated to periods earlier than the contexts in which they were found, but coins of Domitian, A.D. 81-96 (no. 181), and Trajan, A.D. 103-112 (no. 256), came from Stratum II (A.D. ca. 100). The coins of Anthiochus III and Selecuid IV (nos. 29, 72, 177) could be from the Stratum IV occupation and Hyrcanus' building operations (the Plaster Building in the Village and the Qasr with its related structures) although they were found in later deposits. The Ptolemy II coin (no. 28) may witness to early Hellenistic activity in the area. Of interest also are the three Nabatean coins of Aretas IV (nos. 175, 217, 243); his coins were in common use in this area during the first century A.D., but no. 217 is a unique type.

Some of the coins from Qasr are important for the dating of the Byzantine occupation (fig. 8). Only one Hellenistic coin was recovered, a Ptolemaic-ace (no. 30) found in Byzantine Stratum I. Near the Square Building a coin of Constantine I (no. 180), dated A.D. 335-337, was found in the Stratum II floor providing a *terminus post quem* for the stratum. A coin from Arcadius (no. 179), A.D. 383, was lying on the Stratum I floor inside the Square Building. In the Qasr a coin of Theodosius I (no. 51), A.D. 393-395, and one of Zeno (no. 24), A.D. 476-491, help date the latest stratum and Byzantine occupation at Araq el-Emir. There were also a number of small bronze coins that probably date to the fourth century A.D. (nos. 13, 183, 184, 185, 186, and 236) and support the Early Byzanitne occupation along with an unstratified coin of Valens A.D. 364/9-378 (no. 178). In surface and disturbed debris, Arabic, Turkish, and Mandate coins (nos. 285, 182, 4) suggest later squatters or shepherds.

Following are tables listing the coins by date and complete descriptions by registration numbers.

Table 1.   Coins from the Village (Field I)

Reg. No.	Provenience	Stratum	Period	Date	Fig.
28	I.1.18	I	Ptolemy II	271-246 B.C.	7:1
29	I.1.26	I	Antiochus III	223-187 B.C.	7:2
72	I.2.67	II	Antiochus III	223-187 B.C.	7:3
177	I.9.15	II	Seleucus IV	187-175 B.C.	7:4
234	I.3.19	I	Seleucid	2nd cen. B.C.	7:5
257	I.3.34	I	Alexander Jannaeus	103-76 B.C.	7:6
175	I.9.3	unstr.	Aretas IV	9 B.C.-A.D. 40	7:7
217	I.23.1	sf.	Aretas IV	9 B.C.-A.D. 40	7:8
243	I.3.23	sf.	Aretas IV	9 B.C.-A.D. 40	7:9
176	I.9.9	I	Valerius Gratus	A.D. 15-26	
242	I.1.118	sf.	Herod Agrippa I	A.D. 42/43	7:10
181	I.5.37	II	Domitian	A.D. 81-96	7:11
256	I.3.32	II	Trajan	A.D. 103-111	7:12
63	I.2.48	intru.?	Early Byzantine?	2nd half 4th cen.	
216	I.23.1	sf.	Early Byzantine?		
214	I.1.110	sf.	Arabic		
264	I.5.69A	I	?		
267	I.23.31	III	?		
269	I.3.35	II	?		

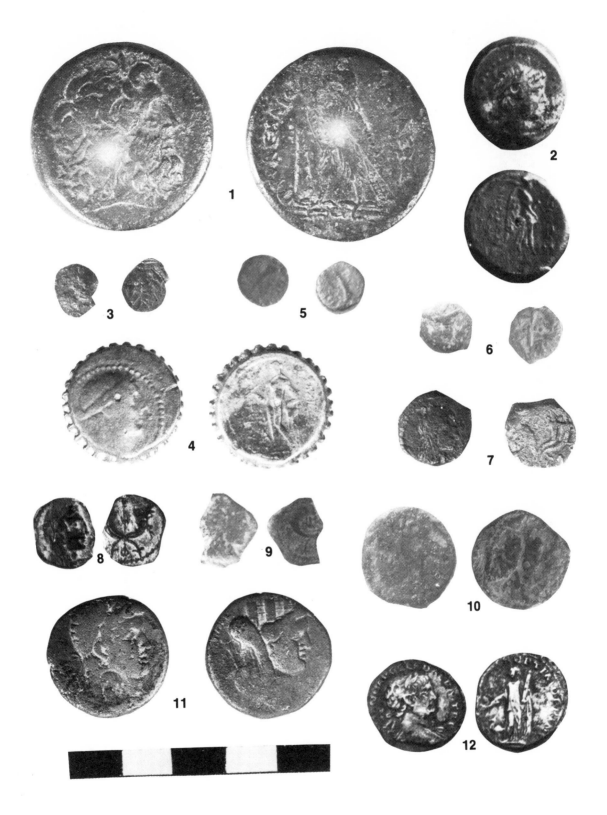

7. Coins from the Village (Field I).
1 = reg. no. 28, 2 = 29, 3 = 72, 4 = 177, 5 = 234, 6 = 257, 7 = 175, 8 = 217, 9 = 243, 10 = 242, 11 = 181, and 12 = 256.

Table 2.   Coins from the Qasr (Field II) and Square Building (Field III)

Reg. No.	Provenience	Stratum	Period	Date	Fig.
30	II.1.13	I	Ptolemaic-Ace	2nd cen. B.C.	8:1
212	II.7.54	unstr.	Late Roman?	2nd cen. A.D.?	
180	III.3.6	II	Constantius II	A.D. 335-337	8:2
178	II.4.13	unstr.	Valens	A.D.364-378	8:3
13	II.1.4	unstr.	Early Byzantine	2nd half 4th cen.?	
179	III.2.14	I	Arcadius	A.D. 383	8:4
236	II.15.3	unstr.	Early Byzantine	4th cen. A.D.	8:5
183	II.7.63	unstr.	Early Byzantine	4th cen. A.D.?	
184	II.7.61	I	Early Byzantine	4th cen. A.D.?	
185	II.8.11	unstr.	Early Byzantine	4th cen. A.D.?	
186	II.7.65	I	Early Byzantine	4th cen. A.D.?	
51	II.1.23	I	Theodosius I	A.D. 393-395	8:6
24	II.1.4	unstr.	Zeno	A.D. 476-491	8:7
285	II.21.2	sf.	Mamluk?		8:8
182	II.7.49	unstr.	Turkish	A.D. 1758	8:9
4	II.11.2	sf.	Palestinian	A.D. 1935	8:10

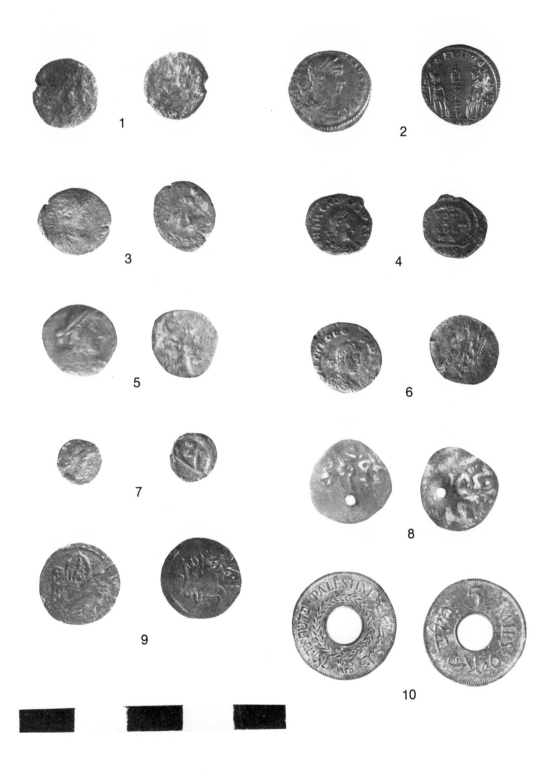

8. Coins from the Qasr (Field II) and the Square Building (Field III).
1 = reg. no. 30, 2 = 180, 3 = 178, 4 = 179, 5 = 236, 6 = 51, 7 = 24, 8 = 285, 9 = 182, and 10 = 4.

Table 3.   Registered Coins

4. II.11.2, surface; 20 mm., 2.8 gm.; fig. 8:10.
Palestine, A.D. 1935, 5 mils.

13. II.1.4, unstratified; 11 mm.; poor condition.
Early Byzantine, second half 4th cen. A.D. (?)
   Obv. Diademed head r.
   Rev. Nike, details effaced.

24. II.1.4, unstratified; bronze, 9 mm., .8 gm.;
fig. 8:7.
Zeno, A.D. 476-491.
   Obv. Bust r., draped, pearl diademed.
   Rev. Monogram ⚲ ; Mint: Constanti-
       nople.
Cf. Carson and Kent 1960: 91, no. 2281.

28. I.1.18, Str. I; large bronze, 35 mm., 37.7 gm.;
fig. 7:1.
Ptolemy II, 271-246 B.C.
   Obv. Bearded head of Ammon r., border
       of dots.
   Rev. PTOLEMAIOU l., BASILEOS r.;
       center: eagle with folded wings, facing l.,
       clutching thunderbolt with talons; club of
       Tyre in field l. Monogram illegible.
Cf. Svoronos 1904: 103, no. 705, pl. 20:14.

29. I.1.26, Str. I: bronze, 20 mm., 9 gm.; fig. 7:2.
Antiochus III, 223-187 B.C.
   Obv. Head of Apollo r., laureate, border
       of dots.
   Rev. BASILEOS r., ANTIOXOU l.; cen-
       ter: Victory marching to r., with palm
       branch over left shoulder.
Cf. Babelon 1890: 57, no. 440, pl. 10:18.
To Department of Antiquities of Jordan.

30. II.1.13, Str. I; bronze, 13 mm., .8 gm.; fig. 8:1.
Ptolemaic-Ace, 2nd cen. B.C.
   Obv. Two heads r., jugate; worn.
   Rev. Cornucopiae; worn.
Cf. Hill 1910: 128, nos. 1-7.

51. II.1.23, Str. I; bronze, 14 mm., .8 gm.; fig. 8:6.
Theodosius I, A.D. 393-395.
   Obv. DN THEODO - SIVS PF [AVG],
       bust r., draped, pearl diademed.
   Rev. Legend illegible, Victory l., trophy
       on shoulder , dragging captive (?); Mint:
       [ ] N [ ] (Antioch?).
Cf. Carson and Kent 1960: 102, nos. 2771-
2775.

63. I.2.48, Str. II; 11 mm.; poor condition.
Early Byzantine, second half 4th cen. A.D.?
   Obv. Diademed bust of emperor r.
   Rev. Nike advancing l.

72. I.2.67, Str. II; small bronze, 9 mm., .6 gm.;
fig. 7:3.
Antiochus III, 223-187 B.C.
   Obv. Head of Apollo r., laureate; dam-
       aged.
   Rev. Apollo, nude, standing l., holding
       arrow in r. hand, l. hand resting on arch;
       damaged.
Cf. Babelon 1890: 54, no. 405, pl. 10:6.

175. I.9.3, unstratified; small bronze, 13 mm.
1.9 gm.; fig. 7:7.
Aretas IV, 9 B.C.-A.D. 40.
   Obv. Bust of Aretas IV r., with long hair,
       laureate (wearing ornament on top of
       head?), border of dots.
   Rev. Two cornucopiae and palm branch;
       in field r., פצ (may represent פצאל, one
       of the children of Aretas IV).
Cf. Hill 1922: xviii, pl. XLIX.9; Meshorer
1975: pl. 4:61B.

176. I.9.9, Str. I; bronze, 16 mm., 2 gm.
Valerius Gratus, A.D. 15-26.
   Obv. Within wreath, inscription:
               TIB
             [K]A[I]
             [C]A[P]
   Rev. Palm branch; across field:
           I[O]U   [LIA]
           L   [C]?
Cf. Reifenberg 1965: 55-56, nos. 128-30.

177. I.9.15, above Str. II; bronze, 23 mm.,
10.9 gm., scalloped edge; fig. 7:4.
Seleucus IV, 187-175 B.C.
   Obv. Head of Apollo r., laureate, border
       dots.
   Rev. BASILEOS r., SELEUKOU l.; cen-
       ter: Apollo, nude, standing toward l.,
       r. hand holding arrow, l. elbow resting on
       tripod. Monogram ⚔ in field l.
Cf. Babelon 1890: 63-64, nos. 479-91.

178. II.4.13; fill; bronze, 13 mm., .8 gm.; fig. 8:3.
Valens, A.D. 364-378.

Obv. DN VA [LE] NS [PF] AV [G], bust
r., draped, pearled diadem.
Rev. R [ESTITVTOR REIPV] BL ICAE,
emperor facing, head r., holding standard
and victoriola; Mint: ANTA (Antioch).
Cf. Carson and Kent 1960: 100, nos. 2649-52.

179. III.2.14, above Str. I floor; bronze, 13 mm.,
1.6 gm.; fig. 8:4.
Arcadius, A.D. 383.
Obv. DNARCADIUS [PF] AV[G], bust
r., draped, pearl diademed.
Rev. In wreath VOT/X/MVLT/XX;
Mint: ANS (Antioch).
Cf. Carson and Kent 1960: 101, nos. 2738-44.

180. III.3.6, to Str. II-I floor; bronze, 15 mm.,
1.7 gm.; fig. 8:2.
Constantius II, A.D. 335-337.
Obv. FLIVLCO [NSTA]NTIVSNOBC,
bust r., laureate, cuirassed, in paluda-
mentum.
Rev. GLOR IAEXERC ITVS, one standard; Mint: [S]MHA (Heraclea).
Cf. Hill 1960: 23, no. 937.

181. I.5.37, Str. II; bronze, 22 mm., 12.5 gm.;
fig. 7:11.
Domitian, A.D. 81-96.
Obv. Bust, laureate, r., counter stamp hu-
man head on neck. Legend illegible.
Rev. Tyche of city, r., turreted, draped,
earring; palm rising from back of shoulder.
Legend illegible. Local mint, perhaps
Philadelphia or Gadara.
Cf. Saulcy 1874: 388, pl. 22:3.

182. II.7.49, mixed debris; 15 mm., .44 gm.; fig. 8:9.
Turkey, 1171 A.H. (A.D. 1758); 5 paras.

183. II.7.63, unstratified; bronze, 12 mm., poor
condition.
4th cen. A.D.?

184. II.7.61, Str. I; bronze, 10 mm. (?), very poor
condition.
4th cen. A.D.?

185. II.8.11, unstratified; bronze, 14 mm., very
poor condition.
4th cen. A.D.?

186. II.7.65, Str. I; bronze, 14 mm., very poor
condition.
4th cen. A.D.?

212. II.7.54, disturbed debris; bronze, 17 mm.,
very poor condition.
2nd century A.D.?

214. I.1.110, surface; bronze, 21 mm., poor condition.
Arabic.

216. I.23.1, surface; bronze, 9 mm.; .99 gm.
Early Byzantine?
Obv. Male bust r., diademed; traces of
letters around edges.
Rev. Partly mistruck. Nike walking l. (?);
at l., traces of letters.

217. I.23.1, surface; bronze, 14 mm.; fig. 7:8.
Aretas IV, 9 B.C.-A.D. 40.
Obv. Bust of Aretas IV r., with long hair,
wearing laurel wreath; in front of head M.
Rev. Two cornucopiae crossed and fil-
leted; between them in center H and be-
low O, intersected by long staff (?).
Cf. Hill 1922: 10, nos. 32-33.
To Department of Antiquities of Jordan.

234. I.3.19, Str. I; bronze, 10 mm., 1.2 gm.; fig. 7:5.
Seleucid, 2nd cen. B.C. (type is known for
several kings).
Obv. Diademed male bust r.
Rev. Apollo standing l. holding bow;
inscription illegible.

236. II.15.3, disturbed debris; bronze, 14 mm.,
1.4 gm.; fig. 8:5.
4th cen. A.D.
Obv. Male bust r.
Details unclear.

242. I.1.118, surface; bronze, 18 mm., 2.7 gm.;
fig. 7:10.
Herod Agrippa I, A.D. 42/43.
Obv. Umbrella with fringe.
Rev. Three ears of barley; across field is
date, LS (year 6 = A.D. 42/43).
Cf. Reifenberg 1965: 46, no. 59.

243. I.3.23, surface; bronze, 13 mm., partially
preserved, 1.5 gm.; fig. 7:9.
Aretas IV, 9 B.C.-A.D. 40.
Obv. Bust of Aretas IV r., long hair,
laureate (and ornament on top of head
and/or border of dots?).
Rev. Two cornucopiae crossed and fil-
leted, between them 7 M (?).
Cf. Hill 1922: 10, nos. 28-31.

256. I.3.32, Str. II; denarius, 18 mm.; fig. 12.
Trajan, A.D. 103-111.
   Obv. Bust of Trajan, laureate, r., with
   drapery on l. shoulder, front and back;
   IMP TRAIANO AVG GER PAC P M
   TR P.
   Rev. Arabia, draped, standing front head
   l., holding branch in r. hand extended
   over camel standing l. and bundle of
   canes (?) upright in l.; - - - - - - S/P/Q/R
   OPTI MO PRINC
Cf. Mattingly 1966: 73, no. 297.
To Dept. of Antiquities of Jordan.

257. I.3.34, Str. I; bronze, 10 mm., .6 gm.; fig. 7:6.
Alexander Jannaeus, 103-76 B.C.

   Obv. Upright anchor with inscription.
   Rev. Wheel of eight rays.
cf. Hill 1914: 210-11, nos. 1-18; Reifenberg
1965: 41, nos. 14, 15.

264. I.5.69A, Str. I; bronze, 14 mm., poorly preserved, indistinguishable.

267. I.23.31, Str. III; bronze, 16 mm., very poorly preserved, indistinguishable.

269. I.3.35, Str. II; bronze, 12 mm., poorly preserved, indistinguishable.

285. II.21.2, surface; bronze, 16 mm., fig. 8:8.
Mamluk (?).

BIBLIOGRAPHY

Babelon, E.
   1890   *Les Rois de Syrie*. Paris: Rollin and Feuardent.
Carson, R. A. G., and Kent, J. P. C.
   1960   Bronze Roman Imperial Coinage of the Later
           Empire, A.D. 346-498. Part II in *Late Roman
           Bronze Coinage*, by R. A. G. Carson. London:
           Spenk.
Hill, G. F.
   1910   *Catalogue of Greek Coins of Phoenicia*. London:
           British Museum.
   1914   *Catalogue of Greek Coins of Palestine*. London:
           British Museum.
   1922   *Catalogue of the Greek Coins of Arabia, Meso-
           potamia, and Persia*. London: British Museum.
Hill, P. V. and Kent, J. P. C.
   1960   *The Bronze Coinage of the House of Constantine,
           A.D. 324-346*. Part I in *Late Roman Bronze
           Coinage*, by R. A. G. Carson. London: Spenk.

Mattingly, Harold
   1966   *Coins of the Roman Empire in the British
           Museum*. Vol. 3, Nerva to Hadrian. London:
           British Museum.
Meshorer, Y.
   1975   *Nabataean Coins*. Qedem 3. Jerusalem: Institute
           of Archaeology, Hebrew University.
Reifenberg, A.
   1965   *Ancient Jewish Coins*. 4th ed. Jerusalem: Rubin
           Mass.
Sāulcy, F. de
   1874   *Numismatique de la Terre Sainte*. Paris: Roths-
           child.
Svoronos, J. N.
   1904   *Ta Nomismata toy Kratous tōn Ptolemaiōn*. Vol.
           2. Athens: Sakellariou.

Chapter 2
Stamped Rhodian Amphora Handles

NANCY L. LAPP

Fragments from Rhodian amphorae were very common in the Hellenistic debris in the Village, and significant fragments were recovered from the Qasr and Square Building (Lapp 1979: figs. 1:10, 2:18). Eight stamped handles came from the Village, four of which are legible.

All except one were from a stratified context, but as usual the handles date considerably earlier than the occupational horizon in which they were found (Grace 1950: 137). Two handles datable between 200 and 180 B.C. came from Stratum I debris and a handle dating between 280 and 220 B.C. came from Stratum III B (figs. 9, 10: 4-6). In the final study of the Village stratification the

significance of the handles will have to be considered.

All handles with enough form preserved indicate a sharp angle in the bend between the upper and lower arm and have a rounded section; these are late characteristics (Grace 1950: 136). They have the typical Rhodian amphora ware: reddish yellow with pinkish white or pink surfaces, very well levigated and without mica inclusions.

Full descriptions and readings, where they are possible, follow for the eight stamped handles. Acknowledgement is due Fr. William Fulco, S.J. For the drawings and aid in reading the stamps.

Table 4. Stamped Rhodian Amphora Handles

1. I.1.3, surface (pot. no. 74); fig. 9:1.
   Complete upper arm of angular, left (?)
   handle, length ca. 7 cm.
   Ware: 5 YR 7/6 reddish yellow; sf. 7.5 YR
   8/4 pink.
   Circular stamp (rose?); possibly 4 letters pre-
   served.
   ] OḲ [   ] EĊ [

125. I.1.94, Str. III B (pot. no. 306); fig. 9:2.
   Fragmentary upper arm of left handle, pre-
   served length ca. 5 cm.
   Ware: 7.5 YR 8/4 pink with 7/5 YR 8/2
   pinkish white sf.
   Rectangular stamp, partially chipped.
   ΑΓΟΡΑΝΑ
   ΚΤΟΣ
   ΑΓΡ[ΙΑΝΙ]ΟΥ
   Maker: Agoranaktos; month: Agrianios.
   Cf. Reisner, Fischer, and Lyon 1924: 18,
   no. 530; 312, no. II.2. Macalister 1901:
   28-29, no. 9 (Tell Sandahannah). Nils-
   son 1909: 356, no. 19.

158. I.1.105, Str. IV (pot. no. 307); fig. 9:3.
   Complete upper arm of angular right handle

length ca. 9 cm.; small portion of lower
arm; ca. 6 × 7.5 cm. neck attached.
Ware: 7.5 YR 8/6 reddish yellow with 7.5 YR
8/2 pinkish white sf.
Long rectangular stamp, few legible letters;
rose or rayed head symbol to 1.
C Ṭ[   ]A
Ẹ[ ]ΦΑИΕΥΣ̣

173. I.7.6, Str. I (pot. no. 308); fig. 9:4.
   Partial upper arm of angular right handle,
   preserved length ca. 5 cm.
   Ware: 7.5 YR 8/2 pinkish white sf.
   Chipped rectangular stamp.
   ΕΠΙ ΘΕCΤΟ [ΡΟΥ]
   ΘΕΜΟΦΟΡΙΟΥ
   Eponym: Thestor; month: Thesmophorios.
   Date: 220-180 B.C.

   Cf. Grace 1934: 229, no. 53 ("220-180, common"); Macalister 1901: 40-44, no. 117 (Tell
   Sandahannah); Hiller von Gaertringen 1931:
   838, no. 157 (group V, 220-180); Nilsson
   1909: 431, no. 236; Crowfoot 1957: 381
   (period III, c. 220-180, p. 379).
   To Dept. of Antiquities of Jordan

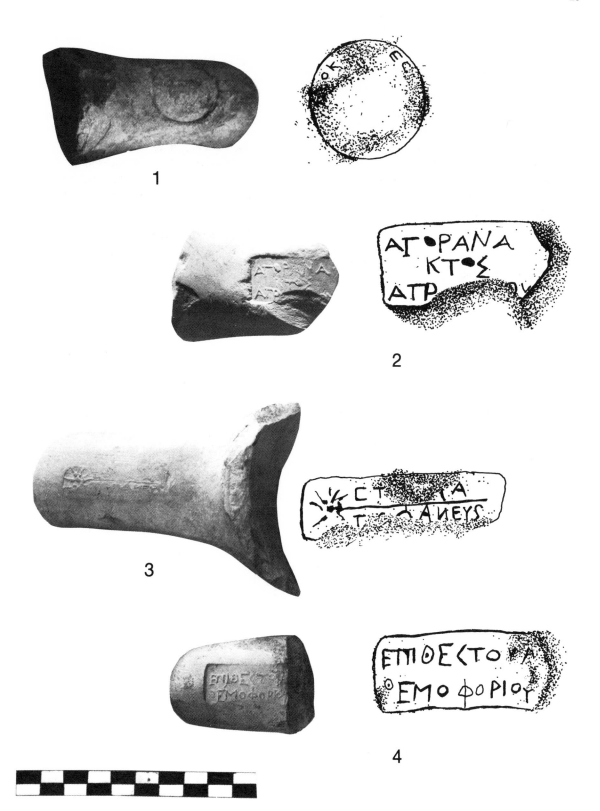

9. Stamped Rhodian Amphora Handles.
1 = reg. no. 1, 2 = 125, 3 = 158, and 4 = 173.

Table 4, *continued*

262. I.3.34, Str. I (pot. no. 309); fig. 10:5.
Complete upper arm of angular right handle,
length ca. 8 cm.; small portion of lower arm;
5-6 cm. neck attached.
Ware: 5 YR 7/6 reddish yellow with 7.5 YR
8/2 pinkish white sf.
Circular stamp, ? in center.
ΕΠΙΑΙΝΗ [ΤΟ] ṚọṢ
ΘΕΣΜΟ[ΦΟΡΙ]ΟῪ
Eponym: Ainetor; month: Thesmophorios.
Date: 220-180 B.C.
Cf. Reisner, Fischer, and Lyon 1924: 314,
no. V.6; Crowfoot 1957: 380 (period III,
dated c. 220-180, p. 379); Hiller von Gaer-
tringen 1931: 835, no. 23 (group IV, frequent
220-180); Nilsson 1909: 360-61, no. 31.
To Dept. of Antiquities of Jordan

292. I.14.37, Str. III B (pot. no. 310); fig. 10:6.
Upper arm of angular left handle, preserved
length ca. 6 cm.; small portion of lower arm.
Ware: 7.5 YR 8/6 reddish yellow with 7.5 YR
8/2 pinkish white sf.
Rectangular stamp.
ΕΠΙΕΡΕΩΣΣΩΔΑΜΟΥ
ΚΑΡΝΕΙΟΥ

Eponym: *hereōs* Sodamos; month: Kar-
neious.
Date: 280-220 B.C.
Cf. Crowfoot 1957: 382 (period II, 280-220,
p. 379); Nilsson 1909: 481, no. 381.
To Dept. of Antiquities of Jordan

293. I.14.37, Str. III B (pot. no. 311); fig. 10:7.
Complete upper arm of angular left (?) handle
except side chip, length ca. 10 cm.; ca. 6 × 6
cm. neck attached.
Ware: 5 YR 6/6 reddish yellow with 7.5 YR
8/4 pink sf.
Circular stamp; illegible.

294. I.14.42, Str. I (pot. no. 312); fig. 10:8.
Partial upper arm of angular left handle, preserved length ca. 3 cm.; 12 cm. lower arm with
uneven longitudinal undulations (cf. Grace
1934: 203).
Ware: 7.5 YR 6/6 reddish yellow with 7.5 YR
8/4 pink sf.
Chipped rectangular stamp; illegible.

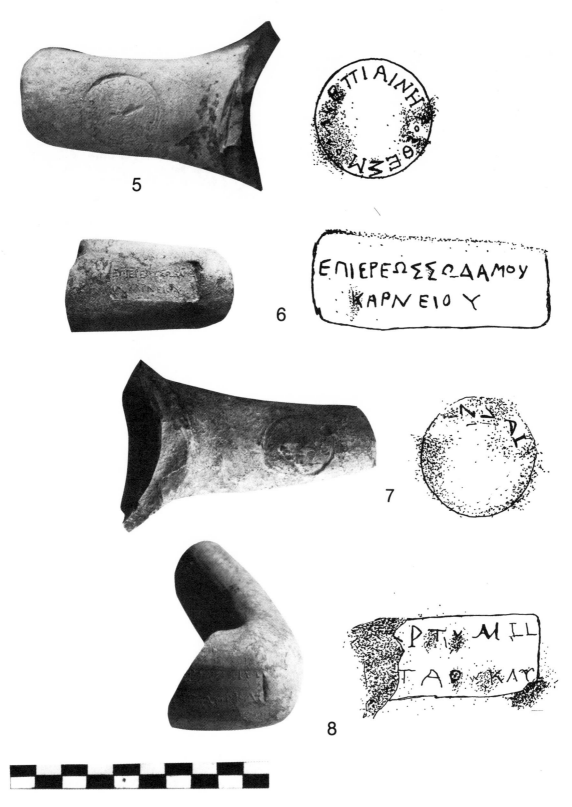

10. Stamped Rhodian Amphora Handles.
5 = reg. no. 262, 6 = 292, 7 = 293, and 8 = 294.

BIBLIOGRAPHY

Crowfoot, J. W.
1957 Potters' Stamps. Pp. 379-88 in *Samaria-Sebaste: The Objects from Samaria*. Reports of the Work of the Joint Expedition in 1931-1933 and of the British Expedition in 1935, by J. W. Crowfoot, G. M. Crowfoot, and K. M. Kenyon. London: Palestine Exploration Fund.

Grace, V.
1934 Stampled Amphora Handles Found in 1931-1932. *Hesperia* 3: 195-310.

1950 The Stamped Amphora Handles. Pp. 135-48 in *Excavations at Gozlu Kule, Tarsus*, Vol. 1, The Hellenistic and Roman Periods, ed. H. Goldman. Princeton, N.J.: Princeton University.

Hiller von Gaertringen, Friedrich
1931 Rhodos. Cols. 818-840 in *Paulys Real-Encyclopädie der Classischen Altertumswissenschaft*, Supplement 5, ed. G. Wissowa. Stuttgart: Metzler.

Lapp, N. L.
1979 The Hellenistic Pottery from the 1961 and 1962 Excavations at ᶜIraq el-Emir. *Annual of the Department of Antiquities of Jordan*, 23: 5-15.

Macalister, R. A. S.
1901 Amphora Handles with Greek Stamps from Tell Sandahannah. *Palestine Exploration Fund Quarterly Statement*: 25-43, 123-43.

Nilsson, M. P.
1909 *Timbres Amphoriques de Lindos*. Vol. 5 in *Exploration Archéologique de Rhodes*. Copenhagen: Lund.

Reisner, G. A., Fischer, C. S., and Lyon, D. G.
1924 *Harvard Excavations at Samaria, 1908-1910*. Cambridge, MA: Harvard University.

Chapter 3
An Inscribed Weight

Frank M. Cross

A large stone weight was discovered in the excavations in the "Village" of ʿArâq el-ʾEmîr in 1961. The weight is identified as object I.6.22 no. 19, and was turned up "on or in a Stratum I dirt floor." It weighs 7700 grams, and measures 24.0 × 13.4 × 16.5 cm. The surface of the weight appears rounded and smoothed save for the area through which a hole was punched in its upper end; no doubt this hole was made to permit the suspension of the weight by cord on a balance beam.

The weight is inscribed in clear Jewish characters, of Late Herodian or early Post-Herodian date, chiseled in its surface. The inscription reads (see figs. 11 and 12):

rḥmnr prs

Evidently *rḥmnr* is the personal name of the owner of the weight, and *prs* the designation of value of the weight. The name may belong to a well-known pattern of Aramaic names: *raḥīm-nūr*, "Beloved of Nūr."[1] It is also possible to read *raḥ(h)am-nūr/nir*, "Nūr/Nir has shown compassion."[2] The theophorous element appears to be *Nūr* in Aramaic, *Nir* (*Nēr*) in Amorite and Canaanite, including the familiar Hebrew names, *Nēr*, *Nērīyahū*, *Nērāʾ Nirīyaw*,[3] etc. The element *nr* appears as a divine epithet paired with *šmš* in

the Sefire Inscription (I, A.9). The writing without *matres lectionis* suggests that the name is *raḥ(h)am-nēr*, and perhaps Ammonite.[4] We note that two Ammonite names are known bearing the element *nr*, *ʾdnnr*, and *ʾlnr*.[5]

The name *rḥmnr* is written with a final *mêm* in the medial position; one could argue that we should read *rḥm* (*bn*) *nr*. However, the name is written without space between *m* and *n*, and the use of final *mêm* in medial position (as well as medial *mêm* in final position) is well-known from ossuary inscriptions and from Qumrân manuscripts of this period, and is the occasion of no surprise.

Prs, Aram. *pĕrēs* or *pĕrās*, Akk. *parisu* (or *parīsu*), Ugar. *prs̄*, Phoen. *prs*, ordinarily means "half unit" of a weight or measure. *Prs* in the sense of "half-mina" is widely distributed. Obviously so small a weight does not come into consideration here.[6] So far as I am aware, *prs* is not used to mean "half-talent," and in any case, the several standard talents in the Hellenistic-Roman era are all much

---

[1] Compare such names as (H)adad-raḥīm, ʾAbī-raḥīm, Raḥīm-ʾil, Raḥīm-(H)adad-milk. (For references, see Zadok 1977: 104, 109.)

[2] Cf. (H)adad-raham (Zadok, 1977: 81), and the West-Semitic names in Egypt: *rḥm rḥmrʿ* (Kornfeld, 1978: 71).

[3] Cf. Zadok 1977: 100; Tallqvist 1966: 176.

[4] The biblical name *rḥwm* found also in the Brooklyn Museum papyri (10, 19; 11, 14; 12, 34) is a hypocoristicon of such a name, presumably the relatively rare *qatūl* pattern to judge from the Massoretic pointing.

[5] *ʾdnnr* is found in the well-known Ammonite seal, *lʾdnnr ʿbd ʿmndb* found in an ʿAmmān tomb (Herr 1978: Ammonite No. 1, p. 59). *ʾlnr* is found in the Ammonite name list from Nimrud (Naveh 1979-80: 163-71; cf. P. Bordreuil, 1979: 313-17).

[6] In the Hellenistic and Roman periods the several minas in use varied roughly between 524 g. (Attic) and 873 g. (Jewish). See Segrè 1945: 357-375, esp. pp. 368-369.

11. Inscribed weight, reg. no. 119.

12. Inscribed weight, drawing.

too large to conform to a unit of 15.4 kg. (2 ×
7.7 kg., the weight of our *prs*). *Prs* is also used
widely as a measure of grain. At Ugarit we find *prš
ḥtm* and *prš qmḥ*. In the Inscription of Panamuwa
II, we find *prs* as a measure of grain, to judge by its
context: *wqm prs bšql*, i.e., a *prs* of grain cost a
šeqel.[7] The passage must be compared with 2 Kg.
7:1, *sᵓh slt bšql wsᵓtym śᶜrym bšql*. Both passages
speak of inflated prices, and the juxtaposition of
the texts suggests strongly that the *prs* is a half
ephah (= 1 1/2 seahs). In the Bauer-Meisner
Papyrus we find *ḥmr qbl ḥmr pr[s qbl p]rs*.[8]
Especially useful are two passages in the Brooklyn
Museum Papyrus 11: *kntn prsn 2 sᵓn 2* (l. 3),
parallel to *sᵓn 5+1* (l. 4). The two *prsn*, two *sᵓn* of
spelt are otherwise reckoned as six *sᵓn* of spelt,

yielding the value of the *prs* as 1 1/2 seahs, or a
half-ardab (= a half ephah).[9]

Being unable to find a suitable unit of weight, I
am tempted to speculate that the ᶜArâq el-ᵓEmîr
weight was used to weigh up an amount equivalent
to a half-ephah (or ardab) of grain. Such a correlation of weight and measures of capacity is most
convenient when storing or packaging commod-
ities in non-standard-size containers, e.g., in sacks,
which to judge from large stamp-seals, were in
wide use.[10]

[7]Donner and Röllig 1962-69: 215, 6.
[8]Bauer and Meissner 1936: 414-24 [1. 5].

[9]Kraeling 1953: 263.
[10]See Cross 1969: 26f. A reading in the Ben Sira Scroll from
Massada may bear on our discussion. At IV,9, the text reads *ᶜl
šḥqy mznym wpls / wᶜl tmḥy ᵓyph wᵓbn*: "Of the dust of scales
and balance, of the polishing of ephah and weight." In the
sequence, the polishing of the ephah stands alongside three
elements in weighing, and could be taken as an ephah weight
rather than an ephah-sized container.

The *ephah* or *bath* in the Hellenistic period appears to have contained 21.83 l.[11] It has been reported to me that a liter of Jordanian barley weighs about 720 g. This would give a figure of 15717.6 g. to an *ephah*, 7858.8 g. for the half-ephah or *pĕrās*. The Notre Dame "ephah" of 21.25 l. would correspond to a *pĕrās* of 7650 g. The two values bracket the value of the ʿArâq al-ʾEmîr weight: 7700 g.

The script, as we have noted above, is a formal exemplar of the Late Herodian or early Post-Herodian period, ca. A.D. 100 ± 30 years.[12]

Certain details of the script merit comment. The *ḥet* is chiseled with a conscious attempt to portray the triangular "corners" of Late Herodian and early Post-Herodian forms. The (final) *mêm* is diagnostic. It is a form emerging at the very end of the Herodian Age, the ticked top-bar has devolved into a vestigial, sharply-pointed right shoulder; it has not yet become the simplified, squared form of the latest Second-Revolt and later types. The *nun* is inscribed with the "sharp keraia" (hooked downward) that begins in the late Herodian Period (4Q Dan[b]) and continues in the Post-Herodian script.[13] The *pê* is unusual only in the openness of its head. Most *pês* of this period are more tightly curled. It may be a surviving early trait. The *samek* is inscribed imitating the triangular, left-top *keraia* of the late Herodian and post-Herodian formal script.

The context in which the weight was found sets a probable *terminus ad quem* of A.D. 200, and a probable *terminus post quem* of the mid-first century of the common era (the suggested date for the beginning of Stratum II). The palaeographical dating of the weight conforms with these data, and suggests that the weight was found *in* rather than *on* the Stratum I floor, or in any case, ultimately derived from the Stratum II occupation.

[11]This is the figure of Segrè (cited above n. 6) based on data from an Egyptian papyrus describing Palestinian usage (the papyrus dates from 259 B.C.), and conforms to other data. For the discussion, see Trinquet 1957. The jar from Qumrân, inscribed *s 2 lg 7*, presumably 2 seahs, 7 logs, has been used to calculate a higher value. This inscription, however, is a crude graffito (unlike the *bt* and *bt lmlk* inscriptions), and may represent not the size of the jar, but an amount added to (or removed from) the jar. Cp. Milik, 1962: 37-41. Ruth Hestrin has reminded me of the jar recently found at Lachish from the early sixth century B.C. labeled *b at 1* which contains between 20.85 and 21.15 l. when full. This would seem to settle the matter since its capacity corresponds closely to the Tell Beit Mirsim, Notre Dame, and Hellenistic values for the bath. See D. Ussishkin, "Excavations at Tel Lachish, 1973-1977," *Tel Aviv* 5 (1978), 85-88.

[12]See my discussion of scripts of this date in Cross 1961: 133-202, esp. pp. 166-181 and Fig. 2, scripts 7-10; and 1962: 217-221 and Fig. 12. For the latest scripts of the Herodian and Post-Herodian periods, see especially Avigad 1957: 77-87.

[13]It should be noted that the *nun* is a perfect exemplar of the formal script used in the other letters of the weight's inscription. The reading is certain. It cannot be read as a cursive, topless *bêt*.

BIBLIOGRAPHY

Avigad, N.
    1957   The Palaeography of the Dead Sea Scrolls and Related Documents. Pp. 77-87 in *Aspects of the Dead Sea Scrolls, Scripta Heirosalymitana* IV, Jerusalem.
Bauer, H. and Meissner, B.
    1936   Ein aramäischer Pachtvertrag aus dem 7. Jahre Darius I, *Sitzungsber. d. Preussischen Akad. d. Wiss. zu Berlin* phil.-hist. Kl: 414-24.
Bordreuil, P.
    1979   Les noms propres transjordaniens de l'Ostracon de Nimroud. *Revue d'histoire et de philosophie religieuses* 3-4: 313-17.
Cross, F. M.
    1961   The Development of the Jewish Scripts. Pp. 133-202 in *The Bible and the Ancient Near East: Essays in Honor of W. F. Albright*, ed. G. E. Wright. Garden City, New York: Doubleday.
    1962   Excursus on the Palaeographical Dating of the Copper Scroll. Pp. 217-221 in *Les 'petites grottes' de Qumrân. Discoveries in the Judean Desert III*. Oxford: Clarendon.
    1969   Judean Stamps. *Eretz-Israel* 9.
Donner, H. and Röllig, W.
    1962-1969   *Kanaanäische und aramäische Inschriften*. Wiesbaden: Harrassowitz.
Herr, L.
    1978   *The Scripts of Ancient Northwest Semitic Seals*. Missoula, MT: Scholars.
Kornfeld, W.
    1978   *Onomastica aramaica aus Ägypten*. Wien.
Kraeling, E. G.
    1953   *The Brooklyn Museum Aramaic Papyri*. New Haven, Conn: Yale University.

Milik, J. T.
    1962   *Les 'petites grottes' de Qumrân. Discoveries in the Judean Desert* III. Oxford: Clarendon.
Naveh, J.
    1979-80   The Ostracon from Nimrud: An Ammonite Name-List. *Maarav* 2: 163-71.
Segrè, A.
    1945   A Documentary Analysis of Ancient Palestinian Units of Measure. *Journal of Biblical Literature* 64: 357-75.

Tallqvist, K. L.
    1966   *Assyrian Personal Names.* Hildesheim: Olms.
Trinquet, J.
    1957   Métrologie biblique. Cols. 1222-1238 in *Dictionaire de la Bible, Supplément V.* Paris.
Zadok, R.
    1977   *On West Semites in Babylonia During the Chaldean and Achaemenian Periods.* Jerusalem: Wanaarta and Tel-Aviv University.

Chapter 4
Jewelry

Nancy L. Lapp

Most of the jewelry recovered from the 1961 and 1962 campaigns was relatively modern (see figs. 13, 14). A few pieces may be singled out because of their stratigraphy and interest.

Of copper or bronze are the dangling earring, reg. no. 111 (fig. 15:1 and also fig. 13, upper left two pieces), the piece of a bracelet with spiral striations, reg. no. 228 (fig 15:2)—both from Village Stratum I, and the fibula, reg. no. 229 (fig. 5:3 from stratum III B. Unstratified but of interest is the tiny spoon, reg. no. 213 (fig. 15:4). A piece of a glass button or bead, reg. no. 271, also came from Stratum III (fig. 15:5).

From the Qasr a piece of a ridged glass bracelet, reg. no. 80 (fig. 15:6) was probably from Stratum I. A piece of a glass ring, no. 378 (fig. 15:7), was unstratified, and of colored glass or faience are the glass bracelets, nos. 286 and 287, found with the burials underneath the stairwell (II.21, fig. 14, upper left).

The table below summarizes the jewelry of interest. For an amulet, see below, and for the beads, see ch. 5.

Sacred Eye Amulet (no. 115)

The *wedjat* or eye of Horus amulet has a long history both in Egypt and in Palestine. Horus, the ancient sky and sun god, was represented by both human and falcon forms. The sacred eye is a combination of the human eye with the marks of the feathers of a falcon around the eye. The Egyptian hieroglyph, ⟨glyph⟩ = wdȝt, to which the amulet is related, stands for the wedjat-eye or uninjured eye of Horus. The Egyptian kings of the First Dynasty are best known by their Horus names, written in a rectangular form surmounted by a falcon.

The earliest sacred eye amulets go back to the Old Kingdom, the Sixth Dynasty, and appear in various forms down to Ptolemaic times (Petrie 1914: 32). In Palestine the peak popularity was probably reached in the ninth-eighth centuries B.C. (Megiddo Strata IV-III and Lachish Tombs 1002 and 224 and ossuary groups 107 and 120, cf. Tufnell 1953: 379; Beth Shan Upper Level V, James 1966: fig. 113:4). Iron I examples are not unknown though; note those from Megiddo Strata VI, V, and V A (Lamon and Shipton 1939: pl. 75, Loud 1948: pl. 206), and Ain Shems (Mackenzie 1912-1913: pl. 28: 1-16). One was found in a tomb at Lahun dated by a scarab to Shishak I (Petrie, Brunton, and Murray 1923: pl. 55:18 and p. 36).

Both right and left eyes appear, and sometimes they are found on both the front and the back of the amulet. They are made from a variety of materials, including haematite, steatite, limestone, glass, and faience, decorated with blue and green glazes, black paint, and gold or other inlays (Petrie 1914: 33). Most Iron II examples seem to be of faience (cf. Lachish, Megiddo, and other examples below). The amulets range in size from less than 1 cm. in length to 4.5 cm. or longer.

The Araq el-Emir amulet (no. 115, fig. 16) is of blue faience and measures 2.4 × 3.2 cm., about average in size. It is a right eye with feather marks on the brow above; feathers typically hanging below are broken off. Close parallels are from

Megiddo Stratum IV (Lamon and Shipton 1939: pl. 75: 16, 19, 23, 25), Stratum V (Lamon and Shipton 1939: pl. 75: 20, 30), and Stratum V A (Loud 1948: pl. 206: 58, 59); Lachish Locus 120 (Tufnell 1953: pl. 34: 10) and Locus 224 (pl. 35: 37); Gezer, "Fourth Semitic" (Macalister 1912: pl. 210: 21, 27, 34); Ain Shems Tomb 1 (probably, at least, Mackenzie 1912-1913: pl. 28: 2,3); Atlit Tomb L 19 (ca. 400 B.C.; Johns 1833: 60, pl. 17:419); and perhaps Beth Shan Upper Level V (9th century B.C.; James 1966: pl. 113: 14). These are variously described as faience, blue and green glazed, green-glazed paste, green enamel, or glazed faience.

The Araq el-Emir amulet comes from a Stratum III (late Hellenistic) context in the Village (I.10.38). Since there was early material in the deposit and an amulet may have been prized for many years for both its superstitious and antique value, it could be from considerably earlier times.

13. Necklace, no. 159, found with burial underneath megaliths inside the Qasr walls (II.7.55). Other jewelry, clockwise from upper right, reg. nos. 96, 237, 222, 171, 254, 238, 301, 296, and 111.

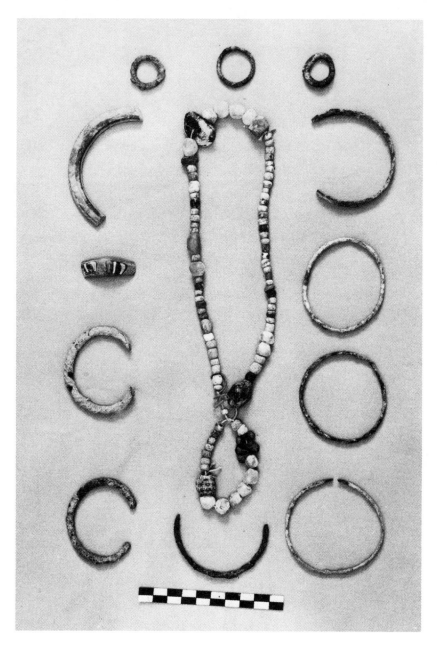

14. Necklace, no. 274, and various pieces of jewelry (nos. 275-287) from under the fallen stairwell in the northeast area of the Qasr (II.21.2) with six relatively recent burials.

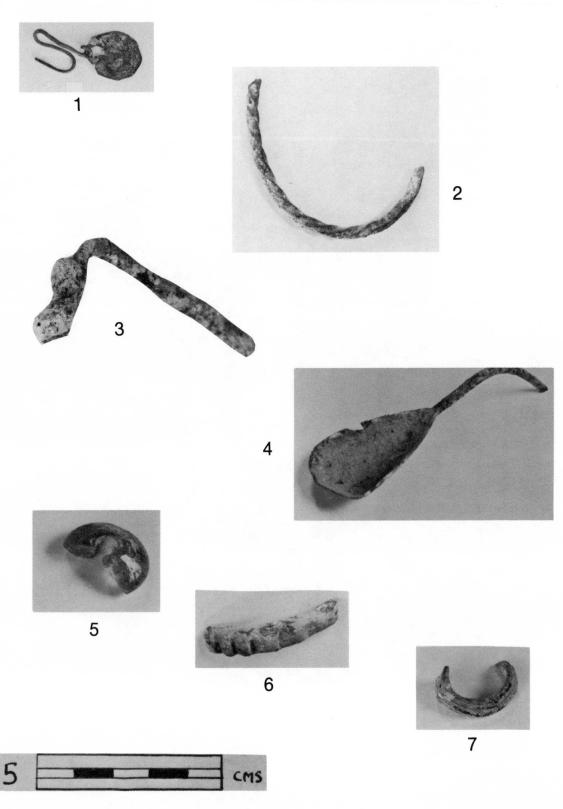

15. Jewelry.
1 = reg. no. 111, 2 = 228, 3 = 229, 4 = 218, 5 = glass reg. no. 271, 6 = 80, and 7 = glass reg. no. 378.

16. Sacred eye amulet, reg. no. 115.

Table 5. Jewelry

reg. no.	prov.	stratum	description	figure
Village (Field I)				
96	I.1.78	-	bronze earring	13
111	I.5.12	I	bronze 2-piece earring	13; 15:1
228	I.9.97A	I	bronze bracelet	15:2
229	I.2.35	III B	bronze toggle pin	15:3
glass 271	I.6.71	III	glass button or bead	15:5
Qasr (Field II)				
80	II.4.7	I	glass or faience bracelet	15:6
171	II.7.55	-	bronze bracelet with recent burial: fig. 43	13
222	II.15.1	-	bracelet	13
237	II.17.1	-	bronze earring	13
238	II.17.1	-	bronze ring	13
254	II.10.4	-	bronze ring on finger of burial: fig. 42	13
275-281	II.21.2	-	bracelets with stairwell burials	14
282-284	II.21.2	-	rings with stairwell burials	14
286, 287	II.21.2	-	glass bracelets with stairwell burials	14
296	II.11C.3A	-	ring	13
glass 378	II.10.3	-	glass ring	15:7
Cave sounding (Field IV)				
301	IV.2.7	-	bronze earring	13

BIBLIOGRAPHY

James, F. W.
    1966   *The Iron Age at Beth Shan*. Philadelphia: University Museum, University of Pennsylvania.
Johns, C. N.
    1933   Excavations at 'Atlīt (1930-1): The Southeastern Cemetery. *Quarterly of the Department of Antiquities in Palestine* 2: 41-104.
Lamon, R. S. and Shipton, G. M.
    1939   *Megiddo I*. Seasons of 1925-34. Strata I-V. Chicago: University of Chicago.
Loud, G.
    1948   *Megiddo II*. Seasons of 1935-39. Chicago: University of Chicago.
Macalister, R. A. S.
    1912   *The Excavation of Gezer*. 3 vols. London: Palestine Exploration Fund.

Mackenzie, D.
    1912-   *Excavations at Ain Shems*. Palestine Exploration
    1913   Fund. Annual 2. London: Palestine Exploration Fund.
Petrie, W. M. F.
    1914   *Amulets*. London: Constable.
Petrie, W. M. F., Brunton, G., and Murray, M. A.
    1923   *Lahun II*. London: British School of Archaeology in Egypt.
Tufnell, O.
    1953   *Lachish III*. The Iron Age. London: Oxford University.

Chapter 5
Beads

GARY COOKE AND NANCY L. LAPP

Only a few of the beads were found in stratified contexts (see Table 6). Most interesting were several from Hellenistic contexts. From the Village Stratum IV (ca. 175 B.C.) came a barrel-shaped amethyst, no. 247 (fig. 17:7). From Stratum IIIb (ca. 100 B.C.) came two others, nos. 108 and 75, of quartz composition (smoky quartz and chert), as well as one of Aragonite, no. 194 (fig 17:6 and see below), and a tiny one of turquoise-blue glass, no. 162 (fig. 17:2). The one bead dating to the Iron age, Village Stratum V, no. 164 (fig. 17:4), was finely decorated with patterned circles and analyzed as ceramic or very porous glass. Two groups of beads were found with fairly recent burials. Beneath megaliths inside the Qasr walls, II.7.55, 55 of 71 beads found with a skeleton were of glass (no. 159, individual beads numbered with prefix N, see fig. 18, above fig. 13, and below fig. 43 for the skeleton). Included were two German church tokens of the 16th and 17th century (N-17 and N-53, see Table 7). Under the fallen stairwell in the northeast area of the Qasr, II.21.2, were six relatively recent burials with various pieces of jewelry (nos. 274-287; see above fig. 14). The beads analyzed were all glass (no. 274, individual beads numbered with prefix M; however most beads remained with the Jordan Department of Antiquities and were not available for study).

The composition of the beads was studied by Gary A. Cooke of the Gulf Research and Development Company, Pittsburgh, Pa., and his report follows. It is interesting to note that most of the beads with mineral content came from Hellenistic contexts. Those from mixed or surface loci were almost all of glass. No glass beads came from contexts necessarily earlier than Roman or Byzantine times except the tiny bead, no. 162.

The Composition of the Beads

Gary A. Cooke

A number of beads from Araq el-Emir were examined by non-destructive methods in order to determine their composition. The results for twenty-one of the beads are reported in Table 6, and additional beads found with the relatively modern burial inside the Qasr (II.7.55) are included in Table 7.

The beads were examined visually and the color and estimated hardness were noted (see tables). Hardness was not precisely determined as damage to the beads might have resulted. Pyncno-meter measurements determined the specific gravity (density) of the beads. X-ray diffraction data indicated the crystalline nature of the beads. The specimens were also individually photographed (fig. 17).

The density data are, perhaps, the most informative. The highest value obtained was 2.76 g/cc (no. 81) which eliminates many minerals from consideration. The majority of the beads have densities less than 2.5 g/cc. Only a very few common minerals hard enough to make into beads have densities this low. One bead (no. 84) has a remarkably low density of 1.03 g/cc. The only naturally occurring material consistent with this low density is some type of tree resin. Modern plastics also have densities this low.

Table 6. Registered Beads and their Composition

Reg. no.	Provenience	Stratum	Size (in cm)	Shape	Color	g/cc density	Hardness	Composition	Comments
108	I.10.38	IIIb (ca. 100 B.C.)	1.6	spherical	Grey Trans-lucent	2.63	>5.5	Quartz	Smokey quartz
103	I.10.36		1.7 × .4	wheel-shaped	Brown Opaque	2.65	5	Quartz	Silicified fossil??
247	I.12.43	IV (ca. 175 B.C.)	1.1 × .9	barrel-shaped	Violet-Clear	2.69	>5.5	Quartz	Amethyst (fig. 17:7)
81	II.7.3		1.1	spherical	Reddish-Opaque	2.76	<5.5	Quartz	Agate
75	I.2.71	IIIb (ca. 100 B.C.)	.6	spherical	Red-Brown	2.73	>5.5	Quartz	Chert
194	I.4.45	IIIb (ca. 100 B.C.)	1.5 × 1.0 .1 thick	oblong, flat	White	2.73	4	Aragonite	$CaCO_3$ shell fragment (fig. 17:6)
192	III.4.14		1.2	spherical, faceted	Yellow-Trans-lucent	2.44	5.5	Glass	(fig. 17:5)
163 a	II.7.57		1.0	irregular,	White	2.40	5	Glass	Coated with calcite (fig. 17:3, 9)
b	II.7.57		.9	faceted	over grey	2.48	5	Glass	Coated with calcite (fig. 17:3)
83	II.7.6	Ib (ca. A.D. 500)	.6 × .8	cylindrical	Pink-opaque	2.43	>5.5	Glass or ceramic	(fig. 17:1)
8	I.1.17		.6	spherical	Greenish-opaque	1.91	5	Ceramic	Porous
164	I.6.65	V (ca. 1000 B.C.)	.8 × 1.0	spherical	Yellow-white-opaque	1.92	~3	Ceramic	Porous-blue color appears when immersed in water (fig. 17:4)
129	I.5.17		.9 × .5	biconical	Green-yellow Iridescent	2.17	~3	Glass	Extremely fragile, flakey coating
M-4	II.21.2		.6	spherical	Cobalt-blue Trans-lucent	2.47	>5.5	Glass	Partially covered with surface coating (patina)
M-1	II.21.2		.6 × .4	cylindrical	Cobalt-blue Trans-lucent	2.55	>5.5	Glass	Mostly covered with patina (fig. 17:8, 10)
110	I.2.126		.6	irregular sphere	Blue-Trans-parent	2.50	>5.5	Glass	
M-2	II.21.2		.6 × .4	cylindrical	Tan-Brown Trans-parent	2.57	~5.5	Glass	Some patina
M-3	II.21.2		.5 × .3	cylindrical	Blue-Trans-lucent	2.41	>5.5	Glass	Completely covered with patina blue appears in water
86	I.2.83		.4	spherical	Turq-uoise-Blue	2.55	5.5	Glass	
162	I.4.31	IIIb (ca. 100 B.C.)	.5	spherical	Turq-uoise Blue	2.37	5	Glass	(fig. 17:2)
84	I.10.7		1.4	spherical	Yellow-Trans-parent	1.03	~3.5	Resin or Plastic	Density is probably closer to 1.2 (one large bubble)

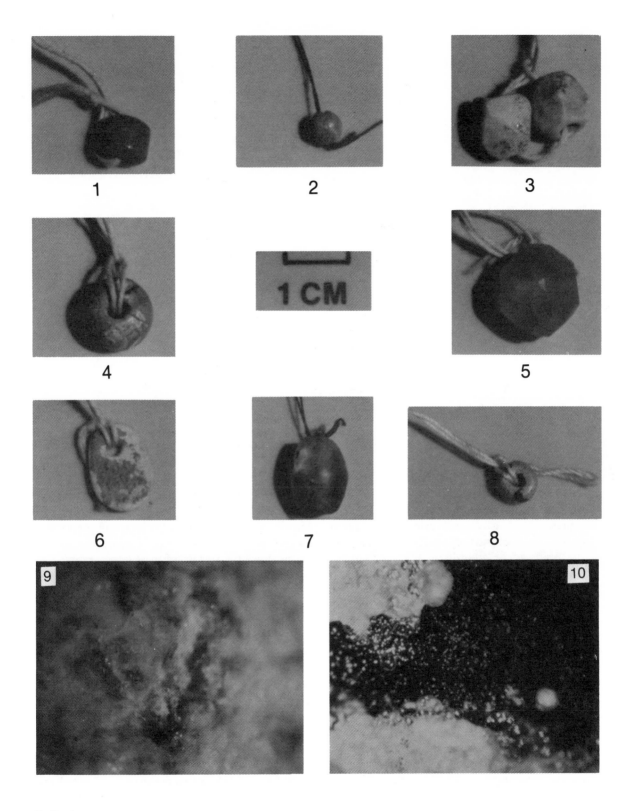

17. Beads.
1 = reg. no. 83, 2 = 162, 3 = 163, 4 = 164, 5 = 192, 6 = 194, 7 = 247, 8 = M-1; 9 = 163a, enlarged 100 ×, light zone is calcite coating; 10 = M-1, enlarged 100 ×, light zone is patina, dark zone is glass; note numerous bubbles.

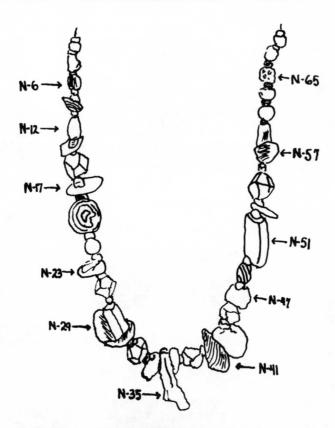

18. Necklace, no. 159 (individual beads with preface N), found with
a skelton (fig. 43) beneath megaliths inside the Qasr walls. See fig. 13
above.

The most common minerals available for bead manufacture and consistent with the density data are quartz (2.65 g/cc) and calcite (2.71 g/cc). However, x-ray diffraction analysis showed most of the beads to be amorphous (non-crystalline). Beads which did show crystalline reflections were 103, 247, 75, 194, and 163 a & b.

Beads 103, 247, and 75 gave x-ray results consistent with quartz. Beads 108 and 81, which are too large to fit the x-ray machine, also have color, density, and hardness consistent with quartz. The average density of these five beads is 2.69 g/cc and the range is 2.63 to 2.76. The high value of 2.76 g/cc is within 4% of the actual value for quartz (2.65 g/cc).

Sample 194 gave an x-ray pattern consistent with $CaCO_3$, but not the common variety (calcite). This sample, which appears to be a shell fragment, is composed of aragonite. Aragonite has a different crystralline structure than calcite and is not stable during geologic burial and fossilization. Consequently, this bead was probably made from a contemporarily living shell rather than a fossil. Beads 163 a & b also have a $CaCO_3$ pattern, but of calcite. However, the density (2.40-2.48 g/cc) is too low. Closer examination (fig. 17:9) showed that the calcite coats the surface of these beads, preventing determination of the crystalline nature of the underlying material by x-ray diffraction.

Excluding the five quartz beads and the shell fragment, the remaining 15 beads all have densities less than 2.57 g/cc and are x-ray amorphous (non-crystalline). Many of these beads also have surface coatings or patinas. Closer examination under a microscope (fig. 17:10) reveals numerous small to large bubbles. The bubbles and the patinas are consistent with glass. Glass has a density of approximately 2.45. Thus 10 samples (192, 163 a & b, M 1-4, 110, 86, and 162) with an average density of 2.47 g/cc, and a range of 2.37 to 2.57, are probably glass. Sample 129, with a density of 2.17 g/cc has a very well developed, flakey patina and is also glass. Sample 83 (with a density of 2.34 g/cc) is probably glass or ceramic. Beads no. 8 and no. 164 have

Table 7. Necklace, reg. no. 159, with burial II.7.55

Reg. No.	Composition	
N-47	fired clay	
N-37	shell (cowrie)	
N-57	shell	
N-41	shell	
N-29	shell	
N-10	shell	
N-51	obsidian	
N-56	obsidian	
N-35	iron slag (magnetic)	
N-13A	copper coin	
N-17	brass coin	German Rechenpfennigs (Tokens)
N-53	brass coin	probably 16th or 17th century*
N-12	quartz (agate)	
N-19	quartz (agate)	
N-27	quartz (agate)	
N-43	quartz (agate)	

All of the other 55 beads are glass

*Inscription on coins N-17 and N-53:
Obverse: *LAZAR GOTTL.LAUFFERS.RECH.PF
(Lazar . . . and Gottl . . ., bishops, penny counter)

Reverse: *GOTTES.REICH.BLEIBT.EWIG
(God's empire lasts forever)

densities of 1.91 and 1.92 g/cc, respectively. These beads are either ceramic (fired clay) or very porous glass.[1]

Bead no. 84 has an unusually low density and some bubbles. The one large bubble which is present will result in an error in the density determination. The true value is probably near 1.25 g/cc. It is either made of resin or is of modern origin (plastic).

In summary (Table 6), five of the beads are composed of quartz, one is aragonitic shell material and the remainder (except no. 84) are either glass or ceramic. Bead no. 84 is either some type of tree resin or a plastic material.

[1]All the beads were shown to Carolyn Hessenbruch, University of Pittsburgh, who confirmed that the majority of the beads are glass. Thanks are due her for confirming and elaborating the conclusions.

Chapter 6
Ancient Glass

Nancy L. Lapp

Unfortunately all the glass recovered from the three campaigns was quite fragmentary and it has not been possible to reconstruct the complete profile of a single vessel. But a good representation of glass forms for the first five centuries of the Christian era come from the Village (Field I) and the Qasr (Field II). Although the glass from stratigraphically sound loci was limited, it is worthwhile to publish some of the fragments by stratum in hopes that they may contribute to future glass studies. As in the case with pottery and other artifacts, each stratum may contain earlier glass fragments, but dated strata should provide *termini a quo*. A selection of the best preserved fragments has been made for publication from the 513 pieces in the glass registry. All fragments were compared to those published to be certain a fair sampling is presented. In the discussion which follows mention is made of comparable unpublished fragments when pertinent. Some parallels to published glass from other sites are mentioned, especially when they are chronologically significant.

For preliminary classification and study the writer is much indebted to her late husband, and to Miss Dorthea Harvey, a member of the 1961 (fall) excavation staff. Her studies form the basis for the present work. For more recent advice and suggestions, Mrs. Carolyn Hessenbruch of the University of Pittsburgh has been of great help and encouragement.

The classification and terminology is that of D. B. Harden, especially his publication of the Roman glass from Karanis (Harden 1936). In the figure descriptions, the color and preservation are mentioned first, and for this the writer is especially indebted to Mrs. Hessenbruch who checked and corrected many descriptions. Measurements are given across the vessel first, then the height, in an effort to note the size of the fragment from which the classification and description is derived. Information is given about the shape, technique, and decoration which supplements the drawings. The writer is thankful for all the help she has received from colleagues, but the final presentation is her full responsibility.

Plates and Bowls

Folded rims of plates and bowls were sometimes hollow in cross-section (Harden 1936: 13-14) and Araq el-Emir shallow and deep bowls had this type of rim throughout the Roman and Byzantine occupation. Plates and shallow bowls, and perhaps oval dishes (cf. especially fig. 23:1), with folded hollow rims are shown in figs. 19:1, 22:1, 23:1, 24:1, 2. Similar vessels are published from Jerash (Kraeling 1938: no. 242, 4th-5th cen.), Samaria (*SS III* 417: fig. 98:5, 4th cen., and others from the 5th cen.), the Judean Desert (Avigad 1962: 178, fig. 6:3, first third of the 2nd cen.), and Karanis, Egypt (Harden 1936: 52, 53, pl. 11:1, 15, 4th-5th cen.—oval dishes). The fold is usually outward, but fig. 22:1 is folded inward (cf. Harden 1936: 55, pls. 11:27—oval dish, and p. 109, pl. 14:242—deep bowl). Note also fig. 24:1 showing a hollow rim and a second tubular ring below, probably from a vessel with double folded hollow rim as those from El Bassa (Iliffe 1933: 88, figs. 19, 20). The cross-section shows that the rim of the vessel was folded

VILLAGE (Field I), Stratum II (ca. A.D. 100)

fig. 19:	reg. no.	prov.	description
1	54	I.1.33	shallow bowl or plate rim greenish, colorless; some frosting & dark iridescence frag. 4.3 × 1 cm; dia. 16 cm folded outward, hollow
2	253	I.5.37	deep bowl rim bluish green; frosty, some iridescence frag. 5.5 × 2.2 cm; dia. 16 cm folded outward, hollow
3	2	I.1.14	deep bowl rim greenish colorless; milky weathering, iridescence frag. 8 × 4 cm; dia. 13 cm outsplayed, rounded
4	466	I.1.120	shallow bowl or plate rim bluish-green; milky weathering frag. 2.2 × 1.6 cm; dia. 23 cm molded; rounded
5	224	I.2.116	deep bowl rim greenish; slight pitting frag. 2.3 × 1.8 cm; dia. 15 cm slightly outsplayed rim, unworked but ground, with bulging vertical ribbing at 1.5 cm below edge
6	436	I.11.73A	side of bowl greenish blue; frosty and enamel-like weathering, iridescence frag. 2 × 4 cm pillar-molded; ribbed, convex
7	4	I.1.15	bowl base bluish green; milky weathering & some dark iridescence frag., half base, 5 × 2/5 cm; dia. 5 cm pushed-in, tubular base ring, concave bottom with pontil mark
8	69	I.2.41	bowl base bluish-green; some enamel-like (brownish-black) weathering & pitting; iridescence reconstructed complete base; dia 5.4 cm pushed-in, tubular base ring, convex bottom with pontil mark
9	264	I.5.37	bowl base pale green; some milky weathering, dark iridescence frag. 4 × 1.5 cm; dia. 4 cm tubular base ring, very fragmentary; very thin ware
10	3	I.1.14	beaker or goblet rim greenish colorless; slight weathering frag. 4 × 4.5 cm; dia. 8 cm rounded & slightly outsplayed

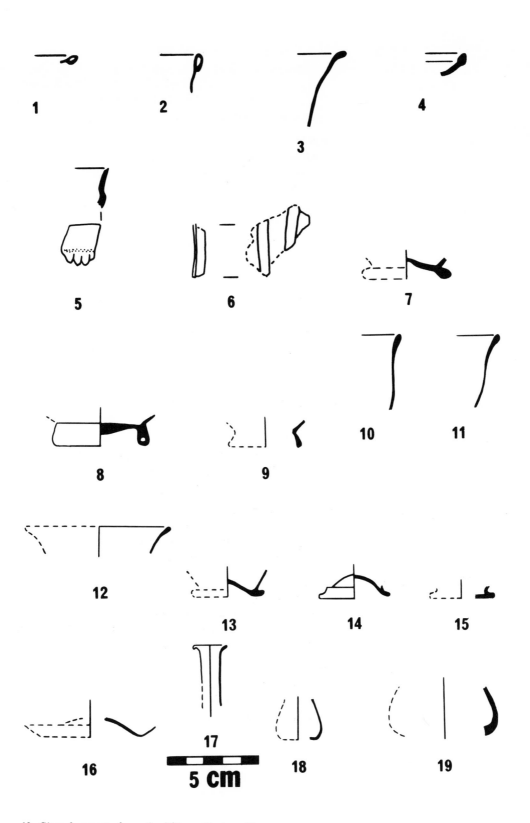

19. Glass fragments from the Village, Stratum II.

fig. 19, cont.:	*reg. no.*	*prov.*	*description*

11	53	I.1.33	beaker or goblet rim and side
			  greenish colorless; slight weathering
			  3 frags. 4 × 4, 2.5 × 4, 2.5 × 1.5 cm; dia. 8 cm
			  rounded outsplayed rim with trailed on zigzag thread
			    of same fabric; very thin ware

12	254	I.5.37	beaker or goblet rim
			  greenish; pitting, iridescence
			  frag. 3.5 × 2 cm; dia. 8 cm
			  rounded, outsplayed

13	257	I.5.37	beaker or goblet base
			  bluish; frosty enamel-like weathering; iridescence
			  reconstructed base; dia. 4 cm.
			  pushed-in, folded solid; concave bottom

14	268	I.4.38	beaker or goblet base
			  green; milky & enamel-like weathering; iridescence
			  complete base; dia. 4 cm
			  pushed-in, folded solid; concave bottom

15	467	I.1.120	beaker or goblet base
			  yellow-greenish colorless; pitted, enamel-like weathering,
			    iridescence
			  frag. 3 × 1 cm; dia. 3.8 cm
			  folded solid; flat bottom

16	97	I.1.61	flask base
			  greenish colorless; pitting, some frosting & iridescence
			  frag. 3.5 × 3 cm; dia. 5.8 cm
			  plain concave; very thin ware

17	354	I.9.104	bottle rim and neck
			  greenish colorless; iridescence
			  frag. 2 × 3.5 cm; complete rim, dia. 2 cm
			  outsplayed rim, infolded lip; very thin ware

18	353	I.9.103	bottle bottom
			  greenish colorless; frosting, iridescence
			  frag. 2.2 × 2.4 cm; dia. 2 cm
			  inverted piriform body, concave base; very thin ware
			  (probably part of no. 354, fig. 1:17)

19	185	I.10.25	bottle bottom
			  green; pitted, iridescence
			  frag. 2.5 × 2.2 cm
			  inverted piriform body

over to form the hollow rim, then melted alongside the exterior of the plate, and finally turned up to form the lower tubular decoration. Preliminary observation may seem to indicate that it is from a very shallow plate with a hollow rim and a tubular ring base below (for deeper bowls like this cf. Harden 1936: pl. 12:117, 118, and *SS III*, 417 fig. 98:5), but close scrutiny of the vessel's construction indicates otherwise.

Folded deep bowl rims with hollow cross-sections are shown in figs. 19:2, 20:1, 23:2, 3, and 24:3-5. From the fragment it is impossible to tell whether fig. 23:4 is from a shallow bowl with short straight sides (cf. Harden 1936: pl. 12:83-108) or from a deeper bowl. Deep bowls with rims folded outward are shown from Karanis (Harden 1936: 105-108, pl. 14: 231-237, probably not pre-Constantinian), the Judean Desert (Barag 1962: 209-10, fig. 4, early 2nd cen.), Jerash (Kraeling 1938: 529, fig. 22:380, 4th-5th cen.—"probably . . . hanging lamps"), and Samaria (*SS III*: fig. 99:2, 3, 6th-15th cen.—beaker lamps). This common rim treatment, folded over leaving a hollow cross-section, appears in stratified contexts at Araq el-Emir from ca. A.D. 100-500. Besides those published there were numerous others from stratified and unstratified context, particularly at the Qasr. Comparative material indicates a long history other places as well.

A few bowl rims from the Araq el-Emir occupation were folded solid or rounded off by reheating (figs. 19:3, 21:1, 23:5, 24:6-8; cf. Harden 1936: 13). The fragment, fig. 23:5, is from a delicate small bowl in thin ware. Comparable to the rim in fig. 21:1 is a rim from an oval dish from Karanis (Harden 1936: pl. 11:28). The outsplayed rounded rims in fig. 19:3 and 24:8 are similar to the early second century rims from the Judean Desert (Barag 1962: 209-10, figs. 3, 8, 9) and the Wadi ed-Daliyeh (Weinberg and Barag 1964: 104, fig. 39:5, 6).

Several different rim forms which are probably mold-pressed came from the Village (figs. 1:4, 2:2-5, and a number of comparable fragments from Stratum I). None came from the strata or debris of the Qasr (mainly 4th and 5th centuries), and their appearance in the Village strata fit well with the evidence that they belong to an early fabric that disappeared after the second and third centuries A.D. (Harden 1936: 64 [shallow bowls], 96 [deep bowls]). From Stratum II of the Village (ca. A.D. 100) came the fragment of a bowl with vertical

ribbing on a bulging body below its unworked rim (fig. 19:5). The bowl base and side fragment from Stratum I, fig. 20:8, probably came from the same kind of bowl. Possible parallels come from Karnis (Harden 1936: 92, pl. 13:215, or p. 123, pl. 15:355), Samaria (*SS III*: 406, fig. 93:3), and similar bowls are in the Carnegie Museum collection, dated to the first century A.D. (Bergman and Oliver 1980: nos. 22-28). From the same statum came the side piece of a ribbed pillar-molded bowl, fig. 19:6. A complete mid-first century A.D. pillar-molded bowl is shown in the British Museum publication (Harden *et al* 1968: 45, no. 52). This is a prevalent type in the Near east usually considered as belonging to the first century A.D. (cf. Harden 1936: 99-101, 118, pl. 14: 310; Reisner, Fisher, and Lyon 1924: 330, fig. 203, II 1 K and II 1 l), and the Village Stratum II evidence supports this dating.

The molded rims from Stratum I (ca. A.D. 200), fig. 20:2-5, included a broad out-turned rim (fig. 20:2) which is similar to some from the Judean Desert (Yadin 1963: 106, fig. 39:10, 11, and Barag 1962: 210-11, fig. 6), dated to the early part of the second century, and from Karanis (Harden 1936: 60, pl. 11:73; p. 83, pl. 12:166). The mold-pressed bowl of heavy ware, fig. 20:4, is comparable to a number found at Samaria that date to the first century B.C. or early 1st century A.D. (*SS III*: 406, no. 2, fig. 93:2) and fig. 20:3 is similar to another Samaria deep bowl (fig. 93:6). The rim, fig. 20:5, has been carefully smoothed and polished (cf. Harden 1936: 13) and has a tiny groove slightly below the rim on the inside; in a similar manner is one from the Judean Desert (Barag 1962: 209, fig. 7) which is rounded and polished with a wheel-cut line just below the rim on the interior, but its sides are slightly concave.

Bowl rims, fig. 24:9 and 10, are unworked, similar to the bowl form Karanis (Harden 1936: 123, pl. 15:331). According to Harden, bowls with plain-cut or polished rims and a constriction just below are very prevalent from the 2nd century to the fifth; and outside Europe, particularly later, the sides tend to be straighter and bowls higher (Harde 1936: 101).

Several kinds of bowl bases are represented, and the fragmentary samples do not make it certain that the following are all from the shallow or deep bowls. But these types are typical of Roman and Early Byzantine vessels. Most common is the pushed-in base forming a tubular base ring (for method see Harden 1936: 16). The majority were

VILLAGE (Field II), Stratum I (ca. A.D. 200)

fig. 20:	reg. no.	prov.	description
1	229	I.6.39	deep bowl rim greenish blue colorless; little weathering frag. 4.5 × 1.7 cm; dia. 12 cm folded outward, rounded, hollow
2	380	I.5.12A	deep bowl rim greenish blue; milky weathering, iridescence frag. 2.9 × 1.5 cm; dia. 14 cm molded; broad out-turned
3	141	I.10.4D	deep bowl rim green; milky weathering; dark iridescence frag. 3.5 × 3.2 cm; dia. 12 cm molded (?), thick ware; interior groove 1.2 cm from top edge, irregular horizontal tool marks on exterior
4	216	I.1.82	deep bowl rim yellowish; pitting, iridescence frag. 3.2 × 3 cm; dia. 14 cm molded; plain with ground edge; interior groove 1 cm from edge
5	258	I.5.39	deep bowl rim colorless; pitting, enamel-like weathering, iridescence frag. 3.5 × 2.5 cm; dia. 14 cm plain, polished; tiny groove .1 cm below inner edge
6	209	I.10.17	bowl base greenish; pitting, milky & enamel-like weathering; iridescence frag. 6 × 2.3 cm; dia. 6 cm pushed-in, tubular base ring, concave bottom
7	8	I.2.11	bowl, beaker, or flask base greenish; frosting, some milky weathering; iridescence frag. 6.5 × 5.5 cm; dia. 8 cm pushed-in, tubular base ring, concave bottom with pontil mark
8	165	I.10.15	deep bowl base and side yellowish green colorless; pitting, milky weathering, iridescence frag. 3.5 × 2.8 cm; dia. 10 cm molded; rounded base & side; vertical ribs & ridge around vessel bottom
9	208	I.10.22	deep bowl base and side bluish green; milky weathering, iridescence frag. 4.5 × 2.3 cm rounded bottom & lower side with parallel raised fine horizontal lines (trailed threads ?)

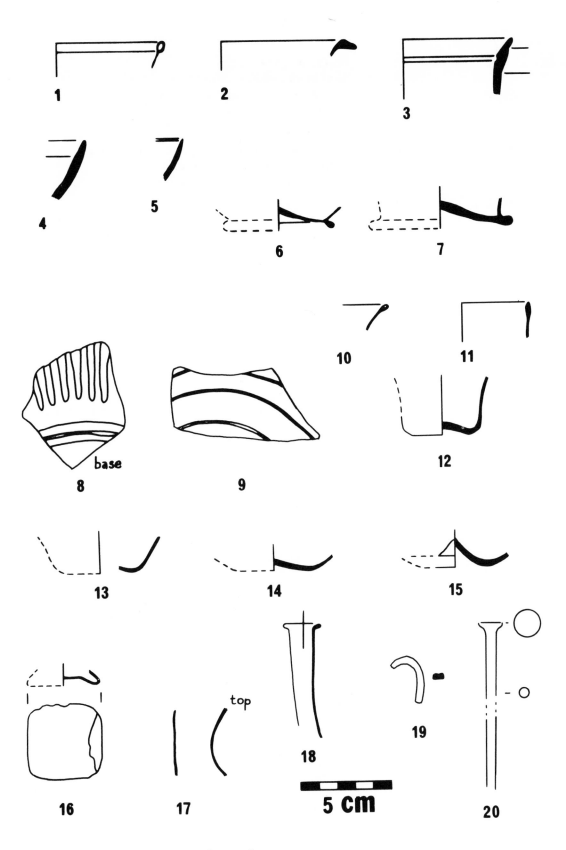

20. Glass fragments from the Village, Stratum I.

fig. 20, cont.:	*reg. no.*	*prov.*	*description*
10	182	I.1.81	beaker or goblet rim greenish; frosting, iridescence frag. 3.2 × 1.6 cm; dia. 10 cm rounded, outsplayed
11	183	I.1.81	beaker rim greenish colorless; pitting, milky weathering frag. 2. × 1.8 cm; dia. 8 cm rounded rim, vertical sides
12	374	I.9.113A	beaker base greenish colorless; milky weathering, dark iridescence frag. 5.2 × 3 cm; complete base, dia. 4 cm plain concave
13	247	I.4.8	beaker base bluish green colorless; milky weathering, iridescence frag. 4.5 × 2.4 cm; dia. 4 cm plain concave
14	222	I.5.12	beaker, flask, or bowl base bluish; milky weathering, iridescence frag. 5.6 × 3.4 cm; dia. 5 cm plain, slightly concave
15	210	I.10.19	flask base greenish; milky weathering, iridescence frag. 5 × 2.4 cm; dia. 3.5 cm concave with sharp kick
16	59	I.1.32	jug or bottle base greenish colorless; enamel-like weathering, pitting, iridescence reconstructed complete base, 4 × 4 cm rectangular concave; very thin ware
17	202	I.10.26	flask or bottle side piece colorless; iridescence frag. 3.8 × 4 cm body frag. of 8(?)-sided vessel; mold-blown (?); very thin ware
18	142	I.10.4D	bottle neck and rim bluish greenish; iridescence frag. 2.2 × 6 cm; complete rim, dia. 2.2 cm long narrow neck with outsplayed infolded rim; very thin ware
19	300	I.11.7	small vessel handle greenish; frosting, pitting, iridescence frag. 2.8 × 7 cm flat, ribbed, in simple C-curve, apparently two coils melted together
20	223 260	I.5.12 I.5.39	fragments of stirring rod yellowish green; milky weathering, iridescence 2 frags. .7 × 4.1 cm, 4 × .8 cm; dia. head 1.3 cm solid, faint diagonal toolmarks & flat butt end

from the Village strata (figs. 19:7-9, 20:6, and 20:7 which may be from a beaker or flask, cf. Harden 1936: pl. 19:709), but there were also unstratified fragments from the Qasr (fig. 24:11-13). Usually a hollow ring shows in cross-section, but in a number of bases from the Qasr area the type was solid (fig. 24:13 and several comparable fragments). Also unstratified from the Qasr is a complete base which may be the pad type (fig. 24:14), and a fragment of a large vessel from Qasr Stratum II, fig. 22:2, is either a pad or a true ring base (made by adding either a pad or a ring of glass; see Harden 1936:16). There were also several coil bases (fig. 24:15) from the Qasr, including an unpublished one from Stratum II.

Most interesting are the rounded bases from decorated bowls, fig. 20:8, 9, from Stratum I in the Village (ca. A.D. 200). Fig. 20:8 shows the base of a fragment with vertical ribbing quite similar to that of fig. 19:5, although the fragment is more weathered (cf. the parallels mentioned there). The sherd, fig. 20:9, has finely raised horizontal lines which may be an early example of trailed threads. A similar decoration on a bottle in the Palestine Archaeological Museum, Jerusalem (exhibit no. 1242), is described as perhaps transitional between the earlier style of the inlaid and the later style of the applied thread (Gallery Book 1943: 50).

Beakers, Globlets, and Flasks

Fragments of rounded rims with fairly wide mouths and straight or slightly curved sides probably came from beakers or goblets. A rounded outsplayed rim was very frequent in all strata at the Village in the Qasr (figs. 19:10-12, 20:10, 22:3, 24:16-18, and many similar fragements). Rims 19:12, 20:10, 22:3, and 24:16, from Village Strata II, I, Qasr Stratum II and unstratified, respectively, are especially similar.

The more straight-sided vessels, figs. 20:11, 23:6-8, are probably beakers (cf. Harden 1936: 132). One smaller vessels has a rounded, but infolded, rim (fig. 24:19). A number of the vessels have a trailed on thread for decoration—fig. 19:11 in a slightly zig-zag pattern, fig. 23:7, 8, horizontally around. Two beakers quite similar to the latter two came from Samaria (*SS III*: fig. 94:14, 3rd cen.; fig. 95:20, 4th-5th cen.; they are straight sided and slightly outsplayed at the rim, have trailed on threads horizontally around, and pad bases similar to those of fig. 24:23, 24 (see below).

Several pushed-in, folded solid, bases from the Village Stratum II (fig. 19:13-15) probably belong to goblets or beakers. Unstratified from the Village is a slightly folded base, probably also from a beaker or goblet (fig. 21:2). More obviously from goblets are pushed-in tubular bases from the Qasr, fig. 23:9 (Stratum I), and fig. 24:20-22 (unstratified). A goblet from Samaria illustrates the type (*SS III*: fig. 96:10). Fig. 24:20 and 21 are stemmed, and the latter has a sharp kick.

Also found unstratified at the Qasr are two pad bases, which may belong to beakers (fig. 24:23, 24), although jars and bowls also have this type (cf. the beakers from Samaria mentioned above, *SS III*: figs. 94:14, 95:20).

Plain flat to concave bases are characteristic of beakers (figs. 20:12-14, 23:10, 11; cf. Harden 1936: pl. 15:371-396). Flasks also often have this kind of base (figs. 19:16, 20:15, 24:25; cf. Harden 1936: pls. 17:533-542, 18:594-612). Often from fragmentary Araq el-Emir pieces it is impossible to distinguish the kind of vessel (figs. 20:14, 23:11). Note the flasks from Samaria (*SS III*: 408, fig. 94:8, and also 6, 9, 10, 3rd cen.; fig. 95:4, 9, 10, 4th-5th cen.). The Araq el-Emir flask base, fig. 20:15 has a sharp kick (cf. Harden 1936: pl. 18:594, 599, 600).

Flask rims, outsplayed and infolded, were unstratified in the Village (fig. 21:3) and from the varoius stata at the Qasr (figs. 23:12, 24:26, and comparable sherds). To the flask with a handle (fig. 23:12) compare that from El Bassa (Iliffe 1933: 89, fig. 24, late 4th cen.) and Harden's class of tall-necked flasks with infolded rims (1926: pl. 18:594-600, but these are handleless). Fig. 21:4 represents a large flask with a flaring rounded rim. A large flask with a less flaring rim came from a third century context at Samaria (*SS III*: 408, fig. 94:8). The fragment, fig. 24:27, is from a flask or bottle with a straight cylindrical neck and inward turned rim. It may be comparable to a vessel from Karanis (Harden 1936: 197, pl. 17:530).

Chronologically, the beaker, goblet, and flasks types found at Araq el-Emir are represented throughout the occupation of the site.

Jars and Bottles

Two rim fragments may best be classed with jars (figs. 21:5, 22:4) because of their short necks yet obvious bulbous bodies in relation to their mouths (cf. Harden 1936: 174). The unstratified rim from the Village is outsplayed and rounded; that from

VILLAGE (Field I), Unstratified

fig. 21:	reg. no.	prov.	description
1	7	I.2.10	shallow bowl rim greenish colorless; milky and enamel-like weathering; iridescence frag. 10 × 2.1 cm; dia. 16 cm folded outward
2	236	I.5.23	beaker, goblet, bowl, or flask base greenish colorless; pitting, enamel-like weathering, iridescence frag. 3.5 × 1.5 cm; dia. 5 cm lightly folded, probably concave; fragmentary
3	237	I.4.3	flask rim pale bluish colorless; pitting, enamel-like weathering, iridescence frag. 2.3 × 1 cm; dia. 3 cm outsplayed, infolded
4	66	I.1.35	flask rim light blue; pitting, enamel-like weathering, iridescence frag. 4 × 1.7 cm; dia. 8 cm outsplayed, rounded & ground
5	159	I.9.3	jar rim slightly green colorless; milky weathering; iridescence frag. 5.5 × 1.7 cm; dia. 8 cm outsplayed, rounded

QASR (Field II), Stratum II (ca. A.D. 335-365)

fig. 22:	reg. no.	prov.	description
1	315	II.16.6	shallow bowl or plate rim pale blue colorless; some iridescence frag. 4 × 1.9 cm; dia. 22 cm outsplayed infolded, hollow
2	335 407	II.16.9 II.21.3	large vessel base green; milky weathering, iridescence 2 frags. reconstructed 7.5 × 4.5 cm; dia. 10 cm pad or true ring base, took marks, flat bottom; broadly outsplayed sides, probably shallow
3	157	II.14.9	beaker or goblet rim pale greenish colorless; pitting, milky weathering, iridescence frag. 1.5 × 1.1 cm; dia. 10 cm rounded, outsplayed
4	319	II.16.5	jar rim pale green colorless; iridescence frag. 4.8 × 3 cm; dia 14 cm unworked, incurved
5	274	II.7.64	conical lamp base pale greenish; pitting, iridescence frag. 3.2 × 5 cm; dia. 2 cm conical straight-sided body, small concave base

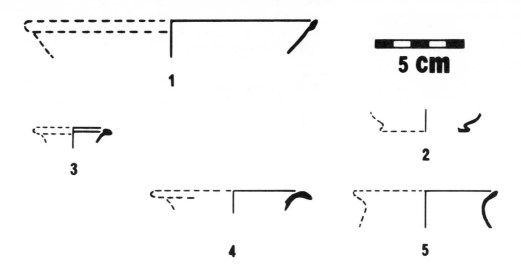

21. Glass fragments from the Village, unstratified.

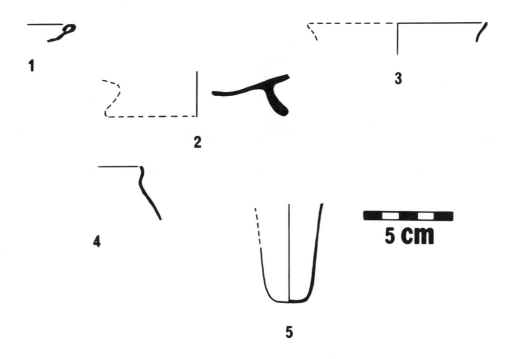

22. Glass fragments from the Qasr, Stratum II.

QASR (Field II), Stratum I (ca. A.D. 365-500)

fig. 23:	reg no.	prov.	description
1	199	II.7.16	plate or dish rim pale greenish colorless; iridescence frag. 8 × 1.4 cm; dia. 35 cm folded outward, hollow
2	197	II.7.16	shallow or deep bowl rim bluish; iridescence frag. 4 × 1.1 cm; dia. 14 cm folded outward, hollow
3	194	II.7.16	deep bowl rim pale bluish-greenish, frosting, iridescence 4 frags. reconstructed, 13 × 2.8 cm; dia. 16 cm folded outward, hollow then joining vessel sides
4	61	II.1.16	bowl rim greenish colorless; frosting, pitting frags. 2 × 5 cm; dia. 15 cm folded outward, shallow, very thin ware
5	26	II.1.8	deep bowl rim pale greenish colorless; milky weathering frag. 1.8 × 1.3 cm; dia. 10 cm rounded
6	47	II.1.15	beaker rim bluish colorless; pitting, dulling, iridescence frag. 3 × 3.2 cm; dia. 10 cm rounded
7	272	II.7.61	beaker rim pale greenish colorless, iridescence frag. 3 × 6 cm; dia. 10 cm rounded; dark blue thread 8 cm from rim; tool marks on inside
8	186	II.1.13	beaker rim bluish colorless, milky weathering, iridescence 3 frags., largest 5.6 × 2.1 cm; dia. 8 cm rounded; horizontal trailed thread design on sides
9	140	II.7.7	goblet base greenish colorless; milky weathering, iridescence complete base; dia. 5 cm pushed-in, tubular, concave bottom; ovoid body
10	200	III.1.3	beaker (?) base greenish colorless, milky weathering, iridescence frag. 3 × 3 cm; dia. 9 cm plain concave (?); fragmentary
11	143	II.7.6	beaker or flask (?) base green, milky weathering, iridescence frag. 3.5 × 1.5 cm; dia. 5 cm plain, sharply concave

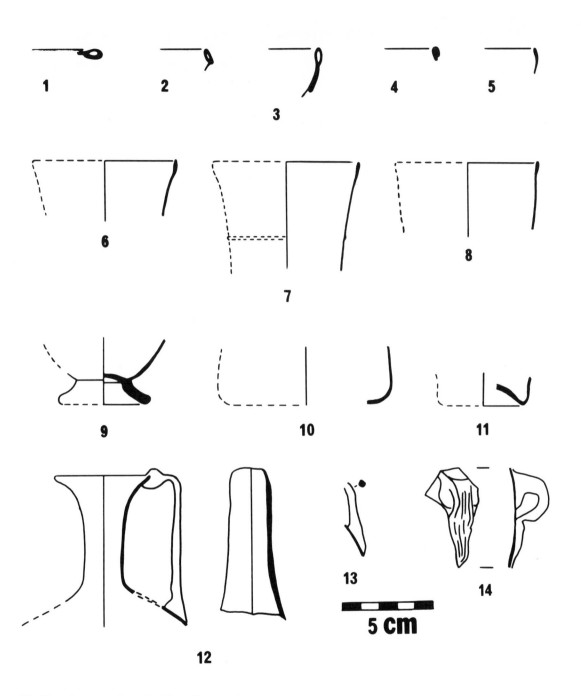

23. Glass fragments from the Qasr, Stratum I.

fig. 23, cont.:	*reg. no.*	*prov.*	*description*

12	138, 147-150, 172	III.1.1
		
		III.1.2
			flask rim, neck, and handle
			    blue; enamel-like weathering, pitting, iridescence
			    reconstructed 7.2 × 9 cm; dia. 5.2 cm
			    outsplayed infolded, rounded & ground rim; cylindrical neck;
			        broad, flat, ribbed handle

13	154	II.7.8	handle
			    blue-green; milky weathering
			    frag. 4.2 × 1.7 cm
			    coil with sharp center ridge

14	207	II.6.7	handle
			    blue-green; iridescence
			    frag. 5.4 × 3 cm
			    flattened, ribbed, with side-whisker

QASR (Field II), Unstratified

fig. 24:	*reg. no.*	*prov.*	*description*

1	133	II.6.2	shallow bowl rim
			    greenish; iridescence
			    frag. 4.6 × 2.1 cm; dia. 20 cm
			    outfolded hollow rim with tubular fold below formed from
			        outside fold

2	400	II.11B.8	shallow bowl or plate rim
			    pale bluish colorless; iridescence
			    frag. 3.5 × 1 cm; dia. 20 cm
			    folded outward, hollow

3	261	II.7.54	deep bowl rim
			    blue colorless; little weathering
			    frag. 5.5 × 2 cm; dia. 14.5 cm
			    folded outward, hollow

4	38	II.2.2	deep bowl rim
			    bluish; pitting, iridescence
			    frag. 3 × 1.2 cm; dia. 20 cm
			    folded outward, rounded, hollow

5	474	II.11B.2	deep bowl rim
			    blue-green; pitting, iridescence
			    frag. 2.6 × 1.6 cm; dia. 24 cm
			    incurved, outfolded, elongated, & hollow

6	391	II.21.2	deep bowl rim
			    pale green; pitting, iridescence
			    frag. 2.9 × 1.6 cm; dia. 12 cm
			    infolded, rounded

7	419	II.21.4	deep bowl rim
			    greenish; pitting, iridescence
			    frag. 3 × 3.1 cm; dia. 12 cm
			    rounded, incurved

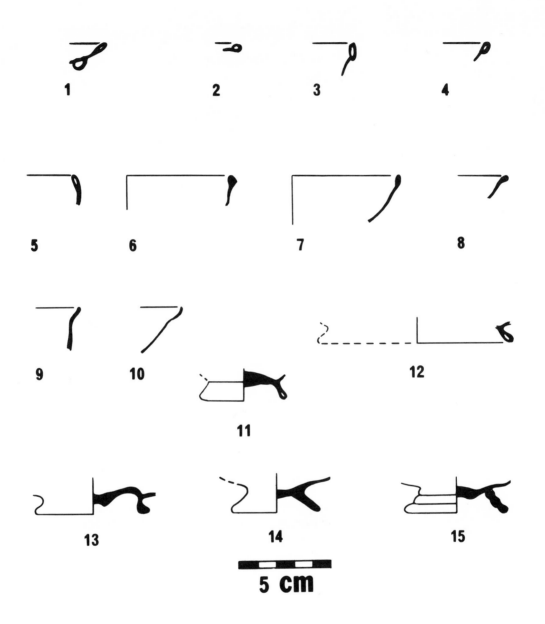

24. Glass fragments from the Qasr, unstratified (*continued p. 59*).

24 *cont.* Glass fragments from the Qasr, unstratified.

8   455   II.16.28   deep bowl rim
                               greenish; pitting, iridescence
                               frag. 2.4 × 1.7 cm; dia. 22 cm
                               rounded, outsplayed, & ground

9   365   II.16.22   deep bowl rim
                               dark greenish; dark iridescence
                               frag. 3.6 × 2.5 cm; dia. 10 cm
                               unfinished, convex

10   478   II.18.2   deep bowl rim
                               pale greenish colorless; pitting, iridescence
                               frag. 3.7 × 3.4 cm; dia. 14 cm
                               unfinished, convex

11   425   II.11C.2   bowl base
                               pale blue-green; pitting, milky weathering, iridescence
                               complete base, dia. 4.8 cm
                               pushed-in, tubular base ring, flat bottom with pontil mark

12   406   II.21.3   bowl base
                               green; pitting, iridescence
                               frag. 5.1 × 1.1 cm; dia. 10.5 cm
                               tubular base ring; very fragmentary

13   357   II.16.22   bowl base
                               blue-green; pitting, milky weathering, iridescence
                               frag. 5.8 × 1.2 cm; dia. 6.3 cm
                               pushed-in, tubular base ring, convex bottom with pontil mark

14   116   II.4.1   bowl base
                               green; milky weathering, pitting, iridescence
                               frag. 5.9 × 1.8 cm; complete base, dia. 5 cm
                               pushed-in or pad, outsplayed, flat bottom with pontil mark

15   326   II.16.3   bowl base
                               blue-green; milky weathering, dulling, iridescence
                               frag. 6 × 1.7 cm; complete base, dia. 6 cm
                               coiled ring, convex bottom with pontil mark

16   94   II.2.30   beaker or goblet rim
                               pale blue colorless; pitting, milky weathering, iridescence
                               frag. 5.2 × 4.8 cm; dia. 5 cm
                               rounded, outsplayed

17   104   II.4.4   beaker or goblet rim
                               greenish colorless; pitting, milky weathering, iridescence
                               frag. 3.8 × 3.1 cm; dia. 8 cm
                               rounded, outsplayed

18   112   II.6.3   beaker or goblet rim
                               greenish colorless; milky weathering, iridescence
                               frag. 4.6 × 2.1 cm; dia. 8 cm
                               rounded, outsplayed

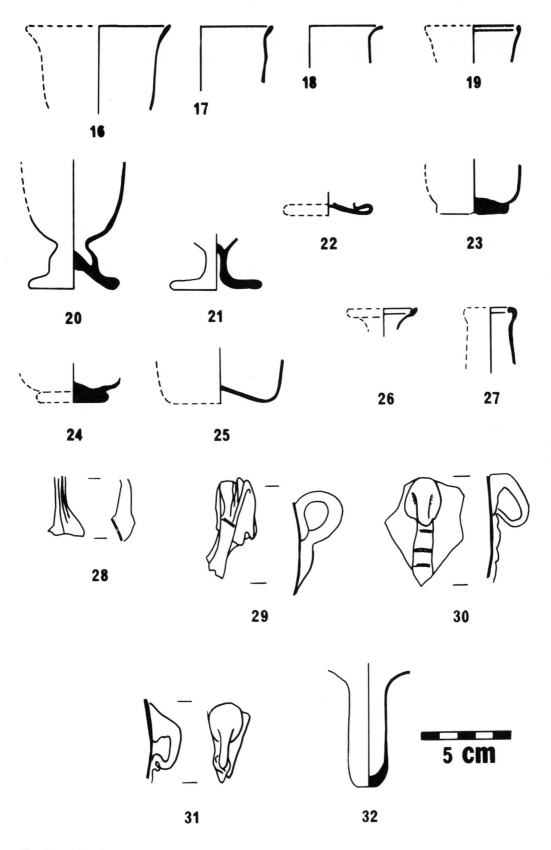

Fig. 24 *continued.*

fig. 24, cont.:	reg. no.	prov.	description
19	131	II.6.2	beaker rim greenish; pitting, iridescence frag. 5.9 × 1.8 cm; dia. 5 cm infolded, rounded
20	234	II.7.32	goblet base and body green; iridescence frag. 5 × 6.5 cm; complete base, dia. 5 cm pushed-in, tubular ring base, concave bottom with kick and pontil mark; tall conical body
21	219	II.7.25	goblet base greenish; enamel-like weathering, iridescence frag. 5 × 2.5 cm; complete base, dia. 5 cm pushed-in tubular ring base, flat bottom with sharp kick; short stem
22	297	II.15.1	goblet (?) base pale greenish; dulling, some iridescence frag. 2.7 × .8 cm; dia. 5 cm pushed-in, tubular ring hollow base, flat bottom
23	443	II.11C.4	beaker, jar, or bowl base bluish; milky weathering, iridescence frag. 5.5 × 2.9 cm; complete base, dia. 4 cm flat pad base with pontil marks; inverted piriform or bulbous body
24	64	II.2.16	beaker or bowl base bluish green; enamel-like weathering, iridescence frag. 1.5 × 5.3 cm; complete base, dia. 4 cm flat pad base with pontil mark
25	220	II.7.25	flask base greenish colorless; milky weathering frag. 4.5 × 2.3 cm; dia. 6 cm concave base with pontil mark
26	233	II.7.36	flask rim pale bluish green; iridescence frag. 2.8 × 1.7 cm; dia. 4 cm infolded, outsplayed
27	371	II.17.5	flask or bottle rim pale bluish colorless; enamel-like weathering, iridescence frag. 2.8 × 3.2 cm; dia. 3 cm infolded, cylindrical neck (?)
28	129	II.6.5	handle blue-green; pitting, iridescence frag. 2 × 3.2 cm ribbed coil

fig. 24, cont.:	reg. no.	prov.	description
29	118	II.8.3	handle pale bluish; milky weathering frag. 2.5 × 5.5 cm ribbed coil with side whisker
30	15	II.1.7	handle blue-green; milky weathering, iridescence frag. 4 × 6 cm plain coil with side whisker, scalloped down side of vessel
31	363	II.16.22	handle blue-green; dulling, iridescence frag. 2.5 × 4.5 cm plain coil, probably with scalloped side whisker which has broken off
32	52	II.2.4	lamp stem greenish colorless; pitting, iridescence frag. 4.3 × 6 cm hollow, rounded on bottom with pontil mark

the Qasr Stratum II is unworked and incurved.

From Stratum I in the Village came the base of a four-sided bottle and the side piece of an 8 or 10-sided vessel (fig. 20;16, 17; cf. the rectangular bottle, Harden 1936: pl. 20:757 and pp. 248-50).

From Village Strata I and II came several fragments of bottles, often called unguentaria (figs. 19:17-19, 20:18), the most widespread and constant shape of Roman glass found all over the Roman Empire from the first to the fifth centuries (Harden 1936: 265). The Araq el-Emir specimens are of thin and fragile ware, probably the reason more fragments were not preserved. Parallels are many, but attention may be drawn to bottles from Samaria (*SS III*: 408, fig. 94:1-10, 3rd cen.; 411, fig. 95:1-11, 4th-5th cen.), Karanis (Harden 1936: class XIII, especially p. 270), and the collection in the Carnegie Museum of Pittsburgh (Bergman and Oliver 1980: nos. 87-111).

Handles

During this period handles appeared on jars, jugs, and some flasks. The only handle fragment from the Village (fig. 20:19) was probably from a small flask; it was made from two coils. A great variety came from the Qasr. Note the broad flat and ribbed handle of the flask, fig. 23:12. Similar handles appeared on late flasks from Karanis (Harden 1936: pl. 19:711, 734, 739). A smaller "celery" ribbed handle, fig. 24:28, is probably from a small flask (cf. Harden 1936: pl. 19:728). The plain handle, fig. 23:13, may be from a tiny flask (cf. Harden 1936: pl. 20: 793 and 796). A particular style of coil handle has been named "side-whisker" because the coil ends in a long tail extending down the side of the vessel, sometimes scalloped at intervals by pinching (Harden 1936: 16). They may be plain or ribbed to varying degrees (cf. Kraeling 1938: 529, fig. 22:57). Note the heavy ribbing of fig. 24:29, "celery" ribbing of fig. 23:14, and the plain handle but even and elaborate scalloping down the side of fig. 24:30. Fig. 24:31 probably represents the latter type but the coil has broken off at the bottom. At Karanis these handles were on "poppy-head" type jars (Harden 1936: 182-83, pl. 17: 509, 511) dating to the 4th and 5th centuries (p. 174).

Except for the one village fragment, all the Araq el-Emir handles are from the Qasr and probably date to the 4th and 5th centuries. This corresponds to the dating of the parallels cited.

Stirring Rod and Lamps

Two pieces of a stirring rod came from Village Stratum I (fig. 20:20). It is of solid glass and has faint diagonal tool markings. The stirring rod is prevalent throughout the Roman Empire (Harden 1936: 286) and at Samaria their findspots suggested an Early Roman date (*SS III*:420).

Two lamp fragments are illustrated, one of the conical type (fig. 22:5 from Stratum II of the Qasr), and the other, a hollow stem lamp (fig. 24:32, Qasr unstratified). Whole specimens of canonical lamps, hollow and with flattened bases as the Araq el-

Emir fragments, are shown from Karanis (Harden 1936: pl. 16:455-460); they developed about the beginning of the 4th century and were very common from then onward (p. 156). A lamp from El Bassa dates from the end of the 4th century (Iliffe 1933: 89, fig. 21). The stem type is best illustrated from Samaria (*SS III*: 414-15, fig. 96:6) where many were found. Fragments come from Jerash (Kraeling 1938: 520, fig. 17). The parallels to both types of lamps come from the 4th and 5th centuries, coinciding with the Qasr occupation at Araq el-Emir.

BIBLIOGRAPHY

Avigad, N.
  1963   The Expedition to the Judean Desert, 1961, Expedition A. *Israel Exploration Journal* 12: 169-83.
Barag, D.
  1962   Glass from the Cave of Horror. *Israel Exploration Journal* 12: 208-214.
Bergman, S. M. and Oliver, A.
  1980   *Ancient Glass in the Carnegie Museum of Natural History, Pittsburgh.* Pittsburgh: Board of Trustees, Carnegie Institute.
Crowfoot, J. W.; Crowfoot, G. M.; and Kenyon, K. M.
  1957   *The Objects from Samaria.* London: Palestine Exploration Fund.
Harden, D. B.
  1936   *Roman Glass from Karanis.* Ann Arbor: University of Michigan.
Harden, D. B., *et al*
  1968   *Masterpieces of Glass.* London: Trustees of the British Museum.
Iliffe, J. H.
  1933   A Tomb at El Bassa of c. A.D. 396. *Quarterly of the Department of Antiquities of Palestine.* 4: 81-91.
Kraeling, C. H.
  1938   *Gerasa, City of the Decapolis.* New Haven, Conn.: American Schools of Oriental Research.

Palestine Archaeological Museum
  1943   Palestine Archaeological Museum Gallery Book. Persian, Hellenistic, Roman Byzantine Periods. (Mimeographed.)
Reisner, G. A.; Fisher, C. S.; and Lyon, D. G.
  1924   *Harvard Excavations at Samaria, 1908-1910.* Cambridge: Harvard University.
SS III
  1957   *The Objects from Samaria* by C. W. Crowfoot, G. M. Crowfoot, and K. M. Kenyon. London: Palestine Exploration Fund.
Weinberg, G. D., and Barag, D.
  1974   Glass Vessels. Pp. 103-105 in *Discoveries in the Wâdī ed-Dâliyeh,* ed. Paul W. Lapp and Nancy L. Lapp. Annual of the American Schools of Oriental Research 41. Cambridge, MA: American Schools of Oriental Research.
Yadin, Y.
  1963   *The Finds from the Bar Kokhba Period in the Cave of the Letters.* Jerusalem: Israel Exploration Society.

Chapter 7

Hellenistic Pottery from the Qasr and Square Building

NANCY L. LAPP

One of the express purposes of the first campaign at Araq el-Emir by Paul W. Lapp in 1961 was to date the construction of the monumental building, the Qasr el-Abd (Lapp 1962: 16). "Hardly a scrap of evidence" resulted from the spring campaign (p. 33), but in the extensive excavations of the second and third campaigns a satisfactory number of sherds from the first half of the second century B.C. was unearthed. Although the sherds were mainly from Byzantine fills, correlating this evidence with the literary and architectural evidence clearly attributed the Qasr to Hyrcanus' building operations in the early second century B.C. (Lapp 1963: 24). In this study the pottery evidence for the dating of the Qasr will be presented in detail (Lapp 1962: 16).[1]

The feline fountain uncovered near the end of P. Lapp's final campaign is near the northeast corner of the Qasr (fig. 25). Although it could not be dated by pottery stratigraphically related to it, artistically and culturally its early second century B.C. creation is certain (Hill 1963: 55). Before its discovery in the east wall extensive clearance had been carried on around the northeast corner. An area had been opened there during the first week of the initial campaign. Two Byzantine floor levels were uncovered running against the outside Qasr wall, but pottery evidence for any Hellenistic occupation was entirely lacking (fig. 26). An attempt to find a Hellenistic floor or closed locus was

a particular aim of the two suceeding campaigns, but only occasional Hellenistic sherds were uncovered. By the time of the discovery of the feline fountain, the excavators were fairly certain that the Qasr had never been completed or actually used by its Hellenistic builders (Lapp 1963: 24). However, the discovery of the fountain near the end of the third campaign did set off an intensive search along the east wall of the Qasr for a possible counterpart to it at the southern end. Nearly the length of the wall was cleared, but only more evidence of the Byzantine walls and floors against the east Qasr wall was uncovered—neither another feline fountain nor any Hellenistic occupation levels. Although very few Hellenistic sherds were noted during the excavation in this area among the limestone chips laid in Byzantine times for a roadbed and in the Early Bronze fill for the Qasr platform, the study of the pottery for final publication has made it possible to recognize parts of about seventeen Hellenistic vessels from the clearance outside the east Qasr wall which can be dated to the first half of the second century B.C. Except for a bowl base (fig. 30:15) which was with the Early Bronze fill, they were all found mixed with later Byzantine sherds, but there were enough Hellenistic sherds to associate them with the early second century construction of the monumental building. Group I, fig. 30:1-17, is from outside the east Qasr wall in which the Hellenistic feline fountain was discovered.

In the second campaign the Square Building was excavated in order to obtain indirect evidence for the dating of the Qasr since architectural fragments indicated contemporary construction (P. Lapp 1963: 33). The original building with foundations

---

[1]This study was first published in part in the *Annual of the Department of Antiquities of Jordan* (N. Lapp 1979: 5-15). However, in that report the stratigraphical significance of Hellenistic sherds in the fill laid for the construction of the Qasr was not noted. See below.

25. The northeast corner of the Qasr during the 1962 excavations. Visible in front of the Hellenistic feline fountain is a
Byzantine wall.

26. Looking north along the east Qasr wall. Note the lower
Byzantine (Stratum II B) floor on the upper right and the
lowest dressed course of the Qasr wall in the upper lefthand
corner.

below the remains of the Byzantine building with
reused Hellenistic blocks can be attributed to the
early second century B.C. on the basis of convincing ceramic evidence (plan 5; P. Lapp 1963: 35-
36). Inside the building (fig. 27) below Byzantine
Stratum II in fill associated with the laying of the
slabs for the Hellenistic floor a Rhodian jar sherd
(fig. 31:18) was found mixed with Early Bronze
pottery. Outside the building in the south trench
(fig. 28) a homogeneous group of Hellenistic sherds
came from below a floor in clayey fill (see section,
fig. 29, nos. 9, 10, 11; sherds fig. 31:23, 28-32, 34).
In hard stoney fill at the west end of this trench a
couple Hellenistic jar rims were found (section, fig.
29, no. 2; sherds, fig. 31:21, 22) and beneath a
burned area there were only Hellenistic sherds
(section, fig. 29, no. 4; sherds fig. 31:20, 24-27). A
sandy layer outside the Square Building which
separated Hellenistic Stratum III from later material above was present in the southern part of the

eastern trench (section fig. 29, no. 6) and below this
in the hard stoney fill at least one Hellenistic sherd
was found (fig. 31:19). However, here the sandy
layer was disturbed in places (see section, fig. 29,
east end no. 2) and late sherds were also present
(reg. nos. 366-368). A Hellenistic jug rim (fig.
31:33) also occurred at about this level north of the
large cistern in the eastern strip outside the Square
Building.

This pottery with stratigraphical significance in
and around the Square Building provides indirect
evidence for the dating of the Qasr. It is shown as
Group II, fig. 31:18-34.

In addition to these Hellenistic groups from
outside the east Qasr wall and the Square Building
excavations, scattered Hellenistic sherds were
found in clearing inside the Qasr walls and selected
areas outside. The significant forms are presented
as Group III, fig. 32:35-58. Some of these (fig.
32:35, 36, 43, 47, 60, and 52) were found along with

27. Looking east at the interior of the Square Building. Near the flat Hellenistic paving stones in the left center a Rhodian jar sherd came from beneath the Byzantine floor.

28. Looking northwest at the south wall of the Square Building. A terrace wall runs south from it (see plan 5 and fig. 29:13).

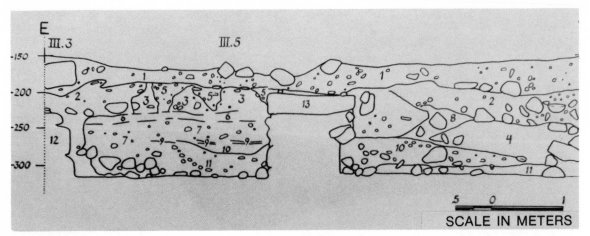

1. black, cultivated
2. hard stoney light brown huwar
3. light white-brown pebbley huwar
4. light white-brown stoney huwar
5. coarse stoney brown
6. white granular, pebbley
7. hard stoney white-brown huwar

8. hard stoney brown
9. light streak floor
10. hard light brown smooth clay
11. light brown clay
12. locus 7 = terrace wall
13. locus 3 = terrace wall

29. The south section of the trench outside the south wall of the Square Building.

Early Bronze sherds in the fill laid for the construction of the Qasr (P. Lapp 1963: 22, n. 25). According to the principle that the latest pottery in a fill established a *terminus post quem* for the deposit of that fill, we thus have evidence for the preparation of the platform for the Qasr dating to the early second century B.C.

Although Hellenistic floors or occupational loci were not uncovered in the 1961 and 1962 excavations at the Qasr, it can be stated with confidence that the pottery and stratigraphy pointed to its Hellenistic construction. Early second century sherds in the platform fill, a Hellenistic stratum at the Square Building, and scattered but significant Hellenistic sherds throughout the excavations is the collective evidence.

The Pottery

Group I

Jar rims are typically out-turned and rounded. Fig. 30:1 has a remnant of an undercut, an early Hellensitic feature (N. Lapp 1964: 17, fig. 1a:1—Balatah Stratum III B, ca. 250-225 B.C.; N. Lapp

1974: pl. 19:3 and p. 31—Wadi ed-Daliyeh, late 4th century B.C.; Zayadine 1966: pl. 27:2, 6—Samaria, first half third century B.C.). The rounded rims, fig. 30:2 and 3, are lengthened and out-turned (PCC: Corpus 11.3; N. Lapp 1964: 19) but only one rim, fig. 30:5, approaches the "collared" type, which becomes popular later in the second century B.C. Rounded rims of a varied type continued to the end of the second century B.C., but are lacking in the first century (TFL: pl. 73:22-38 and text).

Jar handle sections are oval; some come to a point at the side. Fig. 30:9 is from a small jar; the handle has a central ridge, pointed side, and a thumb imprint at the bottom where the handle was attached to the vessel.

Three fragments of a Rhodian jar were found outside the East Qasr wall in the south (fig. 30: 10a-c). They may be from one vessel, although more than one could be represented.

Fig. 30:11-14 are probably jug rims, similar to jar rim forms. They are still rounded (PCC: Corpus 21:1.A-C) and No. 11 is crescent-shaped with an undercut (cf. Zayadine 1966: pl. 28: 20, 22). Rounded jug rims continued at Tell el-Ful down to the end of the second century (TFL: pl. 75: 1-7).

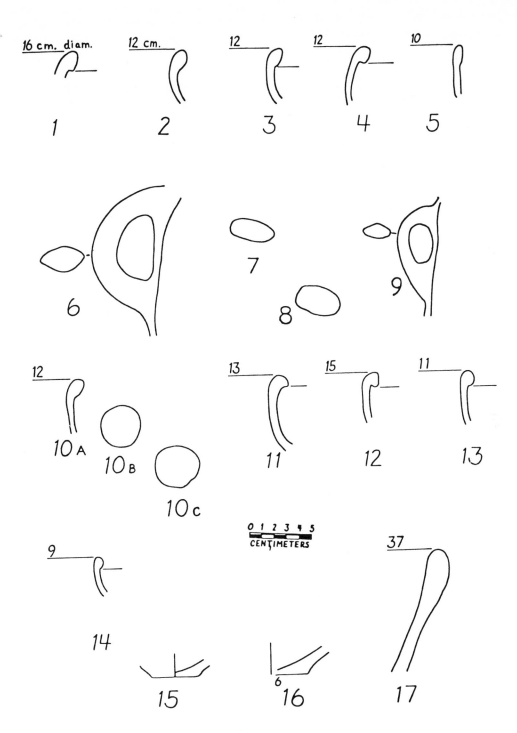

30. Hellenistic pottery from outside the east Qasr wall.
1 = reg. no. 354, 2 = 356, 3 = 338, 339, 4 = 331, 5 = 350, 6 = 333, 7 = 342, 8 = 334, 9 = 330, 10 = 341, 340, 337, 11 = 335, 12 = 336, 13 = 355, 14 = 332, 15 = 329, 16 = 353, and 17 = 463.

Two small bowl bases (fig. 30:15-16) are typically late Hellenistic—flat and carelessly made. They are probably from small incurved rim bowls. These were found in the third century B.C. at Balatah (N. Lapp: 1964: 18) and were popular by late in the century. They continue into Roman times (PCC: Corpus 51.1).

Varied mortarium rims are part of the second century B.C. corpus (PCC: Corpus 41.1). Fig. 30:17 has a plain rounded rim similar to one from the fill for the Hellenistic Fort Wall at Samaria (pre-150 B.C.), but it is from a deeper bowl.

Group II

Unfortunately the Rhodian jar sherd, fig. 31:18, from inside the Square Building was not part of a handle or rim, but the shape indicates it was probably from the neck, and the ware is characteristically orange-pink and very finely levigated.

From outside the Square Building, jar rim fig. 31:19 is typically out-turned and rounded, a form particularly characteristic of the 3rd century B.C. (Zayadine 1966: pl. 27: 1-5). It is fuller and more rounded than most late 2nd century B.C. rounded jar rims (PCC: Corpus 11.3; TFL: pl. 73: 22-38), but may not be out of place in the early 2nd century. Fig. 31:20-24 are flattened on the exterior to varying degrees, a Hellenistic characteristic that begins in the third century B.C. and is the most typical form by the late 2nd century (N. Lapp 1964: 17, 19; TFL: pl. 73: 1-20). Fig. 31:21-23 are of the somewhat squared type, while fig. 31:24 approaches the collared form. Nos. 22 and 23 may be from the same vessel though No. 22 came from above the burned level in the west end of the southern strip outside the building while No. 23 came from beneath the floor to the east. Quite a number of Hellenistic rim, handle, and body sherds came from below the burned level, but it is difficult to tell how many vessels are represented. Several handle sections are illustrated (fig. 31:25-27). A number of other handles (fig. 31:28-31) as well as a fragment of a storage jar base (fig. 31:32) came from a similar depth below the floor in the east.

Jug rim fig. 31:33, out-turned to an upper point, can be compared to those from Balatah Stratum III A (275-190 B.C.) and Stratum II (190-150 B.C.; N. Lapp 1964: figs. 2:9-12 and 3:1). Fig. 3:34 is the section of a cooking pot handle fragment with stub attachment.

Group III

About 23 other Hellenistic sherds were found in the fill laid for the construction of the Qasr and in the debris around the Qasr. The vast majority of them were jar rims—a common phenomenon at sites where Hellenistic occupation occurs (P. Lapp 1968: 78; also noted at TFL). Most of the Hellenistic sherds are represented, fig. 32:35-58. Many of them can be compared to forms already presented in the above groups, but a few other common or important Hellenistic forms will be noted.

Jar rims are rounded and out-turned; most are somewhat lengthened, and these characteristics are those common early in the second century B.C. Some rims are flattened on the exterior (fig. 32:44-48; cf. Nos. 5, 20-24 above) a trend which has begun and will be the dominant type by the end of the second century B.C. Fig. 32:46 and 47 are squared similar to Nos. 21-23 above. Only one sherd (fig. 32:49) of the characteristic Hellenistic collar-rim type—folded over and impressed—has been identified in the excavations (cf. PCC: Corpus 11.21.B-C, dated 175-100 B.C.; N. Lapp 1964: fig. 2:3, Stratum III A, 225-190 B.C.). This became one of the most typical late second and early first century B.C. forms.

Only a couple Hellenistic storage jar handles could be identified and their sections are shown, fig. 32:50, 51. In addition there was another Rhodian jar handle fragment, fig. 32:52, and a nearby Rhodian handle stub fragment most probably came from the same vessel.

Jug rims, fig. 32:53-56, are similar to those above, Nos. 12-14. These rounded, out-turned jug rims are common through the second century. Fig. 32:56 rounds to a decided lower point.

One of the two Hellenistic sherds identified from the first campaign (P. Lapp 1962: 33) is the base of a small bowl of Hellenistic Decorated Ware (fig. 32:27). The offset and the fair quality black paint, place the bowl easily in the first half of the second century B.C. (PCC: Corpus 153.1).

One cooking pot rim and handle is of the high neck type and thick ware (fig. 32:58); it is an early Hellenistic form (N. Lapp 1974: pl. 23:2) with a history back to Exilic times (TFL: pls. 69: 9-22, 78:1).

The total collection of jar rims from the Qasr and Square Building excavations at Araq el-Emir

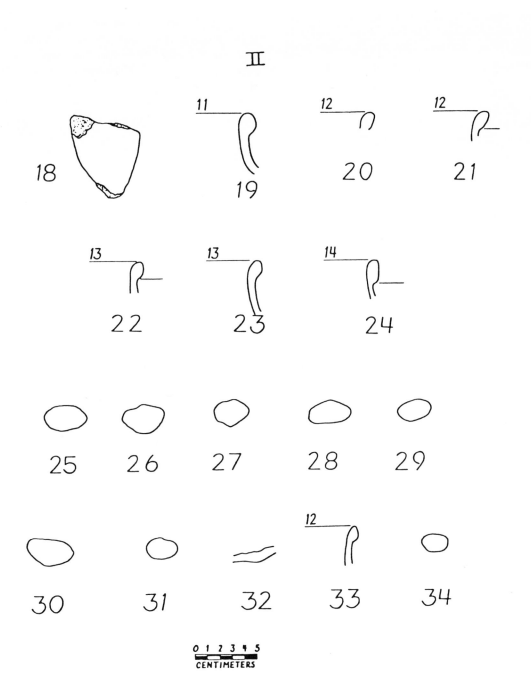

31. Hellenistic pottery from the Square Building.
18 = 364, 19 = 410, 20 = 423, 21 = 420, 22 = 421, 23 = 412, 413, 24 = 422, 25 = 424, 26 = 427, 426, 27 = 428, 429, 425, 430, 28 = 414, 29 = 415, 30 = 416, 31 = 418, 32 = 419, 33 = 411, and 34 = 417.

III

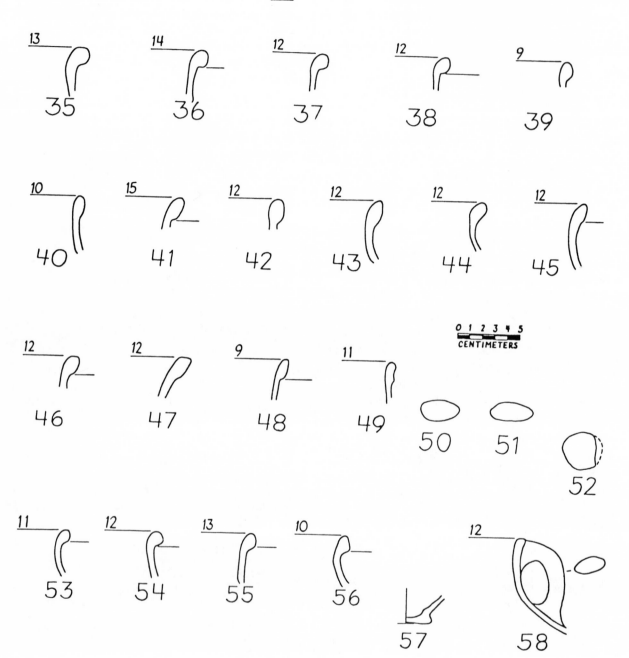

32. Other Hellenistic sherds from in and around the Qasr.
35 = 230, 36 = 327, 37 = 326, 38 = 346, 39 = 320, 40 = 313, 41 = 324, 42 = 343, 43 = 315, 44 = 328, 45 = 314, 46 = 345, 47 = 317, 48 = 352, 49 = 318, 50 = 316, 51 = 344, 52 = 322, 321, 53 = 323, 54 = 325, 55 = 319, 56 = 349, 57 = 203, and 58 = 351.

are perhaps the most certain evidence of the early second century Hellenistic presence at the site. Rims are predominantly out-turned, rounded, and somewhat lengthened. There are a few remnants of the more rounded Early Hellenistic-type rims, and one sherd had a distinctive undercut, a late 4th century and third century characteristic. On the other hand, there are a few somewhat squared rims, common late in the second century, and some collar rims, which becomes the dominant type by the second half of the second century and early in the first century B.C. One sherd was of the most characteristic collared form, folded over and impressed.

Table 8.   Hellenistic Pottery from the Qasr

no.	prov.	form	fig.	ware	inclusions
203	II.2.37	bowl base	32:57	7/5 YR 6/4 light brown; worn 7.5 YR 2.5/ black paint	very fine
230	II.12.9	jar rim	32:35	2.5 YR 5/8 red with 5 YR 5/1 gray core	m, few l
313	II.1.8	jar rim	32:40	5 YR 6/4 light reddish brown with 7/1 light gray core	s, few l
314	II.1.23	jar rim	32:45	5 YR 7/4 pink with 6/1 gray core	s
315	II.1.23	jar rim	32:43	5 YR 6/6 reddish yellow with 6/1 gray core	s, m, l
316	II.1.39	jar handle	32:50	lower attachment; 5 YR 5/6 yellowish red with 5/1 gray core	few s
317	II.2.27	jar rim	32:47	5 YR 6/4 light reddish brown with light gray core	s
318	II.3.1	jar rim	32:49	7.5 YR 6/4 light brown	s
319	II.3.5	jug rim	32:55	7.5 YR 6/4 light brown with 5 YR 5/6 yellowish red toward surfaces	s, few m
320	II.5.4	jar rim	32:39	5 YR 6/4 light reddish brown	s
321	II.6.9	Rhodian handle		stub with attachment; probably same vessel as 322	
322	II.6.10	Rhodian handle	32.52	near attachment; 5 YR 6/4 light reddish brown and 6/6 reddish yellow	very few m
323	II.7.2	jug rim	32:53	5 YR 6/4 light reddish brown	m
324	II.7.20	jar rim	32:41	5 YR 4/4 reddish brown with 4/1 dark gray core	s, m
325	II.8.15	jug rim	32:54	5 YR 6/6 reddish yellow	m
326	II.8.15	jar rim	32:37	5 YR pink	s, m
327	II.8.19	jar rim	32:36	5 YR 6/6 reddish yellow	s, m
328	II.8.23	jar rim	32:44	5 YR 6/6 reddish yellow to 5/3 reddish brown toward center	s, m, few l
329	II.11.13	bowl base	30:15	whole, roughly finished flat base; 7.5 YR 5/4 brown	m

330	II.11A.2	jar handle	30:9	complete handle; smaller than usual, poor lower attachment; 7.5 YR 6/4 light brown	s, few m
331	II.11A.2	jar rim	30:4	7.5 YR 6/4 light brown	s, m
332	II.11A.2	jug rim	30:14	7.5 YR 5/4 brown	few m
333	II.11A.2A	jar handle	30:6	complete handle, non-aligned on body; 10 YR 7/3 very pale brown	s, m
334	II.11A.8	jar handle	30:8	5 YR 6/6 reddish yellow with 7.5 YR N4/ dark gray core	s, m
335	II.11A.3	jug rim	30:11	7.5 YR 6/4 light brown	s, m
336	II.11A.3	jug rim	30:12	7.5 YR 6/4 light brown	s, few m
337	II.11B.1	Rhodian handle	30:10c	lower (?) attachment; 2.5 YR 6/8 light red	very few s, m
338) 339)	II.11B.4	jar rim	30:3	10 YR 7/3 very pale brown	many s, some m
340) 341)	II.11B.7	Rhodian rim & handle frags.	30:10a 30:10b	2.5 YR 6/8 light red	very few s, m
342	II.11C.8	jar handle	30:7	10 YR 6/4 light yellowish brown	s, few l
343	II.12.1	jar rim	32:42	5 YR 7/6 reddish yellow with 6/1 gray core	s, m
344	II.15.5	jar handle	32:51	5 YR 6/8 reddish yellow	s
345	II.16.3	jar rim	32:46	10 YR 7/3 very pale brown	s, m, few l
346	II.17.1	jar rim	32:38	10 YR 6/6 brownish yellow	m
349	II.9.7	jar rim	32:56	5 YR 5/8 yellowish red with 5/2 reddish gray core	s, m, few l
350	II.11C.1	jar rim	30:5	5 YR reddish yellow with 6/1 light gray core	s, few m
351	II.2.1	cooking pot rim & handle	32:58	5 YR 4/6 yellowish red with 4/1 dark gray core	m
352	II.2.2	jar rim	32:48	5 YR 6/4 light reddish brown	s, m
353	II.11.8	bowl base	30:16	roughly finished, discernible wheel marks; 5 YR 5/6 yellowish red	s, few m
354	II.11.9	jar rim	30:1	2.5 YR 5/8 red with 5 YR 5/1 gray core	some m
355	II.11B.5	jug rim	30:13	5 YR 5/1 gray with 6/3 light reddish brown surfaces	s, few m
356	II.11B.9	jar rim	30:2	5 YR 4/2 dark reddish gray with 6/3 light reddish brown surfaces	few s, m
463	II.11B.3	mortarium rim	30:17	7.5 YR 5/2 brown to 6/4 light brown surfaces	s

Table 9. Hellenistic Pottery from the Square Building

no.	prov.	form	fig.	ware	inclusions
364	III.2.25	Rhodian ware	31.18	body sherd, approximately 7 × 5 cm.; 5 YR 7/4 pink	very few s
410	III.3.16	jar rim	31:19	2/5 YR N6/ gray	m, l
411	III.3.18	jug rim	31:33	2.5 YR 6/6 light red	s
412 413	III.5.11	jar rim	31:23	5 YR 6/6 reddish yellow with 5/1 gray core	s, m, l
414	III.5.5	jar handle	31:28	10 YR 6/3 pale brown	many s, m
415	III.5.5	jar handle	31:29	10 YR yellowish brown	many s, m
416	III.5.5	jar handle	31:30	5 YR 6/8 reddish yellow to 5/1 gray	s, m
417	III.5.5	cooking pot handle	31:34	5 YR 4/8 yellowish red	few m
418	III.5.5	jar handle	31:31	7.5 YR 5/4 brown with N6/ gray core	s, m
419	III.5.5	jar base	31:32	7.5 YR N5/ gray core with 5/6 strong brown surfaces	few s
420	III.5.11	jar rim	31:21	5 YR 6/4 light reddish brown	s
421	III.5.11	jar rim	31:22	5 YR 6/1 gray, 6/6 reddish yellow toward surfaces	s, m, l
422	III.5.12	jar rim	31:24	10 YR 6/3 pale brown	s, m
423	III.5.12	jar rim	31:20	fragmentary; 10 YR 6/3 pale brown	s, few m
424	III.5.12	jar handle	31:25	2.5 YR 5/6 red	s, m, l
425	III.5.12	jar handle fragment	31:27	probably 428, 429, 430 same vessel; 2.5 YR N5/ gray with 5 YR 5/6 yellowish red surfaces	m, l
426 427	III.5.12	jar handle	31:26	2.5 YR 5/6 red with N5/ gray core	s, m
428 429 430	III.5.12	jar handle & ware frags.	31:27	probably same vessel as 425; 2.5 YR N5/ gray with 5 YR 5/6 yellowish red surfaces	m, l

BIBLIOGRAPHY

Hill, D. K.
 1963 The Animal Fountain of 'Araq el-Emir, *Bulletin of the American Schools of Oriental Research* 171: 45-55.

Lapp, N. L.
 1964 Pottery from some Hellenistic Loci at Balâṭah (Shechem). *Bulletin of the American Schools of Oriental Research* 175: 14-26.

 1974 The Late Persian Pottery. Pp. 30-32 in *Discoveries in the Wâdī ed-Dâliyeh*, eds. P. W. Lapp and N. L. Lapp. Annual of the American Schools of Oriental Research 41. Cambridge, MA: American Schools of Oriental Research.

 1979 The Hellenistic Pottery from the 1961 and 1962 Excavations at 'Iraq el-Emir. *Annual of the Department of Antiquities of Jordan* 23: 5-15.

1981   *The Third Campaign at Tell el-Fûl*. Annual of the
        American Schools of Oriental Research 45. Cam-
        bridge, MA: American Schools of Oriental Re-
        search.

Lapp, P. W.
    1961   *Palestine Ceramic Chronology 200* B.C.—A.D. 70.
            New Haven: American Schools of Oriental Re-
            search.

    1962   Soundings at 'Arâq el-Emîr (Jordan). *Bulletin of
            the American Schools of Oriental Research* 165:
            16-34.

    1963   The Second and Third Campaigns at 'Arâq el-
            Emîr. *Bulletin of the American Schools of Oriental
            Research* 171: 8-39.

1968   Bethel Pottery of the Late Hellenistic and Early
        Roman Periods. Pp. 77-80 in *The Excavation of
        Bethel (1934-1960)*, ed. J. L. Kelso. Annual of the
        American Schools of Oriental Research 39. Cam-
        bridge, MA: American Schools of Oriental Re-
        search.

PCC   See P. W. Lapp 1961.
TFL   See N. L. Lapp 1981.

Zayadine, F.
    1966   Early Hellenistic Pottery. *Annual of the Depart-
            ment of Antiquities of Jordan* 11: 53-64.

Chapter 8
Wall Decoration

Jennifer Groot

The preliminary reports on Araq el-Emir have barely noted the abundance of painted plaster and white wall stucco found during the three seasons of excavation. This evidence of sophisticated taste in wall decoration has been over-shadowed by the more pressing need to understand the purpose of the architectural monuments themselves. Yet, the very individual nature of the plaster does warrant a closer look. A better understanding of this plaster and what might have been its original appearance can only enhance what is already known about the structures and might further aid in understanding life-style at Araq el-Emir.

Throughout history Palestine has assimilated the cultural influences of neighboring lands and adapted them to its own culture. This was especially true during the Hellenistic period when Palestine was surrounded by Hellenization. To the southwest was the Egypt of the Ptolemies whose government was dominated by the Greeks and the Macedonians. The Nabataeans in Transjordan and cities such as Tyre and Sidon to the north were particularly successful in adopting this new culture. The Hellenic traits were most apparent in their buildings, sculpture, and painting. With an extensive network of trade routes crossing the region and the Greeks visiting as tradesmen and officials, Palestine remained in constant contact with all of her neighbors and the prevailing Hellenistic culture (Tcherikover 1959: 90).

It was during this age of Hellenization in the Near East that Araq el-Emir underwent its most extensive period of building. From about 175 B.C. through 100 B.C. a group of people at the site erected a complex of very sophisticated and distinctively Hellenized houses. This village complex

(Field I) yielded a substantial corpus of plaster which reveals the elegance with which these houses were decorated.

In contrast the Byzantine plaster from Araq el-Emir is less revealing. The Qasr el-Abd (Field II) provided an excellent collection of painted plaster dating from the period after the earthquake of A.D. 365. Although it does not indicate the function of the Qasr during this period, the plaster does reveal that the structure was important enough that it may have been decorated with a painted mural.

The Village (Field I)

The evidence to date indicates settlements at Araq el-Emir as early as the Bronze Age and the early Iron Age, but it was not until the Hellenistic period, particularly around 100 B.C., that there is evidence of a vigorous building program.[1]

House A

In the first phase, Stratum IV (ca. 175 B.C.), almost the entire area bounded by Walls W-1 and N-1 was leveled in preparation for the laying of a thick plaster floor (plan 2). There is little to indicate how the structure may have appeared except for an isolated column base located in the southwest corner of the field (plan 2:15, fig. 33).

The most extensive remains recovered belong to Stratum IIIb (ca. 100 B.C.). Major walls N-1, N-2, N-3, W-1, W-2b, W-3 and W-4c were erected at

---

[1]The discussion of the stratigraphy and the installations of the various strata is based upon the preliminary reports of P. W. Lapp (1962 and 1963).

33. Column base in the Village (I.2.Locus 44) looking down and west. Note layer of plaster.

this time (plan 2) and represent the original Hellenistic plan prior to the alterations of later occupants. The plan of House A corresponds with some of the grand houses of second century Greece in which the living quarters were arranged around a central courtyard (Robinson and Graham 1938: 141-151). House A is a variation of the Hellenistic couryard house whose principle rooms generally consisted of the andron, kitchen, and bathroom on the north side and a portico in front of them. The portico bordered a courtyard with rooms on one or more of the three sides. House A is similar in plan to House XXXIII at Priene (Robertson 1971: fig. 24). One entered on the south side through a recessed doorway, and in the case of House A, this main entrance may have been flanked by a pair of plastered columns. All that remains is the plastered column base first set down during the Stratum IV period and subsequently plastered and decorated with a red tempera wash during the III B phase (fig. 33). In relation to the plan of the house, this column may have been used as a doorpost marking the main entrance into what must have been a "grand" house.[2] The main doorway gave access to a long corridor which directed the visitor to the principle living rooms. The east wall (W-2b) of the passageway bordered the courtyard; but rather than consisting of a row of columns as in House XXXIII, the corridor was enclosed either by a solid wall or a waist high wall on which were short pillars reaching to the ceiling. Access to the paved courtyard was probably through a wide doorway at the north end of Wall W-2b.

Although this phase at Araq el-Emir did yield some evidence of painted wall plaster, the most significant with regard to the style of interior decoration was the white modeled plaster. All of this recovered was basically of the same composition: a thick brown coat with a temper of small

[2]Contrast Lapp 1963:11 who thought it was used for grinding grain.

34. The Plaster Building, looking northwest.

pebbles overlaid by a thin quartz sand finish coat.[3] Most of the fragments were modeled into similar shapes through the build-up of plaster layers and none had any surface embellishment aside from the smooth white finish.

The Plaster House

Ceramic evidence from the east corridor floor and the interior courtyard indicate that the "Plaster House" (plan 4, fig. 34) was probably built during the Stratum IV occupation and at the time of the large-scale building program of Hyrcanus. It is the most significant discovery in the Village for it reveals the first concrete indication of the type and quality of domestic architecture during this period.

The style of the Plaster House was derived from the "Corridor Villa," a variety of country house which originated during the Hellenistic period in Greece and lasted until the late first century A.D. (Robertson 1971: Insula XIV).[4] The plan was a simple rectangular block with either a closed corridor or open portico running either along one side or around all four sides of a central courtyard. The corridor gave access to the courtyard through a number of doorways. Located along three or four sides of the corridor were the living quarters.

The walls of the Plaster House, thicker than those of House A, were not of the same large block quality but of medium to small-sized stones, dirt, and rubble. This common building technique necessitated the use of a plaster facing. The interior faces of Walls P-1 and P-2 were coated with two thin layers of white plaster and etched with a symmetrical arrangement of lines (fig. 35).

The plaster remains from the Plaster House strongly resemble and are similar in composition

[3]Plaster was usually not applied in more than three coats which are called "scratch," "brown," and "finish." The scratch coat is applied first and acts as a bonding agent to attach the body of the plaster to the masonry. The brown coat is applied second and forms the main body of the plaster. The finish or third coat is applied when a smooth finish is desired.

[4]This particular example dates from the first century A.D. in Silchester (Calleva Atrebatum), but as Robertson notes, the "Corridor Villa" is anticipated in Thera during the Hellenistic period (Hiller van Gaertringen et al, *Thera*, vol. 3 [Berlin: 1899-1904], pp. 299, 312).

35. Looking north at the Plaster House. Note the plaster still adhering to the wall in the foreground (Wall P-6), the inner face of the outer wall in the upper right corner (Wall P-1), and incised plaster on the interior face of the inner wall to the left of Wall P-1 (Wall P-2).

to the heavy IIIb plaster from House A. The heavy white stucco from the east corridor was fashioned by building up four layers of plaster: a thick scratch coat with a pebble temper was overlaid with a fine white plaster layer; the general shape formed by these layers was finished with a brown coat tempered with fine gravel overlaid with a white quartz sand finish coat. The plaster was laid in such a way as to form an approximate right angle with its sharp edge beveled.

Wall Decoration

Just as the architecture was derived from domestic structures popular in Greece, so also was the method of interior wall decoration borrowed from popular Hellenistic trends. At the time of the construction of the Hellenistic town at Araq el-Emir, the popular Greek style of plaster wall decoration was to divide the wall plane into zones imitating the construction of an actual masonry

wall: the dado which represented the orthostats of masonry, the main field which corresponded to the coursed blocks, and the cornice. This incrustation or masonry style can be divided into three simple types: the zone style in which the decoration consisted of a number of zones of different colors, the incised-line style in which different fields were delineated by the use of fine incised lines, and the relief style in which areas of plaster were raised and modeled in imitation of the details of wall masonry, including the projecting plinth, coping, and cornice.[5]

[5]Prototypes for the incrustation style at Araq el-Emir are found at a number of sites within the Hellenistic world, but those closest in type are at Olynthus. The zone style was the most common method and the three variations from the Village were also used in a number of houses at Olynthus: simple painted zones (Robinson and Graham 1938: 296, fig. 30c); painted zones separated by an incised line (*ibid.*); painted vertical lines (p. 297, fig. 30f). The incised-line style was also

36. Painted plaster from the Village.
Left to right: P-18, P-27, P-28; below: P-29.

In its simplest form the fields of the zone style were differentiated by the use of contrasting colors. Three plaster fragments from the Village P-18, P-27, and P-28 (fig. 36) indicate that there was at least a limited use of this style. Plaster fragment P-27 is representative in its simplest form; the main part of the wall was painted red and the baseboard was plain white plaster. At Araq el-Emir, as elsewhere, there is evidence of variation on this basic scheme. Plaster fragment P-18 (fig. 37)[6] illustrates that the upper and lower zones were further divided by a horizontal incised line which was accented in yellow ochre. Fragment P-28 also indicated the division into zones, and the lower register was further divided by two painted vertical lines possibly simulating the row of blocks used to construct the wall.

Contemporaneous with the zone style was the incised-line style, and as illustrated by P-18, these two methods were often used in combination. Yet one of the simplest forms of wall decoration was the utilization of the incised-line style alone. The only example of this basic method found in the Village was along the interior face of corridor Walls P 1 and P 2 of the Plaster House. Upon these corridor walls a thin coat of plaster was applied

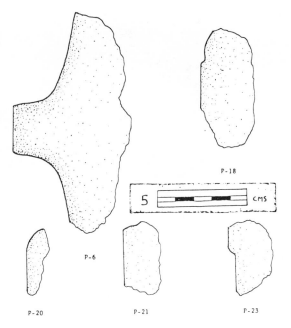

37. Profiles of some fragments of painted stucco from the Village (Field I).

and incised on this was a horizontal line about 1.10 m. above the floor. Intersecting this line was a series of regularly spaced vertically incised lines which started at the floor and continued as far as the plaster was preserved. As with the painted lines on P-28, the incised line method used in the Plaster House suggests the joints formed by the blocks and courses of actual construction.

The greatest proportion of the plaster found in the Village was derived from the third method of wall decoration, the relief style (fig. 38). This method, in which a number of zones were allowed to project from the wall, was often used in combination with the two former styles. This technique is also found as part of the wall decoration in the east corridor of the Plaster House. Modeled plaster fragments P-47, P-48, and P-49 (fig. 39) were found in associatoin with the incised plaster walls at the north end of the corridor. This evidence permits a variety of reconstructions for the east corridor. Since the incised plaster probably represented the dado, it is likely that the modeled plaster functioned as a narrow coping often used to terminate the dado. But if the incised plaster facing ran from floor to ceiling, the modeled plaster probably acted as a decorative cornice.

The relief style within the Plaster House was not limited to the interior of the east corridor. This mode of decoration also embellished the exterior

used at Olynthus on the courtyard wall of House A and in House A vi 7 (pp. 297, 299, fig. 30b, e). This form of wall decoration was also common at Priene and Delos. Olynthus bears no trace of the relief style, but fragmentary examples have been found at Delos and Morgantina. One of few examples to survive in good condition is found at Herculaneum in the House of Sallust of the second century B.C. (Ward-Perkins and Claridge 1978:96).

[6]Thanks are due Bruce R. Gould for the section drawings of the plaster.

38. Modeled plaster from the Village.
Top left to right: P-1, P-8, P-9; bottom left to right: P-10, P-47, P-49.

face of Wall P-7 which looked out onto the couryard. From the Stratum IIIb phase came thirteen plaster fragments (P-29 through P-41; see fig. 39) painted Pompeiian red, some of which were further embellished with raised surfaces. These fragments indicate that the wall was probably decorated with a red dado with the raised surfaces suggesting the block construction of the wall.

The plaster remains from House A (P-1 through P-16; fig. 40) also reflect this mode of interior decoration. Large white plaster fragments such as P-1, P-8, P-9, and P-10 (fig. 38) were probably utilized as either a coping above the dado or the cornice in much the same manner as in the east corridor of the Plaster House. Smaller fragments of plaster such as P-11 and P-12 indicate subtler projections of architectural features such as baseboards or dados. But the fragmentary nature of the Hellenistic plaster from House A does not allow even a tentative reconstruction of the wall decoration.

Roman Period

The Roman occupation (Strata I and II) of the Village was marked by another building surge. The Stratum IIIb walls continued to be used but the open atmosphere of House A was minimized by the addition of subdividing walls. Nearly all of the small rooms from this period contained some plaster but generally not enough remained to draw any conclusions with regard to the decoration.

The Qasr (Field II)

Byzantine wall decoration at Araq el-Emir is best demonstrated by the painted plaster found in the Qasr. In the three seasons of excavation the bulk of painted wall plaster came from Area 7 bounded by Walls ESRU (plan 1).[7] The plaster walls here were built up by the application of three layers of plaster, each of which had a temper of vegetable material[8] and bits of charcoal. The finished surface was then embellished with a painted design utilizing a variety of tempera colors.[9]

---

[7]Area 8 yielded only one fragment. A piece of wall plaster found in Area 2 (P-50) was probably part of the original scratch coat.

[8]It appears that straw was used as a temper. In the course of time the material decomposed leaving only cavities on the finished plaster surface and disrupting the extant painting.

[9]Six tempera colors were used on the walls of the Qasr: green, gold, white, orange-red, pink, and black.

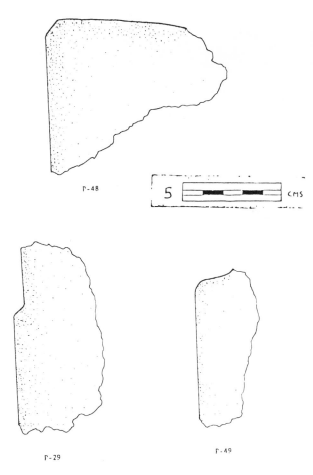

P-48

5 cms

P-29

P-49

39. Profiles of some fragments of stucco from the Plaster House.

The function of the Qasr during the Byzantine period remains enigmatic, but the plaster from Room ESRU (Area 7) does reveal that at least during the period following the earthquake of A.D. 365 (Stratum I) this monument was significant enough to warrant the erection of a painted mural. This room is in the north forehall of the Qasr and during the Byzantine Stratum I occupation three unevenly spaced piers had been erected and are still preserved as high as the springers 2.2 m. above the floor (fig. 41; cf. Lapp 1963: 33). It was during this phase of construction and in association with the laying of Floor 2 that the walls of Room ERSU were plastered and painted.

The plaster from Room ESRU suggests that the painted walls underwent three phases during the early Stratum I occupation (Table 13). After the initial laying of the plaster, the wall was decorated

with a painted design; what remains now only consists of simple horizontal bands, vague tempera washes, and animated lines (P-54 through P-74). At some point, part of the fresco was overlaid with another fine white finish coat of plaster (P-75 through P-83). Due to sever surface erosion, it is not known whether this new plaster received any surface decoration. The reason for the replaster remains unclear, but since it is not a repair, it may have been a later attempt to obscure certain portions of the original composition. Carbon residue visible on a number of the plaster fragments (P-84 through P-96) suggests the final phase of the early Stratum I occupation of Room ESRU. Stratigraphic evidence confirms that this phase of occupation was brought to an end by a violent fire which swept through many of the interior rooms of the Qasr. This fire which brought about the collapse of the north forehall roof probably also caused the painted plaster to expand, buckle, and finally, fall away from the wall. In its wake the fire left nearly a meter of ash in the north forehall. The evidence seems to indicate that this room was never formally reoccupied but rather was left in its ruined state.[10]

Conclusion

The study of the wall plaster from Araq el-Emir contributes to our knowledge of the history of Araq el-Emir. An important occupation is suggested during the Byzantine period and the wealth of the Hellenistic settlement is reflected by the houses in the Village. Although the plaster from the Qasr reveals little about the composition of the wall painting, it does confirm events after the earthquake of A.D. 365 as revealed by stratigraphy and implies that this was a building meriting an extraordinary attempt at decoration. The Hellenistic houses brought to light in the Village excavation contribute significantly to the virtually nonexistent knowledge of domestic architecture in the Near East during this period. It is hoped that before long renewed excavation efforts might be undertaken at the site to further augment the understanding of Hellenistic domestic architecture in the Near East.

[10]This fire also destroyed the early Stratum I occupation of Areas 6, 8, and 9, but not to such a devastating extent. These areas were subsequently reoccupied as evidenced by the construction of a later floor (Lapp 1963: 32-33).

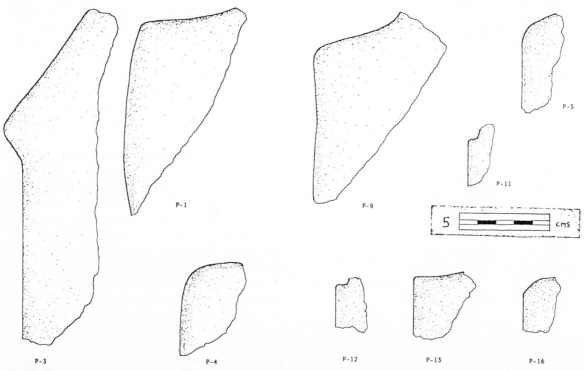

40. Profiles of some fragments of white stucco from the Village (Field I).

41. Looking west into Byzantine Room ESRU (II.7) inside the Qasr. Much plaster showing evidence of a painted mural was found in this room.

Table 10.   Unpainted Plaster of House A in the Village (Field I)

No.	Provenience	Stratum	Description and Remarks
P-1	I.2.56	IIIa	Large, white. Two layers: brown coat approx. 4 cm. thick with temper of small pebbles and very fine finish coat 1 mm. thick with quartz sand temper. Modeled shape. Some surface erosion (fig. 38, 40).
P-2 P-3	I.2.92	IIIb	Both hard white, two layers: brown coat ca. 3.5 to 4.5 cm. thick with temper of small pebbles and very fine finish coat 1 mm. thick with quartz sand temper. Both modeled (P-3, fig. 40).
P-4	I.2.105	IV	Small, hard beige. Two layers evident: 3 cm. brown coat with temper of stone fragments and pebbles and fine, smooth finish coat ca. 1 mm. thick with quartz sand temper. Modeled shape (fig. 40).
P-5	I.2.126	mixed	Similar to P-4 in plaster composition and modeled shape. Some surface erosion (fig. 40).
P-6 P-7	I.3.30	I	Both heavy gray tempered by small sharp stones. P-6, only this brown coat. P-7, finished with fine white finish coat ca. 1 mm. thick. Both modeled (P-6, fig. 37).
P-8 P-9	I.4.26	IIIb	Like P-1 and P-2 in plaster composition and modeled shape (P-8, fig. 38; P-9, fig. 38, 40).
P-10	I.4.28	IIIb	Like P-1 and P-2 in plaster composition and modeled shape (fig. 38).
P-11	I.4.46	III	Small, white, with sand temper. Finish surface either eroded or never applied (fig. 40).
P-12	I.7.2	surface	Small. Four thin layers make up modeled shape: 5 mm. thick brown coat with temper of sand and gravel overlaid with very fine 6 mm. thick finish coat with temper of sand. Part was subsequently covered with two more similar layers: brown coat 6 mm. thick and 2 mm. thick finish coat. Along one edge, faded blue line (fig. 40).
P-13	I.9.7	I	Heavy beige. 2.5 cm. brown coat with temper of pea-sized pebbles and very fine 2 mm. thick finish coat with sand temper. Modeled shape (fig. 40).
P-14	I.10.25	II	Small, white. 9 mm. thick brown coat with temper of small stream pebbles and 1 mm. thick finish coat.
P-15	I.12.23	I	Large. Three coats; 4.5 cm. scratch coat with temper of small stream pebbles; 5 mm. thick brown coat tempered with fine gravel; 1 mm. thick quartz sand finish coat. Some surface erosion.
P-16	1.12.36	IIIb	Small gray. Two layers: 1.4 cm. thick brown coat with temper of small pebbles and 2 mm. thick fine finish coat with sand temper. Modeled to form angle with sharp edge beveled (fig. 40).

Table 11.   Painted Plaster of House A in the Village (Field I)

No.	Provenience	Stratum	Description and Remarks
P-17	I.1.42	IIIa	White. Three layers: scratch coat 6 mm. thick with temper of small pebbles; brown coat 8 mm. thick with temper of fine gravel and sand; very thin finish coat. Painted deep red and subsequently plastered with another very thin layer which was painted with gray and rose colored lines. Finally, given a transparent plaster wash.
P-18	I.2.62	IIIa	Much eroded. Three layers: gray scratch coat—what remains of it approx. 5 mm. thick with temper of small pebbles; brown coat, 1.9 cm. thick with fine gravel and sand temper; very fine finish coat. Decoration of free surface: two painted registers, upper in orange, lower in white; panels separated by deeply incised line accented in yellow ochre; remainder of orange paint wash in corner of upper panel (fig. 36, 37).
P-19	I.3.31	II	Small fine white, 6 mm. thick with quartz sand temper. Entire surface painted yellow ochre.
P-20	I.4.54	Unstr.	Identical in type to P-19 but with one rounded edge. Painted yellow ochre (fig. 37).
P-21	I.6.4	I	Thick. Two layers; brown coat approx. 1 cm. thick with temper of fine gravel and 6 mm. thick finish coat with quartz sand temper. Two sides smoothed off and painted: narrow edge yellow ochre, broad side red (fig. 37).
P-22	I.6.10	I	Small red painted. Brown coat approx. 1.4 cm. thick with temper of stream pebbles and very fine finish coat. Red painted surface much eroded leaving only red strain.
P-23	I.11.7	I	Identical to P-22 except a 5 mm. thick layer of fine white plaster applied forming a raised strip 1.5 cm. wide. Much eroded red painted surface (fig. 37).
P-24 P-25 P-26	I.11.67	III	Fine white. Two layers: brown coat 7 mm. thick with temper of fine gravel, 8 mm. thick finish coat with temper of quartz sand. All painted yellow ochre.

Table 12.   The Plaster House in the Village (Field I)

No.	Provenience	Stratum	Description and Remarks
P-27	I.14	probably IIIb	Small. Two layers: brown coat 1 cm. thick with temper of small to large stream pebbles, 7 mm. thick finish coat with temper of small stream pebbles. Surface divided into two registers: one painted red, other simply the white stucco surface (fig. 36).
P-28	I.14	probably IIIb	Large. Two layers: rose colored brown coat approx. 6 mm. thick with temper of small stream pebbles, coarse white finish coat 4-7 mm. thick with temper of fine gravel. Back indicates some of finish plaster on same level as brown coat, seeming to indicate repair. Painted surface divided into two registers:

upper painted red, lower simply the white stucco surface painted with two red vertical lines, one of which is a very light wash. Upper register subsequently replastered with a thin gray plaster and lower with a thicker gravel tempered plaster since broken away (fig. 36).

No.	Provenience	Stratum	Description
P-29 through P-37	I.16.4	I *	Large, hard white. Cut sections reveal three layers: heavy brown coat approximately 2.5 cm. thick with temper of pebbles; finish coat about 9 mm. thick with temper of very fine gravel; portions of finish layer have been overlaid with another 7 mm. of finish plaster to form raised surface. One edge of raised surface beveled. All painted deep red with some surface erosion (P-29, fig. 36, 39). Earlier pottery also present. These fragments are strikingly similar to P-39 through P-41, Stratum IIIb.
P-38	I.16.4	I	Fine white finish plaster tempered by quartz sand. Painted with rose red wash.
P-39 through P-46	I.16.7	IIIb	Identical to P-29 through P-37 in plaster type. All painted red but none feature the built-up finish forming the decorative relief.
P-47 P-48	I.21.7	I	Heavy white. Section reveals four layers: scratch coat about 2 cm. thick with temper of large pebbles; overlaid with fine 8 mm. thick quartz sand finish plaster; this covered with 5 mm. thick brown coat with temper of fine gravel; finally 4 mm. thick quartz sand finish coat. These four layers built up to shape an approx. right angle. Sharp edge beveled to a flat surface 1 cm. wide. Unpainted and some surface erosion (P-47, fig. 38; P-48, fig. 39).
P-49	I.21.20	IIIb	Heavy white. Section reveals three layers; 1.2 cm. thick scratch coat with temper of medium-sized pebbles; brown coat approximately 9 mm. thick with temper of small pebbles; 3 mm. thick quartz sand finish coat. Modeled shape like P-47 and P-48. Sharp edge beveled to form 5 mm. wide surface. Unpainted and some surface erosion (fig. 38, 39).

Table 13.   Plaster from the Qasr (Field II)

No.	Provenience	Stratum	Description
P-50	II.2	IIb*	Very heavy gray with temper of large pebbles and flint. Free surface reasonable true and etched with 3 parallel lines; only complete line 9.3 cm. long, 5 mm. wide; lines spaced about 3.5 cm. apart. *Adhering to west side of Wall S.
P-51	II.7.8	Ib	Small. Finish coat. White matrix binding temper of vegetable material. Free surface partially painted with bright red tempera wash.
P-52	II.7.25	surface	Matrix similar to P-51. Free surface painted overall pale orange and embellished with red-orange mark resembling a V.

Table 13, *continued*

No.	Provenience	Stratum	Description and Remarks
P-53	II.8.13	Ia	Matrix similar to P-51. Badly damaged. Surface embellished with two colors: red-orange and green.
P-54 through P-74	II.7**	I	Section reveals 3 distinct layers: gray scratch coat, brown coat, and the finish coat. All with temper of vegetable material and small bits of charcoal. All painted: P-54 through P-67 embellished with lines of gold, red and brown washes; P-68 through P-74, generally deep red-orange; P-68 and P 69 also have areas in dark gold.
P-75 through P-83	II.7**	I	Three distinct layers. Painted in shades of red, gold, white, green, and black. P-83 only example from site using bright pink tempera. All evidence of replaster with up to 3 mm. of fine white plaster with quartz sand temper.
P-84 through P-96	II.7**	I	Matrix same as P-54 through P-74. All painted with red, orange, orange wash, gold, white, and black wash. Carbon residue evident. Much surface erosion.

    **Plaster from Area 7 from Loci 2, 3, 4, 15, 25, and 27 was consolidated in the initial sorting. Here it is separated into three categories according to type: P-54 through P-74, painted; P-75 through P-83, painted with signs of replastering; P-84 through 96, painted with signs of burn.

Table 14.   Selected Glossary

Andron: In Greek architecture, an apartment in a house reserved for men; usually a dining room.

Coping: A finish cap to a wall. In the case of Hellenistic wall decoration, it was used as a finishing touch to terminate the dado.

Cornice: Projection ornamental moulding used as a finish along the top of a wall.

Dado: The finishing of the lower part of an interior wall from floor to waist height.

Orthostats: Large masonry slabs on the outer side of a wall forming a sort of dado below the more normally constructed upper parts.

Plinth: Projecting base of a wall.

Stucco: An exterior finish for masonry which is laid on wet; also, fine plaster for decorative work and moldings.

BIBLIOGRAPHY

Brett, Michael J. B.
    1963   "The Qaṣr el-'Abd: A Proposed Reconstruction." *BASOR* 171: 39-45.
Lapp, Paul W.
    1962   "Soundings at 'Arâq el-Emîr (Jordan)." *BASOR* 165: 16-34.
    1963   "The Second and Third Campaigns at 'Arâq el-Emîr." *BASOR* 171: 8-39.
Robertson, D. S.
    1971   *Greek and Roman Architecture*. 2nd ed. Cambridge: University Press.

Robinson, D. M. and Graham, J. Walter
    1938   *Excavations at Olynthus*. vol. 25, pt. 8, *The Hellenic House*. Baltimore: John Hopkins.
Tcherikover, Avidor
    1959   *Hellenistic Civilzation and the Jews*. 1st ed. Philadelphia: Jewish Publication Society of America.
Ward-Perkins, John and Claridge, Amanda
    1978   *Pompeii: A.D. 79*. vol. 1. Boston: Museum of Fine Arts.

Chapter 9
Skeletal Remains

Michael Toplyn

Work directly linked to the classification of the skeletal material from Araq el-Emir was undertaken in the archaeological laboratory of Yale University. Extensive use was made of the Yale Peabody Museum's osteological comparative collection housed in the Kline Geology Building.[1]

Procedure

The analyst's primary goal was to extract as much useful data as possible without transgressing the limitations imposed by the meager number of bones and their generally poor state of preservation. The study was necessarily narrowed by a lack of firsthand knowledge concerning the site itself and the excavation procedures employed. The fundamental aim of analysis consisted of accurate species and element identification.

Procedural steps were eightfold:

1) Separation of bones into respective element categories.
2) Identification according to species.
3) Determination of appropriate body half when possible.
4) Designation of element portions (proximal end, distal end, shaft).
5) Designation of fused or unfused specimens.
6) Approximate age determination based on rates of epiphysial union and tooth eruption.
7) Calculation of minimum numbers of individuals by excavation area and stratum.

8) The recording of artificial alterations in the physical state of the bones due to burning, butchering, retouch (polishing or carving), and the actions of carnivores.

Due to the poor state of preservation evinced by most skeletal specimens, it was deemed necessary to base MNI (Minimum Number of Individuals) calculations largely on totals of disparate element types, taking into account such variables as relative size, age, and position of the axial skeleton. Measurements relevant to the differentiation of sexes were not taken due to the small number of complete and sexually diagnostic elements present in the skeletal assemblage. It was also impossible to accurately distinguish bones of Ovis aries from those of Capra hircus. The postcranial elements essential to the creation of such a division were found in neither the abundance nor state of preservation needed to make the fine distinction. Bones of both caprine species are listed in Tables 15 through 26 under the general heading of Ovis-Capra.

The Nature of the Faunal Assemblage

Caprine remains constituted the great majority of animal bones from Araq el-Emir, or 76% of the 145 identifiable specimens (Table 15). All major components of the caprine skeleton were represented by at least one bone with the exceptions of the calcaneus and constituents of the manus and pes (carpals and tarsals).

The thirteen bovine remains, eight of which were associated with the skull or mandible, comprised a scanty sample by comparison, amounting to only

[1]This paper was written as a Senior Thesis in partial fulfillment of the requirements for the Bachelor of Arts degree in Archaeology at Yale University.

9% of the identified bone total (Tables 15 and 16). The presence of pig at Araq el-Emir was confirmed by nine mandibular, maxillary, and dental fragments accounting for 6% of the faunal aggregate (Tables 15 and 16).

Evidence for the occurrence or utilization of camel, dog, donkey, hyrax, fish, and chicken was meager; only the hyrax was represented by more than one bone, while the single fish jaw was so pitted and friable that precise identification could not be carried beyond the class level. The combined bones of these five species and one class amounted to a mere 5% of the faunal assemblage (Table 15).

A classificatory designation, Large Mammal, was arbitrarily created to denote six fragments which could not be safely assigned to discrete species categories. These bones, although badly shattered and friable, are believed to belong to the genera Bos or Equus (Tables 15 and 16).

The physical condition of the faunal remains was generally poor; nine complete elements of sheep-goat, horse, and cow were noted, but the vast majority of animal bones were fractured, fragmented, or eroded. No conservation measures had been taken in the field. In no instance was a completely articulated skeleton encountered, nor was there a single example of a mandible or maxilla exhibiting complete dentition. Scrap, or twenty-five slivers of bone debris largely lacking in diagnostic features, was recorded and later discarded (Table 15).

The Species Inventory

Carnivora

Dog (Canis familiaris): 1 specimen MNI = 1.

One dextral canine lacking root structure was recovered from a Stratum II deposit in the village (I.5.56). Its surface enamel exhibited some slight wear.

Hyracoidea

Hyrax (Procavia capensis): 2 specimens, MNI = 1.

Two maxillary fragments, one dextral and the other sinistral, were found in disturbed surface debris in the Qasr (II.7.48). Both bones closely approximated each other in size, retained partial dentition, and were unusually well-preserved.

Perissodactyla

Donkey (Equus asinus): 1 specimen, MNI = 1.

One complete dextral metacarpus from an adult donkey was unearthed in Village Stratum I (I.11.24).

Artiodactyla

Two size classes of Artiodactyla were distinguished: small artiodactyls such as caprines and pigs and large artiodactyls including camels and cattle.

Small Artiodactyls

Sheep-goat (Ovis aries-Capra hircus): 110 specimens, MNI = 68.

Caprine remains were distributed throughout all major strata of the village and Strata I and II of the Qasr. Mandibles and teeth were the most frequently occurring element types, accounting for sixty-four identified pieces. No completely intact caprine mandibles were found. Teeth which had been dislodged or broken off from their original positions in the tooth row exhibited vertical fractures, extensive flaking of surface enamel, or loss of root structure.

Collectively, all caprine teeth displayed moderate to high degrees of cuspidal wear. This observation indicates a mature status for most of the sixty-eight caprine individuals and also supports the average age estimate for sheep-goat of approximately 2.6 years. It suggests, moreover, a diet of rather coarse edibles.

A total of ten specimens representing five element types provided distinct evidence of butchering:

Village (Field I):   Stratum V - 1 Phalange (I.5.62)
                      Stratum IIIb - 3 Humeri (I.1.104)
                                     3 Ribs (I.1.104)
                                     1 Phalange (I.1.104)
               Surface Deposits - 1 Femur

Qasr (Field II):   Surface debris - 1 Mandible (II.7.55)

Two pelvic fragments from the Village Stratum IIIb (I.1.104) and two mandibles from surface debris in the Qasr (II.7.55) were badly charred. Stratum IIIb of the village (I.1.104) yielded a broken scapula which showed some signs of having been polished.

Of the thirty-nine postcranial remains, all but specimens of the phalange and astragalus were found in a fragmentary state. One cranial bone, a piece of the premaxilla, was recovered from Stratum II of the Village (I.5.56).

Pig (Sus scrofa domesticus): 9 specimens, MNI = 8.

A handful of pig remains was retrieved from Stata I, III, IIIb, and V in the Village. One mandible came from Stratum Ib in the Qasr (II.6.19). All of the pig bones from Araq el-Emir were either mandibles, maxillae, or teeth. The few specimens which could be aged were judged to belong to animals slightly over two years old.

Large Artiodactyls

Camel (Camelus dromedarius): 1 specimen, MNI = 1.

One caudal vertebra, unfused and badly pitted, came from Iron I Stratum V in the Village (I.7.25). Although its damaged condition prevented a high degree of certainty in identification, it has been tentatively classified as Camelus due to its affinities with complete comparative examples.

Cattle (Bos taurus): 13 specimens, MNI = 12.

Diagnostic bones of cattle were rare and almost always badly damaged or crushed. Elements were sparsely scattered throughout Strata I, II, III, IIIb, and V of the Village. They also occurred in Village surface deposits, but were absent from Qasr deposits. Bones yielding age criteria, with the exception of one mandible, apparently came from animals under 3 1/2 years of age (Stratum I, I.7.37). Evidence for butchering was confined to one dextral astragalus and one dextral humerus from Stratum IIIb (I.23.19 and I.1.104). The same astragalus had also been burned.

Large Mammal (Bos or Equus): 6 specimens, MNI = 3.

Fragments of ribs and long bone shafts constituted a tiny sample of bones which could not be allocated precise species identifications. These remains were found in Village Strata II (I.5.56) and V (I.7.22), and also in surface deposits of the Qasr excavations (II.IIc.1). The rib segment from Stratum II retained traces of the butcher's blade. One of the ribs from Stratum V had been deliberately polished, perhaps in preparation for ultimate use as a utensil.

In addition to the mammalian remains, two examples of the classes Aves and Pisces were identified:

Aves

Chicken (Gallus gallus domesticus): 1 specimen, MNI = 1.

One dextral chicken femur displaying tiny gashes caused by the gnawing of a small car-nivorous animal was found in surface deposits near the Qasr (II.IIc.1).

Pisces

Fish: 1 specimen, MNI = 1.

From Stratum I in the Qasr (II.8.5) came a fragmentary fish mandible in extremely friable condition.

The Human Remains

The human remains preserved from Araq el-Emir constituted, as did the faunal assemblage, a meager and fragmentary sample. In the village, Stratum V (I.5.47) yielded an incomplete skeleton represented by ninety-six specimens, sixty-two of which were cranial components. The humerus, radius, ulna, tibia, palatal dentition, and most of the vertebral column were missing entirely, while the skull had been smashed into dozens of tiny pieces (Table 27). Due to the partial preservation of parietal, temporal, and orbital fragments and the alignment of the deciduous teeth it was possible to attribute the bones to a child of no more than two years of age (Table 27).

Two skulls from burials of recent date, unearthed in the Qasr excavations, were also examined (figs. 42, 43). The associated postcranial remains were not available for analysis. One skull (II.10.4, fig. 42) had to be partially reconstructed. It lacked the dextral temporal and parietal bones as well as portions of the occipital and frontal bones. Palatal dentition, consisting of the second premolar and first and second molars of the dextral side, exhibited a high degree of cuspidal wear. The mandible accompanying the skull was structurally intact and possessed an almost complete adult dentition, lacking only the sinistral canine (Table 27). The individual was almost certainly a male who had probably not survived his sixtieth year; based on rates of tooth eruption, cranial suture obliteration, and tooth wear an age of forty-plus years was determined (Table 27).[2]

[2]The description of the excavation of this skeleton (cf. fig. 42) which is in the field notes of the field supervisor, Dr. John Zimmerman, are worth quoting in part: "Skeleton lies with feet to sw [se]. Appearing also: teeth, human and other.... Bird bleak, and tiny bone fragments from birds or small field animals. These all from location approximately in skeleton's hands. [Actually, were these a bird, or tiny finger bones?]

"Skull in good condition. Lower jar in two pieces, fit together. Lower jaw teeth complete except one incisor. Upper jaw has no teeth left side—may have fallen out of bone and may

42. Skeleton from the Qasr (II.10.4).

The second skull (II.7.54, fig. 43) was complete and belonged to a young female no more than twenty-five years old. A rather prominent inion was present but the facial features were lacking in overall robustness of contour. The sinistral first premolar, both first incisors, and the dextral canine were missing from the palate. The second incisors, sinistral canine, and dextral first premolar had been broken off at the roots (Table 27). The extreme state of wear displayed by the remaining teeth was surprising in light of the individual's estimated age.[3]

Some pertinent anatomical measurements for the skulls from the Qasr appear below.

#1 (II.10.4) *Skull*

      Orbital Breadth - 37.2 mm
      Orbital Height - 33.0 mm
      Orbital Index - 89.1 mm

      Nasal Breadth - 23.0 mm
      Nasal Height - 51.0 mm
      Nasal Index - 45.1 mm

      Upper Facial Height - 70.0 mm

Mandible

      Bicondylar Breadth - 112.2 mm
      Bigonial Breadth - 116.0 mm
      Minimum Breadth of Ascending Ramus - 32.00 mm
      Height of Ascending Ramus - 59.00 mm
      Height of Mandibular Symphysis - 34.00 mm

---

be within skull. Skull pushed down onto shoulders, spine somewhat curved inward. Upper arm, left—34 cm; femur, left—44 cm. Hips broken, due to poor condition of bone. Left leg extended, fragments of toes only. Right leg in fragments. Right arm extended down toward hips, to right of body; left arm extended across body at angle so that both hands near together . . ."

With the skeleton was found a copper ring with the stone missing (reg. no. 254, fig. 13).

[3]With these skeleton remains (fig. 43) were a bracelet (reg. no. 171) and a string of beads (reg. no. 159; fig. 13). The remains

from six relatively recent burials in the stairway ruins of the Qasr (II.21.2) were not preserved. With these were a string of beads (reg. no 274) and a number of bracelets and rings (reg. nos. 275-287). See fig. 14.

43. Skeleton from the Qasr (II.7.55).

#2 (II.7.54) *Skull*

       Orbital Breadth - 33.2 mm
       Orbital Height - 29.0 mm
       Orbital Index - 87.8 mm

       Nasal Breadth - 24.0 mm
       Nasal Height - 46.0 mm
       Nasal Index - 52.3 mm

       Facial Width - 119.0 mm.
       Upper Facial Height - 63.0 mm
       Upper Facial Height - 53.0 mm

       (Internal Palate)

       Palatal Breadth - 37.0 mm
       Palatal Length - 44.2 mm
       Palatal Index - 84.1 mm

       (External Palate)

       Palatal Breadth - 59.2 mm
       Palatal Length - 55.0 mm
       Palatal Index - 107.6 mm

Interpretive Conclusions

The skeletal assemblage from Araq el-Emir was severely limited in size, there being a total of only 244 identifiable bones available for study.[4] Well-preserved specimens were extremely rare, while the element diversity of most identified species was minimal or practically nonexistent. The following suggestions are quite tentative.

A total of 127 diagnostic animal bones were identified from the Village as contrasted with 18 from the Qasr. This discrepancy is not particularly surprising when one recognizes that the Qasr was used for habitation only during part of the Byzantine period while the Village was a center of daily communal activity during several periods. The ruins of the Qasr had been used in recent times for human burials. The paucity of skeletal remains was due in some measure to the vagaries inherent in the processes of post-depositional decay and preservation. Dried chunks of compacted soil adhering to many of the bones had to be pried free with dental

[4]At the time of excavation a determined effort was not made to save all skeletonal material, and undoubtedly material that would have been helpful for this study was discarded. It is hoped that included here is a fair sampling of the total amount. —NLL

picks. The hard, inelastic composition of the soil may help to explain not only the badly broken condition of most elements, but also the preponderance of mandibular fragments. Mandibles and teeth, elements which are ordinarily quite resistant to decay, were found with much greater frequency than postcranial bones. Fragile specimens from small creatures such as hyrax, chicken, and fish were encountered only in surface or upper stratum contexts.

In addition to the effects of post-depositional bone breakage and disintegration, the sparsity of the skeletal assemblage may be attributed to a minimal utilization of livestock within the boundaries of the settlement and the clearing away of refuse before new floors were laid.

Human agency was largely responsible for depositing most of the skeletal material. This supposition is strongly suggested by the fact that bones of sheep-goat and cattle, the domestic animals most commonly eaten in the Near East, constituted 85% of the identified faunal remains. Dogs and hyraxes may also have deposited a small number of specimens. Livestock were probably butchered prior to consumption. Evidence for butchering of sheep-goat occurred in the Village as early as Iron I Stratum V. No fully articulated animal skeletons were discovered at Araq el-Emir.

The stratigraphic distribution of species appears below:

Village (Field I)

Stratum I: Sheep-goat, cattle, pig, donkey.
Stratum II: Sheep-goat, cattle, dog, large mammal.
Stratum III: Sheep-goat, pig, cattle.
Stratum IIIB: Sheep-goat, cattle, pig.
Stratum IV: Sheep-goat.
Stratum V: Sheep-goat, cattle, large mammal, pig, camel.

Qasr (Field II)

Stratum I: Sheep-goat, fish, pig.
Stratum IIb: Sheep-goat.

Sheep-goat, cattle, and pig were consumed during the latest Roman phase of Village occupation. The same meat preferences were indicated for other Village strata except Stratum II (Roman phase), which failed to provide evidence of pig, and Stratum IV (Hellenistic phase), from which only sheep-goat bones were recovered. The Qasr's Byzantine strata yielded sheep-goat and pig remains but did not confirm the presence of cattle. Chicken and fish may also have been eaten in Byzantine times.

In spite of its limitations, the faunal evidence clearly designates caprines as the principal source of meat during all major phases of occupation at Araq el-Emir. Cattle and pig, although poorly represented, may also have served as important sources of nourishment.

The human skulls and mandible from the Qasr were the results of modern burials in surface deposits. It is surprising that the extremely fragile infant bones survived in the Iron I stratum of the Village. No pathological abnormalities were discovered during the examination of the human skeletal material; hence, exact causes of death cannot be deduced.

An Explanation of Tables 15 through 27

The data appearing in Tables 15 through 27 reflect the greatest degree of identification possible. Tables 17 through 26 progress by provenience. They refer only to the faunal remains. Table 27 deals exclusively with the human bones. Vertical axes indicate the fields, areas, and baskets where particular specimens were found. The horizontal column headings, clarified in the Table Key, signify species and element identifications. Included with the tables are minimum number counts of individual animals (MNI) per excavation unit and stratum.

Key for Tables 15 through 27

Prov.	Species	E	EM	P-D-S	S-D	F-Unf	Age	Burned	B-C-R
(Provenience)		(Element)	(Element Modifier)	(Proximal-Distal-Shaft)	(Sinstral-Dextral)	(Fused-Unfused)			(Butcher-Carnivore-Retouch)

MNI =
Minimum Numbers
  Individuals

UD =
Unidentified Bones

ID =
Identified Bones

Max = Maxilla

Premax. =
Premaxilla

Acet. =
Acetabulum

Table 15. Village and Qasr (Fields I and II)
Species abbreviations, species and element percentages of ID bone total, and ID bone and assemblage totals.

Element	Element Count	% of ID Bone Total		Abbreviations		Identified Species and Class
Skull	1	1%		Ovis-Capra	=	Ovis aries-Capra hircus
Maxilla	10	7%		Bos	=	Bos taurus
Mandible	51	35%		Sus	=	Sus scrofa
Tooth	30	21%		L. Mammal	=	Large Mammal
Vertebra	3	2%		Hyrax	=	Heterohyrax syriacus
Scapula	2	1%		Camelus	=	Camelus dromedarius
Rib	14	10%		Canis	=	Canis familiaris
Humerus	5	4%		Equus a.	=	Equus asinus
Radius	3	2%		Gallus	=	Gallus gallus domesticus
Ulna	1	1%				Pisces
Pelvis	6	4%				
Femur	2	1%				
Tibia	3	2%				
Metacarpus	2	1%		Field		ID Bone Total
Metapodial	3	2%				
Astragalus	3	2%				
Phalange	4	3%		I		ID Bones: 127
Long Bone	2	1%		II		ID Bones: + 18

						ID Bone Total: 145

Identified Species	Element Count	% of ID Bone Total				
Ovis-Capra	110	76%		Field		Assemblage Total
Bos	13	9%				
Sus	9	6%				
L. Mammal	6	4%		I		ID Bones: 127
Hyrax	2	1%		II		ID Bones: 18
Camelus	1	1%				Scrap: + 25
Canis	1	1%				
Eqquus a.	1	1%				Assemblage Total: 170
Gallus	1	1%				

Table 16. Village and Qasr (Fields I and II)
Element counts per species.

Element	Ovis-Capra	Bos	Sus	L. Mammal	Hyrax	Camelus	Canis	Equus a.	Gallus
Skull	1								
Maxilla	6	1	1		2				
Mandible	42	2	6						
Tooth	22	5	2				1		
Vertebra	1	1				1			
Scapula	2								
Rib	10			4					
Humerus	3	2							
Radius	3								
Ulna	1								
Pelvis	5	1							
Femur	1								1
Tibia	3								
Metacarpus	1							1	
Metapodial	3								
Astragalus	2	1							
Phalange	4								
Long Bone				2					
Totals	18	110	13	9	6	2	1	1	1	1

Table 17. Village (Field I)
Mammal bone from surface or mixed contexts.

Species	E	EM	P-D-S	S-D	F-Unf	Age	Burned	B-C-R
Ovis-Capra	Mandible	2 3 1 2 3 P P M M M		D		3		
	Mandible	2 3 4 1 2 3 P P P M M M		D		3		
	Mandible	2 3 M M		D		3		
	Mandible	4 1 P M		D		3		
	Mandible	2 3 4 P P P		D		3		
	Mandible	2 M		D		2-1/2		
	Mandible	4 1 2 P M M		S		3		
	Mandible	2 3 4 1 2 3 P P P M M M		S		3		
	Maxilla	1 2 M M		S		2-1/2		
	Maxilla	2 M		S				
	Maxilla	1 M		S				
	Maxilla	1 M		S				
	Tooth	3 M						
	Tooth-Max	1 M		S				
	Tooth-Max	2 P		S				
	Femur		D	S	Unf	2-1/4		B
Bos	Tooth	1 M		S				
	Vertebra	Thoracic						

MNI

10 Ovis-Capra
2 Bos

Table 17, *continued*

Prov.	Species	E	EM	P-D-S	S-D	F-Unf	Age	Burned	B-C-R
I-3-17	Ovis-Capra	Mandible	3 1 P M		S		3		
I-3 -18		Mandible	2 3 1 2 3 P P M M M		S		3		
I-5-20	Ovis-Capra	Mandible	2 3 4 1 P P P M		S		3		
I-5-34		Mandible	3 4 P P		S		3		
I-12	Ovis-Capra	Tooth	2 m		S				

MNI

5 Ovis-Capra

Table 18. (Village (Field I)
Mammal bone from Stratum I.

Prov.	Species	E	EM	P-D-S	S-D	F-Unf	Age	Burned	B-C-R
I-2-3	Ovis-Capra	Maxilla	4 1 2 3 P M M M		D		2-1/2		
I-2-135		Mandible	2 3 m m		S		2		
I-3-7	Ovis-Capra	Mandible	2 3 M M		S		3		
I-3-9		Mandible	3 M		D		3		
I-3-23	Sus	Mandible	2 3 P P		D		2-1/2		
I-3-29		Mandible	4 1 2 P M M		S		2-1/2		
I-3-29		Mandible	4 1 2 P M M		S		2-1/2		
I-5-8	Ovis-Capra	Mandible	2 3 4 1 2 P P P M M		D		3		
I-5-24		Mandible	1 2 3 M M M		D		3		
I-7-5	Ovis-Capra	Mandible	2 3 4 1 P P P M		S		3		
I-7-6		Mandible	2 3 M M		S		3		
I-7-37	Bos	Mandible	2 P		D		3-1/2		
I-10-22	Ovis-Capra	Pelvis	Ischium			Unf	1/2		
I-10-23		Metacarpus			D	Unf	2		
I-11-5	Ovis-Capra	Mandible	1 2 3 M M M		D		3		
I-11-24	Equus a.	Metacarpus			D	F	3		

MNI

10 Ovis-Capra
3 Sus
1 Bos
1 Equus a.

Table 19. Village (Field I)
           Mammal bone from Stratum II.

Prov.	Species	E	EM	P-D-S	S-D	F-Unf	Age	Burned	B-C-R
I-5-49	Ovis-Capra	Mandible	3 4 1 2 P P M M		S		3		
I-5-56		Skull	Premax.		D				
I-5-56		Ulna		D	D	Unf	3-1/2		
I-5-56		Rib							
I-5-56	L. Mammal	Rib							B
I-5-56	Canis	Tooth	C		D				
I-11-27	Ovis-Capra	Mandible	3 4 P P		S		3		
I-11-47		Tooth	1 m		S				
I-11-47		Tooth	3 P		D				
I-11		Tooth	3 P		D				
I-11-47		Tooth	3 m		S				
I-11-52		Pelvis	Pubis		D	Unf	1/2		
I-11	Bos	Mandible	1 2 m m		D		2		

MNI

5 Ovis-Capra
1 L. Mammal
1 Canis
1 Bos

Table 20. Village (Field I)
           Mammal bone from Stratum III.

Prov.	Species	E	EM	P-D-S	S-D	F-Unf	Age	Burned	B-C-R
I-5-59	Ovis-Capra	Mandible	2 3 P P		S		2-1/2		
I-5-44		Mandible	4 1 2 P M M		D		2		
I-5-60		Mandible	2 3 P P		D		3		
I-3-48	Sus	Mandible	2 3 m m		D		1		
I-3-52	Bos	Tooth	2 I		S				
I-3-52	Ovis-Capra	Mandible	2 3 M M		D		3		

MNI

1 Sus
1 Bos
3 Ovis-Capra

Table 21. Village (Field I)
Mammal bone from Stratum IIIb.

Prov.	Species	E	EM	P-D-S	S-D	F-Unf	Age	Burned	B-C-R
I-1-90	Ovis-Capra	Mandible	4 1 2 3 P M M M		D		3		
I-1-104		Tooth	3 M		D				
I-1-104		Tooth	1 I		D				
I-1-104		Vertebra	Thoracic			Unf	2-1/2		
I-1-104		Rib							B
I-1-104		Rib							B
I-1-104		Rib							B
I-1-104		Rib							
I-1-104		Rib							
I-1-104		Rib							
I-1-104		Rib							
I-1-104		Scapula		P	D				R
I-1-104		Humerus		D	D	F	2		B
I-1-104		Humerus		S	D				B
I-1-104		Humerus		S	S				B
I-1-104		Radius		S	D	F	3-1/2		
I-1-104		Radius		S					
I-1-104		Radius		S					
I-1-104		Pelvis	Ilium-Acet.		D	Unf	1/2	B	
I-1-104		Pelvis	Ilium		D	Unf	1/2	B	
I-1-104		Tibia		S					
I-1-104		Tibia		S					
I-1-104		Tibia		S					
I-1-104		Metapodial		S	S				
I-1-104		Metapodial		S	S				
I-1-104		Phalange	1st		D	F	2-1/4		B
I-1-104		Phalange	1st		D	F	2-1/4		
I-1-104	Bos	Humerus		P	D	Unf	2		
I-1-104		Humerus		P	D	Unf	2		B
I-1-91	Sus	Mandible	2 3 4 1 P P P M		D		2		
I-1-104		Tooth	C		D				
I-1-104		Tooth	C		S				
I-16-7	Ovis-Capra	Mandible	4 1 2 3 P M M M		S		3		
I-23-24	Bos	Tooth-Max	2 M		S				
I-23-19		Astragalus			D			B	B

MNI

12 Ovis-Capra
4 Bos
2 Sus

Table 21, *continued*

Probable IIIb

Prov.	Species	E	EM	P-D-S	S-D	F-Unf	Age	Burned	B-C-R
I-1-88	Ovis-Capra	Mandible	$\overset{2\ \ 3}{M\ M}$		D		3		
I-2-85	Ovis-Capra	Mandible	$\overset{3}{M}$		S		3		
I-2-85		Tooth	$\overset{1}{M}$		S				

    MNI

    2 Ovis-Capra

Table 22. Village (Field I)
          Mammal bone from Stratum IV.

Prov.	Species	E	EM	P-D-S	S-D	F-Unf	Age	Burned	B-C-R
I-1-105	Ovis-Capra	Mandible	$\overset{3}{M}$		S		3		

    MNI

    1 Ovis-Capra

Table 23. Village (Field I)
          Mammal bone from Stratum V.

Prov.	Species	E	EM	P-D-S	S-D	F-Unf	Age	Burned	B-C-R
I-1-75	Ovis-Capra	Mandible	$\overset{1\ \ 2\ \ 3}{M\ M\ M}$		S		3		
I-1-77	Bos	Maxilla	$\overset{1\ \ 2\ \ 3}{m\ m\ m}$		D		1		
I-2-89	Ovis-Capra	Mandible	$\overset{3\ \ 4}{P\ P}$		S		3		
I-2-89		Tooth	$\overset{3}{i}$		D				
I-2-89		Tooth	$\overset{1}{m}$		D				
I-2-97	Bos	Tooth	$\overset{1}{M}$						
I-2-97		Tooth	$\overset{2}{M}$						
I-5-46	Ovis-Capra	Mandible	$\overset{2\ \ 3\ \ 4}{P\ P\ P}$		D		3		
I-5-62		Tooth	$\overset{2}{m}$						
I-5-62		Tooth	$\overset{3}{M}$		S				
I-5-62		Metapodial		D	D	F	3		
I-5-62		Astragalus			S				
I-5-62		Phalange	1st		S	F	2-1/4		B
I-5-62		Phalange	2nd		S	F	2-1/4		
I-5-46	Sus	Maxilla	$\overset{2}{P}$		D		2		
I-7-25	Ovis-Capra	Mandible	$\overset{2\ \ 3\ \ 1}{P\ P\ M}$		D		3		
I-7-25		Mandible	$\overset{2\ \ 1}{P\ M}$		D		3		

Table 23, *continued*

Prov.	Species	E	EM	P-D-S	S-D	F-Unf	Age	Burned	B-C-R
I-7-28		Tooth	$\overset{3}{\text{I}}$		D				
I-7-29		Scapula		D	S				
I-7-22		Rib							
I-7-22		Rib							
I-7-28		Pelvis	Ilium-Acet.		S	F	2-1/4		
I-7-29		Astragalus			D				
I-7-22	Bos	Pelvis	Ilium		S				
I-7-25	Camelus	Vertebra	Caudal			Unf			
I-7-22	L. Mammal	Rib							
I-7-22		Rib							R
I-7-22		Long Bone		S					
I-10-47	Ovis-Capra	Mandible	$\overset{4}{\text{P}}$		D		3		
I-10-47		Mandible	$\overset{1}{\text{M}}\overset{2}{\text{M}}\overset{3}{\text{M}}$		S		3		

MNI

14 Ovis-Capra
1 Sus
3 Bos
1 Camelus
1 L. Mammal

Table 24. Qasr (Field II)
Bone from Surface Deposits.

Prov.	Species	E	EM	P-D-S	S-D	F-Unf	Age	Burned	B-C-R
II-7-48	Hyrax	Maxilla	$\overset{3}{\text{P}}\overset{4}{\text{P}}\overset{1}{\text{M}}\overset{2}{\text{M}}\overset{3}{\text{M}}$		D				
II-7-48		Maxilla	$\overset{2}{\text{P}}\overset{3}{\text{P}}\overset{1}{\text{M}}$		S				
II-7-55	Ovis-Capra	Mandible			S			B	B
II-7-55		Mandible			S			B	
II-7-55		Tooth-Max	$\overset{1}{\text{M}}$		S				
II-7-55		Tooth-Max	$\overset{2}{\text{M}}$		S				
II-7-55		Tooth	$\overset{1}{\text{m}}$						
II-7-55		Tooth	$\overset{2}{\text{m}}$						
II-7-55		Tooth	$\overset{2}{\text{m}}$						
II-11c-1	Gallus	Femur		P	D				C
II-11c-1	L. Mammal	Rib							
II-11c-1		Long Bone		S					
II-17-7	Ovis-Capra	Mandible	$\overset{2}{\text{M}}\overset{3}{\text{M}}$		D		3		

MNI

1 Hyrax
3 Ovis-Capra
1 L. Mammal
1 Gallus

Table 25. Qasr (Field II)
Mammal bone from Stratum I.

Prov.	Species	E	EM	P-D-S	S-D	F-Unf	Age	Burned	B-C-R
II-6-19	Sus	Mandible	3 M		S		2-1/4		
II-7-37	Ovis-Capra	Mandible	1 2 3 m m m		D		1		
II-8-5	Pisces	Mandible			S				
II-9-4	Ovis-Capra	Maxilla	2 M		D		2-1/2		

MNI

1 Sus
2 Ovis-Capra
1 Pisces

Table 26. Qasr (Field II)
Mammal bone from Stratum IIb.

Prov.	Species	E	EM	P-D-S	S-D	F-Unf	Age	Burned	B-C-R
II-7-21	Ovis-Capra	Tooth	2 m		S				

MNI

1 Ovis-Capra

Table 27. Human Remains
from Village (Field I) Stratum V and Qasr (Field II) surface deposits.

Prov.	Species	E	EM	P-D-S	S-D	F-Unf	Element— Fragment Counts	Age
I-5-47	Homo sapiens	Skull	Parietal			Unf	3	1+
I-5-47		Skull	Temporal			Unf	4	
I-5-47		Skull	Orbit		S		1	
I-5-47		Skull	UD				54	
I-5-47		Mandible	Ramus		S		1	
I-5-47		Mandible	Ramus		D		1	
I-5-47		Mandible	Coronoid		D		1	
I-5-47		Mandible	Tooth Row				1	
I-5-47		Mandible	Tooth Row				1	
I-5-47		Tooth	1 m				1	
I-5-47		Tooth	1 m				1	
I-5-47		Tooth	2 m				1	
I-5-47		Tooth	2 m				1	
I-5-47		Tooth	1 i				1	
I-5-47		Tooth	2 i				1	
I-5-47		Vertebra	Cervical				2	

Table 27, *continued*

I-5-47	Vertebra	Thoracic			2
I-5-47	Sacrum			Unf	3
I-5-47	Rib				14
I-5-47	Femur		P	D	1
I-5-47	Calcaneus		D		1

MNI   Element—
                                                                       Fragment
                                                                       Total

1 Homo Sapiens

                                                                       96

Prov.	Species	E	EM	S-D	Sex	Age
II-7-54	Homo sapiens	Skull	2 2 I I -Roots	S+D	Female	17-25
			C -Roots I	S		
			P -Roots	D		
			1 2 3 2 M M M P	S		
			1 2 3 2 M M M P	D		
II-10-4	Homo sapiens	Skull	2 1 2 P M M	D	Male	40+
II-10-4		Mandible	1 2 1 2 I I P P	S		
			1 2 3 M M M			
II-10-4		Mandible	1 2 1 2 I I C P P	D		
			1 2 3 M M M			

MNI

2 Homo sapiens

BIBLIOGRAPHY

Bass, W. M.
   1971   *Human Osteology: A Laboratory and Field Manual of the Human Skeleton.* Columbia, Mo.: University of Missouri.
Chaplin, R. E.
   1971   *The Study of Animal Bones from Archaeological Sites.* London: Seminar Press.
Cornwall, I. W.
   1968   *Bones for the Archaeologist. London: Phoenix House.*
Ellenberger, W.; Dittrich, H.; and Baum, H.
   1956   *An Atlas of Animal Anatomy for Artists.* New York: Dover.
Lapp, P. W.
   1962   Soundings at ⁽Arâq el-Emîr (Jordan). *Bulletin of*

the American Schools of Oriental Research 165: 16-34.
Lapp, P. W.
   1963   The Second and Third Campaigns at ⁽Arâq el-Emîr. *Bulletin of the American Schools of Oriental Research* 171: 8-39.
Schmid, E.
   1972   *Atlas of Animal Bones.* Amsterdam, London, and New York: Elsevier.
Sisson, S., and Grossman, J. D.
   1950   *The Anatomy of the Domestic Animals.* 4th edition. Philadephia and London: Saunders.

Chapter 10
Ancient Plant Remains

DAVID MCCREERY

Of the three campaigns at Araq el-Emir undertaken in 1961 and 1962, only a few plant remains were recovered during the two 1961 excavations. The scarcity of material is probably to be explained by the fact that all plant specimens were recovered by simple visual detection during the course of excavation without the aid of a water flotation system.

The Samples

1. From an Iron I, ca. 1050 B.C. context (the Village, I.5.42, Stratum V), the fragmented remains of a carbonized olive pit, *Olea europaea*. The damaged condition of the specimen makes exact measurements of the stone impossible but it can be said that the stone was longer than 12 mm. and about 5 mm. in breadth. This pit is longer and narrower than specimen #4, but is no doubt also the product of a cultivated tree.

2. From an Iron I, ca. 1050 B.C. context (the Village, I.5.42, Stratum V), 2 lentils, *Lens* sp., one carbonized and one not carbonized. The seeds are small with diameter measurements of only 2.8 mm. (uncarbonized specimen) and 2.5 mm. (carbonized specimen). These lentils could be *Lens culinaris/ esculenta* var. *microsperma* which are often found in ancient contexts (Renfrew 1973: 113-15), but the wild *Lens nigricans* cannot be ruled out.

3. From an Iron I, ca. 1050 B.C. context (the Village, I.5.42, Stratum V), 6 uncarbonized achene of Fumitory, *Fumaria* sp. The seeds range from 1.3-1.8 mm. in diameter with an average of 1.45 mm. Both *Fumaria arabia* and *F. thymifolia* are found in the region around Araq el-Emir today but

the size and morphological characteristics of these seeds suggest they belong to the species *Fumaria arabia* (Cf. Zohary 1972: 345-47, pls. 510, 511). Helbaek (1970: 235) points out that Fumitory is an extremely widespread weed which often occurs along with pulse crops and in vineyards. Although it is not commonly found in archaeological contexts, it has been reported from as early as 5050 B.C. at Hacilar (Helbaek 1970: 235).

4. From a Hellenistic, 100 B.C. context (the Village, I.2.84, Stratum IIIB, above floor), one carbonized and broken olive pit, *Olea europaea*. Although the specimen is badly damaged, length (12.0 mm.) and breadth (6.2 mm.) measurements were obtained from half of the stone which was still intact. The stone is slightly smaller than those of modern cultivated olives but slightly larger than most ancient carbonized specimens (Cf. Renfrew 1973: 133). Since the stones of wild olives are significantly smaller than this pit (Renfrew 1973: 133), there is little question that it belongs to the cultivated species *Olea europaea*.

5. From a Roman, 100 A.D. context (the Village, I.5.37, Stratum II, removing floor), the carbonized remains of the fruit and stone of Date Palm, *Phoenix dactylifera*. Because of the damaged condition of the specimen, only length measurements are obtainable. The length of the stone is 16.0 mm. and the length of the fruit is 20.0 mm. Similar finds of carbonized whole dates have come from the Cave of the Pool in the Wadi Sder (Naḥal David) (Zaitschek 1962: 184, pl. 21B: 5, 7-9).

6. From a Byzantine, pre-365 A.D. context (Square Building, III.4.13, Stratum II, sub-floor), nine carbonized grape pips. Of these, 6 are completely

intact and can therefore be measured accurately. The averate length is 4.93 mm. (4.5 mm.-5.2 mm.), breadth 3.17 mm. (2.8 mm.-3.5 mm.) and L/B index .64 mm. (.57 mm.-.73 mm.). Although the number of pips measured is quite small and the L/B indices cannot be used as a decisive criterium for distinguishing between wild and domesticated grapes (Renfrew 1973: 129), the general morphological characteristics, i.e., oblong endocarps, with distinct stalks and indistinct dorsal shields, indicate that these pips come from cultivated grapes, *Vitis vinifera* (Hjelmqvist 1970: 329).

7. From a Byzantine, probably pre-365 A.D. context (Qasr, II.1.19, Stratum Ia/II, sub-floor), two uncarbonized field peas, *Pisum sativum*. Both seeds are reddish-brown in color, spherical in shape and have well defined hilums. The diameters measure 4.8 mm. and 6.5 mm. and the length of the hils are 1.5 mm. and 2.0 mm. respectively. These peas are larger than most ancient specimens which have shrunk due to carbonization but are comparable in size to fresh peas (Cf. Renfrew 1973: 111, 112). The size, shape, and color of these specimens is very similar to that of *Pisum sativum* L. ssp. *syriacum* which grows in the area today (Zohary 1972: 222, pl. 316).

8. From a Byzantine, probably pre-365 A.D. context, (Qasr, II.1.19, Stratum Ia/II, sub-floor), 54 uncarbonized chickpeas, *Cicer arietinum*. These seeds are dark reddish-brown and slightly more spherical in shape than the modern angular seeds. Nevertheless, the distinctive dice-like shape and protruding radicula makes the chickpea identification certain. The diameters of the 54 specimens range from 3.0 mm.-4.2 mm. with an average of 3.67 mm. These specimens are much smaller than modern chickpeas grown in Jordan but are comparable in size to ancient carbonized chickpeas

found at Lachish, Assyrian Nimrud, and Salamis (Renfrew 1973: 119).

9. From an unknown context, one intact and one broken cereal grain. Both caryopses have been damaged by carbonization and are not accompanied by rachis or other spikelet components so it is not possible to refine the identification beyond saying that the specimens belong to the genus *Hordeum*. This identification is based on the gross morphology of the grains. The convex sides of the grains, narrow lateral profile and angular cross-section, distinguish these specimens from *Triticum* (cf. Renfrew 1973: 34; and van Zeist and Herres 1973: 25, 26, fig. 4). The dimensions of the one whole specimen: length 6.0 mm., breadth 3.3 mm., and thickness 2.8 mm., indicate that it belongs to a cultivated rather than a wild species of barley but it is impossible to determine whether it is a 2-row *Hordeum distichum* or 6-row *Hordeum vulgare*.

In spite of the small size of this plant assemblage, it throws significant light on the agricultural practices of the people of Araq el-Emir during the Iron Age, Hellenistic, Roman, and Byzantine periods. It comes as no real surprise that grapes, barley, olives, peas, lentils, dates and chickpeas were being cultivated during these periods for they have all been found in contexts much earlier than the Iron Age in Palestine and elsewhere in the Near East. All of these crops could have been grown locally as they still are today (Cf. *Agric. Stat. Yrbk.* 1976: 16-18), with the exception of dates which were probably brought up from the Jordan Valley just a few kilometers away. It is also reasonable to assume that wheat, the most important cereal crop of the area today (*Agric. Stat. Yrbk.* 1976: 16), along with figs, an important fruit crop (*Agric. Stat. Yrbk.* 1976: 18), were cultivated in ancient times at Araq el-Emir.

BIBLIOGRAPHY

Agric. Stat. Yrbk.
   1976   *Agricultural Statistical Yearbook and Agricultural Sample Survey, 1976.* Hashemite Kingdom of Jordan, Department of Statistics. Amman: Department of Statistics.
Helbaek, Hans
   1970   The Plant Husbandry of Hacilar. Pp. 189-244 in *Excavations at Hacilar.* Vol. 1. By James Mellaart. Edinburgh: Edinburgh University.
Hjelmqvist, H.
   1970   Some Carbonized Seeds and Fruits from the Necropolis of Salamis. Pp. 329-335 in *Excavations in the Necropolis of Salamis.* Vol. 2. By V. Karageorghis. Nicosia: Zavallis.

Renfrew, Jane M.
   1973   *Paleoethnobotany: The Prehistoric Food Plants of the Near East and Europe.* New York: Columbia University.
Zaitscheck, D. V.
   1962   Remains of Plants from the Cave of the Pool. *Israel Exploration Journal* 12.3-4: 184-185, Pl. 21B.
Zeist, Wilhelm van., and Heeres, J. A. H.
   1973   Paleobotanical Studies of Deir 'Alla, Jordan. *Paléorient* 1: 21-37.
Zohary, Michael
   1972   *Flora Palestina.* Vol. 2. Jerusalem: The Israel Academy of Sciences and Humanities.

Part II
Excavations of the 1970s

Chapter 11
The 1976 ASOR Soundings

Robin Brown

Introduction

In October of 1976 the American Schools of Oriental Research sponsored a one-month excavation of the site of Araq el-Emir in Jordan, during which time soundings were made both inside and outside of the Qasr el-Abd. Excavation costs were shared between the American Center of Oriental Research in Amman, which provided tools and housing, and the Department of Antiquities of the Hashemite Kingdom of Jordan, which supplied a labor force and transportation. The project staff extends its gratitude to the Department of Antiquities and its former Director General, the late Mr. Yaquob Oweis, for their generous assistance. From the Institute Français d'Archéologie du Proche-Orient we wish to extend out thanks to Dr. Ernest Will for his kind support of the project and to Mr. François Larché for making available his surveying skills and the surface survey ceramic corpus which has been catalogued below. The excavation and the analysis of its results were greatly facilitated by Prof. Nancy Lapp of Pittsburgh Theological Seminary who provided recommendations and much needed materials including plans, notes, and photographs which would have been otherwise unavailable. Dr. James A. Sauer, Director of the American Center of Oriental Research, contributed much of his time and expert advice in reviewing the preparation of this manuscript and for this the author is deeply grateful.

The project staff included: Mr. Mujahid Muhaisin, Inspector for the Department of Antiquities and field archaeologist; Ms. Jane Muhawi, draftswoman and field archaeologist; Dr. James A. Sauer, project advisor and ceramic typologist, and Ms. Robin Brown, field director.

The objective in initiating soundings at Araq el-Emir was to obtain greater clarification of the dating of the phases represented within the Qasr el-Abd, the sequence of which had been established by the late Dr. Paul W. Lapp during his excavation of the site in 1961 and 1962. Specific aims included the isolation of controlled ceramic groups from as many phases as possible and, on the basis of refinements in the ceramic typology of Transjordan subsequent to Lapp's work, it was hoped that additional confirmation of the Late Hellenistic stratum and more precise dating of the Byzantine phases would be achieved.

The stratigraphic profile was analyzed by Lapp for the Qasr el-Abd and the Square Building as follows (Lapp 1963: 21, 33; above Introduction):

Stratum III	Hellenistic	ca. 200-175 B.C.
Stratum II	Early Byzantine	ca. A.D. 335-365
Stratum I	Early Byzantine	ca. A.D. 365-500

The stratification of two of Lapp's areas excavated within the Qasr is particularly relevant to the discussion of the 1976 soundings (see section, fig. 44). Area II.1 was located just west of the center of the Qasr interior and Area II.2 lay contiguous and to the west, intercepting the exterior wall line, Wall A.

Area II.1

Stratum Ia Floor 1 (above Banded Earth and Stones)

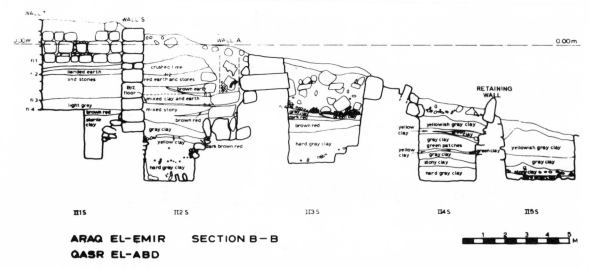

ARAQ EL-EMIR   SECTION B—B
QASR EL-ABD

44. Looking south at the east-west section through the center of the Qasr, Areas II.1, II.2, II.3, II.4, and II.5.

Stratum Ib Floor 2 (inclusive of Banded Earth and Stones
              below) structural collapse, possibly earthquake
Stratum IIa Floor 3 (above Light Grey)
Stratum IIb Floor 4 (above Brown Red)

Area II.2
  Stratum Ia
  Stratum Ib Floor 2 (possibly a temporary pavement,
              above Red Earth and Stones and Brown
              Earth)
              structural collapse, possibly earthquake
  Stratum IIa Floor 3, plaster and rough hewn wall (above
              Mixed Clay and Earth)
  Stratum IIb Floor 4, plaster (above Mixed Stony)

In the material presented below all references to
chronological periods and absolute dates follow
Sauer (1973: 3-4) and where abbreviated in the text
they appear as follows: Hellenistic-H, Late Helle-
nistic-LH, Early Roman-ER (63 B.C.-A.D. 135),
Late Roman-LR (A.D. 135-324), Early Byzantine-
E Byz. (A.D. 324-491), Byzantine-Byz. (A.D.
324-640). Other abbreviations include Early
Bronze-EB, Ottoman-Ott., and "unidentified"-UD.
Alphabetic wall designations follow Lapp (plan 1).
Although the compass orientation of the long axis
of the Qasr el-Abd is approximately 18° west of
north, for convenience all directions cited in the
text refer to north as if it were directly along the
axis. Descriptions of the size of geological inclusions within the loci follow the Wentworth Scale
(Lahee 1961: 38-39). The color classification cited
on the Ware Analysis lists follows Munsell (1954).

Square AE 76.1

Square 1 was a 2.00 m × 2.00 m sounding
located in the northwest corner of the interior of

the Qasr el-Abd. The selection of this location for
excavation was dictated by the massive fallen
blocks and thick rock rubble which obscured much
of that portion of the interior which had not been
excavated previously. The north balk consisted of
Lapp's Wall E which is aligned along an east-west
axis and the west balk was established along the
Wall A alignment. Due to the hazardous condition
of the east and south balks, excavation was terminated before the founding levels of either of the
walls could be ascertained.

Stratum III Late Hellenistic

Stratification. Wall 1:1, Lapp's Wall E (see plan
1), which formed the north balk of Square 1, was
oriented east-west and consisted of a single huge
cyclopean and rectangular cut limestone block,
only a portion of the face being exposed through
excavation (fig. 45). It lay at right angles to the
West Qasr Wall 1:2. That portion of the Wall 1:1
block which lay within the square measured 1.68 m
east-west and 2.50 m in height. The lower, eastern
corner of the block had been broken away leaving
a gap .94 × .74 m.

Wall 1:2 extended along the north-south alignment of the exterior west Qasr Wall A (fig. 46). It
was exposed for a depth of 1.48 m, extended the
full 2.00 m length of the west balk, and continued
into the south balk. The wall consisted of a single
row of dry laid, square, and rectangular cut limestone blocks, three courses of which were exposed.
The blocks ranged in size from 0.30 × 0.54 m to
0.64 × 1.02 m. The blocks of the uppermost course
included a drainstone whose channel lay along an
east-west axis (figs 45, 46).

45. Square AE.76.1 looking north. Note Wall 1:2 (Wall A) on the west and the channel in its top course.

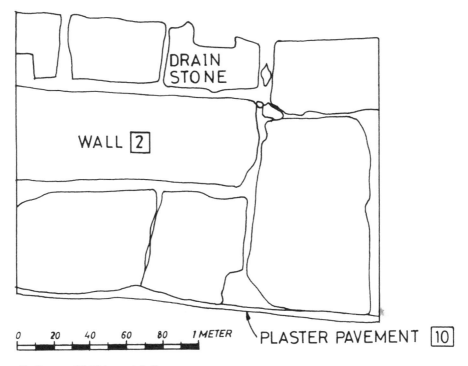

46. Square AE.76.1, west balk.

47. Looking west at Pavement 1:10 next to Wall 1:2 (Wall A) in Square AE.76.1.

Plaster Pavement 1:10 lay adjacent to Wall 1:2 at the depth excavated (fig. 47). It averaged 0.03 m in thickness and lay beneath Gray Soil Layer 1:8B and Clay, Limestone and Earth Layer 1:8A. In the north it lay adjacent to Wall 1:1 except where cut by Clay, Limestone, and Earth Layer 1:8A, and in the south and east it lay perpendicular to the base level of the uppermost course of Wall 1:9 (fig. 48). The plaster, composed of a roughly ground limestone paste with inclusions of small rounded limestone pebbles, contained no artificial remains. Imbedded into the surface of the plaster were a few flat, smooth, limestone cobbles.

Interpretation. Wall 1:1 (Lapp's Wall E) and most probably Wall 1:2 (Lapp's Wall A) are among the original Stratum III blocks which make up both the exterior of the Qasr as it stands today and the principal interior partitions. While no direct dating evidence for this stratum resulted from the 1976 Sounding, these Walls are assigned to Stratum III by their obvious continuity with the rest of the original Qasr walls which are dated 2nd century Hellenistic (1963: 24, and see ch. 7). The excavated part of Wall 1:1 is part of a typical Qasr megalith and this wall forms the south partition of a chamber which flanks the west side of the front or north entrance portico.

Wall 1:2 extended along the alignment of Lapp's Stratum III Wall A and can probably be identified with it. The second feline fountain lies flush against the exterior of Wall 1:2, parallel to the first found in East Qasr Wall B (Lapp 1963: 26). The smaller

stones of Wall 1:2 seem to have filled out the thickness of the wall as on the east (Lapp 1963: 27 and plan 1). The drainstone situated in the uppermost preserved course of Wall 1:2 (figs. 45, 46) formed the channel leading to the animal's mouth which is severely damaged (figs. 49, 50).

Excavation could not go below Pavement 1:10, but most probably it is to be associated with the fountain as a small plastered basin for storing water. There was some evidence for a similar basin

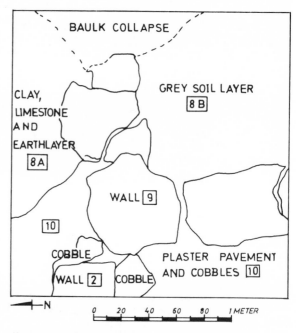

48. Square AE.76.1, top plan.

on the east side (Lapp 1963: 27). Similarly, fragments of channel stones were among the debris in both areas. The extent of Pavement 1:10 was disrupted by Stratum II Wall 1:9.

Stratum II Early Byzantine.

Stratification. Along its north-south axis, Wall 1:9 lay parallel to Wall 1:2 and extended into the south balk, and along its east-west axis it lay parallel to Wall 1:1 and extended into the east balk (fig. 48). Along both axes Wall 1:9 lay at an average distance of 0.40 m from Walls 1:1 and 1:2. To the west and northwest between Wall 1:9 and balk Walls 1:1 and 1:2 lay Plaster Pavement 1:10. Wall 1:9 was constructed of roughly cut boulder size limestone blocks set a single row in width and at least two courses in depth. It measured 1.45 m north-south, 1.68 m east-west, and averaged 0.50 m in width. Situated beneath Layers 1:8A and 1:8B the wall was also bordered by the continuation of the deep fill 1:8B which lay in the south-east corner of the square. The thin layer of debris which lay

between the courses of the wall contained a few sherds.

Pottery

Locus 9 4 sherds (Byzantine body sherds, 1 possible H, 1 UD body sherd); fig. 56: 117.

Interpretation. Wall 1:9 appears to have been a secondary support wall which skirted the inner faces of the Walls 1:1 and 1:2. The rough cut, though uniformly proportioned, blocks paralleling principal wall lines are also a feature of Lapp's Area II.2 where a similar rough hewn wall had been set just inside the Wall A alignment. Lapp found such walls against the entire length of Wall A and could only surmise that they were necessary to support roofs (1963: 32). The ceramic evidence from between the first and second courses of Wall 1:9 confirms that it is a Byzantine feature. In the construction of Wall 1:9, the builders cut through Plaster Pavement 1:10. Within the angle of Wall 1:9 the pavement had been destroyed, but on the

49. Looking southeast at Wall A and the west side feline fountain. Note the channel leading from the broken mouth through Wall A into Square AE.76.1.

50. Looking east at the partially destroyed west side feline fountain.

west and north it extended into the joining of the two exposed courses (fig. 51). In the room formed by Wall 1:9 the Stratum II Byzantines probably went below the Stratum III level, similarly to Areas II.1, II.2, and other places excavated in the Lapp campaigns.

Stratum I Early Byzantine

Stratification. Green Brown Sediment Layer 1:3-6, lying beneath Topsoil 1:3A, covered the entire 2.00 m × 2.00 m probe area and varied in thickness from ca. 0.50 m to 0.75 m (fig. 52). The debris consisted of compacted brown soil and banded gray-green clay. Interspersed throughout the sediment were localized patches of ash and reddish soil, *huwwar* pebbles, and pebbles, cobbles, and boulders of limestone. Also present were cut limestone architectural blocks which lay at random amid the earth and clay.

Red Brown Sediment Layer 1:7 lay beneath Green Brown Sediment Layer 1:6, extended across the entire square and varied in depth from 0.06 m to 0.60 m. The debris included compacted red brown soil mixed with limestone pebbles, cobbles,

and boulders.

Clay, Limestone, and Earth Layer 1:8A lay beneath Red Brown Sediment Layer 1:7 and extended over the northern portion of the area. It measured 2.00 m east-west, an average of 0.40 m north-south and reached a maximum depth of 0.80 m. The southern portion of the locus lay over part of Wall 1:9. This uncompacted layer was characterized by the loose granular brown soil mixed with yellow clay and pebbles of limestone.

Gray Soil Layer I:8B lay beneath Red Brown Sediment Layer 1:7 and extended from the south balk northward where it met Clay, Limestone, and Earth Layer 1:8A and Wall 1:9 (fig. 48). To the west, where it covered Wall 1:9, it averaged 0.08 m in depth and to the southeast it measured 1.40 m in depth, the latter being the point of arbitrary termination. It measured 2.00 m east-west and averaged 1.60 m north-south. The matrix contained loose, granular gray soil mixed with charcoal flecks and small cobbles and boulders of limestone. Cut limestone architectural fragments were also included and these averaged 0.05 × 0.25 × 0.40 m. Scattered throughout were air pockets where the soft soil had subsided.

51. Looking east in Square AE.76.1 at Wall 1:9 going south and east.

52. Square AE.76.1, east balk.

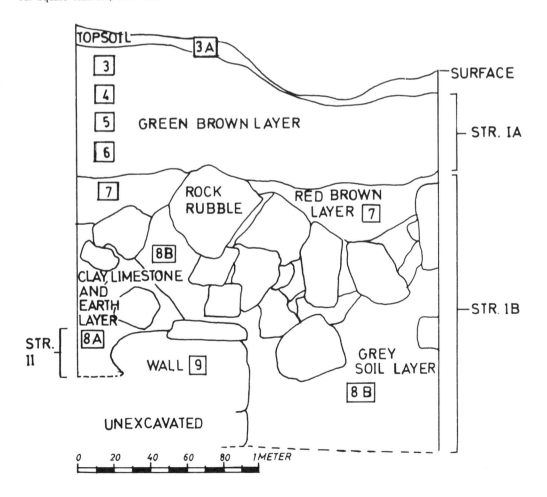

Pottery

Locus 3 90 sherds (E. Byz III-IV dominant, 1 possible Iron); fig. 56: 106, 107, 109, 113, 135, 145, 146, 149.

Locus 4 488 sherds (E. Byz. III-IV dominant, few possible E. Byz. I-II, 1 Iron ?, 1 H ?, body sherds);
fig. 56: 99-105, 107, 108, 110, 111, 113, 114, 123-126, 129-134, 138, 139, 141, 144, 147, 151.

Locus 5 49 sherds (E. Byz. III-IV dominant, few LR III-IV ? body sherds, UD body sherds);
fig. 56: 118-120, 148.

Locus 6 114 sherds (E. Byz. III-IV, few H ? body sherds, few EB ? body sherds, UD);
fig. 56: 115, 116, 122, 142, 155.

Locus 7 25 sherds (E. Byz. I-II, probable Byz. body sherds, UD body sherds).

Locus 8A 3 sherds (E. Byz.)

Locus 8B 58 sherds (E.Byz. I-II dominant, few ER/H body sherds, probably Byz. body sherds);
fig. 56:140.

Objects

Locus 4 glass
Locus 6 glass
Locus 7 glass
Locus 8B glass, painted and unpainted plaster

Interpretation. Although no surfaces were extant in Stratum 1, the presence of fills mixed with occupation debris may be analyzed in terms of the stratification from Lapp's excavation. Similar to the results from the previous excavation, the interior of the Qasr provided evidence of occupation but the ceramic corpus and object collection remain small. Ceramic correlations with the distinctive earth layers indicate two major fills within Stratum I.

The uppermost, Green Brown Sediment Layer, 1:3-6, was a thick compacted homogenous deposit which may have had an upper pavement or beaten earth surface. If floored it was probably cobbled for no plaster was included in the debris. That this fill is a Stratum Ia feature is indicated by the dominance of Early Byzantine III-IV wares which appear consistently throughout the layer.

Red Brown Sediment Layer 1:7, Clay, Lime-and Earth Layer, 1:8A and Gray Soil Layer 1:8B represent a series of concurrent fills. The very loose soft Gray Soil Layer, 1:8B contained a high percentage of rock rubble, much of which was either cut limestone architectural blocks or fragments derived from such. This thick random rubble scree suggests collapse of the interior Byzantine walls which were constructed of such square and rectangular blocks. This soft earth was poured over the rubble to serve as a post-collapse fill which was concentrated in the southeast portion of the square where it extended to an undetermined depth. Overlying Plaster 1:10 and part of Wall 1:9 was the substantial compacted Clay, Limestone, and Earth Layer 1:8A which was also assisted in raising the level of the room, but contained less architectural rubble. Levelling and sealing over these fills was a third layer, apparently designed to provide a firm basis for a surface. Although of variable depth, this Red Brown Sediment Layer 1:7 was consistently compacted and contained far less rubble than the preceeding Layer 1:8B. It probably functioned as an informal packed earth surface or held some form of pavement.

That this and the two lower fill loci are features of Stratum Ib is confirmed by the ceramic analysis. In each of these layers the dominant wares were Early Byzantine I-II and no Early Byzantine III-IV sherds were present. The fill was thus debris from the preceeding period, Stratum II, and perhaps the early part of Stratum I, and would suggest rather immediate filling and levelling off after the earthquake, probably close to A.D. 365. Absolute dates for Stratum Ib and Ia could therefore by ca. A.D. 365-392 and A.D. 392-491 respectively.

Topsoil Modern-Ottoman

Stratification. Sediment Layer I:3A consisted of the uppermost surface soil which covered the whole area of the square and averaged 0.10 m in depth (fig. 52). The debris included soft powdery earth mixed with cobbles and cut architectural blocks of limestone, vegetation, and modern refuse.

Pottery

Locus 3A 75 sherds (E.Byz., 1 possible LR IV body sherd, 1 Ott. pipe fragment);
fig. 56: 112, 121, 127, 128, 136, 137, 143, 150.

Interpretation. This layer represents a post-occupation accumulation of earth and refuse from the modern period and retains no relationships with architectural significance. In reference to Area II.2, which held a thick deposit of topsoil, Lapp noted that "the present topsoil was brought from nearby to prepare a gradual slope for agricultural purposes" (1962: 27). It appears that such a topsoil deposit, if placed over Square AE.76.1 as well, is no longer in evidence, for Lapp further notes in his description that "large pottery caches" were present in the topsoil (1962: 15) and such caches were not characteristic of 1:3A. The architectural rubble which cluttered the surface of the square may have served as a deterrent to agriculturalists. A clay tobacco pipe fragment is an indicator of Ottoman presence, for as discussed below, such pipes are ubiquitous in Ottoman occupation. The nature of the Ottoman occupation at Araq el-Emir appears to have been temporary and possibly squatter, for Lapp cites a similar Ottoman presence in the Square Building (1963: 37) which also lacked fixed structural remains. The Ottoman sherds collected from the surface of the site and those present in the 1976 soundings total a half dozen or less, a circumstance which supports the contention that while clearly present, the Ottoman occupation was brief and unsophisticated.

Square AE 76.2

Square 2 consisted of a probe which measured 1.00 m north-south by 2.00 m east-west. The south balk was located against the outer face of the northern arm of the retaining wall which surrounds the terrace upon which the Qasr el-Abd had been built. Above that section of the retaining wall against which Square 2 was opened stood a Late Ottoman-Modern house, the foundations of which were provided by the retaining wall.

Strata I-II Early Byzantine I-IV

Stratification. Clay and Sediment Layer 2:4-6 covered the whole probe area, 2.00 m × 1.00 m and averaged 1.20 m in depth. The tightly compacted clay and earth mixture was banded and varied in hues which included brown soil, orange-red soil, gray and black clay, brown and white clay, yellow clay, and gray silt. Among the inclusions were pebbles, cobbles, and boulders of limestone, patches of decomposed limestone, and fossils. To the south this Clay and Sediment Layer lay adjacent to the first course of Wall 2:1 and its foundation courses, the bottom of which was not fully articulated (fig. 53). While the wall proper consisted of roughly squared blocks measuring an average of 0.60 m × 0.60 m the foundation stones were small boulders and large cobbles packed together with clay.

Pottery

Locus 4   26 sherds (body sherds: 4 probable E. Byz., 2 E.Byz/LR, 1 H ?, 2 EB ?, UD); fig. 56: 157, 158.

Locus 5   10 sherds (body sherds: 1 Byz., 2 probable H, 1 EB, UD).

Locus 6   16 sherds (1 probable E. Byz., 8 E. Byz. body sherds, 2 H ?, 1 EB body sherd, 1 EB ?, 3 UD); fig. 56: 155.

Interpretation. The moist and tightly compacted thick layering of clay is indicative of water laid

53. Looking south at the north face of the retaining wall in Square AE.76.2.

deposition. The presence of fossils is probably due to weathering of the limestone cliffs above the Qasr to the west. The ceramic assemblage represents several periods including wares from the Byzantine period which were present throughout the sounding. Lapp recognized the possibility of the accuracy of the reference of Josephus to a moat attributed to Hyrcanus (*Ant.* 12.4.11 § 230) and indeed the excavation of Square II, outside of the platform enclosed by the retaining wall has confirmed this reference. At the present day, during heavy winter rains, the basin in which the Qasr platform sits may fill with water as the drainage pattern is unchanged. It is likely that the engineering of a permanent or seasonal moat was easily accomplished during the Hellenistic construction of the Qasr. The Clay and Sediment Layer 2:4-6 attests ceramically that either the maintenance of the water channeling system into such a moat, via the aquaduct which follows the cliffs in which the caverns were carved out, or the heavy seasonal inundation of the area, continued during the Byzantine occupation. Whether the retaining wall, Wall 2:1 which would have protected the Qasr platform from erosion, was a feature of the original Str. III construction or whether it was introduced in the Byzantine period cannot yet be determined.

Topsoil Modern-Ottoman

Stratification. Topsoil Layer 2:2-3 covered the entire 2.00 m × 1.00 m probe area and averaged 0.30 m in depth. Along the south balk this topsoil lay adjacent to the lower portion of the second course of the retaining wall. The upper locus, 2:2, consisted of compacted clay, granular brown soil and dung. The lower locus, 2:3, contained patches of loose granular brown soil mixed with boulders and large cobbles of limestone followed by compacted soil laminae.

Pottery
Locus 2   75 sherds (7 E. Byz., 1 Byz.?, 3 probable H body sherds, 1 Iron I ? body sherd); fig. 56: 153, 154, 156.
Locus 3   45 sherds (body sherds: E. Byz. dominant, few H ?, 1 probable Iron I).

Objects
Locus 3   glass

Interpretation. The topsoil loci consisted of relatively modern deposition and while reflecting a mixture of ceramic types, attested the Ottoman occupation which has been noted above in the Qasr, in the Square Building (Lapp 1963: 37), and from the survey of the region immediately around the Qasr (see below). The presence of Iron Age sherds indicated that the Iron Age occupation at Araq el-Emir was not confined to the village site. As today, the Iron Age villagers may have farmed the basin land enclosed by the hills around the Qasr.

Summary

Although the objectives which the project had forwarded initially became impractical with the impediment of unsafe balk conditions, the successful correlation of architectural features and sediment layers uncovered during the 1976 Soundings with the stratification of the previous excavation is significant. Although differences are apparent as they are between the individual areas excavated by Lapp in and around the Qasr as well, the overall phasing scheme which Lapp presented after his final season of excavation (1963:21) was confirmed by the 1976 season. The smallness of the ceramic corpus limits the scope of conclusions with respect to the clarification of the relationship between ceramic groupings and the phasing sequence. Nevertheless the material from the Square 1 sounding within the Qasr does present clear cut divisions which correlate with the various substrata. The Square 2 sounding did not contribute to a stratified body of ceramic data in that the Byzantine sherds which were present in all loci below topsoil were not always substantial enough to enable identification with reference to a specific sub-phase within the Byzantine period. This sounding did, however, serve to present a full picture of the occupational history of the site which includes: Early Bronze Age, Iron Age, Hellenistic, possible Roman period (whose representation is confirmed from the village site and the Qasr surface survey), Early Byzantine, and Ottoman. The extensive clay pan which lay beneath the topsoil has demonstrated conclusively that throughout the Byzantine period, and probably in earlier periods as well, a large standing body of water existed in the area around the Qasr, if not all year round at least on a seasonal basis.

Summary of Loci

AE 76.1

locus	description	stratum
1:1	East-west wall forming north side of area (= Wall E)	III
1:2	North-south wall forming west side of area (= Wall A)	III
1:3A	Uppermost surface soil, whole area	surface
1:4-6	Green Brown Sediment, sub 1:3A whole area	I
1:7	Red Brown Sediment, sub I:6	I
1:8A	Clay, Limestone, and Earth Layer, sub 1:7 in north	I
1:8B	Gray Soil, sub 1:7 south of 1:8A and 1:9	I
1:9	Wall parallel Wall 1:2 extending into south balk and parallel Wall 1:1 extending to east balk	II
1:10	Plaster Pavement between Wall 1:9 and Walls 1:1 and 1:2	III

AE 76.2

locus	description	stratum
2:1	Retaining wall forming the south balk of the area	III?
2:2-3	Topsoil, uppermost layers, whole area	surface
2:4-6	Clay and Sediment Layer, whole area, adjacent Wall 2:1 in south	II-I

Ceramic Analysis

A typological analysis of surface sherds from a survey both inside and outside of the Qasr el-Abd is presented below, nos. 1-98 (figs. 54-55). Sherd nos. 99-158 (fig. 56) represent the assemblages from Sounding 1 and 2. References to sherds and vessels from other sites have been introduced into the text for comparative purposes. Sherds identified with a specific historical period or date may be traced to coin controlled loci or sealed homogenous assemblages.

Surface Survey Sherds

Hellenistic

Sherd nos. 1-2 are thick hooked rims from large bag-shaped storage jars. The former had been quickly fired leaving a thick dark core mixed with coarse, blue and white inclusions while the latter exhibits a well fired orange ware throughout and a buff slipped exterior. These compare closely with Samaria (Crowfoot, Crowfoot and Kenyon 1957: fig. 42:8, 9, 11). Other similar forms include Beth-Zur (Sellers *et al* 1968: fig. 22:8), Balatah (Lapp 1964: fig. 1a:1-2), Heshbon (unpublished) and Amman, Citadel (unpublished). Only one comparable rim is published from the Lapp excavations (see above ch. 7, fig. 30:1). Precedence for this form is documented from the onset of the Helle-

nistic period at Mugharet Abu Shinjeh (Wadi ed-Daliyeh) (Lapp 1970: fig. 9:1) where a parallel vessel dates to 332 B.C. Of the examples cited above, those from Balatah belong to a 250-225 B.C. group, the Beth-Zur rim dates 175-165 B.C. and the Samaria sherds belong to a corpus dating prior to 150 B.C. Exclusive of the prototype form this group sets a chronological framework of 250-150 B.C. encompassing the Ptolemaic era of the Early Hellenistic period to the beginning of the Hasmonean era of the Late Hellenistic.

Lamp no. 3 features folded over sides which have been pinched together from the nozzle opening to the back and a sloping body which terminates with a flat base. Similar lamps with flat or squared bases include: Jerusalem, Rehavia (Rahmani 1967: fig. 9:1-3), Jerusalem, Shahin Hill (Rahmani 1958: fig. 2:5), Jerusalem, Dominus Flevit (Bagatti and Milik 1958: fig. 25:1), Jerusalem, Temple Mount (Mazar 1971: fig. 17:27), Bethany (Loffreda 1969: fig. 2:8 and Saller 1957: fig. 33:3), Beth-Zur (Sellers 1933: fig. 41 and Sellers *et al* 1968: pl. 32B:3), Ain Shems (Grant 1932: pl. L:26), Ramat Rahel (Aharoni *et al* 1962: fig. 21:4-5 and 1964: fig. 11:5), Tell Goren (Mazar, Dothan, and Dunayevsky 1966: fig. 25:9), Gezer (Seger 1976: fig. 3), and Maliha (Kennedy 1963: pl. XX:481). The recently published pottery from the third campaign at Tell el-Ful includes one flat-based lamp (Lapp 1981: pl. 80:11) from Stratum

Fig. 54.   Surface Survey

Sherd No.	Reg. No.	Ware	Surface	Inclusions	Core	Diameter
1	119	5YR 6/1 Gray	2.5YR 6/6 Light Red	large	thick	12
2	118	2.5YR 6/6 Light Red	7.5YR 8/4 Pink	large	none	14
3	168	5YR 8/3 Pink	5YR 8/2 Pinkish White	medium	----	
4	75	7.5YR 4/6 Red	7.5YR 4/6 Red	fine	slight	12
5	150	5YR 5/1 Gray	2.5YR 6/4 Light Reddish Brown	fine	thick	19
6	114	5YR 5/1 Gray	5YR 5/2 Reddish Gray	fine	thick	8
7	95	2.5YR 6/6 Light Red	10R 5/6 Red	medium	none	16
8	144	10R 6/4 Pale Red	10R 5/2 Weak Red	medium	thick	
9	94	5YR 7/6 Reddish Yellow	5YR 5/2 Reddish Gray	medium	none	11
10	97	5YR 6/4 Light Reddish Brown	5YR 5/1 Gray	medium	medium	11
11	102	5YR 7/4 Pink	5YR 5/1 Gray	fine	none	12
12	98	5YR 7/6 Reddish Yellow	5YR 5/1 Gray	medium	slight	11
13	93	2.5YR 6/6 Light Red	2.5YR 5/2 Weak Red	fine	none	15
14	99	5YR 7/3 Pink	5YR 5/2 Reddish Gray	fine	none	12
15	91	2.5YR N6/ Gray	2.5YR N5/ Gray	fine	none	14
16	92	2.5YR 6/6 Light Red	2.5YR 4/2 Weak Red	fine	none	14
17	89	5YR 7/6 Reddish Yellow	5YR 5/2 Reddish Gray	fine	none	13
18	90	2.5YR 6/4 Light Reddish Brown	5YR 5/1 Gray	fine	slight	12
19	103	5YR 7/4 Pink	5YR 5/2 Reddish Gray	fine	none	12
20	107	5YR 7/4 Pink	2.5YR 5/2 Weak Red	fine	none	24
21	117	5YR 7/4 Pink	7.5YR 8/2 Pinkish White	fine	none	9
22	129	5YR 7/6 Reddish Yellow	2.5YR 6/6 Light Red	medium	slight	10
23	155	5YR 7/4 Pink	5YR 8/3 Pink	medium	medium	11
24	121	2.5YR 6/4 Light Reddish Brown	7.5YR 8/2 Pinkish White	large	slight	10
25	110	2.5YR 6/6 Light Red	5YR 7/3 Pink	large	none	11
26	116	5YR 7/2 Pinkish Gray	7.5YR 8/2 Pinkish White	medium	thick	11
27	96	5YR 6/1 Light Gray	5YR 5/1 Gray	fine	slight	10
28	151	2.5YR N6/ Gray	5YR 6/1 Gray	large	medium	12
29	106	5YR 8/4 Pink	5YR 8/4 Pink	fine	none	10
30	125	5YR 8/1 White	7.5YR 8/2 Pinkish White	fine	none	13
31	149	5YR 7/4 Pink	5YR 5/2 Reddish Gray	fine	thick	5
32	118	5YR 7/6 Reddish Yellow	5YR 8/4 Pink	medium	thick	14
33	143	5YR 7/3 Pink	5YR 5/2 Reddish Gray	fine	none	3
34	88	5YR 8/4 Pink	5YR 5/2 Reddish Gray	fine	none	4
35	142	5YR 7/4 Pink	2.5YR 6/4 Light Reddish Brown	fine	none	4
36	109	2.5YR 6/8 Light Red	2.5YR 6/8 Light Red	fine	none	20
37	124	10R 6/6 Light Red	5YR 5/2 Reddish Gray	fine	none	18
38	152	2.5YR 6/4 Light Reddish Brown	5YR 5/2 Light Reddish Brown	medium	none	16
39	157	5YR 6/6 Reddish Yellow	5YR 5/2 Reddish Gray	medium	none	24
40	111	5YR 7/4 Pink	10 R 6/6 Light Red	medium	slight	34
41	159	5YR 7/4 Pink	5YR 6/2 Pinkish Gray	fine	none	22
42	158	5YR 7/6 Reddish Yellow	5YR 7/6 Reddish Yellow	fine	none	17
43	163	5YR 7/4 Pink	2.5YR 6/4 Light Reddish Brown	fine	none	22
44	164	2.5YR 6/4 Light Reddish Brown	2.5YR 6/4 Light Reddish Brown	fine	none	22
45	160	5YR 8/4 Pink	5YR 6/1 Gray	fine	none	29
46	156	5YR 7/4 Pink	5YR 5/2 Reddish Gray	medium	none	21
47	161	5YR 7/4 Pink	2.5YR 6/4 Light Reddish Brown	medium	none	18
48	137	5YR 7/4 Pink	10R 6/6 Light Red	medium	slight	13
49	154	2.5YR 6/6 Light Red	2.5YR 6/6 Light Red	fine	none	30
50	130	7.5YR 6/4 Light Brown	5YR 6/1 Gray	medium	slight	10

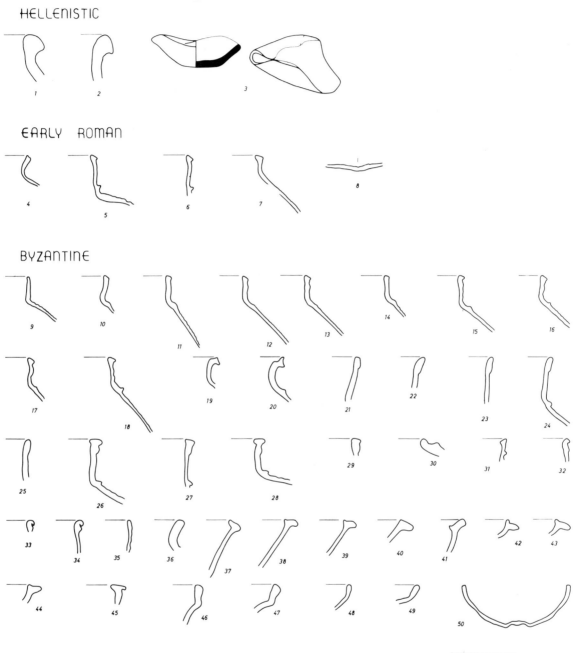

54. Surface sherds from a survey in and around the Qasr.

IV B (ca. 135-100 B.C.), and it is suggested there that the folded lamps with rounded bases may date with Exilic material (pp. 98, 105). Folded lamps with round bases are represented at: Ramat Rahel (Aharoni *et al* 1962: fig. 21:6 and Aharoni 1956: fig. 8:1), Beth-Zur (Sellers 1933: fig. 41) and Ain Shems (Grant 1932: pl. L:24). Other instances include Bethel (Albright and Kelso 1968: pl. 72:5), Jerusalem, Temple Mount (Mazar 1971: pl. XXII: 3-4), Jerusalem, Jewish Quarter (Avigad 1970: pl. 34:C) and Bethany (Loffreda 1969: fig. 2:8).

Comparable flat based lamps which may be dated are from Bethany (Saller 1957:165:5) 75-50 B.C., Jerusalem Citadel (Johns 1950: fig. 14:5) 37-29 B.C. and Jerusalem, Tyropoeon Valley (Crowfoot and Fitzgerald 1929: pl. XVII:2) 37-4 B.C. This form is consistently absent from Early Roman III and IV sites such as Heshbon, Judean Desert Caves, Wadi Murabbaat and Araq en-Nasaneh, implying a chronological distribution from the end of the Hasmonean era to the close of Early Roman II, 75-4 B.C. This form is frequently present in assemblages from Jerusalem and neighboring towns. From the East Bank there are no published examples of folded lamps and the example from Maliha, a village east of Damascus, remains a curiosity.

Early Roman

Represented in no. 4 is the rim of a closed globular cooking pot which features a short incurved neck with a groove upon the edge of its outturned rim and a brick red colored fabric. Parallel sherds are illustrated from Jerusalem, Sanhedriyya (Rahmani 1961: fig. 5:8), Jerusalem, French Hill (Strange 1975: fig. 14:19) and Ein el Ghuweir (Bar Adon 1977: fig. 14:4). Observations of Early and Late Hellenistic cooking pot forms, Samaria (Crowfoot, Crowfoot, and Kenyon 1957: fig. 41:1) and Bethany (Saller 1957: fig. 47:1) respectively, indicate that no. 4 is not associated with the Hellenistic styles. While a related, though possibly later, form from Alayiq (Pritchard 1958: fig. 58:3) dates to an Early Roman III stratum, no similar cooking pots have been associated with such strata at Heshbon or Qumran. Early Roman IV forms, Judean Desert (Yadin 1963: fig. 41), share no morphological resemblance to no. 4. It is therefore most probable that this form belongs among the Early Roman I and II types of cooking pots, although it may carry over into Early Roman III.

Nos. 5-6 belong to a genre of large bag-shaped storage jars which are apparent from the Hellenistic to the Byzantine periods and are characterized by narrow, cylindrical necks, a hooked rim and a ridge at the base of the neck. Forms which anticipate nos. 5-6 have longer straighter necks, as shown in Early Roman III examples; Masada (Yadin 1966:97), Jerusalem, North Wall (Hamilton: 1944: fig. 14:3) and Alayiq (Pritchard 1958: fig. 58:29) of which the latter belonged to a stratum dated 30 B.C.-A.D. 50. Other seemingly early forms include Bethel (Albright and Kelso 1968: pl. 70:13), Samaria (Hennessy 1970: fig. 7:32) and Ein el Guweir (Bar Adon 1977: fig. 21:1). The subsequent development, represented by nos. 5-6, involved a shortening and concave bowing of the neck, as further illustrated by Araq en-Nasaneh (Lapp and Lapp 1974: pl. 29:6-7) and Judean Desert (Aharoni 1962: fig. 3:2). Both of these sites have an A.D. 135 *terminus ad quem*, thus establishing an Early Roman IV framework for this form as it appears at Araq el-Emir. That this form continues into the mid-4th century A.D. is suggested by Cafarnao (Loffreda 1974: fig. 44:6), which although thickened and less angular, is notably similar.

Possibly from a cooking pot form, no. 7 is without parallels in the literature. Its shallow ribbing and light red ware suggest an Early Roman date.

The base of a closed cooking pot, no. 8 is unribbed, slightly curving and comes to a faint point. The red color of the ware compares with that of no. 4. In reviewing the typology of classical cooking pot forms, Bethany (Saller 1957: fig. 47:1) and Samaria (Crowfoot, Crowfoot and Kenyon 1957: fig. 69:7) demonstrate that the Hellenistic and Early Roman I vessels were perfectly rounded from neck to base. With the Early Roman III cooking pot the slightly pointed base appears, Qumran (deVaux 1953: fig. 3:11). By the end of Early Roman IV the bases have become distinctly pointed and ribbed (Judean Desert, Yadin 1963: fig. 41). This evolution indicates an Early Roman III context for no. 8.

Byzantine

Presented in nos. 9-18 is a group of closed globular cooking pots. Distinct from the rest of the group, the neck of no. 9 narrows into a thin, almost pointed rim and lacks carination where it joins with the shoulder. This example is paralleled at Bethany (Saller 1957: fig. 47:10, 12). The rest of the group is generally slightly concave on the interior of the neck, convex or bulging on the exterior, have hooked rims and are marked by carination at the junction of the shoulder and neck. These may be compared to the cooking pots from Jerusalem, North Wall (Hamilton 1944: fig. 23:18), Pella (Smith 1973: pl. 43:1326), Khirbet al-Kerak (Delougaz and Haines 1960: pl. 53:36) and Tell er-Ras (Bull and Campbell 1968: fig. 11:1-7). The mid 3rd to mid 4th centuries A.D. Tell er-Ras corpus suggests an Early Byzantine I-II date for this form. A Late Roman III-IV date is excluded by Heshbon (Sauer 1973: fig. 2:45-50) whose pots bear no resemblance.

Open cooking pot rims, pictured in nos. 19-20, feature an incurved neck and splayed, hooked rim.

A homogenous group of high collared storage jar rims is presented in nos. 21-25. These rims are thickened, folded over and flattened on their exterior faces. The neck is plain and cylindrical and, in the instance of no. 24, marked at the base by a ridge. Other examples of this type are from Samaria (Crowfoot, Crowfoot and Kenyon 1957: fig. 72:3 and Hennessy 1970: fig. 10:21), Cafarnao (Loffreda 1974: fig. 1:3), Magdala (Loffreda 1976: fig. 10:21), Caesarea (Riley 1975: no. 16) and Khirbet Shema (Meyers *et al* 1976: fig. 7.20: 17-19, 30). From among the Khirbet Shema examples no. 17 is associated with a pre-2nd century A.D. layer and nos. 18-19 are from the first half of the 3rd century A.D. The citation from Cafarnao is pre-mid 4th century A.D.

The storage jar rims shown in nos. 26-29 are knob thickened, profiled at the top and retain a ridge at the base of the neck. This form appears in a variety of ware colors ranging from pink to black. Dibon provides several comparisons (Tushingham 1972: figs. 4:3, 93; 12:29).

The grooved, hole mouth jar rim, no. 30, is distinguished by its light grey ware. From Bethany (Saller 1957: fig. 41:3926, 7038) are parallel examples.

No. 31, a small decanter rim, is characterized by a pronounced ridge around the neck and grey brown slipped orange ware. Other small forms are represented by rolled rim juglets nos. 32-34 with an orange fabric; nos. 33-34 are grey brown slipped, no. 32 is buff slipped. A thin ribbed neck sherd from a small jug is shown in no. 35. The orange ware is red-orange slipped on the exterior. An enigmatic and possibly unique form, no. 36, is

thick, slightly splayed, rounded at the top and has an apparent convex curving of the neck. The fabric is bright orange.

Small bowls nos. 37-39 feature sloping sides and hooked rims pointing both outward, as shown by nos. 38-39 and inward, as shown by no. 37. The latter has a dark grey brown slipped exterior and red slipped interior while the former two are of an orange-pink ware and grey brown exterior slip.

The rim from a large bowl form, no. 40, has a light red-orange ware covered on the exterior with a shiney red slip. The thick flaring lip is known from Bethany (Saller 1957: fig. 50:3479) and Beth She'arim (Avigad 1955: fig. 3:18). Although this specific shape is not included in Hayes's corpus, his late fifth century A.D. Form 85:H approaches this and may be related (Hayes 1972: fig. 85:H). The treatment of the ware and this resemblance to an Egyptian Red Slip form (*ibid*) suggest that no. 40 is a local imitation of the Red Ware style which became popular in Jordan during the Byzantine period.

A group of various small bowl types is presented in nos. 41-49. Small bowl no. 41 displays a high upward projecting blunt lipped rim which is peaked toward the interior. Its ware is pink-orange and covered with a grey brown slip on both the interior and the exterior. Two other small bowls, shown in nos. 42-43, have rims with peaked tops and outward flaring lips. The gentle curves of the necks indicate these to have been shallow, wide mouthed dishes. The wares are orange and red-orange slipped upon both the interior and exterior faces. Small bowl no. 44 also reflects the blunt outflaring lip and peaked rim-top but is less exaggerated than nos. 42-43. The ware is the same as above. Flat topped and flaring both inward and outward, bowl rim no. 45 consists of a grey brown slipped pink-orange ware. Carinated bowls nos. 46-47 share similar features, including a thick rounded rim, pink-orange ware and red-orange slip. Smaller bowls of the same fabric are represented in nos. 48-49. Silet edh-Dhahr (Sellers and Baramki 1953: fig. 31:9) parallels the latter of these.

Vessel no. 50, referred to in the literature as both a cup and a bowl, is a small open form characterized by an umbellicus base and indented exterior side walls. The pink-orange ware is dark grey brown slipped on both the interior and exterior. Identical vessels have been published from excavations on both sides of the Jordan River: from

Fig. 55. Surface Survey

Sherd No.	Reg. No.	Ware	Surface	Inclusions	Core	Diameter
51	141	2.5YR 6/4 Light Reddish Brown	5YR 8/4 Pink	large	thick	37
52	138	5YR 7/3 Pink	7.5YR 8/2 Pinkish White	medium	slight	40
53	174	5YR 7/4 Pink	7.5YR 8/4 Pink	medium	slight	40
54	170	5YR 7/3 Pink	5YR 7/3 Pink	fine	slight	33
55	140	5YR 7/6 Reddish Yellow	7.5YR 8/4 Pink	medium	thick	29
56	166	7.5YR 8/4 Pink	10YR 8/4 Very Pale Brown	fine	slight	33
57	139	5YR 7/4 Pink	5YR 6/2 Pinkish Gray	medium	thick	22
58	165	2.5YR 6/6 Light Red	2.5YR 6/6 Light Red	fine	none	23
59	132	10R 6/6 Light Red	10R 6/6 Light Red	fine	medium	32
60	153	10R 6/6 Light Red	10R 6/6 Light Red	fine	slight	30
61	113	10R 6/8 Light Red	10R 6/8 Light Red	medium	none	31
62	80	5YR 7/3 Pink	5YR 5/2 Reddish Gray	medium	none	
63	76	5YR 8/3 Pink	5YR 6/2 Pinkish Gray	fine	none	
64	77	7.5YR 7/4 Pink	5YR 5/1 Gray	medium	medium	
65	82	5YR 7/4 Pink	5YR 5/2 Reddish Gray	medium	medium	
66	78	10R 6/6 Light Red	10R 6/6 Light Red	fine	none	
67	83	2.5YR 6/6 Light Red	2.5YR 6/6 Light Reddish Brown	medium	slight	
68	79	2.5YR 5/6 Red	2.5YR 5/6 Red	fine	none	
69	127	5YR 6/4 Light Reddish Brown	7.5YR 8/2 Pinkish White	medium	slight	
70	84	5YR 7/6 Reddish Yellow	2.5YR 6/4 Light Reddish Brown	medium	thick	
71	87	2.5YR 6/6 Light Red	7.5YR 7/4 Pink	large	thick	
72	115	7.5YR 6/4 Light Brown	10YR 8/3 Very Pale Brown	large	thick	
73	81	5YR 7/4 Pink	7.5YR 8/2 Pinkish White	medium	none	
74	101	7.5YR 7/4 Pink	5YR 7/4 Pink	medium	none	
75	85	5YR 7/4 Pink	7.5YR 8/4 Pink	medium	slight	
76	86	5YR 7/4 Pink	5YR 8/4 Pink	large	thick	
77	175	5YR 7/4 Pink	5YR 6/1 Gray	medium	none	
78	176	2.5YR 6/6 Light Red	5YR 5/2 Reddish Gray	fine	none	
79	173	2.5YR 6/6 Light Red	5YR 5/2 Reddish Gray	fine	none	
80	122	5YR 7/4 Pink	5YR 7/4 Pink	large	none	
81	123	2.5YR 6/4 Light Reddish Brown	7.5YR 8/4 Pink	large	none	
82	120	5YR 7/4 Pink	5YR 7/4 Pink	large	none	
83	136	5YR 7/4 Pink	5YR 8/4 Pink	fine	none	
84	126	2.5YR 6/4 Light Reddish Brown	2.5YR 5/2 Weak Red	fine	none	
85	133	5YR 7/4 Pink	5YR 6/2 Pinkish Gray	fine	none	
86	134	5YR 7/2 Pinkish Gray	7.5YR 8/2 Pinkish White	fine	none	
87	135	2.5YR 6/6 Light Red	5YR 6/2 Pinkish Gray	medium	medium	
88	146	5YR 7/3 Pink	5YR 7/3 Pink	medium	none	
89	147	7.5YR 7/2 Pinkish Gray	5YR 7/3 Pink	large	thick	
90	145	5YR 7/2 Pinkish Gray	5YR 7/2 Pinkish Gray	medium	none	
91	172	2.5YR 6/4 Light Reddish Brown	2.5YR 6/4 Light Reddish Brown	fine	none	
92	167	5YR 7/4 Pink	2.5YR 6/6 Light Red	fine	none	
93	178	5YR 6/4 Light Reddish Brown	7.5YR 8/2 Pinkish White	medium	slight	
94	171	5YR 8/4 Pink	5YR 8/1 White	large	none	
95	162	5YR 7/3 Pink	5YR 7/4 Pink 10R 5/4 Weak Red (Paint)	fine	none	34
96	112	5YR 7/4 Pink	2.5YR 6/4 Light Reddish Brown	large	thick	
97	169	5YR 7/3 Pink	5YR 7/3 Pink 5YR 4/1 Dark Gray (Paint) 10R 5/4 Weak Red (Paint)	large	none	
98	177	5YR 6/2 Pinkish Gray	5YR 6/2 Pinkish Gray	large	none	

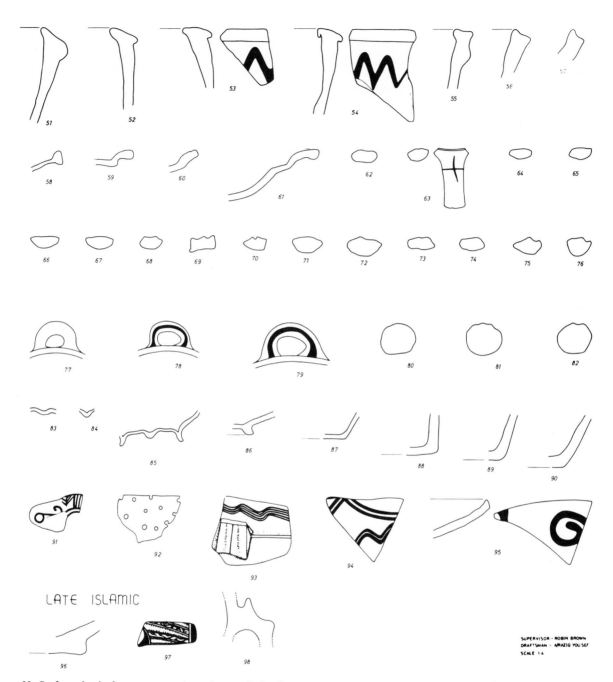

55. Surface sherds from a survey in and around the Qasr.

Ramat Rahel (Aharoni *et al* 1964: fig. 7:3) and Mt. Nebo (Schneider 1950: fig. 13:2).

Presented in nos. 51-57 is a corpus of basin rims. These thick, heavy hand-made vessels are all characterized by a round cylindrical body and a flat base. At Araq el-Emir basins are represented by two different rim types; nos. 51-54 have thickened rims with flat sloping tops which project both inward and outward, and nos. 55-57 are thickened, squared and grooved at the top. Two of the examples of the former type, nos. 53-54 are decorated with a grooved horizontal band in a zig-zag line pattern which rings the exterior pot wall beneath the rim. The squared rim profile appears at several other sites including Dibon (Tushingham 1972: fig. 10:49-52), Cafarnao (Loffreda 1974: fig. 14:6-7 and Corbo, Loffreda and Spijkerman 1970: fig. 5:3, 6) and Magdala (Loffreda 1976: fig. 10:22); these sloping rims are identical to nos. 56-57. Projecting rims nos. 51-53 are comparable to Dibon (Winnett and Reed 1964: pl. 65:20). The bulging exterior wall which characterizes no. 55 is attested at Pella (Smith 1973: pl. 44:1248). The basin fragments from Cafarnao are stratified to 4th century A.D. contexts but that this form continued throughout the Byzantine period is attested by even later stratified examples from the Umayyad Period: Amman, Citadel (Harding 1951: fig. 2:40, 53). No Late Roman layers have yielded basins as such.

The group of plates shown in nos. 58-60 seem to represent locally manufactured vessels in the style of Red Ware pottery. No. 58 is marked by a thickened, triangular knobbed rim with a flattened exterior face. Similar imitations of this style have appeared at Heshbon (unpublished) but the majority of parallels are with the true Red Ware plates which are included in the corpora of Samaria (Crowfoot, Crowfoot and Kenyon 1957: fig. 84:24), Ramat Rahel (Aharoni *et al* 1964: fig. 7:9) and Khirbet al-Kerak (Delougaz and Haines 1960: pl. 52:3). Hayes discusses this type as his Form 104 (1972:160-166 and fig. 31:22). Nos. 59-60 are splayed, thickened rims from step-sided open dishes.

Red Ware plate no. 60 shows the profile of a deep step-sided dish with a flaring, thickened, horizontal rim. This form is well documented from sites on both sides of the Jordan River, including Petra (Hammond 1965: pl. LIII:3a-6), Bethlehem (Tzaferis 1975: pl. 11:1-11), Dibon (Tushingham 1972: fig. 11:14), Ramat Rahel (Aharoni *et al* 1962: fig. 18:9 and 1964: fig. 7:9), Antioch (Waage 1948:

pl. IX:871A-871P) and Mt. Nebo (Schneider 1950: fig. 12:2). Hayes presents a full discussion of this type under his Form 67 in which he cites a number of examples from the Mediterranean world (1972: 112-116 and fig. 19). These plates, although frequent, demonstrate variability of form; Hayes notes "The shape of individual pieces does not reveal any very consistent development" (p. 115). Hayes also refers to a communication with Paul Lapp in which Lapp confirmed that this form was present at Araq el-Emir (p. 116). Comparisons with stratified examples include Cafarnao (Loffreda 1974: fig. 21:7), dated to A.D. 341 and Kellia (Egloff 1977: pl. 99:6) from strata encompassing the years A.D. 390-450.

The cooking pot handles shown in nos. 62-68 are of three types. No. 62, associated with the open cooking casserole, is a straight horizontal handle which may have terminated in a loop turned up and over upon itself. Vertical cooking pot handles nos. 63-65 are small, ovoid in section and feature a pink-orange ware with a grey brown slip. The cross upon the surface of no. 63 was incised subsequent to firing. This is a group analogous to that represented by handles nos. 124-128. The remainder of the vertical cooking pot handles, nos. 66-68, are larger and are either flattened on the top face, as nos. 66-67, or multifaceted, as no. 68. The latter has a coarse grainy deep red fabric while others share a pink-orange ware. A handle from Cafarnao (Loffreda 1974: fig. 32:2) parallels no. 68.

Jar handles nos. 69-76 exhibit a multiplicity of shapes. A unique form within the corpus and without parallels in the literature, no. 69 has a rectangular shape, three distinct ridges across the upper face and a lip seen projecting from the left or the underside. For more detailed discussion refer below to no. 93. No. 70 is sharply grooved across the upper face, a feature of the Late Roman cooking pot handles, as attested at Heshbon (Sauer 1973: fig. 2:82). This however, appears at Araq el-Emir as a jar handle and therefore the similarity may be regarded as superficial. A comparison of this type to a jar form may be cited from Khirbet al-Kerak (Delougaz and Haines 1960: pl. 55:7). Handles nos. 71-72 are the largest, and both consist of a coarse, gritty ware while the other handles of the group have an orange ware. All of the handles are grooved across the top and most retain vestiges of a buff slip.

Handles nos. 77-79 represent the open lid cooking casserole, a form which varies in depth but usually is characterized by body ribbing and horizontal handles bonded just beneath the rim. No. 77, attached to an unribbed, gently sloping section of the body, had been pulled from a single stand of clay and rather than being positioned horizontally it had been pushed up over the rim slightly. Among the comparisons which document the frequency of this style are: Samaria (Hennessy 1970: fig. 7:31), Beth She'arim (Avigad 1955: fig. 3:14), Pella (Smith 1973: pl. 30: 1127, 1128, 1328) and Bethany (Saller 1957: fig. 48:3338, 4003). This same type, although twisted, has been noted at Caesarea (Riley 1975: nos. 26-27) and a similar, though possibly typlogically later example is from Alayiq (Pritchard 1958: pl. 28: N 169). Handles nos. 78-79, associated with ribbed cooking casseroles, were made from two stands of clay pressed together producing a distinctive ridge upon the upper face. Both were tilted upward over the rim to a slight degree. Similar handles are known from Khirbet Shema (Meyers et al 1976: fig. 7.12:28), Dibon (Tushingham 1972: fig. 5:29, 33 and 9:30, 32-36 and Winnett and Reed 1964: pl. 14:9), Jerash (Fisher and McCown 1931: pl. 14:B2 xl) upon which the exaggerated omphalos base and heavy ribbing may indicate a later development, and Jerusalem, North Wall (Hamilton 1944: fig. 23:14). Groups from Nazareth (Bagatti 1969: fig. 226:7-11) and Cafarnao (Loffreda 1974: fig. 11:1, 3, 12) share some features with the Araq el-Emir group but illustrate regional variations of stylistic detail. As indicated in Heshbon (Sauer 1973: fig. 2:51-53) and Cafarnao (Loffreda 1974: fig. 11:13) by the presence of lids, the first period to witness this form of open cooking pot is the Late Roman period. That this form continues throughout the Byzantine period is documented by Umayyad examples, Amman, Citadel (Harding 1951: pl. IV:69), which are pushed high up over the rim into a vertical position.

The thick, heavy spherical zir handles pictured in nos. 80-82 are marked by single or multiple grooves across their upper surfaces and a consistently pink-orange ware. Comparisons may be drawn with examples from Dibon (Tushingham 1972: fig. 12:61-62), Heshbon (Sauer 1973: fig. 3:102), Qasr el-Abd (Bagatti 1968: fig. 7:11-12) and Abu Gosh (deVaux and Steve 1950: fig. 3:9). There is a clear transition from the ovoid Early Roman IV handles, Judean Desert (Yadin 1963: fig. 43:A12) to the form illustrated in the examples cited above which compare with Mt. Nebo (Saller 1941b: pl. 144:2, 7) from a Byzantine layer. In the Umayyad period this handle type is similar though

less symmetrical (Heshbon, Sauer 1973: fig. 3:130).

Nos. 83-85 are ring bases which have a small center omphalos. The orange ware was grey brown slipped on the exterior. Frequently appearing on jug forms, such bases may be compared with Caesarea (Riley 1975: Nos. 134-135) and Cafarnao (Loffreda 1974: fig. 4:10). With a notably higher omphalos, a precursor to these examples (Judean Desert, Bar Adon 1961: fig. 1:9) has a *terminus ad quem* of A.D. 135 which places it at the end of the Early Roman IV period, and an antecedent from the Byzantine stratum at Mt. Nebo (Schneider 1950: fig. 11:3) illustrates a departure from the distinct ring base pictured in no. 85. Within these limits the ware type indicates that this sherd is from an Early Byzantine rather than Late Roman vessel.

The ring base from a bowl, or similar open form, is represented in no. 86. The grey buff ware of this base appears on the same form at Dibon (Tushingham 1972: fig. 10:83). The source of inspiration for these locally made grey buff pieces may be sought abroad, for identical Red Ware bases are also included in the corpus from Dibon (Tushingham 1972: fig. 11:19, 21, 24). As noted above, the advent of the popularity of Red Ware and its consequent imitations by provincial workshops is characteristic of the Byzantine period in Jordan.

The thin, flat base pictured in no. 87 is an uncommon form although the ware, bright orange with a dark grey brown exterior slip, is well represented by a variety of sherds from Araq el-Emir. The form suggests a possible affinity with flat based lanterns from Jerash (Fisher and McCown 1931: pl. 14:A 24) and Jericho (Sellin and Watzinger 1913: pl. 44:A 19).

Base sherds nos. 88-90 are associated with the hand made basin form, discussed above under nos. 50-56. Direct parallels to these flat bases include Dibon (Tushingham 1972: fig. 10:48) and Cafarnao (Corbo, Loffreda and Spijkerman 1970: fig. 5:11).

Sherd no. 91 consists of the upper portion of a mold-pressed lamp which preserves a portion of the nozzle and part of the body around the filling hole. Other examples of this lamp are: Amman, Jebel Jofeh el-Sharqi (Bisheh 1972: pl. III: fig. 2), Amman, Jebel Luweibdeh (Dana 1970: pl. IV: J12459, J12460) and Ramat Rahel (Aharoni et al 1964: fig. 32:3), the distribution of which indicate it to be primarily an East Bank form. It is characterized by a rounded body, elongated nozzle and raised molded decoration. Depicted upon this lamp fragment are a volute, which curves from the nozzle's wick hole to the filling hole, and, flanking the filling hole, schematized olive branch or tree followed by straight ray lines. These motifs frequently accompany this lamp form although their arrangement upon the lamp surface is variable. In addition to exhibiting these motifs, the handle of the Jebel Luweibdeh lamp was impressed with a cross. A chronological definition of this type of lamp is assisted by a review of the typology of Palestinian and Jordanian lamps. From the Judean Desert (Yadin 1963: fig. 42) are Early Roman IV lamp types, which include the late Herodian spatulate nozzle form as well as a form dominated by a spherical body with a small bulb nozzle which protrudes from the body only slightly. The Late Roman lamp is well represented in Amman, Jebel Jofeh (Harding 1950: pl. XXV) and reflects a larger nozzle but one which still appears as an appendage upon an essentially round body. From Mr. Nebo, Saller records the presence of a candlestick lamp (1941a: 325. Nos. 1461, 1922) in a clear Byzantine context. Umayyad lamps, also of the candlestick type, are exemplified at Heshbon (Sauer 1973: fig. 3:126-127). Another Umayyad form, the channel nozzle lamp, is illustrated by Amman, Citadel (Harding 1951: pl. III:55-56). The distinctive Late Byzantine and Umayyad forms exhibit an eliptical body in which the nozzle had been absorbed into the overall ovoid shape; features which are not common to the lamp from Araq el-Emir. As the elongation of the nozzle increases through the Late Roman period it probably continued to do so into the Early Byzantine period. The form shown in no. 91 appears as part of this gradual transition which, prior to the development of the eliptical form, manifested itself as a basically rounded body with the nozzle emerging as a distinct element.

A section of a strainer is presented in no. 92. Wheel thrown and slightly concave, this thin disc of clay is marked by frequent perforations. The characteristic bright orange ware is unslipped. A strainer from Mt. Nebo (Saller 1941b: pl. 157:22) illustrates similar perforations although this handmade utensil bears no overall morphological resemblance to no. 92. Other examples of boring at Mt. Nebo appear on lanterns (Saller 1941b: pl. 157:26-30).

Sherd no. 93 has a sharply ridged shoulder beneath which is a handle stump broken at its lower point of attachment. The ware, coarse grained, poorly fired and reddish brown in color,

was white slipped on the exterior. The concavity of the sherd, which lends it a biconical profile, and the steep attachment angle of the handle indicate that it belongs to a closed jug form. The squared, deeply ridged handle appears to be without parallel in Transjordan or the Levant. Jugs with deep shoulder ridging are known from other East Bank assemblages including Dibon (Tushingham 1973: fig. 6:28), an example which is marked with vertical, straight line combing which covers much of its surface, and Mt. Nebo (Schneider 1950: fig. 2:3 and 11:5). It is noteworthy that the same deep ridging is attested upon bowl forms as well, examples of which include Ramat Rahel (Aharoni *et al* 1964: fig. 22:20), Jerusalem, Dominus Flevit (Bagatti and Milik 1958: fig. 32:1) and Khirbet al-Kerak (Delougaz and Haines 1960: 54:12). Several features of no. 93 point to a Byzantine period of origin, including the ware type which is totally alien to those known from the Late Roman and Umayyad periods; combing, while predominantly a feature of the Umayyad period, has been attested in Byzantine contexts at Mt. Nebo (Saller 1941b: pl. 155:49, 51) and Dibon (Tushingham 1972: fig. 4:95), as well as the parallel jug cited above from Dibon (fig. 6:28) which was stratified with Late Byzantine coins.

Illustrated in no. 94 is a thick body sherd from a handmade exterior white slipped vessel whose slight concavity and thick wall indicate that this vessel was very large. The surface is marked by three bands of double line grooving running at right and oblique angles to one another. Dibon pl. 15:18 (Winnett and Reed 1964) parallels this style of grooving. That this sherd may have belonged to a basin is suggested by Mt. Nebo (Saller 1941b: pl. 152:26-29, 31-32). Of these grooved basin fragments two (nos. 27, 32) are dated by their Byzantine contexts.

The simple bowl rim which is depicted in no. 95 is a red painted orange fabric decorated on the interior with a clockwise spiral and cross bands upon the face of the rim; the latter are 1.0 cm in width and evenly spaced 1.5 cm apart. Although red paint is most commonly a characteristic of the Umayyad period, of the 83 examples of red painted sherds, including both interior and exterior painting, recorded at Mt. Nebo, 19 were from stratified Byzantine deposits. Among those examples, a Mt. Nebo basin (Saller 1941b: pl. 153:22) is decorated with identical red spirals on the interior and upon its rim are red painted zig-zag motifs. In this group the examples of red painting appear upon a variety of forms, including jugs, basins and bowls, and in at least one instance it occurs upon a fabric with the same description as no. 95. A post-Byzantine date for sherd no. 95 is precluded by its ware type.

Late Islamic

The hand-made, undecorated base represented in no. 96 consists of a coarse, pink, poorly fired fabric. The heel is rounded and its underside faintly concave. Such bases appear frequently in the literature and are associated with a variety of wheel thrown and hand-made forms, including bowls, jugs, craters, and storage jars. Parallels in the literature are from Pella (Smith 1973: pl. 74:955), Dibon (Tushingham 1972: fig. 7:46 and Winnett and Reed 1964: pl. 66:27), Heshbon (Sauer 1973: fig. 4:159), Aro'er (Olavarri 1956: fig. 3:13) and numerous examples from Tell Abu Gourdan (Franken and Kalsbeek 1975: pls. 174-200). Tell Abu Gourdan well illustrates the variability of the concavity of the base underside and the variety of surface treatments which include paint (*ibid*: fig. 61:38) and glaze (*ibid*: fig. 37:77). Although absent from the Umayyad assemblages of Heshbon and the Amman Citadel, this form appears frequently at Late Islamic sites and has been dated at Heshbon to an Early Mameluk stratum (Sauer 1973: fig. 4:159). At Tell Abu Gourdan Franken records this base type in all levels; Sauer however, in his analysis of the Tell Abu Gourdan evidence suggests a post-Fatimid, possibly Sedjuq-Zengid date for its initial appearance (Sauer 1976:94). In the absence of either coins or ceramics which are clearly Ayyubid or Mameluk from Araq el-Emir, it is probable that no. 96 belongs with the Ottoman assemblage.

Spout no.97 is from a jug similar to those from Hama (Riis and Poulsen 1957: fig. 1033, 1034). The fabric is a coarse pink ware and the exterior decoration consists of a finely executed close bichrome pattern which repeats the same basic design alternating in red and black paint. The motif appears, in part and incorporated with other designs, at: Tell Siran (Hadidi 1973: fig. 2:7), Tell Abu Gourdan (Franken and Kalsbeek 1975: fig. 52:D.1, 9 and fig. 65:27, 28), Heshbon (Sauer 1973: fig. 4:155) and Pella (Smith 1973: pl. 73:24). While it may be conjectured that the close bichrome designs are associated with the Ayyubid period rather than the later Mameluk period, this is pure

speculation and it is equally plausible that it dates to any of the other Late Islamic periods, including the Ottoman, a period which is represented at the site.

No. 98 features a cup and portion of a handle which had been affixed to the shoulder of a large bag-shaped storage jar. This appendage, resting between the neck and one of the shoulder loop handles of the jar, probably held a small rounded dipper juglet. Tell Abu Gourdan (Franken and Kalsbeek 1975: fig. 66:26) illustrates a similar cup device from a stratum which probably dates to the Early Mameluk period (Sauer 1976: 94). The coarse, undecorated ware of no. 98 does not aid in establishing a chronology for this piece.

Sounding I

Cooking pot rims nos. 99-100 represent one of three types of cooking pots present in the 1976 Soundings. They are thickened and rounded at the top, taper downward and are thinned at the base of the neck. At the juncture where the neck and shoulder meet the body of the vessel is ribbed on both the interior and the exterior. Both form and ware, the latter a dark reddish brown, are without parallel.

Another group of cooking pot rims is illustrated in nos. 101-114. These simple rims vary individually but most are rounded and thickened at the top while a few are flattened and hooked. They tend to be concave on the interior wall and faintly ridged on the exterior. Common to each of these examples is a light orange ware and darker burnt orange slip. Among the parallels to this group are: Dibon (Tushingham 1972: fig. 9:1-6), Bethlehem (Tzaferis 1975: fig. 19:1), Meiron (Meyers, Meyers, and Strange 1974: fig. 10:12-21 and Ritterspcah 1974: pl. 1:1-15), Beth She'arim (Avigad 1955: fig. 3:12), Samaria (Crowfoot, Crowfoot and Kenyon 1957: fig. 72:5), Khirbet Shema (Meyers *et al* 1976: fig. 7.13:19-26, fig. 7.14:1-21, fig. 7.15:7, and fig. 7.16:24), Magdala (Loffreda 1976: fig. 2:1, 4, fig. 6:15-21, 24, fig. 8:29 and fig. 19:2) and Abu Gosh (deVaux and Steve 1950: fig. 4:20). Despite the frequent examples of this type of cooking pot, adequate stratification with which to determine a date for this form is limited. Some chronological implications, however, are supplied by a survey of cooking pot vessels from various periods. The grooved rim cooking pot at Heshbon (Sauer 1973: fig. 2:45-50), which is a component of Late Roman

Fig. 56.   AE 76.1

Sherd No.	Reg. No.	Ware	Surface	Inclusions	Core	Diameter	Locus
99	66	2.5YR 5/2 Weak Red	2.5YR 5/2 Weak Red	medium	thick	10	4
100	65	2.5YR 5/2 Weak Red	2.5YR 5/2 Weak Red	medium	thick	14	4
101	64	5YR 8/4 Pink	5YR 7/6 Reddish Yellow	fine	none	13	4
102	59	5YR 7/3 Pink	5YR 7/6 Reddish Yellow	fine	none	12	4
103	62	5YR 8/4 Pink	5YR 7/6 Reddish Yellow	fine	none	13	4
104	48	5YR 8/4 Pink	5YR 7/6 Reddish Yellow	fine	none	14	4
105	44	5YR 8/4 Pink	5YR 6/2 Pinkish Gray	fine	none	16	4
106	18	5YR 7/3 Pink	5YR 7/6 Reddish Yellow	fine	none	15	3
107	60	5YR 8/4 Pink	5YR 7/6 Reddish Yellow	fine	none	22	4
108	49	5YR 8/4 Pink	5YR 7/6 Reddish Yellow	fine	none	14	4
109	25	5YR 7/6 Reddish Yellow	5YR 6/2 Pinkish Gray	fine	none	8	3
110	47	5YR 7/6 Reddish Yellow	2.5YR 6/2 Pale Red	fine	none	17	4
111	46	5YR 7/4 Pink	2.5YR 6/2 Pale Red	medium	slight	12	4
112	41	5YR 7/6 Reddish Yellow	5YR 6/2 Pinkish Gray	fine	none	16	3A
113	24	5YR 7/6 Reddish Yellow	5YR 6/2 Pinkish Gray	fine	none	10	3
114	19	5YR 7/6 Reddish Yellow	2.5YR 6/2 Pale Red	fine	none		4
115	72	10YR 8/1 White	10YR 8/1 White	fine	none	10	6
116	71	5YR 7/4 Pink	2.5YR 6/4 Light Reddish Brown	fine	none	26	6
117	53	7.5YR 7/4 Pink	7.5YR 7/4 Pink	medium	slight	11	9
118	30	5YR 8/4 Pink	2.5YR 6/2 Pale Red	medium	none	4	5
119	28	5YR 7/4 Pink	5YR 5/2 Reddish Gray	medium	none	4	5
120	29	5YR 8/4 Pink	5YR 5/2 Reddish Gray	medium	none	3	5
121	34	5YR 8/4 Pink	5YR 7/6 Reddish Yellow	fine	none	6	3A
122	70	5YR 7/3 Pink	2.5YR 6/2 Pale Red	medium	none	16	6
123	61	5YR 7/4 Pink	2.5YR 5/2 Weak Red	medium	medium	26	4
124	50	2.5YR 6/8 Light Red	5YR 6/2 Pinkish Gray	fine	none		4
125	11	5YR 7/4 Pink	5YR 5/2 Reddish Gray	fine	none		4
126	15	5YR 7/4 Pink	10YR 8/2 White	fine	slight		4
127	42	5YR 7/6 Reddish Yellow	2.5YR 6/4 Light Reddish Brown	fine	none		3A
128	39	5YR 7/4 Pink	2.5YR 6/4 Light Reddish Brown	fine	none		3A
129	43	5YR 7/6 Reddish Yellow	2.5YR 6/8 Light Red	fine	none		4
130	63	5YR 7/6 Reddish Yellow	5YR 7/6 Reddish Yellow	medium	none		4
131	52	5YR 7/6 Reddish Yellow	5YR 5/2 Reddish Gray	medium	none		4
132	51	2.5YR 6/8 Light Red	2.5YR 5/2 Weak Red	fine	none		4
133	56	5YR 7/6 Reddish Yellow	2.5YR 6/4 Light Reddish Brown	medium	none		4
134	7	5YR 7/6 Reddish Yellow	7.5YR 8/4 Pink	medium	thick		4
135	20	2.5YR 6/4 Light Reddish Brown	10YR 8/2 White	medium	medium		3
136	36	5YR 7/6 Reddish Yellow	5YR 7/6 Reddish Yellow	medium	medium		3A
137	35	5YR 7/4 Pink	5YR 7/2 Pinkish Gray	medium	slight		3A
138	16	5YR 7/6 Reddish Yellow	7.5YR 8/2 Pinkish White	medium	slight		4
139	57	5YR 7/6 Reddish Yellow	5YR 8/4 Pink	medium	medium		4
140	69	5YR 7/6 Reddish Yellow	5YR 7/6 Reddish Yellow	medium	none		8B
141	58	5YR 7/4 Pink	5YR 7/4 Pink	fine	none		4
142	74	5YR 6/2 Pinkish Gray	5YR 6/2 Pinkish Gray	fine	none		6
143	40	10R 6/4 Pale Red	5YR 5/2 Reddish Gray	fine	none		3A
144	14	2.5YR 6/4 Light Reddish Brown	5YR 5/1 Gray	medium	none		4
145	22	2.5YR 6/8 Light Red	2.5YR 6/8 Light Red	fine	none		3
146	17	5YR 7/4 Pink	5YR 7/4 Pink	large	thick		3
147	10	2.5YR 6/6 Light Red	5YR 6/1 Gray	medium	slight		4
148	27	5YR 7/3 Pink	10 YR 8/3 Very Pale Brown	fine	none		5
149	26	5YR 7/6 Reddish Yellow	5YR 7/1 Light Gray	medium	medium		3
150	38	5YR 7/4 Pink	5YR 7/4 Pink	fine	none		3A
151	12	5YR 7/4 Pink	5YR 7/4 Pink	medium	medium	5	4
152	13	5YR 4/1 Dark Gray	5YR 7/4 Pink	large	none		3A

AE 76.2

153	5	5YR 7/2 Pinkish Gray	5YR 7/2 Pinkish Gray	fine	none	19	2
154	3	5YR 7/4 Pink	5YR 7/4 Pink	fine	none	8	2
155	67	7.5YR 7/2 Pinkish Gray	7.5YR 7/2 Pinkish Gray	medium	slight	19	6
156	4	5YR 7/4 Pink	5YR 5/2 Reddish Gray	fine	slight		2
157	2	5YR 7/4 Pink	5YR 7/4 Pink	fine	none		4
158	1	5YR 7/4 Pink	5YR 7/4 Pink	medium	none		4

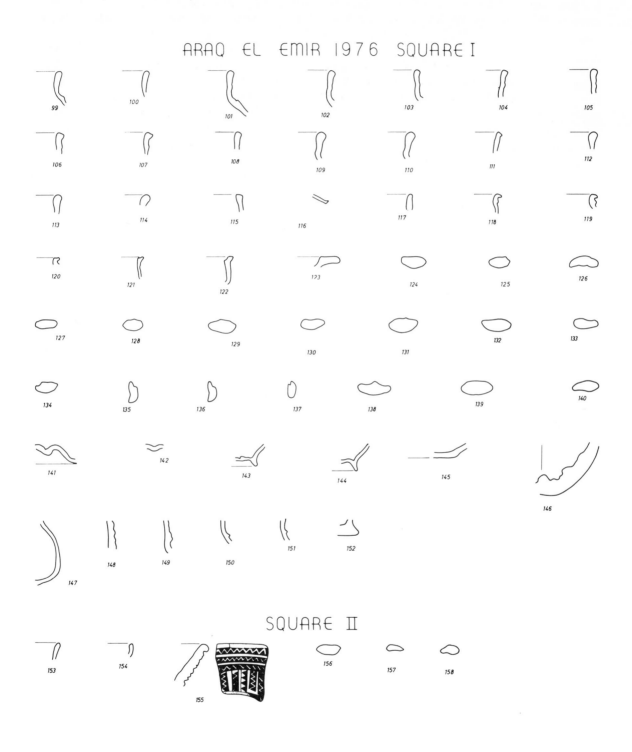

56. Sherds from the soundings in AE.76.1 and AE.76.2.

III-IV assemblages, bears no similarity with the Araq el-Emir group and sixth century A.D. forms; Cafarnao figs. 10:5-6 (Loffreda 1974) also show no resemblance. This typology and the orange ware suggest a possible 4th-5th century date for the group.

No. 115 is a solitary specimen from the third category of cooking pots. It is differentiated from the other examples by both its squared rim and white slipped white ware, a color which is not a feature of any other sherd from the site.

Lid no. 116 is from an open casserole form of cooking pot. The handles which accompany this form of cooking vessel have been discussed above under nos. 77-79. This may be compared with Dibon (Tushingham 1972: fig. 9:46). As a form the open casserole is first introduced in the Late Roman period and the lids associated with the vessels at that time; Heshbon fig. 2:51-53 (Sauer 1973) and Cafarnao fig. 11:13 (Loffreda 1974) were thick and not up-turned at the edges. Some Byzantine examples, possibly from the Late Byzantine period, have a steep curving approach to the lip's edge, as shown by Mt. Nebo (Schneider 1950: fig. 14:2). It is possible that no. 116 with its deep orange colored ware and thin straight form dates to the Early Byzantine period. For further chronological discussion, see above nos. 77-79.

Jar rim no. 117 is of the same form and ware type discussed above under nos. 22-23.

Juglet rims nos. 118-120 are bulbous with hooked rims and share the common orange ware and dark grey brown slip. The closest comparisons are from Dibon (Tushingham 1972: fig. 11:54-57).

Jug rim no. 121 features a widely grooved rim, ribbed neck and light orange ware covered with a exterior darker burnt orange slip.

The rim from a small bowl, no. 122, reflects heavy notching on the interior and a flaring exterior rim profile. Although as a form it is without precedence, the light orange ware and exterior brown slip are typical of Araq el-Emir. It is noteworthy that in comparison to other bowl forms this notched rim is the exact opposite of the exterior notched bowl rims from the Late Roman period as illustrated by Heshbon (Sauer 1973: fig. 2:63).

Plate rim no. 123 preserves a flatly horizontal lip which is slightly ridged along the edge which faces the interior of the vessel. The orange ware has a dark exterior slip. Dibon (Tushingham 1972: fig. 10:35-40) presents a group which is analogous in form.

Two classes of cooking pot handles are represented within the corpus. The first of these includes nos. 124-128 which are similar to nos. 63-65 above, in their relative smallness in aspects of length, breadth, and width. The orange ware is slipped in a variety of colors ranging from dark red brown to black. These compare with Tell er-Ras (Bull and Campbell 1968: fig. 11:2, 3, 5) which date to between the mid-3rd and mid-4th centuries A.D. The second group of handles is pictured in nos. 129-133. The most significant attribute of this category is the larger size which exceeds the first group in all dimensions. The upper surfaces have three flattened faces as is most clearly represented in no. 129. The ware is consistently light orange and covered with a burnt orange slip identical to that of the second group of cooking pots presented above in nos. 101-114. This group compares with examples from Dibon (Tushingham 1972: fig. 9:6-11, 15) and Khirbet Shema (Meyers et al 1976: fig. 7.16:20, 22).

Jug handle no. 134 consists of a poorly fired orange fabric and is marked by three flattened faces on its upper surface.

The horizontal handle profiles presented in nos. 135-137 belong to the cooking casserole form and were made from a single strand of clay turned over upon itself giving the appearance of two strands of clay. For more detailed discussion and comparisons refer to nos. 77-79 above.

Omphalos jar bases are shown in nos. 141-142. The former is pink in both ware and slip and the latter is orange with a brown exterior slip. Close parallel forms include Pella (Smith 1973: pl. 43:1290), Khirbet Shema (Meyers et al 1976: fig. 7.22:30, 39) and Mt. Nebo (Schneider 1950: fig. 11:2). Other similar forms include Magdala (Loffreda 1976: fig. 5:4 and fig. 7:38), Ramat Rahel (Aharoni et al 1964: fig. 27:6), Jerusalem, Tyropoeon Valley (Crowfoot and Fitzgerald 1929: pl. XIII:9), Dibon (Tushingham 1972: fig. 5:59), Balatah (Kerkhof 1969: fig. 18:10) and Heshbon (Sauer 1973: fig. 3:100). Other varient forms which appear in a number of periods attest to the frequency and development of this form. The earliest documented predecessor is from a Hellenistic stratum at Beth-Zur dated 140-100 B.C. (Sellers et al 1968: fig. 25:2-6). From the Early Roman IV period is another prototype: Judean Desert fig. 7:26 (Aharoni 1961). Of the sherds cited above, the Heshbon example is from a 5th century A.D. provenience and the Mt. Nebo jar is from the Byzantine stratum.

Sherd nos. 143-144 are ring bases with a center omphalos and have been discussed above under nos. 83-85.

The flat base no. 145 appears to have been part of a bowl or large platter of orange ware.

The thick rounded base shown in no. 146 is associated with the large zir rims of sherds nos. 1-2. The poorly fired orange ware exhibits a thick core speckled with large bluish and white inclusions. The exterior had been white slipped and the interior left unfinished. For chronological discussion of this as a Hellenistic form see rim nos. 1-2 above.

Illustrated in no. 147 is a portion of a juglet, possibly related to rim nos. 118-120. The ware is a deep red-orange with an exterior black slip.

Sherd no. 148 shows the ribbed neck of a jug. Applied to the exterior over the orange ware was a buff slip identical to that upon handle no. 138. Parallels which demonstrate the complete form are Mt. Nebo fig. 11:2 (Schneider 1950) from the Byzantine stratum and Dibon fig. 5:34 (Tushingham 1972).

No. 149 is a body sherd encompassing the neck and shoulder junction of a cooking pot whose form, deep orange ware and darker exterior slip, define it as among the cooking pots whose rims are represented by nos. 101-114.

Neck fragments, from those jars whose rims are pictured in nos. 22-24, are shown in nos. 150-151. These consist of a buff slipped orange ware. For discussion of chronology see nos. 21-23 above.

The molded base of a pipe bowl, no. 152 is characterized by a dark reddish fabric and shiny black slip. Across the bottom of the bowl are two lines of tiny hatch marks and incised triangles (not illustrated). A grooved mark decorates the side of the pipe bowl. Parallel pipes include Hama figs. 1074 and 1077 (Riis and Poulsen 1957) and a decorative example illustrates mold impressed triangles (fig. 1080). Subsequent to the European discovery of the New World came the introduction of tobacco throughout the Mediterranean and South West Asia. In Jordan the advent of tobacco correlates with the Early Ottoman period and from that time pipes became a constant to all Ottoman assemblages both Early and Late.

Sounding II

Pictured in nos. 153-154 are two bowl rims, the former of gray ware and the latter of orange ware.

The wheel turned bowl which appears in no. 155 is distinctive for its cut out decoration which completely covers the exterior surface of the sherd with triangular incisions. A possible parallel to this decorative style is Mt. Nebo (Saller 1941b: pl. 158:23 B). The analogy here however is limited by the differences in ware and the hand-made technique employed in making the latter. Both the gray ware and the closeness of the design contrast with the Umayyad and other Early Islamic cut ware bowls (Amman Citadel, unpublished), although like these later bowls, no. 155 is probably an imitation of stone bowl carving.

Handles nos. 156-158 are from cooking pots and are all of an orange ware.

Summary

The presence of sherds from the Iron Age and the Roman period in Sounding II, an area removed from the site of village occupation where these periods were represented by strata, indicates that this area was trafficed by the inhabitants during those periods and it is probable that they took advantage of the rich agricultural potential of the basin land there.

While important for their contribution to the small corpus of material culture items which may be ascribed to the initial stratum of the Qasr el-Abd, the few Hellenistic sherds from the 1976 Soundings do not contribute significantly to a perception of Hellenistic culture at Araq el-Emir.

The more representative Byzantine group allows some measure of interpretation. From the consistent ware types and surface treatments there emerges a pattern of homogeneity, apparently reflecting a regional style which represents a local workshop. While similar wares and treatments are frequent at nearby Heshbon (Sauer 1973: 31, fig. 2:87 and unpublished), the Araq el-Emir assemblage retains a distinctive identity. Two other important facts to be considered in the evaluation of the typology of the Byzantine ceramics are that although few, the parallel examples cited in the text above which are associated with specific dates consistently point to 4th-5th century A.D. dates, and features which are frequently characteristic of Late Byzantine pottery (Sauer 1973: 37-39) are not present in the corpus from Araq el-Emir. While a few possible Late Byzantine sherds are included (see above nos. 93, 95), the group as a whole may be assigned to the Early Byzantine period, a conclusion which also correlates with the stratification of the Qasr el-Abd.

Excavations past and recent have demonstrated that the remains from the Late Islamic occupation are limited to a few sherds and artifacts which justify the assertion that there was no significant community in this portion of the Wadi Sir from

the end of the Early Byzantine period until the Modern period.

BIBLIOGRAPHY

Aharoni, Y.
1956   Excavations at Ramath Rahel, 1954 Preliminary Report. *Israel Exploration Journal* 6:137-157.
1961   The Caves of Nahal Hever. *Atiqot (English Series)* 3:148-162.
1962   Expedition B. *Israel Exploration Journal* 12:186-199.

Aharoni, Y. *et al*
1962   *Excavations at Ramat Rahel; Seasons 1959 and 1960.* Rome: Centro di Studi Semitici.
1964   *Excavations at Ramat Rahel; Seasons 1961 and 1962.* Rome: Centro di Studi Semitici.

Albright, W. F., and Kelso, J. L.
1968   *The Excavation of Bethel (1934-1960).* Annual of the American Schools of Oriental Research 39. Cambridge, MA.: American Schools of Oriental Research.

Ant.
Josephus. *Jewish Antiquities.* Trans. Ralph Marcus from Greek, Loeb Classical Library. London: Heinemann and Cambridge, MA: Harvard University, 1943.

Avigad, N.
1955   Excavations at Beth She'arim, 1954 Preliminary Report. *Israel Exploration Journal* 5:205-239.
1970   Excavations in the Jewish Quarter of the Old City of Jerusalem, 1970 (Second Preliminary Report). *Israel Exploration Journal* 20:129-140.

Bagatti, B.
1968   Un'inedita chiesa al Qasr el'-Abd. *Liber Annuus* 18:288-300.
1969   *Excavations in Nazareth.* Studium Biblicum Franciscanum 12. Jerusalem: Franciscan.

Bagatti, B., and Milik, J. T.
1958   *La Necropoli del periodo romano.* Part I: *Gli scavi del "Dominus Flevit".* Studium Biblicum Franciscanum 13. Jerusalem: Franciscan.

Bar Adon, P.
1961   Expedition C. *Israel Exploration Journal* 11:25-35.
1977   Another Settlement of the Judean Desert Sect at 'En el-Ghuweir on the Shores of the Dead Sea. *Bulletin of the American Schools of Oriental Research* 227:1-25.

Bisheh, G.
1972   A Cave Burial Tomb from Jabal Jofeh El-Sharqi in Amman. *Annual of the Department of Antiquities of Jordan* 17:81-83.

Bull, R. J., and Campbell, E. F. Jr.
1968   The Sixth Campaign at Balatah (Shechem). *Bulletin of the American Schools of Oriental Research* 190:2-41.

Corbo, V.; Loffreda, S., and Spijkerman, A.
1970   *La Sinagoga di Cafarnao.* Studium Biblicum Franciscanum, Collectio Minor 9. Jerusalem: Franciscan.

Crowfoot, J. W.; Crowfoot, G. M.; and Kenyon, K. M.
1957   *The Objects from Samaria,* Vol. III: *Samaria-Sebaste.* London: Palestine Exploration Fund.

Crowfoot, J. W., and Fitgerald, G. M.
1929   *Excavations in the Tyropoeon Valley, Jerusalem.* Palestine Exploration Fund Annual 5. London: Palestine Exploration Fund.

Dana
1970   Luweibdeh Roman Tomb. *Annual of the Department of Antiquities of Jordan* 15:37-38.

Delougaz, P. and Haines, R.
1960   *A Byzantine Church at Khirbet al-Kerak.* Oriental Institute Publications 85. Chicago: University of Chicago.

Egloff, M.
1977   *La Poterie Copte.* Tome 2 *Recherches Suisses D'Arc Copte* Vol. III. Geneve: Libraire de L'Universite.

Fisher, S., and McCown, C.
1931   *Jerash-Gerasa 1930.* Annual of the American Schools of Oriental Research, 11. New Haven, Conn.: American Schools of Oriental Research.

Franken, H. J., and Kalsbeek, J.
1975   *Potters of a Medieval Village in the Jordan Valley.* North-Holland Ceramic Studies in Archaeology 3. Amsterdam: North-Holland/New York: American Elsvier.

Grant, E.
1932   *Ain Shems Excavations (Palestine) 1928-1929-1930-1931.* Part II. Biblical and Kindred Studies No. 4. Haverford, PA.: Haverford College.

Hadidi, A.
1973   The Pottery from Tell Siran. *Faculty of Arts Journal* 4. Amman: University of Jordan.

Hamilton, R. W.
1944   Excavations Against the North Wall of Jerusalem, 1937-38. *Quarterly of the Department of Antiquities in Palestine* 10:1-54.

Hammond, P. C.
1965   *The Excavation of the Main Theater at Petra, 1961-1962: Final Report.* London: Colt Archaeological Institute.

Harding, G. L.
1950   A Roman Family Vault on Jebel Jofeh, Amman. *Quarterly of the Department of Antiquities in Palestine* 14:81-94.
1951   Excavations on the Citadel, Amman. *Annual of the Department of Antiquities of Jordan* 1:7-16.

Hayes, J.
1972   *Late Roman Pottery.* London: The British School at Rome.

Hennessy, J. B.
1970 Excavations at Samaria-Sebaste, 1968. *Levant* 2:1-21.

Johns, C. N.
1950 The Citadel, Jerusalem. *Quarterly of the Department of Antiquities in Palestine* 14:121-190.

Kallner-Amiran, D. H.
1950- A Revised Earthquake Catalogue of Palestine.
51   *Israel Exploration Journal* 1:223-246.

Kennedy, C. A.
1063 The Development of the Lamp in Palestine. *Berytus* 14:67-115.

Kerkhof, V.
1969 Catalogue of the Shechem Collection in the Rijksmuseum van Oudheden te Leiden. *Oudheidkundige Mededelingen uit het Rijksmuseum van Oudheden te Leiden* 50:28-109.

Kraeling, C., ed.
1938 *Gerasa: City of the Decapolis*. New Haven, Conn: American Schools of Oriental Research.

Lahee, F. H.
1961 *Field Geology*. New York: McGraw-Hill.

Lapp, N.
1964 Pottery from Some Hellenistic Loci at Balatah (Shechem). *Bulletin of the American Schools of Oriental Research*. 175: 14-26.

1981 *The Third Campaign at Tell el-Fûl*. Annual of the American Schools of Oriental Research 46. Cambridge, MA.: American Schools of Oriental Research.

Lapp, P. W.
1961 *Palestinian Ceramic Chronology 200 B.C.-A.D. 70*. New Haven, Conn.: American Schools of Oriental Research.

1962 Soundings at ʿArâq el-Emîr (Jordan). *Bulletin of the American Schools of Oriental Research* 165:16-34.

1963 The Second and Third Campaigns at ʿArâq el-Emîr. *Bulletin of the American Schools of Oriental Research* 171:8-39.

1970 The Pottery of Palestine in the Persian Period Pp. 179-197 in *Archaologie und Altes Testament: Festschrift fur Kurt Galling*, ed. Kuschke, A., and Kutsch, E. Tubingen: Mohr.

Lapp, P. W. and Lapp, N. L. eds.
1974 *Discoveries in the Wâdī ed-Dâliyeh*. Annual of the American Schools of Oriental Research 41. Cambridge, MA.: American Schools of Oriental Research.

Loffreda, S.
1969 Due Tombe a Betania. *Liber Annuus* 19:349-366.
1974 *La Ceramica. Cafarnao* II. Studium Biblicum Franciscanum 19. Jerusalem: Franciscan.
1976 Alcune Osservazioni sulla Ceramica di Magdala. In *Studia Hierosolymitana, in onore del P. Bellarmino Bagatti*. I. *Studi Archeologici*. Studium Biblicum Franciscanum. Collectio Maior 22. Jerusalem: Franciscan.

Mazar, B.
1971 *The Excavations in the Old City of Jerusalem*. Jerusalem: Israel Exploration Society.

Mazar, B.; Dothan, T.; and Dunayevsky, I.
1966 En-gedi: The First and Second Seasons of Excavation 1961-1962. *Atiqot (English Series)* 5.

Meyers, C. E.; Meyers, E. M.; and Strange, J. F.
1974 Excavations at Meiron in Upper Galilee, 1971-1972: A Preliminary Report. *Bulletin of the American Schools of Oriental Research* 214:2-25.

Meyers, E. M. et al
1976 *Ancient Synagogue Excavations at Khirbet Shema, Upper Galilee, Israel 1970-1972*. Annual of the American Schools of Oriental Research 42. Durham, N.C.: Duke University.

Munsell
1971 Munsell Soil Color Charts. Baltimore: Munsell Color Company.

Olavarri, E.
1965 Sondages a Aro'er sur L'Arnon. *Revue Biblique* 72:77-94.

Pritchard, J.
1958 *The Excavation at Herodian Jeicho, 1951*. Annual of the American Schools of Oriental Research 32-33. New Haven, CT.: American Schools of Oriental Research.

Rahmani, L. Y.
1958 A Jewish Tomb on Shahin Hill, Jerusalem. *Israel Exploration Journal* 8:101-105.
1961 Jewish Rock-Cut Tombs in Jerusalem. *Atiqot (English Series)* 3:93-120.
1976 Jason's Tomb. *Israel Exploration Journal* 17:61-100.

Riis, P. J., and Poulsen, V.
1957 *Les Verreries et Poteries Medievales*. Vol. IV:2 *Hama*. Copenhagen: Nationalmuseet.

Riley, J. A.
1975 The Pottery from the First Session of Excavation in the Caesarea Hippodrome. *Bulletin of the American Schools of Oriental Research* 218:25-63.

Ritterspcah, A. D.
1974 The Meiron Cistern Pottery. *Bulletin of the American Schools of Oriental Research* 215:19-29.

Saller, S.
1941a *The Memorial to Moses on Mt. Nebo*. Part I. Studium Biblicum Franciscanum 1. Jerusalem: Franciscan.
1941b *The Memorial to Moses on Mt. Nebo*. Part II. Studium Biblicum Franciscanum 1. Jerusalem: Franciscan.
1957 *Excavations at Bethany*. Studium Biblicum Franciscanum 12. Jerusalem: Franciscan.

Sauer, J. A.
1973 *Heshbon Pottery 1971*. Andrews University Monographs 7.
1976 Pottery Techniques at Tell Deir Alla. *Bulletin of the American Schools of Oriental Research* 224:91-94.

Schneider, H.
1950 *The Memorial of Moses on Mt. Nebo*. Part III. Studium Biblicum Franciscanum 1. Jerusalem: Franciscan.

Seger, J. D.
1976 The Search for Maccabean Gezer. *Biblical Archaeologist* 39:142-144.

Sellers, O. R.
1933 *The Citadel of Beth-Zur*. Philadelphia: Westminster.

Sellers, O. R., and Baramki, D. C.
    1953   A Roman-Byzantine Burial Cave in Northern Pal-
            estine. *Bulletin of the American Schools of Oriental
            Research, Supplementary Series* 15-16.
Sellers, O. R. *et al*
    1968   *The 1957 Excavation at Beth-Zur.* Annual of the
            American Schools of Oriental Research 38. Cam-
            bridge, MA.: American Schools of Oriental Re-
            search.
Sellin, E., and Watzinger, C.
    1913   *Jericho.* Leipzig: Heinrichs.
Smith, R. H. *et al*
    1973   *Pella of the Decapolis* I. London: Clowes.
Strange, J. F.
    1975   Late Hellenistic and Herodian Ossuary Tombs at
            French Hill, Jerusalem. *Bulletin of the American
            Schools of Oriental Research* 219:39-67.
Tushingham, A. D.
    1972   *The Excavations at Dibon (Dhiban) in Moab, The
            Third Campaign 1952-53.* Annual of the American
            Schools of Oriental Research 40. Cambridge, MA.:
            American Schools of Oriental Research.

Tzaferis, V.
    1975   The Archaeological Excavation at Shepherds's
            Field. *Liber Annuus* 25:5-52.
Vaux, R. de
    1953   Fouille au Khirbet Qumran. *Revue Biblique* 60:83-
            106.
Vaux, R. de, and Steve, A. M.
    1950   *Fouilles a Qaryet el'Enab Abu Gosh.* Paris:
            Gabalda.
Waage, F. O., ed.
    1948   *Ceramics and Islamic Coins.* Vol. IV, Part 1:
            Antioch on-the-Orontes. Princeton, N.J.: Prince-
            ton University.
Winnett, F. W., and Reed, W. L.
    1964   *The Excavations at Dibon (Dhiban) in Moab.*
            Parts I and II. Annual of the American Schools of
            Oriental Research 36-37. New Haven, CT. Amer-
            ican Schools of Oriental Research.
Yadin, Y.
    1963   *The Finds from the Bar Kochba Period in the Cave
            of Letters.* Jerusalem: Israel Exploration Society.
    1966   *Masada*: London: Weidenfeld and Nicolson.

Chapter 12

The Monumental Gateway and the Princely Estate of Araq el-Emir

J.-M. Dentzer, F. Villeneuve and F. Larché

The most complete and spectacular building at the site of Araq el-Emir is the Qasr el-Abd which has been the subject of an extensive study by Prof. E. Will since 1976 in preparation for final publication. The whole site, with the installations in the original caves, the construction of a dam and an irrigation system, the agricultural terraces, as well as the vestiges of several monumental buildings has caught the interest of travelers and explorers since the nineteenth century. This assemblage, which appears to be a coherent arrangement of a large palatial estate, was described by Flavius Josephus (*Ant.* 12.4.11, § 229-236), and his description collaborates remarkably with the present understanding of the landscape (fig. 57).

A general study of the site cannot be undertaken without a certain number of soundings and limited excavations, for, contrary to the Qasr, the other vestiges lay in ruins and are for the most part buried. This enterprise was begun with the excavations conducted by P. W. Lapp in 1961-62 in the village and the "Square Building." In 1976 the monumental gateway (fig. 58), situated about 150 m. to the east-northeast of the Qasr el-Abd, appeared as a first objective because of its rather small dimensions, its state of preservation (four courses remained visible) which permitted significant comparisons with the building techniques of the Qasr, and a hope that this area would help make precise from a statigraphical basis the chronology and the circumstances for which a building clearly related to the Qasr had been erected. In addition, because of its location and function, this gateway could give a clue to the relationship between the area of the Qasr and the rest of the site.

In two campaigns, in 1977 and 1978, enough information was uncovered for publication of the structure due to the generous help and cooperation of the Department of Antiquities of Jordan particularly in providing the heavy machinery necessary to handle several of the large blocks.

This report will be limited to a few conclusions the excavations have determined in the areas of architecture, stratigraphy, artifacts, and chronology, and the relationship between the gateway and the whole estate.

1. Architecture

1.1 Plan

In the two campaigns all the elements have been discovered to restore the gateway to a height of more than 9 m. At ground level the monumental structure has two piles 3.26 m. × 3.35 m., flanking an opening 3.70 m. wide; their height can be restored to 6.35 m. (see figs. 58-61). The passage separating these piles measured 3.35 × 4.40 m., narrowed by the projection of four door-posts. The recess thus made was meant to receive the doors of the open gate. The piles were brought together by a unique facade at the level of the lintel and the courses above and by a series of flagstones covering the doorway, set longitudinally on the lintel, partly inserted in the posterior side of the blocks of the ionic cornice.

1.2 Techniques

In this building two noticeably different techniques are recognized. The most spectacular, the megalithic, is used for the facade. It is characterized not only by the dimensions of the blocks

57. Looking toward the Qasr with the Monumental Gateway to the right and the dam toward the front left.

58. Looking north toward the Monumental Gateway.

59. Looking southwest at the southwest pile and its recess.

(up to almost 3.20 m. long), but also by arranging them on edge. This gives the impression of strength, but it is eventually detrimental to the security of the building. The archaic way of bonding, with tenons and mortises carved in the blocks themselves, is only used in these blocks. The regular alternation of high courses (blocks set on edge) and of low courses (blocks set on their quarry bed) with their ends set to the opening of the gateway, is different from the arrangement in the Qasr. It corresponds to the alternate binder-stretcher edge known in Greek architecture, where its most characteristic forms seem to appear in places which are influenced by oriental building methods. In this

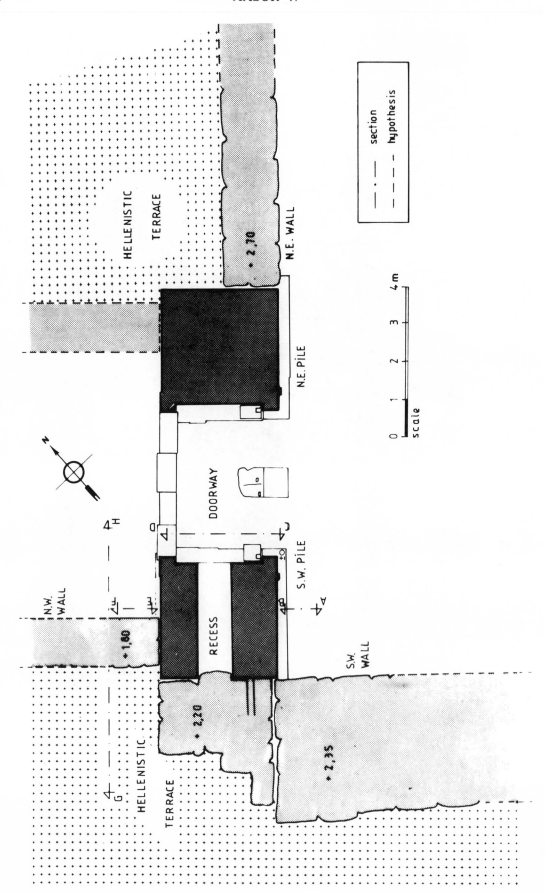

60. Plan of the Monumental Gateway.

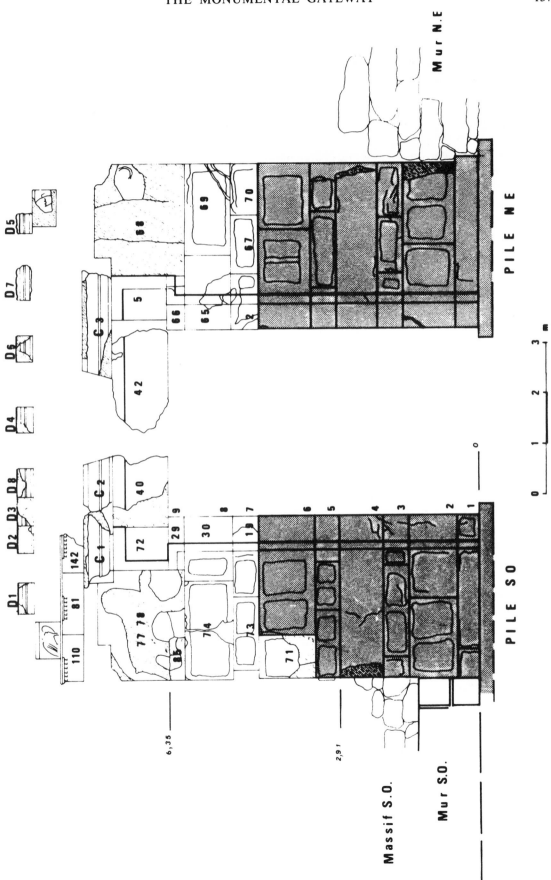

61. Provisional restoration of the Monumental Gateway.

gate the form must probably be interpreted as a sign of Phoenician influence.

The other technique used in the rest of the building consists of less high courses (no more than .58 m. high). If the blocks are laid flat, the limited height of the flagstones provides more stability. The blocks are always assembled with sharp joints and without metallic sealings.

For these two different techniques two different materials are used. Dolomite, hard and quite white, looking very much like marble (cf. *ek lithou leukou, Ant* 12.4.11 § 230), is used only for the facade. In the rest of the building it is used only for a few elements requiring special resistance, such as the lintel of the hallow space of the southwest pile. The other blocks are made of soft chalky and greyish limestone. The difference in materials leads to different techniques in carving. The dolomite blocks result from a very sharp pegging, while the blocks of soft limestone reveal curved oblique incisions which seem to indicate bush hammer cutting.

1.3 Elevation

The courses from 1 to 6 (see fig. 61) are *in situ* and were partly visible above the ground before excavation. The characteristics of the building—alternation of the courses, slight difference in size between the two door-posts, the presence of a fascia outlining the opening—make it possible to put back most of the blocks scattered near the walls and to restore the elevation up to the level of the ionic cornice surmounting the lintel. All blocks necessary for restoration of eight courses have been found, and since there were no additional similar blocks, the number of courses can be limited to this figure. On the top courses of the door-posts there were two smaller blocks (nos. 29 and 66) on which the fascia indicated the form of the gateway. The frame of a doric gate can thus be recognized outlining the lintel. Three elements of the lintel have been found in several pieces (nos. 72, 40, 42, 5). The course of the lintel is completed at each end by a block on which the form of a feline can be reconstructed. The notch at the upper right angle of block 77/78 was probably to receive the left end of the ionic cornice (C 1).

A series of smaller blocks have also been found belonging to a doric entablature—architrave blocks with regulae and guttae and cornice blocks with mutules. Two blocks decorated with an eagle could have been used as metopes. On the other hand, no

triglyph has been found. There is no doubt this aggregation set above the ionic cornice, but it is not known whether it lay directly on the cornice course or whether it was separated from it by one or more standard courses.

1.4 Decoration

The discovery of rich architectural decoration, comparable to that of the Qasr, was the unexpected event of the first campaign in 1977. In addition to the doric frame of the gateway crowned with an ionic cornice, a doric entablature was found. This combination, that was seen in the Qasr where on the staircase door a doric frame joined a cornice with palmettes carved on the same block, is well attested in the Hellenistic period. They are found on the facades of the rock cut tombs at Petra and Jerusalem. C. Watzinger, who would be tempted to see in this combination the influence of Alexandrian art, more precisely compares the style of the palmettes alternating with araceous stems on the ionic cornice with the style of a sima block in the Hieron of Samothrace (around the beginning of the 2nd century B.C.).

2. Stratigraphy and Chronology

2.1 Stratigraphy

(See figs. 62 and 63, section A-F, SE/NW oriented, and section G-H in the back of the gateway, SW/NE oriented; cf. fig. 60).

Six stratigraphic soundings, ultimately connected together, have revealed the stratigraphy and architectural plans. In the following account, the levels refer to a level O; this coincides with the base of the SW pile's SE face, which should be considered as the Hellenistic base level, where the threshhold of the gate would have been if there had been one.

As at the Qasr, the area around the gateway was buried before excavation began in a mass of architectural blocks, stones, and powdery earth which resulted from the seism that destroyed both monuments. The level before digging ranged from 1.50 to 2.70 m., depending on the place.

Behind the gateway, a stratum of humus (stratum 1) was particularly thick (40 cm.) because of lemon trees. It contained a few sherds from all periods represented in the other strata and two Islamic sherds. Stratum 2 resulted from falls and characteristically consisted of many blocks from

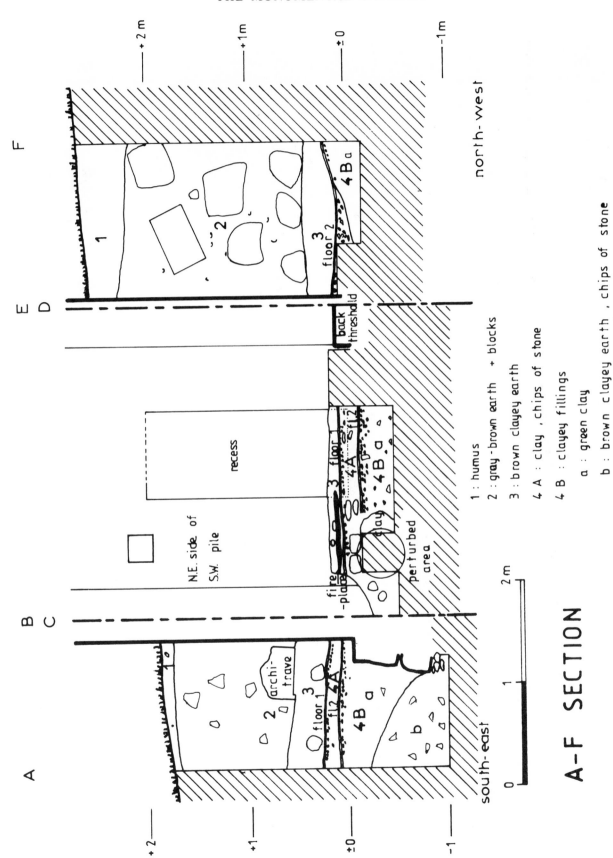

A-F SECTION

1 : humus
2 : gray-brown earth + blocks
3 : brown clayey earth
4 A : clay , chips of stone
4 B : clayey fillings
   a : green clay
   b : brown clayey earth , chips of stone

62. Section A-F, southeast to northwest through the Monumental Gateway.

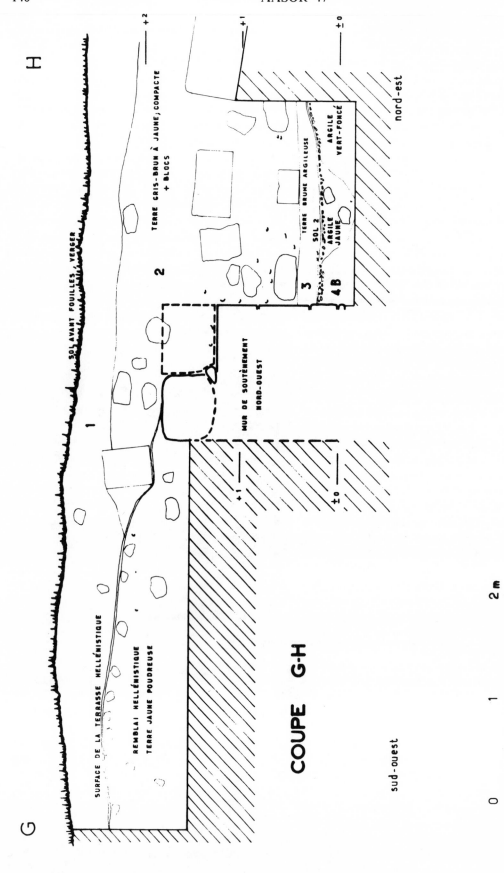

'IRAQ AL-AMIR PORTE

COUPE G-H

échelle

63. Section G-H, southwest to northeast in back of the gateway.

the gateway fallen from the earthquake and of mixed pottery (Hellenistic to Byzantine). Its thickness was uneven, more than 1.50 m. behind the gate and in the passage but only 1 m. in front of the piles. The room of the SW pile was nearly filled by this stratum, only lacking the large blocks.

The first blocks of the gateway that fell, that is the elements from the very top, fell down to a level of .30/.40 m. in most areas. This level was not a floor.

Below, stratum 3 appeared, generally less than .30 m. thick but varying according to place. It was always a brown compact clayey earth, but more or less stoney. This stratum essentially represents a period of abandonment before the earthquake. In the passage and in the small room the lower part of this stratum is characterized by clear traces of burning. The few sherds found in this area (see below, nos. 10, 11) suggest for the very short occupation corresponding to that burning a date about the middle of the 1st century A.D.

Consideration will now be given to the levels related to the gateway structure. There are two superinposed floors, both Hellenistic, but neither of them were the real floor the builders considered for the gateway. The construction was (suddenly?) stopped and neither the flagstones, meant to be related to the base of the pylons in the passage, nor the front threshhold which should be symmetrical to the back threshhold which was uncovered, have been found. What remains is only evidence of hasty work or utilization, nearly level, trodden, and characterized by quite fragmentary but well dated material and chips resulting from the stone cutting.

Seven coins (78/M 1-7) are related to the upper floor (Floor 1). The six identifiable are dated to the reign of Antiochus III (see 2.2); the last years of the third century B.C. are thus the *terminus post quem* for this floor. Since there is no later material on this floor and in the subsequent stratum it does not seem too presumptuous to adopt the chronology of Josephus (*Ant* 12.4.11 § 228-236) and to consider that the construction of the gateway, as well as the Qasr, took place at the end of the reign of Seleucus IV (187-175 B.C.) and was interrupted in 175 B.C.

This floor does not correspond to the architectural levels of the gateway; it is higher than the base underlying the foot of the SW pile. On the other hand, it is related to a hasty closing of the gateway in its unfinished state. Small slabs with metallic sockets against the groove of the gateway on the bases of the piles and a block with a rabbet

may have been horizontally used as an abutment to fix the scanty gateway doors. It is very likely this block that Butler (1919: 19) mistook for a threshhold. Its excavation has somewhat disturbed the stratigraphy of the passage entrance, and it is impossible to know if the hasty closure and Floor 1 correspond to the end of the construction or to reuse a little after 175 B.C.

Under Floor 1 are Hellenistic strata contemporary with the building of the gateway. This contemporaneity is established by the nature of these strata themselves, especially Stratum 4 A (chips of stone, green to brown clayey filling, and behind the back threshhold spoiled architectural block submerged in the clayey ground of Stratum 4 B), rather than the very fragmentary artifactual remains. Floor 2, which is unquestionably a work floor (whereas Floor 1 may be a very neglected utilization level), reveals certain Hellenistic material but only in tiny fragments. Only a very common cooking pot (see below, no. 1) could be restored.

Below, Stratum 4 B, the clayish filling of the foundation trenches, was nearly sterile. Note that in back of the gateway behind the SW pile, Floor 1 and Stratum 4 A are absent, which is evidence in favor of the interpretation of Floor 1 as a utilization level in front of and in the passage.

On the whole the stratigraphy shows that the gateway was only used for a short period of time after the interruption of its construction and was never reused later, except for the ashy layer of Stratum 3. There is no Byzantine reoccupation here as at the Qasr. The area may have been used at that time as an extensive dump, which would explain the presence of Byzantine pottery in Stratum 2 (see below nos. 21-24) along with the rockfall.

As to the date of the building itself, the lack of Byzantine disturbance and the fortunate discovery of Antiochus III coins, as well as the small number of Hellenitic sherds found in situ and at the level of the fall, confirm the witness of Josephus. There is also collaboration for the events happening in 175 B.C., events important enough to prevent the completion of the gateway, which lacks a threshhold and a paving and is simply provided with a derisively weak closing.

2.2 Coins.

Chr. Augé, who graciously agreed to examine the coins found in the excavation, has proposed the following conclusions.

Some evidence is presented by the thirteen coins
brought to light in the excavation of the gateway,
although three are illegible due to wear and corro-
sion: a coin and the fragment of one found under
the small slab with a socket (78/M 8 and 9, see
above 2.1, Floor 1) and one of seven small coins
found together (above 2.1). The other coins could
be identified. There was an unrelated Roman coin
of Constantine struck at Antioch (78/M 10). In the
passage, Stratum 1 yielded two very worn bronze
coins, one of Aprippa I (77/M 2), the other of the
Maccabean period (77/M 3), and also a corroded
second century Seleucid coin. Important are the
homogeneous series of six small bronze coins
(78/M 1-6). Comparatively, these *halves* are in fair
condition and rather neatly struck; they must be
attributed to the Antioch mint under the reign of
Antiochus III. One of them (78/M 2) has the
elephant on the reverse; the five others have Apollo
standing. They all belong to Series III of Newell,
dated a little before 200 B.C.

This representation confirms the observations,
suggested by other local discoveries either sporadi-
cally or from the excavations, concerning the
money circulating in the Araq el-Emir area during
the Hellenistic and Roman periods. Silver coins
are lacking, but some evidence is presented concerning the small bronze coins in use, which came,
depending on their dates, from Palestinian or
North Syrian mints. The lagide bronzes, sporadi-
cally attested until Ptolemy III, are replaced by
numerous Seleucid small bronzes (fourteen examples were examined), principally units or half
units of Antiochus III all produced at Antioch
around the year 200 B.C. (eleven examples), and
then a few small coins of the second century such
as one of Demetrius II. After that the Maccabean
coins appear (one example of Alexander Jannaeus).

After a long interruption during the Idumaean
dynasty, the use of Nabataean bronzes, which are
generally very common in the East, is attested in
the first century B.C. under Aretas IV. Then there
are some coins of the Jewish revolt (one example
of 67/68 A.D.). The later coins are only a few
Roman *folles* of the fourth century struck at
Antioch which are very common throughout the
Near East. Before this, from the end of the first
century until about the second half of the third, the
territories of Transjordania use the bronze coins of
several cities of the Decapolis or the Provincia
Arabia.

In contrast to the rarity and sporadic appearance of these various coins, to be emphasized

among the local discoveries is the number of small
Seleucid coins of Antiochus III, scarcely worn and
only about twenty years older than the constructions of Hyranus.

Pottery and Other Artifacts

3.1 General remarks (see fig. 64)

The study of the pottery of this excavation has
been greatly facilitated by help from several
scholars: Dr. Fawzi Zayadine, Dr. James Sauer,
Mrs. Nancy Lapp, M. Ernest Will, Mlle D.
Orssaud, and Mlle M.-J. Roche. We wish to
express our appreciation to them.

Not all the artifacts found during the excavation
of the gate are presented here but a selection of the
more complete forms. This explains the incomplete
character of the numeration in the text and fig. 64.
For an exhaustive presentation of the pottery one
will be able to refer to the definitive publication
which will appear in *Syria*.

The material is subdivided into five groups on
the basis of (1) the stratigraphy, and (2) material of
the same stratum, but chronologically distinguished on the basis of parallel material.

Group A. Pottery from Stratum 4 (Stratum 4 B,
Floor 2, Stratum 4 A, Floor 1), Hellenistic
(fig. 64:1).

The terminus post quem for the pottery from
this stratum and Floor 1, about 200 B.C., is furnished by coins 78/M 1-78/M 6 found on Floor 1.
This terminus is not necessary for the pottery; since
it is a matter of fills the pottery can theoretically be
more ancient, but nothing is out of place in the first
quarter of the second century B.C.

Group B. Pottery of Stratum 3, Hellenistic and
Early Roman (fig. 64: 4, 10, 11, 12).

With the exception of a small group of Hellenistic sherds from the first quarter of the second
century B.C. remaining in this stratum (see fig. 5:4),
a date for the pottery of this stratum to the middle
of the first century A.D. seems to be indicated. This
is essentially on the basis of known parallels to no.
10 and from Coin 77/M 2, dating to the reign of
Herod Agrippa I (A.D. 37, 40, 41-44), found on the
site but not stratified.

Group C. Hellenistic pottery from Stratum 2
rockfall (fig. 64: 13, 14, 15).

The parallels examined for this group of sherds
(which are a part of a later collection, see Group
D), do not contradict a date in the first quarter of
the second century B.C. Only no. 13 can be dated
legitimately older than this time. But does it wit-

ness to an occupation of the site in the third century B.C. or only to the persistence to the beginning of the second century of a type of jar well known at the end of the fourth century and in the third century B.C.?

Group D. Early Roman pottery and Byzantine of the Stratum 2 rockfall (fig. 64: 20-24).

Only for no. 20 are there helpful parallels. They date it to the first century A.D. so it therefore should be associated with the period of occupation represented by Group B (Stratum 3).

Of the remainder, there exists for no. 23 some late parallels (and also for no. 21, late parallels in northern Syria, according to Mlle D. Orssaud), placing the group before the end of the 5th century B.C. The Constantinian coin, 78/M 10, from an unstratified context, as well as several *folles* of the 4th century found elsewhere at Araq el-Emir (see 2.2 and the coins of the 4th and 5th centuries uncovered by P. W. Lapp (1962: 29; 1963: 32, 37) confirm this date.

Such non-specific evidence by no means determines a precise date for the earthquake which destroyed the gate (was the Byzantine pottery of Group D deposited in Stratum 2 by sliding between the blocks after the earthquake?) nor does it clarify the Byzantine occupation at Araq el-Emir.

Group E. Artifacts from the upper layer (Stratum 1) and unstratified (fig. 64:30, 32-37).

This includes objects related to the phases represented in Group B (no. 30, Early Roman) and Group D (nos. 32-34 and the basin in steatite, no. 36; Byzantine). In addition, nos. 35 and 36 date to the 12th-13th centuries A.D., precisely determining the Late Islamic occupation at the site, along with the evidence published by R. Brown from her work at Araq el-Emir in 1976 (1979: nos. 96-98, and ch. 11 above).

The quantity of pottery found in the course of this excavation is neither exceptionally small nor exceptionally large when considering the function of the building—neither habitation nor tomb. In the layers of fill and on the floors the pottery is extremely fragmentary. It is only in Stratum 2 (the rockfall) that fragments are greater, corresponding to the utilization of the area as a dump and yielding some forms almost completely restorable.

For all the periods represented—Hellenistic construction, short Roman utilization, Byzantine debris—the notable fact is the absence of fine vases (Hellenistic black glazed, Late Hellenistic and Early Roman sigillata, late sigallata, etc.). Again, this fact, considering the nature of the monument,

is not surprising.

The forms found are among the assemblage present in the region. Exceptions, because of the rarity of parallels, are nos. 4 (Hellenistic), 30 (Early Roman), 21, 22, 34 (Byzantine), and especially no. 35 (Islamic). The decoration of no. 36 (Islamic) is well known but it is mainly associated with an Ayyoubid form of mediocre quality and not wheelmade; the Araq el-Emir example is wheel-made, hard, and well baked.

For the Hellenistic phase, the pottery from Araq el-Emir is particularly coarse (nos. 1, 13, 14 especially). Most of the forms are related to a very slow evolutionary tradition which takes root in the Persian period and goes out of use in the second century. Especially abundant were the fragments of crude red orange ware with a rough surface and abundant inclusions (see no. 14). This technology seems to find its origin in the Iron age, and this type of ceramic material still appeared at Araq el-Emir during the Byzantine period (see no. 32); it ought to be a matter of local or regional production. A petrographic study of some thin sections would give some precision in this matter. The plate, no. 14, is an imitation in this manner of a well known form of fine ceramic called a fish plate. The Hellenistic pottery from this excavation is quite comparable to the common pottery of neighboring sites with Hellenistic levels in Transjordan and Cisjordan (earlier excavations at Araq el-Emir, Amman, Balatah, Samaria).

One finds the same characteristics in the pottery of the Early Roman period: everyday pottery exclusively, with the exception of no. 20 of finer ware and with a red slip, now very worn. The geographical context of pertinent comparisons remain the same: local ceramics on both sides of the Jordan and around the Dead Sea.

From the Byzantine era diverse types of pottery are represented: red walled (no. 21), fine gray ware baked to metalic consistency (nos. 22, 34), thick pale yellow (nos. 23, 23a, 33), and red orange already mentioned above (no. 32). For this period comparisons are particularly numerous with sites on the slopes of the Ghor (Mount Nebo), Galilee (Nazareth), especially around Lake Tiberus (Caperneum, Magdala), and Samaria and Judea.

In the assemblage of these periods one notes the rather surprising scarcity of parallels with the pottery of Hesbon and Pella, sites not far from Araq el-Emir. It is true that comparisons based on three dozen pottery forms does not authorize very assured conclusions.

| | *Inventory* | | |
| No. | no. | *Type* | *Ware* |

HELLENISTIC (1st quarter of 2nd cen. B.C.)

1	78IAP10, 21, 24	cooking pot rim	2.5 YR 5/8 red; burned ext.; baked very hard; very irreg. surf.; incl.: small quartz particles.
4	78IAP60/1	cooking pot rim ?	10 YR 8/3 very pale brown; rough surf. but regular; incl.: small quartz particles.
13	78IAP102	jar rim	not wheelmade except for neck; ext. 5 YR 6/6 reddish yellow; int. 5 YR 6/4 light reddish brown; dark gray core; hard; incl.: large white particles.
14	78IAP5/3	"fish plate" rim	5 YR 6/6 reddish yellow; gray core; soft; many incl.: white and black, quartz, grog ? particles; rough surf.
15	78IAP104/2	amphora rim	7.5 YR 7/6 reddish yellow; soft but dense; many incl.: white and quartz particles.

EARLY ROMAN (middle of 1st century A.D.)

10	78IAP52/3, 53/1, 72/3	pot rim	2.5 YR 5/8 red; black core; fairly hard; incl.: fine black and white; smooth surf.
11	78IAP21/1	amphora rim	7.5 YR 6/4 light brown; baked homogeneously; hard; incl.: small quartz particles; slip: 10 YR 8/4 very pale brown.
12	78IAP93/1	jug base	10 YR 6/2 light brownish gray int. to 2.5 YR 7/6 ext.; dark core; hard; incl.: many very prominent white and quartz; rough surf.
20	77IAP5	juglet rim	7.6 YR 8/4 pink; traces of red slip; small whitish incl.
30	78IAP8/1	bowl rim	7.5 YR 6/4 light brown; very hard; smooth bright surf. with several cracks; few calcite incl.

BYZANTINE

21	78IAP28, 33, 41, 42	jug with handle	2.5 YR 6/8 light red; baked very homogeneously; hard, well-baked; rough ribbed surf.; white incl.
22	78IAP42, 50	cooking pot with 2 vertical handles slightly off-center, base probably convex	ext.: 7.5 YR 5/2 brown, int. and core: 7.5 YR 6/6 reddish yellow; baked very hard; rough ribbed surf.; some white incl.
23	78IAP11/2, 3, 104/1	basin	7.5 YR 6/6 reddish yellow, gray core; rough surf.; quartz incl.; the base is not wheelmade and there are vertical traces of modeling.
23a	78IAP41/2	handle of no. 23 ?	see no. 23

(no. 33 below is an example with horizontal handles, but this type exists with vertical handles also: not yet published by E. Will from Qasr)

24	78IAP33/1	cooking pot rim	7.5 YR 7/6 reddish yellow; baked homogeneously; ribbed surf., traces of brown slip; white and quartz incl.
32	78IAP43/1, 3	amphora rim	5 YR 6/6 reddish yellow; gray core; somewhat hard; many large and small incl.: black, very many white, a few quartz and grog; porous surf.
33	77IAP2	basin rim with horizontal handles	see no. 23
34	77IAP1	jug rim, probably with a handle attached to the neck	see no. 22
37	77IAP3	rim of a large receptacle with vertical sides	blackened steatite

ISLAMIC (12th-13th centuries A.D.)

| 35 | 77IAP6 | fragment of basin ? | see no. 23 with slip: 7.5 YR 8/2 pinkish white; decorated with deep combing and incised decoration on lip. |
| 36 | 77IAP4 | storage pot rim | 5 YR 6/4 light reddish brown with grayer core; slip: 10 YR 7/3 very pale brown; paint: 2.5 YR 2.5/4 dark reddish brown; the top of the lip is painted; white incl. |

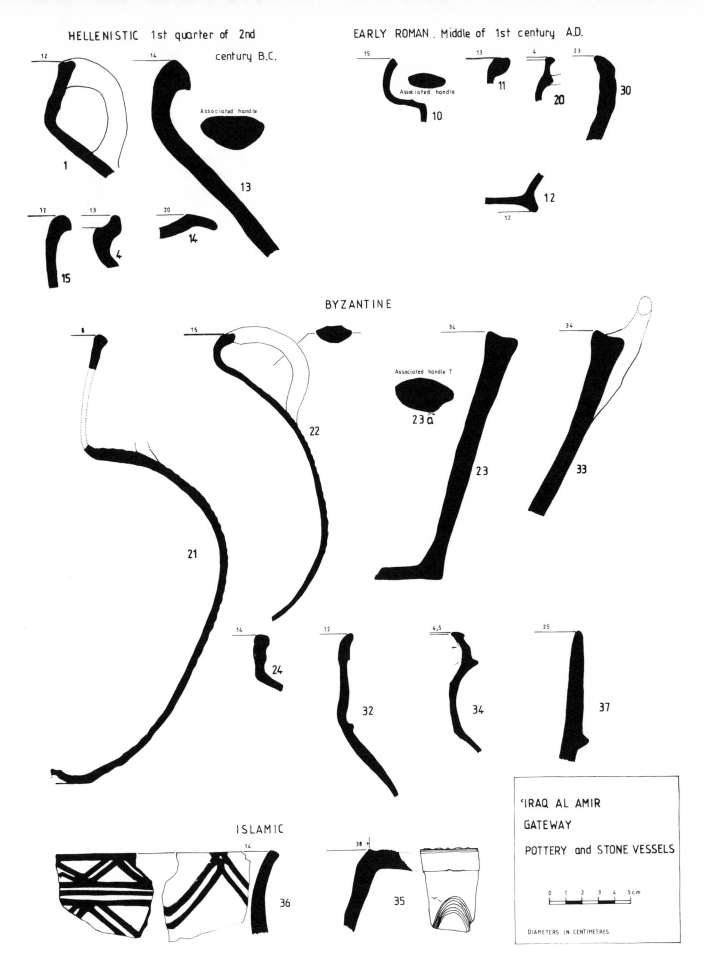

HELLENISTIC 1st quarter of 2nd century B.C.

EARLY ROMAN. Middle of 1st century A.D.

BYZANTINE

ISLAMIC

'IRAQ AL AMIR
GATEWAY
POTTERY and STONE VESSELS

0 1 2 3 4 5cm

DIAMETERS IN CENTIMETRES

64. Selected pottery from the Monumental Gateway excavations.

3.2 Catalogue

In the catalogue opposite fig. 64 the colors of the sherds are given precise designations by reference to the Munsell Soil Color Charts (1971). Except for designated instances, they describe the exterior surface of the vases. The diameters noted in the drawings are from the outer point on the rims. With two exceptions, noted in the catalogue, the pottery described is wheelmade.

4. The Gateway and the Estate

4.1 The function of the gateway and the walls

The operations of 1978 have clarified the relationship between the monumental buildings, of which the Qasr is the center and the gateway is one, thanks to the efforts of Pierre Gentelle in his study of the landscape and its agricultural management. The gateway opened onto an enclosure, the walls forming on the exterior a right-angled bend. A southeast-northwest oriented wall abuts against the south corner of the southwest pile whereas a second wall extends the facade of the northeast pile toward the northeast (see fig. 60). The orientation of the gateway has no relationship with the orientation of the Qasr nor with the way the Qasr relates to the cave area. Rather it corresponds to the axis of a road, rectilinear for about a hundred meters, following the dike which contained the artificial lake around the Qasr (see fig. 57). The gate was therefore a part of the development program which entirely remodeled the area, the climax being the construction of the Qasr. This program can be dated to about 175 B.C. and is the work of Hyrcanus.

The southwest wall set into a notch at the south corner of the southwest pile did not stand higher than the top of course 4. The angular blocks of the fifth and sixth courses revealed an embossment on their southwest side of the same type as those of the facade and were therefore visible. On the other hand, the three blocks behind the stretcher of course 4 are roughly squared and were probably to remain hidden. This very thick (nearly 3 m.) and rather low (2.91 m.) wall had a limited defensive capacity considering the height of the gateway. It was not principally used as a rampart but as a supporting wall. It was also used as a dike in an area where the embankments were quite thick, while the thinner northeast wall was only used as a supporting wall. A sounding made behind the southwest pile revealed another northwest-southeast oriented supporting wall along the road on the axis of the gateway up to the road joining the Qasr to the cave area. A parallel wall abutting the northeast pile can be hypothesized. The direction of the gateway was thus from southwest to northeast, on a heap of earth, the surface being more or less on the level of the top of course 4; the road went through the gate probably between two supporting walls.

The same conclusion is reached when gateway structure is studied. In the Near East a very skillful military architecture developed from the Bronze Age on in which there were numerous devices protecting the approaches to the gates and for trapping the assailants in the passages. It is surprising that there is no special reinforcement to protect this main entrance. Even the piles do not project from the walls. It must be remembered that Hyrcanus had to use the caves as shelters when he was threatened by his brothers' supporters. DeSaulcy and his companion, Captain Gélis, were struck by the mediocre strategic efficiency of the Araq el-Emir complex which is situated in a hollow. His conclusion, however, that the Qasr could only be a sanctuary, was too hasty.

4.2 The agricultural estate

In actuality, a careful examination of the site shows the dominant importance, not of defense works, but of agricultural installations like terraces, supporting and enclosure walls, and canals for irrigation. The choice of the site must be explained by the value and attraction of the perennial stream, the Wadi Sir, in an area where relatively wide spaces could be used at the foot of the cliffs which have a vertical face of 20 to 25 meters. The importance of the site has always been related to the wadi whose name undoubtedly derives from the ancient name of the site, *Tyros*. The site and its surroundings must first be described as an agricultural estate intensively cultivated, more likely in gardens than in fields (cf. fig. 57).

Gentelle has studied the setting and functioning of a coherent farming system covering more than 200 hectares. Inclined fields and terraces supported by dry stone walls were furnished with water by small irrigation ditches, some of which were lined with cut limestone blocks. Two main canals took the water upstream in the perennial bed of the Wadi Sir. The present orchards and cultivation are proof of the richness of the site in antiquity. A man like Hyrcanus, whom Josephus shows as particularly greedy, would have been interested in its economic value. Such richness needed to be protected and the walls and monumental gateway can be considered as a means of limited protection. They were of course of little use against large organized and well equipped siege troops such as the Hellenistic royal armies, but they could be adequate against robbers or nomads with their cattle threatening the fields and gardens.

4.3 The princely residence

All the monuments cannot be explained completely by only agricultural exploitation. The Josephus text emphasizes their attractiveness and their luxury. The megalithic techniques and the choice of materials of the gate establishes the intention of presenting a monumental appearance for the facade. Its dimensions cannot be justified for strategic reasons; they principally wanted to give a high conception of the estate owner's power and wealth. Some architectural forms and decoration are borrowed from an oriental tradition found in sanctuaries as well as in royal palaces. The only decorative figures are eagles and wild beasts which occupy a predominant place also on the Qasr walls. The felines were placed symmetrically and turned towards the gateway opening. The outline of the left feline suggests that its head was facing forward. This emphasizes their apotropaic role of protecting the passage. Although the lion and eagle are often represented in sanctuaries, they basically belong to the royal bestiary. They symbolize the human or divine royal power that demonstrates its strength by destroying its enemies.

The Araq el-Emir estate can be compared to a more specific kind of oriental royal residence, the Iranian *paradeisos*, which combines the luxurious buildings with natural surroundings such as gardens and parks. On a papyrus from the archives of Zenon there is a letter sent by a certain Tobia to Apollonios, dioiketes of Ptolemy II, dated to the year 29 of the latter's reign. It says that Tobia will send several animals to Ptolemy as a gift. In addition to horses, camels, and dogs, there are offsprings of hemionager and onager. The letter emphasizes that all these animals have been tamed. Since beasts were produced in captivity through expert cross-breeding it can be concluded that actual breeding centers for beasts did exist.

On another papyrus which records the sale of a young slave girl to Zenon, the same Tobiah appears; he is a native chief who held a military command in the Birta of Ammanitis, a place generally identified with the Araq el-Emir area. Therefore the Tobiad breeding center must certainly be placed here. It corresponds with one of the most characteristic functions of a Persian *paradeisos*, and Josephus precisely uses the word *paradeisos* in describing the place he named Tyre (Ant 12.4.11 § 233).

The above papyrus suggests that the Araq el-Emir site had been already somewhat arranged for agricultural exploitation around 265 B.C., much before the Hyrcanus period. The Greek cleruchs mentioned as witnesses were soldiers settled on the area and probably given pieces of agricultural land. The inscription *Ṭwbyh* cut on the entrances to two caves can be dated to the third century B.C. paleographically.

The presence of Iron age pottery in the village area could indicate not only a previous occupation of the site but also most probably the beginning of the exploitation of the water from the Wadi Sir. By pursuing the archaeological study of the site through systematic collectoin of the ceramics and by soundings it should be possible to fix precisely the chronology of the various installations. Already it can be concluded that in the first quarter of the second century B.C. a new impulse was given to the development of the site, especially in the Qasr area, orderly arranged according to Josephus' account (new system of terraces and dikes, reorganization of the access roads, creation of a lake, and construction of the Qasr and the monumental gateway). This work can be attributed to Hyrcanus who probably also completed the cave installations. The incompletion of the various projects seem to be due to the historical circumstances described by Josephus, to the short time Hyrcanus was there, and to his prematured death by suicide.

The traits which are borrowed from Hellenism cannot be pressed here. These are more decorative or technical than structural. Even if the lord of the estate depends more or less on the remote authority of a Hellenistic or Seleucid king, his reference is the oriental despot. Hyrcanus tries to impose political authority and probably a tribute on his neighbors (Ant 12.4.11 § 229, 236). The ostentatious expression of this power is probably an attempt to conform to a Persian model, the ideal of the Great King or the Satrap. Hyrcanus has an Iranian name. It is not necessary to suppose that the influence came directly from Persia. The satrap residence at Sidon, where a *paradeisos* is known, could have been a nearer model.

BIBLIOGRAPHY

Ant.   Josephus. *Jewish Antiquities.* Trans. Ralph Marcus
           from Greek, Loeb Classical Library. London:
           Heinemann and Cambridge, MA: Harvard Uni-
           versity, 1943.

Brown, R.
    1979   Excavations at 'Iraq el-Emir. *Annual of the
           Department of Antiquities of Jordan* 23: 17-30.

Butler, H. C.
    1919   *Syria.* Division II, Section A. Publications of the
           Princeton University Archaeological Expeditions
           to Syria in 1904-5 and 1909. Leyden: Brill.

Lapp, P. W.
    1962   Soundings at ꜥArâq el-Emîr (Jordan). *Bulletin of
           the American Schools of Oriental Research* 165:
           16-34.

    1963   The Second and Third Campaigns at ꜥArâq el-
           Emîr. *Bulletin of the American Schools of Oriental
           Research* 171: 8-39.

Munsell
    1971   Munsell Soil Color Charts. Baltimore: Munsell
           Color Company.

Chapter 13

The Recent French Work at Araq el-Emir: The Qasr el-Abd Rediscovered

ERNEST WILL

Jordan is privileged to have remaining on its soil a number of extraordinary monuments, landmarks of its glorious history. Among the least well-known, but not the least important, is the site of Araq el-Emir on the Wadi Sir in the neighborhood of Amman. Where else is to be seen so imposing a building as the Qasr el-Abd, so well preserved and dating back with certainty to the Hellenistic period?

The work carried out there under my direction during the last five years and devoted to the study of the Qasr is now completed, and we can bring into focus the results. We have come a long way since the day when, in the company of Dr. Fawzi Zayadine, I visited the site for the first time in 1975, and we agreed to present to the Director General of Antiquities a project for resuming work there. When our proposal was accepted, considerable technical means were made available to our team due to the kindness of Dr. Adnan Hadidi, the present Director General. Today the visitor, who has reached the end of the narrow road winding from the village of Araq el-Emir, suddenly finds himself in front of the edifice partially rebuilt in 1980; both eastern and western ground-floor walls have been re-erected and the west side view is particularly striking (fig. 65).[1]

The site and its main building were rediscovered at the beginning of the 19th century by two Englishmen, Irby and Mangles and identified by their companion, Bankes, as the Tyrus described by Josephus in his *Antiquities* (12.4.11. § 233).[2] They were then seriously explored about the same date by two Frenchmen, and immediately the many and complex issues raised by both site and edifice were discussed with passion—the general history of the site, the date of the Qasr, the reconstruction of its architectural features, and its purpose.

Count Melchior de Vogüé in 1862 was the first to conduct a close study of the Qasr which was well-balanced and precise; he admitted the Hellenistic date as well as its construction as a palace in conformity with Josephus' testimony, a point of view all the more praiseworthy since he pointed out similarities to the temple of Jerusalem (1864b: 38-43, pls. 34-35; 1864a: 52). Far more reckless in his judgments was Félicien de Saulcy who came to the site as early as November 1863, with a team consisting of Salzmann, Mauss (the architect of St. Anne's Church in Jerusalem), and staff-captain Gélis. They made drawings and maps of the site and the building. They had come up from Jericho along the same road which had led to Araq el-Emir in antiquity (de Saulcy 1867:83).[3]

F. de Saulcy found reasons to disagree with his "learned friend," de Vogué. He and the soldier who

[1] I am glad to have the opportunity to offer my sincere thanks to Dr. Adnan Hadidi for the generous and friendly assistance always offered the French team. Without the important technical means made available by the Director General our results could not have been achieved. For the preliminary account of our work, see Will 1977: 69-85.

[2] Irby and Mangles 1852. Another Englishman, Captain Conder visited and described the site in *The Survey of Eastern Palestine* (1881).

[3] Also de Saulcy 1865: 211-35, with some additional stories, like that of the fight with an unseen panther. It is likely that Zenon took the same road. For a rather comical (given the evidence) relapse into the manner of de Saulcy, see Fritz 1977: 87-91, fig. 18, with a new version of the temple hypothesis.

65. West side of the Qasr rebuilt, 1980.

accompanied him were first struck by the fact that the Qasr could not be a fortress. "We could not help smiling" at such an idea, concluding with this astonishing sentence: "Need I dissert at length to prove that the Qasr el Aabed was not a citadel, but indeed a religious edifice, a genuine temple? I am so far from thinking so that I abstain without the least scruple." He does develop a number of arguments which are far from convincing. A temple dedicated to what divinity? "This Qasr el Aabed is obviously a religious building, a temple of Qamos and Moloch. The idol worshiped there is the lion carved in round whose fragments I discovered."[4] The date, therefore, could not be later than Persian. De Saulcy included in his report the plan of an

edifice reconstructed with three naves and an apse at its southern end.

Although they ignored the ancient text at their disposal and were supported by only slight evidence, these assertions have never been completely given up. The temple hypothesis (of course it is much more attractive to identify a temple) was taken up with no stronger arguments by H. C. Butler (1919), who also recognised Persian capitals, and then by P. Lapp, who was impressed by the comparison with the "temples à escaliers" (1963: 28-32), whose study had just been completed by R. Amy (1950). On the other hand, two German archaeologists, K. Lange in 1885 (p. 149, pl. 5) and later, C. Watzinger (1933: 13, pl. 22), briefly studied the Qasr and followed in de Vogüé's steps in refusing to ignore Josephus' testimony and stuck to the palace identification and the Hellenistic

[4]These fragments belong to one of the lion slabs.

date. Watzinger supported this view with more detailed and precise arguments.[5]

Half a century elapsed before the American H. C. Butler stayed for six days on the site in 1904 and brought back reconstructions of the various facades and the internal structure (Butler 1919) which remained uncontested until our own investigation. Now with the architectural study approaching its conclusion, complete revision is required of Butler's reconstructions.

No doubt Butler himself acknowledged the hypothetical character of some of his ideas. So in 1961 another American, P. Lapp, assisted by an architect, M. Brett in 1962, resumed the exploration of the Qasr approaching it in a more archaeological manner; a number of soundings were made in and around the building, and for the first time the importance of the Byzantine occupation was recognized. Yet there remained the difficulty of identifying with precision the Hellenistic level (Lapp 1962, 1963).[7] But his untimely death prevented Lapp from pursuing this promising line of investigation.

Where do we stand now after five years? F. Larché, who supervised the work on the site during this time[8] and myself are now reaching final conclusions, within the limits of evidence bound to remain incomplete.

We certainly can do away with some unfounded hypotheses. Of these, the first and most important concerns the purpose of the monument. To begin with, it was hazardous to disregard Josephus' testimony, who descibes the building as a palace or manor (a *baris*) built by Hycanus in the years

preceeding his death in 175 B.C. Strong arguments are needed to reject an ancient text: why should Josephus speak of a palace instead of a temple when he precisely mentioned the existence of a Jewish temple at Leontopolis in Egypt, at a date when the history of the Tobiads belonged to the remote past?

The archaeological evidence has entirely justified Josephus. The plan, as reconstructed since de Saulcy and more or less accepted by Butler and Lapp, as a large basilical hall with or without internal colonnade is no longer credible. Rather, the Hellenistic building consisted of a unit of four rooms surrounded by a wide corridor on the ground floor, and above the ground floor there was a second story of the same height. Nothing recalls a temple—at least a temple of a known type: obviously the edifice was intended for secular use.

Of course Josephus may have been mistaken in attributing the monument to the last Tobiad, Hyrcanus, who may simply have reused it. Indeed, even if the Hellenistic date is admitted on the whole, one may hesitate, as some scholars have done, to decide between Hyrcanus and one of his ancestors, who lived a century earlier at the time of the Zenon papyri (Vincent 1920: 182).[9]

To determine the date of the construction of the building is why Lapp carried out his soundings. His main discovery, however, was a thick, unmistakable, Byzantine level. The Hellenistic sherds were few and unstratified.[9a] We must turn to the history of the monument to solve the problems.

Architectural study still provides the only reliable arguments. The architectural ornamentation supports without discussion the Hellenistic date. The prevailing Corinthian order on one side, and the association of a Doric triglyph frieze with Corinthian epistyle and cornice on the other, irrefutably point to this period. C. Watzinger had tried to reach more definite conclusions through the study of the Corinthian capitals to which he assigned an early 2nd century B.C. date (1933: 15 and n. 2).

Two other arguments are conclusive. The architectural analysis of the remains reveals two facts: first, that the Hellenistic building—that is everything except the internal Byzantine level—was

---

[5]Lange's reconstruction presents the Qasr as a Hellenistic or Roman basilica. For other German studies, see Welter 1931: 405, who explained the whole estate as a *paradeisos* on a Persian pattern; it was probably more important as a *Jagdschloss*, but with differences. Another Frenchman, the duke of Luynes, visited the site about ten years after de Saulcy and gave a brief illustrated account in his *Voyage d'exploration à la Mer Morte* (1874: 138, pl. 30-32).

[6]The reconstruction by Butler of the northern facade is unfortunately reproduced in many publications. For a detailed re-examination, see Will 1977: 69.

[7]Brett 1963: 39-45, retains the general outlook of Butler's reconstruction, adding a twofold internal colonnade which does not fit well with the preserved Hellenistic walls. For an isometric projection of this reconstruction, see p. 43 and Lapp 1976: 529.

[8]Full credit for the architectural study of the monument must be given to F. Larché who also directed the re-erection of the east and west walls in 1980.

[9]For the Zenon papyri, see Mittmann 1970: 199.

[9a]Futher study of the material has determined there were some stratified Hellenistic sherds. See above Introduction and ch. 7 (NLL- ed.).

built at one and the same time, and secondly, that it remained unfinished. This twofold finding leads to the inescapable conclusion that the construction of the edifice followed its master's fate, both meeting a brutal end at the same date, 175 B.C.[10]

Important points are thus definitively established: the builder's identity, the purpose of the building, and the date of its construction. There remains the architectural problems.

Regarding the elevation, F. Larché's drawings and studies have provided an entirely new and convincing image of the facade, more reliable for the northern and southern ends than for the intermediate part, and more reliable as always, for the lower than for the upper story. The reconstructions presented by Butler are no longer tenable.

The edifice consisted of two stories of practically equal height: to the ground floor entrance hall with its two columns corresponds the second story two-columned loggia set between two corner rooms with bays and decorated with well known lion slabs at their bases. Lengthwise, the seven large bays in the east and the west sides, which Butler in his reconstruction had filled arbitrarily with half-columns turned toward the interior (a curiously long-lived mistake) were indeed intended to give light to the inside; the same rhythm was repeated on the second floor by a row of small bays divided by mullions decorated with small Corinthian half-columns.[11]

But the most difficult problems are raised by the arrangement of the inside area between the northern entrance block and its southern counterpart. The clearance of this area supplied the plan of the Byzantine level which still occupies it in its entirety. The difficulty was to discover the Hellenistic level under the preserved Byzantine structures.[12] The clearance and a few additional soundings have yielded some final data.

Lapp had indeed seen that the Byzantine level consisted of a large fill reaching up to 1.65 m above level O, the threshhold of the northern entrance hall. As became clear in our recent soundings, the

Byzantine builder, in order to establish the new floor, had leveled down the existing walls to a chosen height; he then set the most important of his partition walls straight above the remains of the Hellenistic walls, but not, as a rule, directly on top of them. A small intervening course of irregular stones marked clearly and indubitably the separation between the two levels. Thus one cannot miss the internal Hellenistic walls preserved everywhere to the same height.

In addition a sounding which I carried out in the southeastern corner clearly revealed the level (0.85 m) intended for the Hellenistic floor inside the Qasr, probably in the form of a slab pavement (Will 1979: 139, pls. 59, 60).[13]

The Hellenistic plan is thus clear: it consists of a central unit surrounded by a horseshoe-shaped corridor lit by the big bays of the east and west sides, as well as by three similar bays to the south (fig. 66). This allows us to discard the preceeding reconstructions, that is those linked to a large basilical hall which seemed to support the temple hypothesis (or its possible alternative, the hypothesis of a princely *aula*). Instead we have some kind of storerooms completed by the two square rooms in the southeast and southwest corners. The brightly lit corridor was intended to make the handling of the stored wares or equipment easy.

This was clearly a purely practical device. But how to reconcile this with the *baris*, the palace or manor of Josephus? There was the upper story. Consider a well known type of oriental house, both ancient and modern, with its ground floor reserved for strangers, storage, or animals in the case of a farmhouse, and its upper story for living quarters (the *harim*).[14] In the Qasr it is worthy to note that a single staircase led to the second story. Obviously the plan of this floor was linked to the walls of the ground floor; but all we can say with certainty is that the upper story was also brightly lit by means of a great number of small decorated bays.

The building remained unfinished, and we know this not just from the architectural decoration.[15]

---

[10]The story as told by Josephus gives the only convincing explanation of the unfinished monument. Moreover, Josephus describes only, and accurately, the external facades without mentioning the inside.

[11]The "blocks in T-form terminating in a half cylinder (Butler 1919: 7, ill. 3) don't "exactly fill the spaces," that is, of the bays. These blocks can be readjusted as two piers which closed the north loggia on the inside.

[12]For the inside strata and the Byzantine fill, see Lapp 1963: 31.

[13]An intermediate level, ca. + 0.40 m, existed in the second vestibule.

[14]This is the case, for instance, in the traditional Lebanese house, see Ragette 1974: 13.

[15]Lapp 1963: 24. In the Roman temples of Lebanon the architectural ornamentation is very rarely finished. That was due, of course, to lack of money. Note that the Monumental Gateway of the estate near the Qasr remained unfinished in Hellenistic times also, as the clearance carried out by J. M. Dentzer has made clear (see ch. 12).

Qasr el-'Abd à 'Iraq el-Emir : plan général

66. General plan of the Qasr (E. Will).

The unfinished state of ornamental embellishment is no proof that the building was not used. There is more convincing evidence. The many bays in the internal, as well as in the external walls, were never equipped with window or door panels. Characteristically, the lintel above the door of the north entrance hall has a socket hole, but there is no corresponding hole in the sill. Likewise, there are no remains of slabs or any other kind of pavement, or any evidence of their setting. The internal walls were leveled down during Byzantine times, but it is hard to believe that the walls ever reached the full height of the lower floor. If they had, why should the Byzantines have dismantled them to set new ones in the same place? It follows that no partitions were erected on the second floor in Hellenistic times and that this central area was never roofed.[16]

We can hardly conclude more. Some day a similar *baris* may be discovered in the Jordanian or Syrian countryside as other manor houses of this oriental type must have existed.[17] But even so, it is unlikely that such a discovery would give us more than a plan or any help in reconstructing an upper story. The luxurious dwelling dreamed about by Hyrcanus will remain unknown forever.

The findings outlined above will be described more fully in a more detailed publication devoted to the Qasr. But the second stage of our program, the exploration of the site of Araq el-Emir, has already begun. Another team of the French Archaeological Institute for the Near East will carry out the survey of all the remains of the large estate of Hyrcanus in close collaboration with the Jordanian Directorate General.[18]

[16]The Qasr remained uninhabited for half a millenium. Another hypothesis could be put forth: during this period the second story collapsed or was dismantled and the blocks and columns were carried away to be reused elsewhere. The result is the same: it is impossible to reconstruct the second floor.

[17]The only possible parallel known to me is a building of the end of the third century B.C. at Shahr-i Qūmis in Iran (Hansmann and Stronach 1970a: 36, figs. 3-5, pls. 2-3, and 1970b 142, fig. 1; Colledge 1977: 55, fig. 25 B). There a central unit of storerooms is surrounded by corridors on the four sides. According to the excavators, a second story for the living quarters certainly existed. Technically the building is entirely different from the Qasr.

[18]This survey is being carried out by F. Larché and F. Villeneuve in collaboration with Dr. Fawzi Zayadine.

BIBLIOGRAPHY

Amy, R.
1950   Temples à escaliers. *Syria* 27: 82-136.
Ant.   Josephus. *Jewish Antiquities*. Trans. Ralph Marcus
from Greek. Loeb Classical Library. London:
Heinemann, and Cambridge, MA: Harvard University, 1943.
Butler, H. C.
1919   *Syria*, Division II, Section A. Publications of the
Princeton University Archaeological Expeditions
to Syria in 1904-5 and 1909. Leiden: Brill.
Colledge, M. A. R.
1977   *Parthian Art*. London: Elek.
Conder, C. R.
1889   *The Survey of Eastern Palestine*. London: Palestine Exploration Fund.
Fritz, V.
1977   *Tempel und Zelt*. Germany: Neukirchener.
Hansman, J., and Stronach, D.
1970a   Excavations at Shahr-i Qūmis. *Journal of the
Royal Asiatic Society* 1970: 29-62.
1970b   A Sasanian Repository at Shahr-i Qūmis. *Journal
of the Royal Asiatic Society* 1970: 142-58.
Irby, C. L., and Mangles, J.
1852   *Travels in Egypt and Nubia, Syria, and the Holy
Land*. London: Murray.
Lange, K.
1885   *Haus und Halle*. Leipzig: Veit.
Lapp, P. W.
1962   Soundings at ᶜArâq el-Emîr (Jordan). *Bulletin of
the American Schools of Oriental Research* 165:
16-34.
1963   The Second and Third Campaigns at ᶜArâq el-
Emîr. *Bulletin of the American Schools of Oriental
Research* 171: 8-39.
1976   ᶜIraq el-Emir. Pp. 527-31 in vol. 2 of *Encyclopedia
of Archaeological Excavations in the Holy Land*,
ed. M. Avi-Yonah. Jerusalem: Israel Exploration
Society.

Luynes, H. T. P., duke of
1874   *Voyage d'exploration à la Mer Morte*, vol. 1. Paris:
A. Bertrand.
Mittmann, S.
1970   Zenon im Ostjordanland. Pp. 199-210 in *Archäol-
ogie und altes Testament*, Festschrift für Kurt
Galling, ed. A. Kuschke und E. Kutsch. Tübingen:
J. C. B. Mohr.
Ragette, F.
1974   *Architecture in Lebanon*. Beirut: American University of Beirut.
de Saulcy, L. F.
1865   *Voyage en Terre Sainte*. Paris: Didier.
1867   Mémoire sur les monuments d-Aâraq el-Emyr.
*Mémoires de Academie des Inscriptions et Belles-
Lettres*, 26, Part 1: 83-115.
Vincent, L. H.
1920   La Palestine dans les Papyrus Ptolémaiques de
Gerza. *Revue biblique* 29: 161-202.
de Vogüé, C. J. M.
1864a   Ruines D'Araq el-Emir. *Revue Archéologique* 10:
52-62.
1864b   *Temple de Jerusalem*. Paris: Noblet & Baudry.
Watzinger, C.
1933   *Denkmäler Palästinas*, vol. 2. Leipzig: Hin-
richs'sche.
Welter,
1931   Arak el-Emir. *Forschungen und Fortschritte*, 7:
405-406.
Will, E.
1977   L'Edifice dit Qasr el Abd à Araq al Amir (Jordanie).
*Comptes-rendus de l'Académie des Inscriptions &
Belles-Lettres*, 1977: 69-85.
1979   Recherches au Qasr el ᶜAbd à Iraq al-Amir. *Annual
of the Department of Antiquities of Jordan* 23:
139-49.

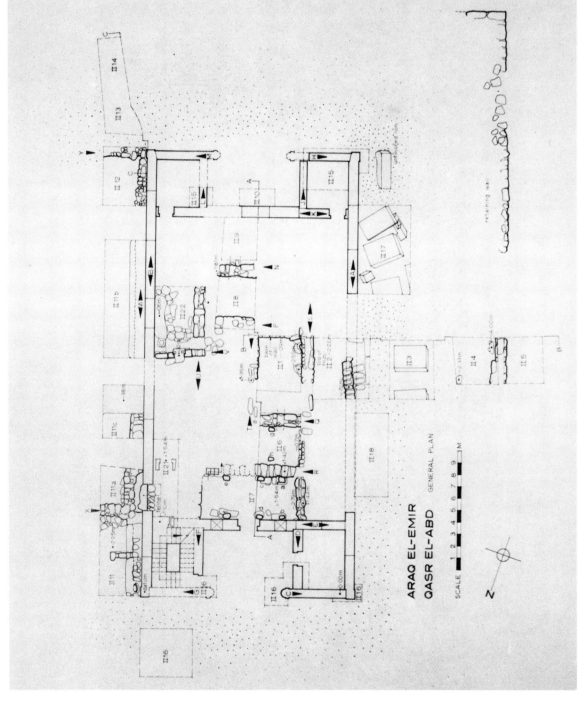

Plan 1. General plan of the 1961 and 1962 excavations at the Qasr (Field II).

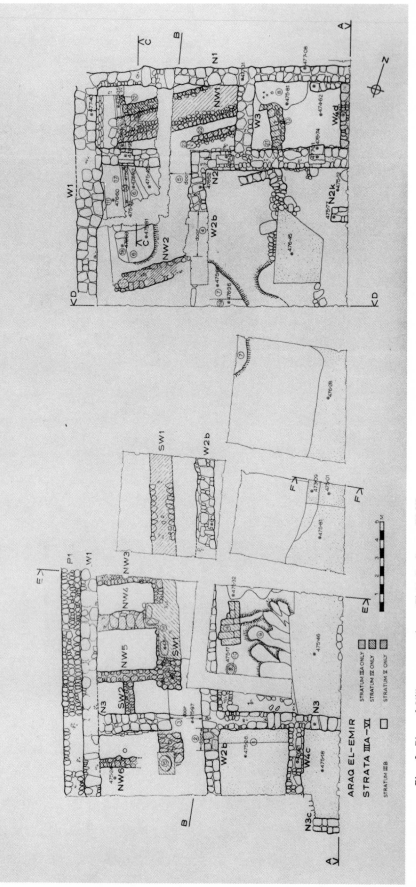

Plan 2. Plan of Village excavations (Field I), Strata III-VI.

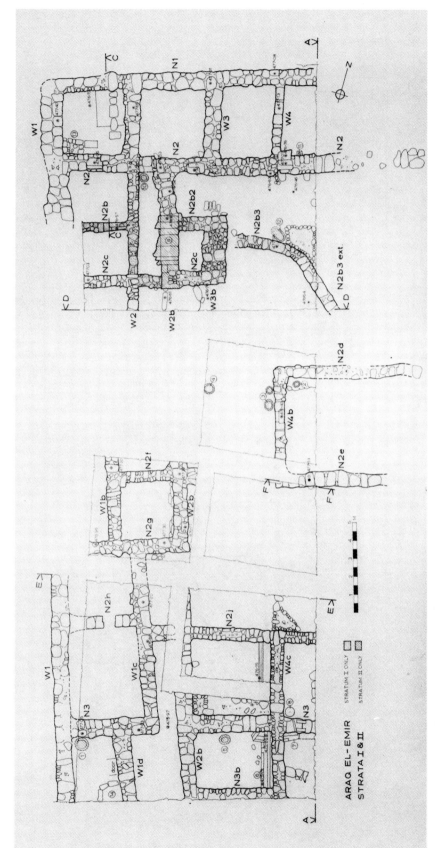

Plan 3. Plan of Village excavations (Field II), Strata I-II.

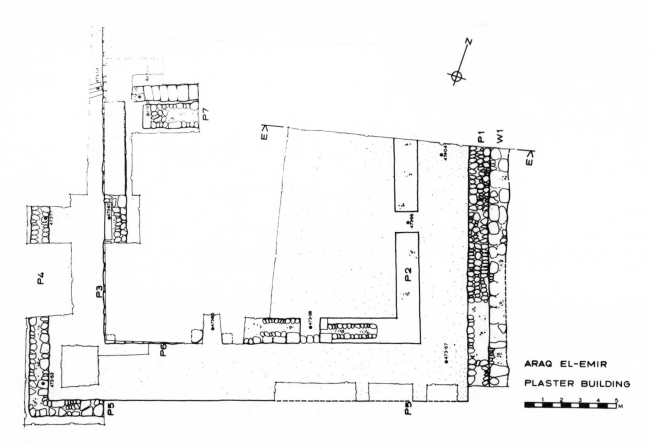

ARAQ EL-EMIR

PLASTER BUILDING

1 2 3 4 5
M

Plan 4. Plan of Village excavations (Field I), The Square Building.

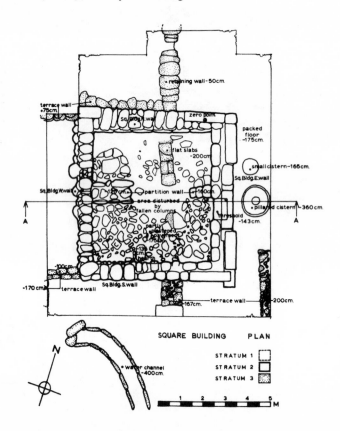

SQUARE BUILDING   PLAN

STRATUM 1 ☐
STRATUM 2 ☐
STRATUM 3 ☐

1 2 3 4 5
M

Plan 5. Plan of the Square building (Field III).

THE AMMAN AIRPORT EXCAVATIONS, 1976

THE ANNUAL OF THE AMERICAN SCHOOLS OF ORIENTAL RESEARCH

Volume 48

Edited by
Joseph A. Callaway

The Amman Airport Excavations, 1976

Edited by LARRY G. HERR

with contributions by
Larry G. Herr, Robert M. Little, Robert Miller and Zeidan Kafafi

Published by the
American Schools of Oriental Research

Distributed by

Eisenbrauns
P.O.B. 275
Winona Lake, IN 46590

Library of Congress Cataloging in Publication Data

Main entry under title:

The Amman Airport excavations, 1976.

    (The Annual of the American Schools of Oriental
Research ; v. 48)
    Includes bibliographies.
    1. Amman Airport Site (Jordan) I. Herr, Larry G.
II. American Schools of Oriental Research. III. Title.
IV. Series.
DS101.A45 vol. 48 [DS154.9.A52] 930s [933] 83-11760
ISBN 0-89757-047-2

Printed in the United States of America
1 2 3 4 5

Table of Contents

LIST OF FIGURES

Chapter 1
Introduction

LARRY G. HERR

Background, Acknowledgments and Staff

When the new runway and apron extension for the accomodation of large, wide-bodied commercial aircraft were first proposed for the Amman Civil Airport, a number of people were concerned about the fate of the Late Bronze Age temple situated very near the runway. One of the more active members of Jordan's Friends of Archaeology at that time, Mrs. Remie Fenske, could do more than simply be concerned: her husband, Mr. Kenneth Fenske, a Pan American Airlines administration official, was a key advisor to the airport expansion program. Mrs. Fenske urged her husband to do what he could to salvage the structure.

Resulting from this public concern and from a conversation Kenneth Fenske had with Lawrence T. Geraty of Andrews University, Director of the Hesban excavations, at a garden party hosted by the American Center of Oriental Research in Amman, it was arranged that Geraty and I should visit the site with Fenske early in June, 1976. After a second visit, which included Siegfried H. Horn, former Director of the Hesban excavations, and a brief conference at the site with His Excellency Sharif Ghazi, Director of the Department of Civil Aviation, it was agreed that further salvage excavations could prove instructive and aid in the preservation of the structure. Sharif Ghazi generously offered funds from his department to meet the expenses of the project, including airline meals for the excavation crew, if Geraty and I would supply the personnel and tools. He was further interested in developing the site for touristic interest because the ruins were easily visible to all planes taxiing to and from the runway. Indeed, the

old apron runway had been somewhat deformed to avoid the structure. Geraty and I suggested that the excavations commence in the third week of August as soon as the Hesban dig, to which we both belonged, was completed so that personnel and equipment connected with that project could be utilized.

With this logistic support in hand, the Department of Antiquities of the Hashemite Kingdom of Jordan, directed by Mr. Yaqoub Oweis and assisted by Dr. Yusef Alami, gave us permission to conduct a salvage excavation for ten days from August 17 to 27, 1976. Thanks must go to Miss Nazmieh Rida Tawfiq, the representative assigned to us from the Department of Antiquities, for smoothing much of the bureaucratic way.

Prof. J. B. Hennessy of the University of Sydney, who excavated the site in 1966, lent his support to the project, mailing us his unpublished plans and sections. The American Center of Oriental Research, directed by Dr. James A. Sauer, provided moral support, work space and housing for some of the project's personnel.

I served as Director of the excavations while Geraty acted as Project Advisor. Square Supervisors included Robert Miller of the Institute of Archaeology at the University of London, Janie Miller from London, Dick Dorsett of Amman, Vincent Clark of the University of Melbourne, Scott Rolston of Amman and, for a few days, Kaye Barton of Dickenson, North Dakota. Rolston, who had been one of the photographers for the Hesban project, and Dorsett were the photographers. Patricia Crawford of Brandeis University worked with the flotation materials and pollen samples; Professor Joachim Boessneck of the

1

Institut für Paleoanatomie, Domestikationsforschung, und Geschichte der Tiermedizin der Universität München made a quick analysis of the few identifiable animal bones; Merling Alomia of Berrien Springs, Michigan helped with the drafting work. All three of these last individuals were also connected with the Hesban project. Janie Miller served efficiently as pottery and object registrar. Again, the services of Nazmieh Rida Tawfiq were greatly appreciated as she actively and energetically took part in every aspect of the field work and aided in post-season processing of the finds. Rafiq es-Saraf, designated to us by the Department of Civil Aviation, helped in our relations with the airport construction crews and with airport working and security protocols. Because the airport could not spare workmen from their construction forces to help us dig, we enlisted the enthusiastic services of volunteers largely from the foreign community in Amman. During free days in S. Thomas Parker's 1976 *limes* survey, Frank Koucky of Wooster College, the geologist for that expedition, briefly analyzed the geomorphology of the site and helped us describe our lithic finds.

Transportation to and from the dig site was accomplished with the aid of a small bus and driver loaned to us by the Department of Civil Aviation and by a Volkswagen microbus provided for our use by the Department of Antiquities. Since supervisors and volunteers lived at home or at the American Center of Oriental Research, these vehicles were invaluable, making their rounds to the homes of the various members of the excavation and driving them through the empty streets of pre-dawn Amman to begin the workday on time.

The attempt to preserve and consolidate the structure for viewing from taxiing aircraft was frustrated. Soon after Mr. Kenneth Fenske finished his work in Amman and contrary to eloquent pleas from the Department of Antiquities the structure was bulldozed to make way for the eastern edge of the new apron runway. Although the structure itself had been completely excavated by Hennessy in 1966 and our excavation cleared what little was left outside, making possible future excavations unnecessary, the loss of such a unique structure from the important Late Bronze period of Transjordan is lamentable.

The local pottery and the non-ceramic artifacts found in the 1976 excavations have been left with the Department of Antiquities of Jordan for storage or exhibit at their discretion. The human

bones, imported ceramic fragments and flints are being stored at the Siegfried H. Horn Archaeological Museum at Andrews University.

Special thanks should go to the preliminary readers of this report, Siegfried H. Horn, Lawrence T. Geraty, Oystein S. LaBianca and William H. Shea, for their suggestions and support.

Previous Excavations

In 1955, while expanding the Amman airport facilities, construction workers operating bulldozers encountered a substantial ancient structure. Fortunately, the then Director of the Department of Antiquities of Jordan, G. Lankester Harding, was in the airport at the time and was able to inspect the discovery immediately. Soon afterward, a quick salvage excavation was conducted by M. Salih (Harding 1956: 80), the area was fenced off and the apron runway was constructed to skirt the site. All debris above a stone pavement floor was removed inside the building during the 1955 excavation, but nothing is reported of excavations outside. Probes were made beneath the paving stones in three of the rooms (Hennessy 1966a: 156). According to preliminary notices several hundred fragments of Egyptian stone vessels, scarabs, cylinder seals and bone and ivory objects were found (Harding 1956; 1958). Unfortunately, most of the local pottery collected at this time seems to have been lost (Hennessy 1966a: 155). On the basis of the imported Mycenaean pottery, Harding dated the site to the Late Bronze Age and suggested that the building's square plan and rich corpus of objects indicated a temple function for the site (Harding 1956, 1958). He further noted the isolation of the site. Nothing more than preliminary announcements regarding this excavation have been published (Harding 1956: 80; 1958: 7-18); some of the objects, however, have appeared: the scarabs and cylinder seals were published by Ward (1964) and the Aegean pottery and stone vessels and objects have appeared together with similar items discovered in 1966 (Hankey 1974a: 1974b).

The building's unique square plan, apparent isolation and plethora of imported ceramics and objects raised important questions which the 1955 excavations did not answer. J. B. Hennessy, therefore, decided to return to the site with the support of the British School of Archaeology in Jerusalem. He completely excavated the building, leaving only the walls, and probed the immediate surroundings, especially the northwest and east sides of the

Fig. 1. The Amman airport structure looking east as it is being cleared in 1966 by J. B. Hennessy's excavation; to the north of
the structure (left) three of his shallow trenches may be seen; in the upper of these trenches a portion of the structured rock pile
may be seen including his probe (our Phase 2 Pit A.4:9) through the western outfall of the structured rock pile (at the very edge
of the photograph); Our Phase 2 Pit A.4:10 is the probe just to the right of the structured rock pile in the same trench; the
depression above these trenches may have been part of the 1955 excavations; our Square A.1 was laid out just above Hennessy's
trenches and included part of the depression.

building from February 21 to March 27, 1966
(Hennessy 1966a; Figs. 1 and 6). This excavation
resulted in several general preliminary reports
(Hennessy 1966a; 1966b; 1970) and two specialist
reports (including also the 1955 material), one on
the Aegean pottery, (Hankey 1974a) and the other
on the stone vessels and objects (Hankey 1974b).
To date, the final publication of the 1966 project
has not yet appeared, but a summary of the results
as presented in the preliminary reports may be
helpful at this point.

Three stages were observed in the development
of the building (Hennessy 1966a). The first stage
included a large, square, leveling foundation
trench dug into the soil, reaching bedrock on the
west but not in the east where bedrock seems to
have deepened. After the first course of the exterior
walls was laid at the edges of this trench, a
yellow clay-and-soil fill layer was deposited for a
depth of ca. .15-.20 m in the interior. This layer

included frequent pockets of burned clay, ashes
and bones (animal, bird and human) with a rich
array of small objects (40 small gold objects including jewelry and gold strips, jewelry in silver
and bronze, hundreds of beads made of various
semi-precious stones with one inscribed in cuneiform, scarabs generally Hyksos or early 18th
Dynasty in date, cylinder seals, bone and ivory
inlay pieces and bronze weapons); pottery was
rare. It is Hennessy's suggestion that these objects
were dedicatory offerings (perhaps associated with
a cult of child sacrifice) which were offered at the
time of construction (Hennessy 1970: 307). The
internal walls of the building were positioned on
top of the "dedicatory fill" and two cylindrical
blocks were placed one on top of the other in the
central room; a foundation trench for the latter
was excavated through the recently deposited
"dedicatory fill." The second and later courses of
all walls were then added and carefully bonded

together as the building was finished. This stage was used long enough for a .02-.03 m surface deposit to build up in which were found more ash pockets from small fires including animal, bird and human bones, as well as many small finds; again pottery was very scarce, although some Mycenaean IIIA-B sherds were found.

The second stage saw a new floor made of flat "tabular" stones (Hennessy 1966a: pl. XXXIIB) but no change in the occurrence of ash pockets and the plan of the building (and therefore its function) was observed. All objects associated with this stage had been removed by the 1955 excavation.

In the third stage, the cylindrical stones in the central room were put out of use when a dividing wall was constructed through the central room and a new door to that room was cut while the old door was blocked (Hennessy 1966a: Fig. 3).

Hennessy agreed with Harding that the basic function of the building was that of a temple. He also maintained the isolation of the structure but noted the existence of a site about 300 m to the east under one of the runways which he was not able to investigate. No certain surfaces were observed on the building's exterior except for a possible surface of crushed rock very near the outer walls. Beyond this only virgin soil was found mixed with a few potsherds. The cylindrical stones in the middle of the central room were identified as the temple's altar and it was suggested that they were put out of use in the third stage when the cult of the temple had probably changed. Hankey has suggested however that the large amount of pottery and objects inside the building would have left little room for cultic rites to be practiced and the building may have served as a storehouse (Hankey 1974b: 168).

Because the founding "dedicatory fill" contained Mycenaean IIIA-B sherds but Mycenaean II forms were rare (Hankey 1974a) Hennessy refined Harding's date to the Late Bronze II period, ca. the early 14th century to the late 13th century (1970: 309).

Fig. 2.   The Amman Airport structure looking north as it appeared just prior to excavation in 1976; in the immediate foreground to the right are a few stones of the south exterior wall of the structure; the most visible walls are those defining the inner, central room; the debris mounds, made by the renewed 1976 airport construction in the upper left corner extended much nearer the structure immediately outside the photograph and threatened to cover it; in the background and just in front of the apron docking area is the beginning of a small wadi, tributary to the Wadi Zerqa, and partially filled by earlier airport construction.

Fig. 3. The Amman airport structure looking east as it appeared just prior to excavation in 1976; in the lower right is the foot of a debris mound, caused by the renewed airport construction, which threatened to cover the outer west wall of the structure; the most visible walls are those defining the inner, central room.

The Site

In 1976 the site of the Amman Airport temple was overrun with weeds and was being threatened with debris mounds pushed up from the near-by runway construction (Figs. 2 and 3). The plan of the structure, however, was easily discernible, and a few meters to the north a line of unexcavated stones that seemed to form a corner was apparent at the surface (Figs. 4 and 5). No other signs of occupation were visible.

Around the structure were several utility trenches excavated by the airport construction crews (Fig. 6); these aided us in our investigation (below). Hennessy's seven trenches (Fig. 6) outside the north and east walls of the structure were easily identifiable as visible depressions though they were silted in with balk tumble and loess deposits and were overgrown with weeds (compare Figs. 1 and 7).

The site is situated near the middle of a long east-west oriented plain, perhaps better described as a gentle, broad valley shelf, which slopes gradually downward (ca. 2°) from the hills on the

south toward the Wadi Zerqa at the extreme northern edge of the valley. According to geologist Frank Koucky the ancient geomorphology of the site may have witnessed a low hill just to the east of the site, although the deepening bedrock may have accounted for his observations; at present the region immediately surrounding the structure is devoid of irregular topography.

Forty-five meters north of the structure a large volume of modern debris has been pushed over an original slope in the terrain which had descended to a small wadi still rudimentarily present today (Fig. 2). Although this material included clearly foreign debris from the original construction of the airport (below), it may also have contained the debris from bulldozed topographical irregularities present on the plain prior to the airport construction, such as the small hill projected by Koucky.

Excavation Goals

Several aspects of the site attracted us to consider salvage excavations: First and most obvious was the threat of destruction to the site due to

Fig. 4. Pre-excavation photograph of the stone line which suggested that more excavations at the Amman airport site might prove profitable (looking north); it turned out to be the western stone line of the structured rock pile.

airport construction. Second, the possible wall to the north of the structure (Fig. 4) suggested a reason for further excavation. Third, a one-period site, at which new methods in biofact retrieval would be implemented, could lend interesting data regarding the flora, fauna and climate of the Late Bronze Age in this region. Fourth, a proper observation and recording of the construction trenches around the structure (Fig. 6) could help solve the debate on the relative isolation of the site. Fifth, further excavation could turn up more clues regarding the nature and function of the site, still debated after two excavations. As will be seen, these goals were realized with varied success.

Excavation Layout

Except for dismantling the walls, Hennessy's excavation had completely excavated the structure in 1966; it merited no more digging. We thus laid out six Squares in three Areas outside the structure (Fig. 6). Area A, on the north side of the structure, was the location of the major thrust of our excavations. The original three Squares of Area A measured 2.00 × 4.50 m (except A.2 which was 5.00 m long), laid end to end with .50 m balks between. Square A.1 extended north from near the northeast corner of the structure, the posited entrance to the building; Squares A.2 and A.3 continued this line northward to intersect a projected east-west line of stones connected with the north-south line of stones observable on the surface to the north of the structure (Figs. 6 and 7). It was hoped that the west balk of these three Squares would serve to connect stratigraphically the structure with the line of stones. As excavation proceeded it became clear that a larger horizontal exposure was necessary to clarify what was emerging. Square A.2 was therefore enlarged 3.00 m to the east in 1.00 m increments and Square A.4 was laid out to the west of A.2 to expose the western extension of the stone line. The latter Square measured 5.00 m east-west by 6.00 m north-south and was separated from A.2 by a .50 m balk. All balks, after having been drawn and photographed, were removed in the final stages of excavation.

Fig. 5.   Pre-excavation photograph of the stone line which suggested that more excavations at the Amman Airport site might
prove profitable (looking west); it turned out to be the western stone line of the structured rock pile; it was originally thought
that the two stones leading upward from the stone line might be a subsidiary wall line; they actually formed part of the outfall
from the structured rock pile bordered on the right by the edge of a 1966 probe (our Pit A.4:9).

Square C.1 was a long trench 2.00 and 1.00 m wide extending eastward from the southeast corner of the structure for 12.00 m until it intersected a very long (178 m) utility trench running north-south (Figs. 6 and 8). C.1 was meant to tie the stratigraphy of the utility trench with that of the structure. Square D.1 was also a narrow trench (1.00 × 8.00 m) extending to the south of the structure to check for hints of occupation in that direction.

The top of the upper stone of the east jamb to the supposed entrance of the structure was given an arbitrary level of 100.00 m. All levels were measured from that datum. This stone has, unfortunately been removed in the regrettable dismantling of the site (above).

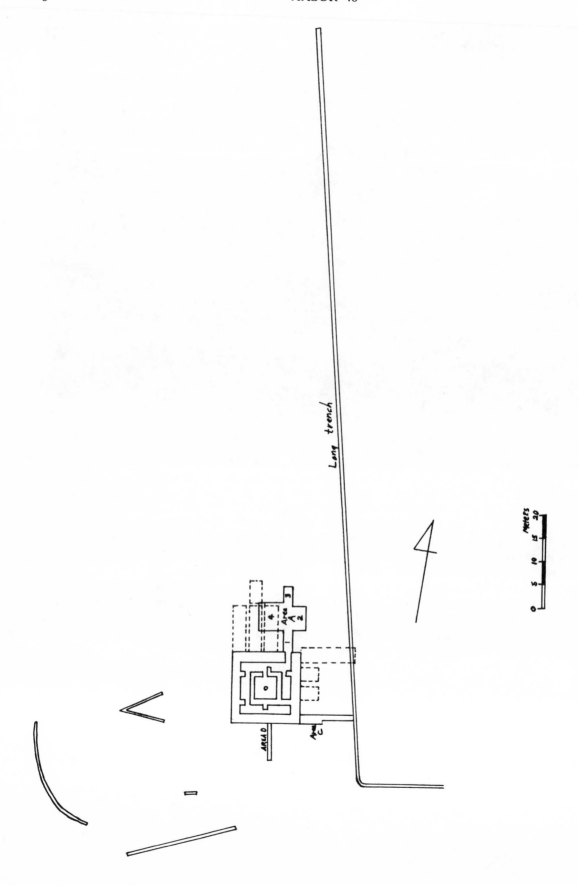

Fig. 6. General plan of the Amman airport site; the 1976 excavation Squares are drawn with solid lines, those of 1966 with dotted lines; to the south, east and north of the structure are shallow utility trenches excavated by the airport construction crews.

Fig. 7. General view of the 1976 Amman airport excavations with balks removed looking south; the north exterior wall of the structure may be seen in the upper part of the photograph; in the upper right and just below the structure's north wall are the outlines of two of the 1966 trenches whose edges are rounded by balk collapse and loess deposition; Square A.1 (extending from the north wall of the structure) has reached virgin soil as has Square A.3 in the left foreground; note the weathered stones within the virgin soil; the structured rock pile lies within Squares A.2 to the left and A.4 to the right; the left edge of the meter stick rests on a stone in the middle of the pile and the west structuring line is just to the right of the meter stick; the western outfall of the structured rock pile has, at the time of this photograph, been removed; the 1966 probe (Pit A.4:9) has been cleaned out to the right of the western structuring line; the western balk line of Squares A.1, 2 and 3 is drawn in Fig. 10.

Fig. 8.   The long utility trench (looking north), 178 m long, stretched north-south
and was situated to the east of the structure (the southeast corner of the structure
is outside the photograph 12 m to the left of the meter stick); Area C joins the
trench in the upper left behind the meter stick; the cement items are airport
construction materials.

Chapter 2
Stratigraphy

LARRY G. HERR

Occupation debris around the Late Bronze Age structure at the Amman Airport was very shallow and extended no further than a few meters from the walls. Indeed, only on the north side did our excavations reveal occupational debris buildup of any kind beneath the topsoil; on the east side in Square C.1 topsoil lay directly over virgin soil; the few artifacts found here were contained totally within the topsoil, thinning out proportionately with increased distance from the structure. On the south side in Square D.1 no artifacts except bone fragments similar to those found in other Areas of the excavation were found. It is unlikely in these sectors that earlier airport construction destroyed significant occupation levels because an extant occupation surface was found north of the structure. Moreover, while the east and south sides of the building could have been set into a low rise (above), the contemporary surface thus being higher than the present topsoil, artifacts were found in the first few centimeters of topsoil in Area C and bones were found in Area D indicating a limited form of ancient debris and material culture deposition. It would thus seem that the building was not heavily used at least on the south and east sides. In antiquity most activity seems to have occurred on the north side where Hennessy projected the structure's entrance (1966a: 156; Fig. 9). For this reason the bulk of our excavation as well as its significant finds were located on the north side of the structure.

Six phases were encountered in the excavation, numbered from topsoil down to virgin soil. They will be discussed in sequential order of deposition from bottom to top. Locus designations include the Area (capital letter), the Square (Arabic numeral following a period) and the locus (Arabic numeral following a colon). A detailed description of each locus is included in the List of Loci.

Phase 6 (Fig. 10)

Layers of virgin soil were found at the bottom of each of our Squares (A.1:7, A.2:4, A.3:3, A.4:7, C.1:4 and D.1:2). In most Squares virgin soil was excavated for a few centimeters so that the lack of occupational debris could be verified. Since this was the layer upon which the Late Bronze Age structure was constructed and upon which the contemporary occupational activities took place (below) a few potsherds were found near its top. This ancient surface was apparently so little used, however, that in no location except A.1 near the structure was the top of virgin soil clearly separable from the layers above it.

About .30 m below the top of virgin soil a very hard-packed soil layer (A.3:3) was encountered, composed of small nari chips cemented together probably by leached calcium carbonate which tends to accumulate in this layer (B2 in soil parlance) in arid regions (Brady 1974: 313). Geologist Frank Koucky observed, however, that these chips could not have been naturally formed, but no artifacts whatsoever were found which could help put this material into an archaeological context. Its presence beneath the virgin soil upon which the Late Bronze Age structure was founded makes it evident that, whatever the layer with the nari chips represented in antiquity, it was not related to the Late Bronze Age materials. Because of the depth of sterile soil on top of the nari chips which accumulated after the latter's deposition, I would suggest that a relatively long period of time elapsed between the deposition of the nari chips and the construction of the Late Bronze Age structure.

Phase 5 (Fig. 10)

Dug into the virgin soil of Phase 6 and sealed by Phase 4 Surface A.1:2 was the foundation trench

Phase 4 Surface. Within this layer were several small patches or lenses of black ash of unknown origin; no outstanding items of material culture were found within these pockets. Seven of the twelve flints found in Square A.1 came from this locus (two more were found on the top of virgin soil [A.1:7] just beneath A.1:3 and probably should be considered part of A.1:3). Layer A.1:6 was a thin (.10 m maximum), patchy layer of fine silt separating A.1:3 below from A.1:5 above; it did not extend any closer to the structure's north wall than .65 m and did not reach any of the balks. Layer A.1:5 was a layer of silt containing many small pebble-sized nari chips, possibly from the preparation of blocks for the structure. Very near the structure it was ca. .20 m thick, but .60 m north of the structure it rose rather sharply over Layer A.1:3 so that it was only .05-.10 m thick. It lay immediately beneath Surface A.1:2 of Phase 4. Although layers A.1:5 and 6 contained more pottery than A.1:3, with, however, few registered indicator sherds, only three flints were found.

These three soil layers illustrate the order and method of fill for the foundation trench. Two interpretive models can account for the data described above as follows. The first model would force a division of Phase 5 into Phases 5A and 5B. Layer A.1:3 may have originally maintained its northern level southward to the wall of the structure. If so, Layers A.1:5 and 6 made up the fill of a second foundation trench excavated into A.1:3 at some point after its deposition, but not necessarily much later. This would indicate a major rebuilding of the structure. The fact that significantly more pottery appeared in Layers A.1:5 and 6 than in A.1:3 would suggest, at first sight, that enough time had elapsed between the deposition of Layer A.1:3 and Layers A.1:5 and 6 for a degree of material culture to accumulate at the site. There are, however, other data which militate against this model. There is no architectural indication whatsoever for two major foundational phases for the exterior walls of the structure. The relatively minor changes which occurred inside the structure would most certainly have not required a second foundation trench (Hennessy 1966a: 157).

The second model would suggest that the builders, after they had dug the foundation trench and constructed at least the first course or two of the walls, began to fill the trench with cobbles and a few boulders easily at hand; soil most likely from the material excavated for the foundation trench (note the indentical Munsell readings for Layer

Fig. 9. Plan of the Amman airport structure based on plans made by the 1966 excavations; in the northeast is a very small entrance; in the middle of the central room is the circular "incense altar" or "column base."

(A.1:9) for the structure. It was a shallow pit (ca. .30 m deep) running along the north wall of the structure; in our excavated area its bottom extended 1.50-1.80 m north of the structure before turning up rather sharply to its lip below Surface A.1:2 of Phase 4.

Three soil layers made up the fill of the foundation trench: Layer A.1:3 was composed of silt with cobbles and a few boulders at or near the bottom except at the west balk where some very small boulders appeared near the top, just below the

A.1:3 and Virgin Soil A.1:7) was then thrown on top of the rocks near the outer edge of the trench. Few items of material culture would have been available at the new site to be included in this material, except for the flint flakes which could have been knapped by a workman during the early stages of the structure's construction before the foundation trench was filled. It is possible that Layer A.1:3 may have been exposed for a short period of time. Layer A.1:6 which might be designated a very soft surface was deposited and may have been exposed for a while during later portions of construction, but more likely, together with Layer A.1:5 above it was simply part of the fill and leveling process preparatory to the laying of the Phase 4 surface. The difference in pottery frequency between layers A.1:3 and A.1:5 and 6 can be explained by the foundational activity which took place inside the structure. Here Hennessy found frequent pockets of burned soil, bones and other various items of material culture. Since all of the activity represented by these soil pockets took place before the second course of building blocks was laid (Hennessy 1966a: 157) a degree of time must have elapsed wherein considerable human activity took place between the earlier stages of the building of the structure and the later stages. If the foundation trench had been partially filled prior to this activity (Layer A.1:3) and then entirely filled after completion of the interior foundation fill, the difference between the pottery frequencies of Layers A.1:3 and A.1:5 and 6 is understandable. The inclusion of probable stonemasons' chips in Layer A.1:5 may indicate that this layer was deposited after a degree of work was accomplished on the stones being prepared for the building. There is, therefore, no necessity to propose two separate, major architectural phases.

Whether the ash pockets with the fill were remains from foundational burnt offerings (Hennessy 1966a: 157; 1970: 307) or simply the remains from workmen's fires sheltered in the trench is impossible to determine. Although Hennessy's ash pockets contained burned bones, ours contained none. Phase 5 should be equated with the first architectural stage designated in the 1966 excavation (Hennessy 1966a: 157).

Phase 4 (Figs. 10 and 11)

Over the debris which filled the Phase 5 foundation trench of the structure and running up to the latter's walls was a very thin (.02-.06 m), soft surface (A.1:2) with a texture of silt, sand and small pebbles and very pale brown (10YR7/4) in color (Figs. 12 and 13). It extended 1.80-2.10 m north of the structure, but was not found at all in Areas C and D on the east and south sides respectively of the structure. Where the surface extended to the north beyond the edge of the structure's foundation trench, it lay directly on virgin soil (A.1:7). When it lensed out, the soil of Phase 3 above it (A.1:4) lay directly on top of virgin soil.

The limited extent of the surface with no stratigraphic or structural reason for its cessation north of the structure, its absence on other sides of the building, its relatively soft consistence and the paucity of occupational debris in general at the site would encourage a conclusion that either the site was inhabited for a only a short period of time or that it was used infrequently at various periods of time; in any case, it is apparent that the site was never intensively occupied.

The structured rock pile (Fig. 11) was the principal find of the 1976 excavation. It had already been partially uncovered by Hennessy's excavation in 1966 (Fig. 1), but very little seems to have been done beyond placing a small probe through its edge (below). Its structuring boulders were the first indication to Geraty and myself that further excavations at the site might be warranted (above— Figs. 4 and 5). This structuring consisted of two north-south lines of unhewn boulders one row wide and one course high laid on top of virgin soil with no mortar (Figs. 14 and 15).

These structuring stone lines were roughly parallel, 4.00 m apart. The line on the west (A.4:4) measured 3.75 m long while the eastern line (A.2:3) measured only 1.50 m long, though the line may have originally been longer to equal the western line. The construction of both lines would seem to have been too irregular and flimsy to have supported walls for a dwelling or other type of building; no east-west stone lines were found, though these may have existed originally.

Between the two structuring lines and not more than .25 m high was an amorphous mass of limestone cobbles mixed with a few small boulders, only one or two approaching the size of the stones making up the structuring lines (Fig. 14). Many of the cobbles were discolored on one side from their usual pinkish and yellowish white to shades of gray as a result of burning; in their present position no uniformity regarding the orientation of the burned sides was found. In the southern part of the rock

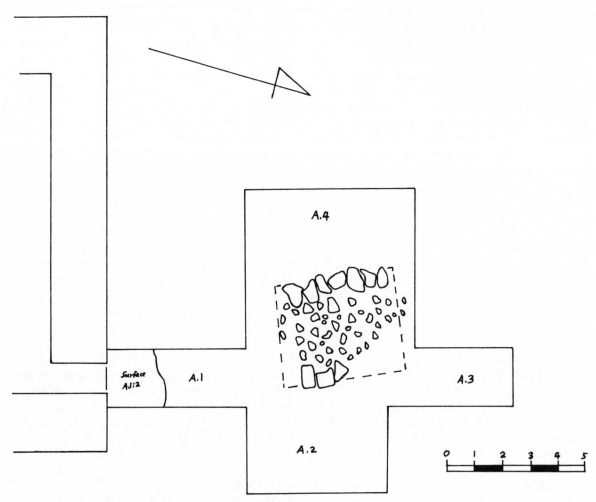

Fig. 11. Plan of Phase 4 remains unearthed in 1976 including the structured rock pile and Surface A.1:2 north of the structure; the numbers correspond to locus numbers discussed in the text.

pile the very hard-packed soil between the rocks contained several small (no larger than .25 × .25 × .05 m) lenses of ashy soil.

While the partially burned stones and the ash pockets could have been imported from elsewhere, the complete lack of other occupational remains near the site (below) would make it difficult to defend such a suggestion. A second model is certainly more realistic: the structured rock pile was constructed at least two or three courses high of field stones and, upon its flat top, activities involving burning took place. When the pile was no longer in use the structuring elements began to decay and, as stones near the edges tumbled out (below), those in the center shifted position resulting in the disorientation of burned sides noted above. Stones with no signs of burning would have originated from the lower levels of the pile. The ash

lenses would be remains from the fires burned on top of the pile.

The soil within the structured rock pile (A.2:3 and part of A.4:4) was found to contain many more pieces of pottery and objects than were found elsewhere in the excavation, even though a relatively minor volume of soil was removed from the stones. Thirteen pieces from different stone vessels were found here. Moreover, the larger number of artifacts found within the Phase 3 rock tumble, which was outside the stone structuring lines (A.2:3 and A.4:2) but which must have originated from the rock pile itself, and the paucity of artifact finds elsewhere outside the structure indicate some connection between the structured rock pile and the pottery and other artifacts. (Note also that the topsoil loci adjacent to or immediately above the rock pile and its debris [A.2:1 and A.4:1] contained

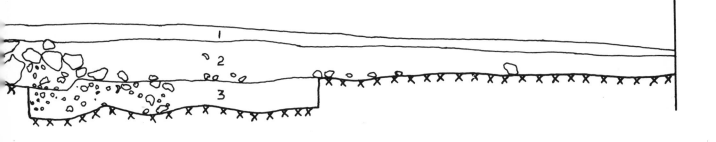

A.3

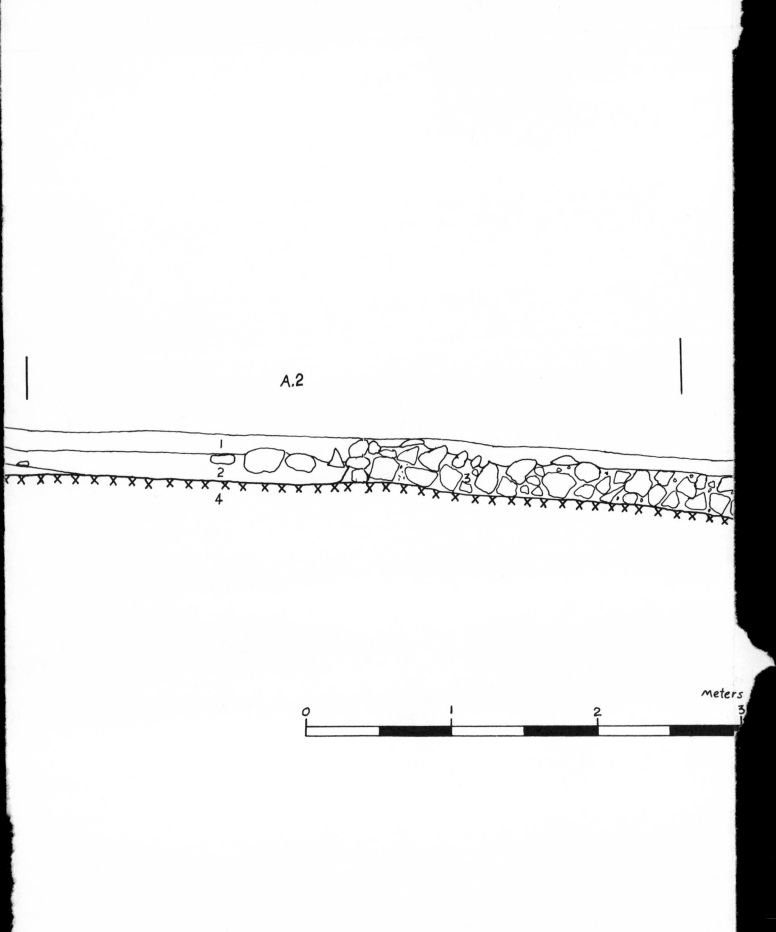

A.2

1
2
4
3

meters

0   1   2   3

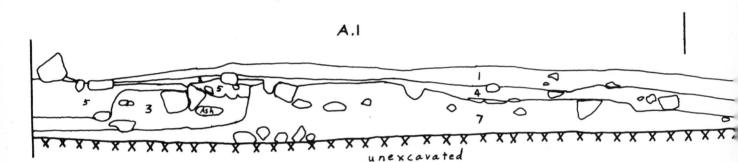

A.1

Fig. 10. The west balk of Squares A.1, 2 and 3; the numbers correspond to locus numbers discussed in the text; Phase 6: A.1:7, A.2:4, A.3:3; Phase 5: A.1:3, 5, 9; Phase 4: A.1:2, A.2:3; Phase 3: A.1:4, A.2:2, A.3:2; Phase 1: A.1:1, A.2:1, A.3:1; nothing of Phase 2 was preserved in this balk.

Fig. 12.   Surface A.1:2 of Phase 4, looking south toward the northern exterior wall of the structure just visible in the upper part of the photograph; the meter stick rests on the patchy, uneven surface.

most of the the other artifact fragments found by our excavation.) No pottery vessels or other artifacts, save the bead and the bronze arrowhead in A.4:2, were found completely preserved.

The objects from the vicinity of the structured rock pile included 10 diorite vessel fragments, 7 gabbro vessel fragments (mostly bowls and platters), 4 travertine vessel fragments, 2 white-limestone vessel fragments, 2 black-limestone vessel fragments, 1 marble vessel fragment, 1 basalt vessel fragment, 1 bead, 1 bronze arrowhead, 1 metal pin, 1 ceramic spindle whorl and a few miscellaneous unidentifiable bronze fragments. Very few other objects were found anywhere else. (Due to the one period nature of the site it is certain that the ancient objects found within stratigraphically later phases were originally contemporary with those in Phase 4. They have therefore been included here.)

There was no observable stratigraphic connection between the Phase 4 surface (A.1:2) near the structure and the structured rock pile in Squares A.2, 3 and 4. However, the stones of the structured rock pile lay directly on virgin soil as did the Phase 4 surface where it extended beyond the foundation trench of the structure while the soil and stones of the Phase 3 debris (below) overlaid the Phase 4 surface and ran up to and partially covered the structured rock pile. This would indicate that the structured rock pile originated prior

to the deposition of the Phase 3 debris. Whether or not it was constructed at the same time as the structure itself thus cannot be proved stratigraphically but it had the same stratigraphic position relative to Phase 3 above and Phase 6 below as the Phase 4 surface. Since there is a complete lack of ceramic and object evidence for another period of occupation at the site, and since the ceramic and object finds within the structured rock pile were of the same typological horizon as those within the Phase 4 and 5 material, it would seem likely that the structured rock pile was contemporaneous with the structure.

Phase 4 should be equated with the post-foundational use of the first, second and third architectural stages found by the 1966 excavation (Hennessy 1966a: 159).

Phase 3 (Figs. 10 and 16)

Partially covering the Phase 4 surface (A.1:2) and running up to and partially over the structured rock pile was a layer of debris composed of light reddish brown loess mixed with pebbles, cobbles and small boulders (A.1:4, A.2:2, A.3:2, A.4:2 = 3 and 12). When the Phase 4 surface lensed out ca. 2.05 m north of the structure, this debris layer was found directly above virgin soil. The portion of the layer closest to the structured rock pile

Fig. 13. Surface A.1:2 of Phase 4, looking north toward the emerging structured rock pile visible behind the meter stick in Square A.2; The surface extended a maximum of ca. 2.00 m north of the structure's northern exterior wall visible at the lower edge of the photograph; the metal stake is a post-1955 fence post.

structuring lines have been preserved than on the north and south where they were not, unless the stones to the north and south were removed at some time in antiquity along with possible east-west structuring lines.

From the above description it would seem that Phase 3 represents the abandonment of both the structure (at least its exterior surface) and the structured rock pile and that the soil was deposited gradually over the centuries as loess while the structured rock pile decayed. The stones "floating" near the top of Layer A.2:2 in Fig. 10 probably fell from the structured rock pile well after abandonment. The top of the Phase 3 soil layer was most likely the topsoil layer encountered by Salih in 1955.

Phase 2 (Fig. 6)

Evidence of Salih's 1955 excavation and Hennessy's 1966 campaign was found only in A.4 and possibly A.1. Several of the latter's trenches were found in A.4, and in A.1 a depression may have been part of Salih's activities (Fig. 1). Locus A.4:9 was a probe within Hennessy's easternmost trench located in the north central part of A.4, barely visible in Fig. 1; it was 1.00×2.00 m and had been backfilled with dump debris (A.4:5 and 8) from the 1966 excavation of the flat paving stones from the interior of the structure (Fig. 17); the cleaned pit is seen in Fig. 7. A few plastic bags were found at the bottom.

Locus A.4:10 was a trench 1.50 m (east-west) $\times$ 1.75 m (north-south) in the south central part of the Square; it was another probe in Hennessy's easternmost trench (Fig. 1: just to the right of the rock pile near the left edge of the photo).

Locus A.4:11 was only 1.00 m wide in the west side of A.4 but it extended farther west outside the Square for about another meter; we had 2.50 m of its north-south length in the northwest quadrant of A.4. It most likely was another probe associated with the middle of Hennessy's three northern trenches. Loci A.4:10 and 11 were not backfilled except by Phase 1 loess and balk collapse.

In the southeast quadrant of A.4 a small lens of debris (A.4:6) just outside the east edge of Hennessy's east trench contained a few modern glass fragments and should probably be interpreted as 1966 (or possibly 1955) dump debris (Fig. 18). It also included partially burned stones like those of Phase 4 suggesting that it originated near the Phase 4 structured rock pile (A.4:2 = 3), perhaps

(A.2:2 and A.4:2) contained many more stones and items of material culture than elsewhere (Fig. 14). The stones were very similar in size and treatment to those found within the rock pile and some had been similarly burned on one side as well.

In Square A.4 Hennessy's excavation had removed almost all of this layer to virgin soil so that rocky debris to the west of the structured rock pile remained only where the 1966 excavation had not probed (A.4:2 = 3). The original rock debris must have been fairly heavy here, similar to that on the east.

The debris layer running up against the structured rock pile on the north (A.3:2 and A.4:12) contained comparatively few stones. Stone deposition on the south also was not heavy. There is no clear explanation why the stone tumble was heavier on the east and west sides where the

Fig. 14. Remains of the structured rock pile as uncovered in 1976 looking west; note the structuring lines above and below the meter stick; the stones outside these lines are probably the result of outfall; at the time this photograph was made a few cobbles had been removed in the lower left; the cobbles ceased entirely just outside the photograph at the bottom; the probe at the right is a probe into virgin soil in Square A.3; lines of the 1966 trenches and probes are also visible near the top; Pit A.4:9 of Phase 2 is visible as a depression above the edge of Square A.4.

from the stones excavated from the probe designated by us as A.4:9.

Phase 1 (Fig. 10)

On the north side of the structure, topsoil (A.1:1, A.2:1, A.3:1, A.4:1) consisted of a distinct layer of loess blown in after the excavation of 1966; it partially filled the project's trenches, blurring the trench lines but not obliterating them (Fig. 7). On the south and east the loess (C.1:1 and D.1:1) was barely more than .02 m deep while at some points in the north, together with the debris from the collapsed balks of the 1966 season, it reached .10 m. As would be expected from such deposits, relatively few artifacts were found, although some had worked their way up from lower levels into the fine, wind-blown soil.

Probably also originating after 1966 (or perhaps near the date of the airport's construction in 1955) were two airport utility trenches, dug from the level of topsoil, which our Area D intersected. D.1:4 was only .15 m deep and .25 m wide and ran

east-west across the width of D.1. Nothing was found within it. D.1:5 was .95 m wide, but its bottom was not reached; it also ran east-west across the width of D.1.

Other Trenches (Fig. 6)

While excavation proceeded there was opportunity to examine several open trenches near the structure which had been recently excavated by the airport construction crews. South and west of the structure were four such trenches, all excavated to a depth of ca. .60 m. In none of these could any signs of occupational debris be seen; the soil profiles consisted of the normal regolithic transition for the region from subsoil to topsoil, indicating an undisturbed state. Certainly no adjacent settlement can be said to have been situated in the sector immediately to the southwest of the structure.

Another similar but much longer trench began southeast of the structure and ran west for 18 m where it turned north for another 160 m. The

Fig. 15.   Remains of the structured rock pile looking north after the outfall has been removed; the western structuring line is just left of the meter stick; the eastern structuring line is made up of the last stones to the right.

Fig. 16.   Plan of the structured rock pile including the outfall; the numbers correspond to locus numbers discussed in the text.

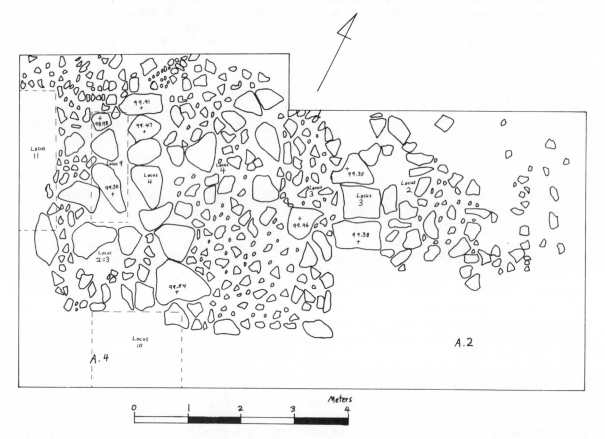

Fig. 17.   Phase 2 Pit A.4:9, a 1966 probe, backfilled with stones from the interior pavement of
the structure, looking south; the meter stick is just outside the pit; the western structuring
line of the rock pile is visible as the left edge of the pit.

southern portion of its north-south extent ran
more-or-less parallel to the east wall of the structure at a distance of ca. 12 m (Fig. 8). Like the
smaller trenches discussed above it consistently
averaged .60 m deep and nothing but virgin soil
could be seen in its profile on either side of the
trench for the first 88 m. From that point (45 m
north of the structure) modern dump, possibly
from earlier airport construction, was all that was
visible in the profile; the modern dump was
characterized by soils of white, pink, and yellow
colors (10YR8/2, 7.5YR8/2, 7.5YR8/4) and contained a few modern objects such as broken glass
bottles and plastic bags. This dump seems to have
been imported to level the ground near the apron
taxiway.

It is thus impossible for an extant settlement
contemporaneous with the Late Bronze Age structure to have existed in its immediate environs on
the north, east, southeast and southwest. The lack
of any observable occupation debris in Area D
would indicate strongly that no settlement existed
in the south as well.

The only sector adjacent to the structure thus
left open for a possible settlement is the northwest
quadrant, which, at the time of our excavations,
was covered with a large mound of dirt placed
there by construction crews. However, Hennessy's
trenches, the western-most of which proceeded
north from the northwest corner of the structure,
encountered no occupational materials. The fact
that material culture finds were made on all sides

Fig. 18.   South balk of Square A.4; the numbers correspond to locus numbers discussed in the text.

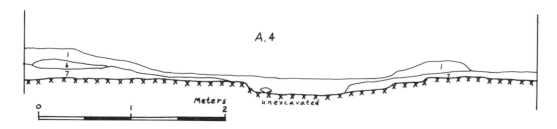

of the structure would suggest that airport construction did not disturb the original top-soil enough to obliterate any architectural remains. It is thus highly unlikely that a contemporary settlement existed contiguous to the Late Bronze Age structure.

Interpretation of the Material Culture Finds

Pottery

Of interest concerning the function of the site is the repertoire of local pottery forms found in 1976. Although the pottery is described and illustrated in detail in Kafafi's paper below, several points should be mentioned here. Bowls were very frequent and appeared in several rim types; jugs were almost as frequent, but were found in a more limited range of rim types; lamps were fairly frequent, certainly more frequent than is usually the case in normal domestic debris. Kraters, however, seem to have been relatively rare, and then only uncertainly ascribed as kraters because most seem to be an otherwise relatively rare narrow-mouthed type; only one certain cooking-pot rim was found; no jar bases whatsoever and no certain jar rims were uncovered; although classified as jugs, nos. 77, 78 and 80 could be flasks (with shoulder handles); and finally, no examples of juglets were unearthed. Thus it should be apparent that the assemblage is not typically domestic. Moreover, the high frequency of imported ceramic forms found at the site in previous excavations would tend to confirm such a conclusion. The ceramic repertoire, therefore, seems to imply some kind of specialized function for the site.

While earlier excavations had found a considerable quantity of imported pottery (especially Mycenaean wares), our excavation found only 14 very small fragments which were most likely imported and nine others which were, judging by the crude ware, probably local imitations of Mycenaean forms. Four small fragments seem to have been Cypriot in origin incuding three probable base-ring fragments and one milk-bowl fragment. All of the above fragments were body sherds and none were large enough to display a coherent pattern of form or decoration. Because this paltry material cannot extend the study already made on the imported pottery by Hankey (1974a) these sherds have not been published. All attempts to have neutron activation studies on the Mycenaean sherds failed for various reasons. A spectroscopic study made on the Mycenaean sherds by Peter Hare of the Carnegie Institution in Washington, D. C. led to "indeterminate conclusions."

Hankey calls attention to the unusually broad chronological range of Mycenaean pottery for a site so distant from the sea and the normal centers of international trade (1974a: 142). She notes that vessels from Mycenaean II A to III B have been found in similar quantities only at large and important centers of trade, such as Hazor, Gezer, Lachish and Gaza. Such observations, along with the imbalance of types in the local assemblage, serve to emphasize the special nature and function of the site.

The relatively great quantity of imported Aegean vessels found *inside* the structure (Hankey 1974a) compared with the infrequency and fragmentary nature of such finds *outside* the structure indicates that the structure must have served as a repository for these highly valuable imports. Whether they were kept for trading purposes or were used at the site ceremonially is unknown. At any rate, one of the reasons for the building's thick walls may have been to provide protection from theft and pillage for these valuable items.

The frequent lamp finds, virtually all from near the structured rock pile, would indicate a specialized site function, as well. Lamps could be used for outdoor ceremonies at night when there was little or no wind as is often the case in this region. Their dispersal around the structured rock pile would suggest some use in conjunction with its function (below).

It should also be noted that the copious presence of bowls and jugs at a specialized non-domestic site, apparently several kilometers distant from the nearest settlement (below), could be either an important functional indicator or could mean nothing more than a "picnic" style of sustenance when treks to the site, for whatever reason, took place. Since no water source is to be found at the site and the Wadi Zerqa is about a kilometer away, water would have to be transported, possibly in jugs (the absence of flasks is however, significant). Trips to the isolated site may have involved a whole day or more; food would thus have to be brought as well, possibly in bowls. For a different, more likely model see "Interpretations and Implications" below.

After the 1955 excavations Harding dated the site to the Late Bronze Age (without being more specific) on the basis of the Mycenaean pottery discovered (Harding 1958: 10-12). Following the 1966 campaign Hennessy refined that date to the Late Bronze II period (ca. 1400 through the 13th century B.C., Hennessy 1966a: 162). Later he narrowed the chronological range to include the period from the early 14th century to the late 13th century B.C. (Hennessy 1970: 309). Hankey's study of the Mycenaean pottery from the 1955 and 1966 excavations emphasized a Mycenaean III B I sherd found in the foundational fill of the building (Hankey 1974a: 133) which, following her chronological scheme for Mycenaean pottery in Palestine (Hankey 1974a: 140), would be the Late Bronze IIB period (13th century B.C.). Although her study does not explicitly state it, it would seem the she would thus suggest that the date of the construction of the site should have been within the 13th century. Since no Mycenaean III C sherds were found, she would imply that the site ceased to function before the Iron I period which began ca. 1200 B.C. (Hankey 1974a: 132). Because much of the Aegean pottery is Mycenaean III A 2 and earlier (Hankey 1974a: 136) she suggests that these imported vessels were already antiques when they were stored at the Amman site (Hankey 1974a: 142), some as old as 200 years: Mycenean II A pottery was apparently found above the latest floor. Thus the imported pottery, while including a wide chronological range of forms, points to a rather narrow date for the structure wholly within the 13th century B.C., when the stratigraphic data is taken into consideration.

The local ceramic materials excavated in 1955 have apparently been lost (Hennessy 1966a: 155) and the 1966 materials have yet to be published. Although it is difficult to determine the beginning date for the 1976 local pottery (the one indicator sherd [no. 23] found in the foundation trench does not lend itself to close chronological scrutiny), the latest forms are beginning to reflect the transition from the LBII to the Iron I horizons. The "hammer" rim on the large shallow bowl (no. 24) and the vertical walls on bowls 50-57 reflect an Iron I tendency. Bowls with high carination (nos. 3, 4, 42-45) are very similar to forms from Gezer Field II Stratum 13, also from the very end of the LB period (Dever. et. al. 1974: 49). To be noted is the rarity of the typical MB/LB carinated bowl forms, although the slight "S" shape carinated bowls (nos. 4, 56, 57) may represent forms in transition from the MB/LB tradition to the Iron I forms. The one sherd that is possibly in the

MB/LB tradition (no. 5) does not go far enough down the profile to display the carination; it could be simply a typical LB platter bowl with the interior rim slightly thickened. Lamp rims which are strongly flanged also encourage a date late in the LB period (Dever et. al. 1970: 24).

Very little can be said about the jugs except that the preponderance of wide-mouthed forms and the lack of trefoil rims may turn out to be significant, possibly more in terms of geography than chronology.

Hankey notes the remarkable rarity of imported Cypriot wares at the site (1974a: 142); she could count only 50 sherds. She notes that at most Palestinian sites where Mycenaean pottery is frequent, the Mycenaean sherds are rare relative to Cypriot imports but the opposite is true at the Amman site. The key to this enigmatic situation is two-fold. First, whereas Mycenaean pottery seems to have been valued as antiques and *objets d'arts* by the people using the Amman site, the more common Cypriot pottery had no such value and therefore was not preserved anachronistically like the Mycenaean wares. Second, there is a growing consensus that Cypriot imports did not extend beyond the 14th century B.C. in Egypt (Merrillees 1968: 202). The importation of Cypriot wares may have already been on the decline, or indeed had already ceased, when the Amman site was begun. The 13th century date for the site would thus fit in well with the lack of Cypriot imports at the site.

The observations made above, especially on the bowl types, along with the general lack of painted sherds and the rarity of Cypriot imports would point to a period near the end of LBIIB for the *floruit* of the site. Most of the forms are paralleled in Gezer Field II Stratum 13, Megiddo VII B and Hazor I A (Lower City). The date of the assemblage should thus be attributed to the 13th century B.C., with its main *floruit* toward the end of that century.

Non-ceramic Artifacts

Most artifacts other than pottery from the 1976 excavations were made of stone, although a few bronze artifacts and a ceramic disk were found. Since these items are described and illustrated in a separate paper below, their significance will simply be summarized here.

Whereas platters and bowls of magmatic stone (basalt, gabbro and diorite) can be considered domestic artifacts, the large quantity of such pieces from one building is not typical of domestic dwellings. Expensive, heavy stone vessels were unlikely to be used in such quantity by a single domestic establishment: The 1955 excavation alone found between 280 and 290 fragments of stone vessels, both local and imported (Hankey 1974b: 161). It should also be noted that, like the pottery, a large proportion of these artifacts were imported primarily from Egypt and, to a lesser extent, Crete (Hankey 1974b: 163-64). Such a proportion of imported items has never been found in a single domestic dwelling in the Late Bronze Age.

The intended use of the most frequent stone vessels found in 1976, the magmatic stone platters and bowls, is enigmatic, but a few suggestions, which also relate to the function of the structured rock pile, may be put forward. Within and around the structured rock pile there was a much larger percentage of magmatic stone platters and bowls in the overall stone artifact corpus than was the case inside and immediately outside the structure. Of the stone objects found in 1976 when excavations centered around the structured rock pile 59% were magmatic stone platters and bowls, while only 8% of the stone vessels published from the 1955 and 1966 expeditions, when excavations concentrated on the structure itself, were similar types (Hankey 1974b). (Only the 1966 excavation touched a corner of the structured rock pile; it is tempting to speculate that some of the magmatic stone vessels published by Hankey came from that region; note that some of the stone objects were burned [Hankey 1974b: 172] and that only two of them came from inside the structure [Hankey 1974b: 177].)

In the ceremonial model for the site, the platters could have been used to hold votive collections of grain during rituals performed there, especially in the vicinity of the structured rock pile. Although the function of the structured rock pile will be discussed below, it may be noted at this point that the burned stones within the pile indicate burning activities of some kind. Some of the stone platters and bowls may have been placed close to or indeed within, these fires causing them to shatter with the heat. This would account for the comparatively large quantity of these vessels in and around the structured rock pile while other forms were relatively infrequent. The fact that very few of the fragments came from the same vessel would indicate, moreover, that the practitioners of the cere-

monies intended to keep a clean burning area for at least some attempt seems to have been made to clear the area of the broken vessels. An alternate explanation for the presence of these fragments is less likely: the fragments could have been mixed with stones used for the structured rock pile before it was constructed; Hennessy's two phases for the structure could fit in with this, if the structured rock pile is conceived as having been constructed from materials taken from the first phase. However, one should then expect a higher proportion of other stone vessel types within the assemblage and there is no indication that the structure was destroyed or dismantled at the end of its first phase.

Although many flints were found, most were simply waste flakes (see Miller's paper below for details). No certain tools were discovered. This lack of evidence for agriculture associated with the site fits in well with the non-domestic ceramic and stone vessel repertoires. Of interest is the observation noted above with the discussion of Phase 5 that nine of the twelve flints in Square A.1 came from the lower levels of the foundation trench. These flints, can, therefore, have played no role in the utilization of the site; rather, they are to be associated only with the early activities of the construction of the structure.

The bronze arrowhead found in 1976, the bronze weapons, and the quantities of beads and gold jewelry found in earlier seasons (Hankey 1974a: 131) likewise do not fit a typical domestic site. Some of the stone platters could be mortars, but the appearance of only one grinder would tend to suggest that the remaining pieces were not, for the most part, intended to grind grain. The nonceramic artifacts thus lead to the same conclusion as the pottery: the site performed some kind of specialized non-domestic function.

Bone Remains

Animal Bones. The quickly identifiable animal bones found during the 1976 excavation were examined by Joachim Boessneck who was in Amman at the time of our excavations working on the Hesban animal bone material. From our total bone collection (2.090 kg.) he separated the immediately apparent animal bones (.080 kg.) observing to us that a much more detailed analysis would probably find a few others in the hundreds of small fragments making up the collection (see Little's paper below).

Whereas many of the human bones showed signs of burning almost none of the animal bones did. Sheep-goat bones were, as usual, in the majority, though there was one cattle tooth, evidence of one small rodent and a bird, possibly a pigeon or a dove. The animal bones found by Little's detailed study are separate from these, but tend to show similar types, that is, sheep-goat and possible bird.

Of note were the disproportionately large quantity of sheep-goat astragali which, Boessneck pointed out, played an important part in ancient divination. These astragali may have been the only animal bones found in 1976 which clearly suggest a human connection. The other bones may have been unassociated with the Late Bronze Age use of the site; because of the shallow nature of the excavations these bones could even be modern.

Human bones. Of much more interest were the large quantities of human bones (total: 1,127) found in a high degree of fragmentation (the total weighed only 2.010 kg.); only one bone was complete. These bones were found in the topsoil of Areas C and D, and in every soil locus of Area A, but they were especially frequent around the structured rock pile. None of the bones were in any way articulated.

Of particular importance were the signs of burning exhibited by many if not most of the bones; even many of the bones described by Little as "tan" in color were not quite the usual color of unburned bones although burning may not necessarily result in discoloration. This slight discoloration and the extreme fragmentation of all of the bones (some still intact fracture lines) suggest that the human bones were remnants from bodies which had been burned. Of interest was the tendency for the bones of the upper trunk and head to show heavy signs of burning, whereas the extremities showed little, if any, such signs. Apparently, when the bodies were burned, the upper trunk and head were deemed the most important parts for burning. It would also imply that the bones were articulated when burned from which the conclusion may be inferred that the burning took place relatively soon after death, at least prior to the complete decay of the flesh; primary burial would therefore not have previously occurred, since bones from such burials would have been burned in a heap and thus would have shown indiscriminate signs of burning on all bones. This would further indicate that the persons whose bodies were burned most probably did not die a long distance from the site. At times, relatively unburned bones may be found from the head and upper trunk which would mean that the fire was probably hot enough to burn the flesh but not hot enough to discolor the bones significantly. Minimal fires may therefore be postulated.

William H. Shea has pointed out to me (in a personal communication dated June 1, 1980) that, for the upper vertebrae to be burned to the extent that some seem to have been, some preparation of the corpse for burning may have been done. While skull bones could be easily burned through the thin skin of the scalp, the thick paravertebral muscles running down the length of the spine would allow signs of burning to be visible on the tips of the vertebrae only (unless the fire reached the temperature of an incinerator) if no corpse preparation had occurred.

The ceramic and artifact remains show that the site had a specialized function in antiquity; the bones may be considered a major indication of what that function was. Quantities of burned bones usually mean one of three things: human sacrifice (Hennessy 1970: 307); cremation; or local accidental burning. Because of the bone quantities and the wide dispersal of the bones the last alternative can most certainly be rejected. Moreover, since virtually none of the human bones could be identified as infant bones and since most clearly-documented human sacrifices involved infants (below) it would seem that at least part of the function for the site was to provide for and to perform cremation rites for persons who had died nearby. The disarticulated, random distribution of the fragments may thus be accounted for. Indeed, the fragments appeared as if they were the small, unseen pieces left over from a pyre where bodies were burned when the bones and ashes were gathered for disposal. The presence of human bones on all sides of the structure in spite of the rarity of artifacts in Area C and their complete non-existence in Area D may indicate that the remains of burned corpses were either inhumed near the foundations of the structure (Hennessy 1966: 357) or simply scattered to the winds about the building.

Seeds

Soil samples from every locus were floated for seed retrieval to aid our goal of reconstructing the Late Bronze ecosystem of the region. The samples were analyzed by Patricia Crawford, who had been working with the flotation materials of the Hesban excavations. She found no seeds whatsoever, though several samples contained a great quantity of grass root hairs, to be expected in shallow excavations. Some of the samples had small, modern beetles; none had bones, shells or any other carbonized material of any kind. Although she was unaware of the stratigraphy of the site, she suggested in a letter to me that this could indicate a lack of any significant quantity of archeological remains.

Pollen

The excavations had begun with high hopes of obtaining a significant pollen fraction to aid in the reconstruction of the Late Bronze Age ecosystem of the region. However, because the excavations were so shallow and because of the large quantity of modern organic debris found in the flotation samples, it was decided that we could not be certain that the pollen samples taken were positively clean of modern material. No samples were therefore considered.

Interpretations and Implications

Settlement Patterns

The 1976 excavations did not have time to send out an archeological survey into the region around the airport. However, no previous surveys have found contemporary materials any closer to the Amman airport than Amman itself, where a few Late Bronze Age remains have recently been found (Bennett 1978: 8).

Until the 1970's Glueck's conclusion that there was virtually no settled occupation in Transjordan throughout the Middle and Late Bronze Ages was more-or-less normative in archeological circles. However, in the last several years, more detailed surveys have discovered a growing number of sites with LB remains (see, for example, Miller 1980: 51); it now appears that, while not heavily populated, most of Transjordan had enough settlements to be considered at least sparsely settled. In terms of overall settlement patterns, therefore, the Amman airport structure no longer seems quite the unique site that it initially was thought to be.

However, the 1976 excavations confirmed earlier reports that the site was utterly isolated from other contiguous or nearby buildings. The shallow occupational debris outside the structure, its complete disappearance within a few meters of the structure

and the smooth transition from virgin soil to topsoil with no occupational debris in the profile of nearby airport construction trenches indicate the isolation of the site. There can be no doubt any longer that the site was completely isolated from any kind of immdeiately contiguous, contemporary site.

Hennessey's assumption (1970: 307) that an associated settlement existed 300 m to the east beneath the runways is inexplicable until further evidence is published. A distance of 300 m to the east of the structure would put one at least 100 m beyond the edge of the farthest runway. A casual investigation in this region by our team revealed no remains whatsoever but this would not deny the existence of a small site under the present runways (if the site were larger than 50 m in diameter, however, it would be visible on either side of the runway and thus investigable). However, it is questionable that a very small site alone would have been able to support economically and functionally such a structure as the Amman airport building.

Function of the Structured Rock Pile

It should again be stated that there is no stratigraphic proof that the structure and the structured rock pile were utilized contemporaneously. The fact that both were founded atop virgin soil is stratigraphically meaningless at a shallow, lightly-used site. More meaningful, however, is the fact that the Phase 3 post-abandonment debris clearly post-dated both the structure and the structured rock pile. Moreover, the pottery and other artifacts found within and around the structured rock pile match perfectly the finds found within and around the structure, though to which of the structure's three phases (Hennessy 1966b: 357) the structured rock pile may belong cannot be ascertained.

A structured rock pile 7.5 m distant from the entrance of a structure commonly identified as a temple immediately suggests the model of an exterior (courtyard) altar. Add to this the fact that many of the stones found within and around the structured rock pile showed signs of burning on one side with the presence of frequent ash pockets on the south side of the pile and the model becomes more compelling. Although all four sides of the structured rock pile cannot be certainly defined, its dimensions were at least 3.75 m (N-S) by 4.00 m (E-W). It is possible that at least part of the northward extension of the west alignment of stones beyond the northern termination of the eastern line (Fig. 11) could have been part of a stairway. No positive indications were present to suggest such an interpretation however.

The prevailing winds in the valley where the site is situated consistently come from either the east or the west. It is for this reason that the airport runway is oriented east-west. If the structured rock pile was an altar of some kind with smoky fires burning on it, its situation to the north side of the pile is explainable: The wind would keep the smoke away from the building.

It is possible to become more specific about the function of this altar. If bloody sacrifices were offered there, the type of sacrifice should be apparent from an analysis of the burned bones found in the immediate area. Interestingly enough, 96% (1,117 in number) of the bones found in 1976 were human, many of which showed signs of varying degrees of burning. The finds from the 1966 season must have been similar because Hennessy has concluded (1970: 307) that worshipers at the temple practiced a cult of human sacrifice. If so, it would be the first such cult center found in the Levant that I know of.

One problem with such an interpretation is that human sacrifices were usually infants or very small children as was the case in the later Phoenician western colonies. Biblical references to the rite as ordinarily practiced also seem to limit the victims to children, although this is not specifically stated. One or two cases may have included older children (Ju. 11:34-40 and 2 Kings 3:27), but these stories may have been included in the biblical record precisely because they were exceptional. Green's discussion of human sacrifice (1975) includes many adult examples, but it is never clear whether these are burials strictly from human sacrifices or simply special or ritual burials resulting from deaths due to other means. A quick perusal of Robert M. Little's report of the human bones found in 1976 (below) shows that very few of the bones could have been from pre-adolescents and virtually none from infants.

The only other model that could fit such quantities of burned adult human bones found in 1966 and 1976 with a structured rock pile is that of cremation. In this model, the structured rock pile would not be an altar but a pyre. Unfortunately, no other cremation pyres that I know of have been found in the Ancient Near East which may be used for comparative purposes.

If the head was placed toward the south, one would then expect the heaviest accumulation of ashes to have been deposited on that side and perhaps to have been removed in that direction. Since several pockets of ash were found at the southern edge of the rock pile, this may very well have been the case. Since, moreover, cremation has a funerary aspect about it, it is very plausible that at least some grave goods or offerings were placed on the pyre while cremation was in process. This may account for the large number of broken stone vessels found within and near the rock pile; they may have contained grain or other offerings burned at the same time as the body was being cremated. The fact that these vessels tended to be platters and bowls made of magmatic stone, which would withstand heat variables better than vessels made from other stone materials, would fit such a ritual use.

Function of the site

Before setting forth arguments for the function of the site suggested by our excavation a review of previous interpretations will be instructive. Following the prompt excavations by M. Salih in 1955 G. L. Harding suggested that the building was a temple because of its rich collection of imported pottery and its square plan which he thought was too symetrical for a profane function; he further noted that it was evidence for settlements during the Late Bronze Age in Transjordan (Harding 1956; 1958).

Most writers have followed Harding's interpretation and have sometimes added strengthening arguments. G. R. H. Wright called attention to similar square temples of the Nabataeans in the Hauran (1st and 2nd centuries A.D.) as well as to the "fire temples" from Achaemenid Persia (G. R. H. Wright 1966; 1968). Although he notes the significant chronological gap between these structures and the Late Bronze Age Amman airport building, he suggested that the Amman plan served as a proto-type of the square-plan idea for both the Achaemenid and Nabataean square temples. He noted that the architectural concept of the square had sacral connotations, especially among the Semites, and gave the Meccan Kaaba and the Biblical Most Holy Place as examples (1966: 355). For a more ancient example he pointed out the similarity of the plan of the Amman building with that of a structure excavated by the Germans at the foot of Mt. Gerizim and identified by both Welter and Sellin as a temple (1966: 356; Fig. 19) because of certain ritual objects found there, such as

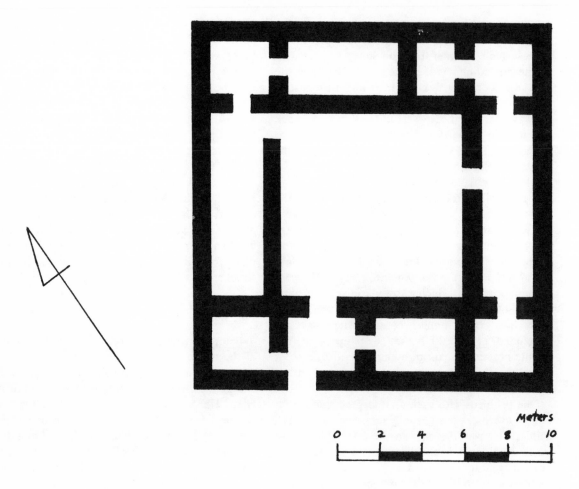

Fig. 19.   Plan of the Tananir site based on plans of the 1968 ASOR excavations.

incense stands, a stone idol, a "fetish," and a model of a phallus (1968: 11).

After his excavations in 1966 Hennessy considered the temple function confirmed (1966: 157) and was followed by G. R. H. Wright in a second discussion of the Amman building (1968: 13). Hennessy noted that, in the earliest phase of the building, the large foundation trench was filled with soil containing pockets of burned clay, ashes and bone, presumably dedicatory offerings as construction work progressed (1966: 157). In this "dedicatory fill" were abundant small objects: 40 small gold objects, jewelry in silver and bronze, beads "by the hundreds," scarabs, cylinder seals, bone and ivory pieces and bronze weapons; pottery was very rare. On the subsequent surface there was ample evidence for small, isolated fires, many

bones (animal, bird and human) and many small finds (1966: 159). The great quantities of burned bones and other evidence for frequent fires suggested to Hennessy that some form of a fire cult was practiced at the site (1966: 161). Later analysis of the human bones seemed to indicate that it was only children which had been burned (Hennessy 1970: 307) leading to the suggestion that the cult practiced at the site involved child sacrifice. He called attention to a cylindrical bead in onyx with a four-line cuneiform inscription from the Kassite period which also seems to depict something like human sacrifice and noted that the story of Jephthah in Judges 11 and 12, which involved human sacrifice, took place in this region (this information seems to have come from a study by M. Ottosson 1980: 103-104 [thanks to Joe Callaway for calling this to my attention]). For the problems with such a view see above. Hennessy's interpretation is followed with little discussion by Hankey in her publication of the Aegean pottery and the stone objects (1974a: 131).

A joint article by E. F. Campbell and G. E. Wright agreed with the temple interpretation (1969: 109) and identified the practitioners of the cult with an unknown league of nomad or semi-nomad tribes who used the structure in a similar fashion as the early Israelite tribes used Shiloh (1969: 111). They noted the association of Shechem with covenent ideologies and suggested that the Gerizim building (now called Tananir), and therefore its parallel at Amman, was used for purposes of league covenants. They suggested that the central pillars of both structures were bases for *massebot* commemorating and celebrating these covenants (1969: 111).

Although R. G. Boling did not discuss the function of the Amman building in either his preliminary report (1969) or his final report of the American excavations at Tananir (1975) except in passing, he seems to side with a religious interpretation for the Tananir building (1975: 56). He cites ashy foundation debris containing a copper needle and an alabaster vase and large quantities of "under-sized" bowls similar to types found in the Balata temple area (compare 1969: 101 with 1975: 54). Boling suggests these may have been used in religious festivals. Because he seems to support the comparison of the Tananir building with the Amman structure (1969: 94) he would probably also supply a religious interpretation for the Amman structure.

In discussing a building in Area F at Hazor dated to the Late Bronze I period with a plan apparently similar to the Amman structure, Yadin accepted the interpretation of Campbell and Wright, even suggesting nomadic roots for the Hazor building (Yadin 1972: 98-100).

Although many scholars have expressed doubts about the religious function of the Amman site, very few have done so in print. V. Fritz (1971) clearly demonstrated the lack of proof supporting the identification of the building as a temple. He maintained that the objects were not typical of temples; square temple plans are not found in Palestine during the 2nd and 3rd millenia B.C. and G. R. H. Wright's comparison with Nabatean and Achaemenid temples was far-fetched because of the chronological gap. He disagreed with Campbell's and Wright's conclusion that nomads used

the site because of the rich finds and the very strong construction of the building which do not reflect nomadic involvement. He maintained that the central "altar" was really a column base and that the ash remains there were carbonized leftovers from the wooden column; if this was not an altar, argued Fritz, then the building lacked an altar and was not necessarily a temple. He further noted that the plans of the Tananir and Amman buildings cannot really be compared because of a basic difference in room communication: the side rooms at Tananir opened into the central court much like a domestic dwelling while at Amman the central room was closed from the side rooms and so was not a court but an "inner room" (Fig. 9). Because of the strong walls and the careful construction techniques used on the building, Fritz proposed that the building was a tower similar to those found around Amman during the Iron Age and the Roman period. He suggested that the square plan and the isolation of the site fit this model. He made nothing of the extraordinary finds.

Fritz's objections to the temple interpretation are certainly cogent; when a sacred interpretation cannot be proven, it is best to look for a secular, more mundane function (Fritz 1971: 151). But an interpretation of the building as a tower in no way accounts for the great quantities of imported pottery, stone objects and other rich finds, nor does it account for the curious pockets of ash and burned bones in the foundation layer. Moreover, if a tower had been inhabited in antiquity one would expect more of an exterior surface than was found both by Hennessy's excavation (1966: 159) and ours (above).

However, Fritz's basic objections to a temple interpretation still stand. Two may be added: First, the fact that the "dedicatory fill" needed to be reexcavated to give a foundation to the circular stones in the central chamber may indicate that the circular stones were originally intended to support a considerable weight; structurally, an incense altar would not need a significant foundation. Second, the Kassite cylinder seal possibly depicting human sacrifice cannot be automatically assumed to be relevant to the function of the Amman site. From this review of the literature it should be clear that the commonly accepted temple interpretation of the building is not certain.

It was shown above that the ceramic and artifact repertoires of the Amman airport site represent some kind of specialized non-domestic function.

With the discovery of a pyre for cremation just outside the building (above) it is possible to suggest that the specialized function of the site was connected in some way with funerary ceremonies; the obvious model would be that of a mortuary institution. Those utilizing the site for mortuary purposes need not have practiced cremation exclusively; other ceremonies and/or rituals connected with various funerary procedures may have been conducted inside and/or around the building (Hennessy's "altar" [1966b: 358] may have been used as an incense altar for such purposes).

Connected with a mortuary institution would have been specialized, ritual utensils, used either during the mortuary ceremonies or supplied for use as tomb furnishings. The structure thus may very well have been a repository for tomb furnishings supplied to the bereaved family at the time of burial. (Note Hankey's observation that some of the finds from a Late Bronze Age tomb at Sahab [Dajani 1970] are identical to those found at the airport site [1974a: 131] and that in Mycenae, some of the forms found at Amman were made specifically for funerary uses [1974a: 139].) Common, everyday tomb items need not have been reposited within the building, whose thick walls and narrow entrance would have served admirably to thwart the ambitions of thieves and raiding tribesmen from access to the expensive imported items connected with mortuary and burial practices. (The Mycenaean vessels and fine stone vessels found outside the structure seem to have come from interior debris scraped out by the bulldozers [Hankey 1974a: 139].) It should be noted that Mycenaean vessels, bronze weapons, beads, gold jewelry and imported stone vessels, while possible at ordinary temple sites and found only rarely in domestic dwellings, are, however, typical tomb furnishings, especially of the more well-to-do tombs dating to this period. Moreover, when local pottery is used for burial accoutrements, the forms frequently found at the airport site such as bowls, jugs, lamps, and, more rarely, kraters are typical of such tomb pottery; on the other hand, infrequent forms at our site, such as storejars and, to a lesser extent, cooking pots and juglets, are often not typical tomb items. (Compare the finds in Tomb C at Sahab [Dajani 1970: 29-34]; the LB1 tomb at Kataret es-Samra [Leonard 1979: 53-65]; the LB tombs at Jericho [Kenyon 1960: 1965], Beth Shan [Oren 1973] Megiddo [Guy and Engberg 1938],

Lachish [Tufnell 1958], Ajjul [Tufnell 1962] and Dan [Biran 1974]. The 13th century tombs at Deir el-Balah are associated with storejars, but the burials are exceptional on almost every other score as well [T. Dothan 1979].) Although the Sahab finds included a multitude of flasks which were rare, if present at all, at the airport site, it should be noted that the occurrence of flasks in tombs is irregular. A mortuary function for the site thus admirably fits the pottery, artifacts and bones.

This conclusion is confirmed by the large cylindrical onyx bead from the Kassite period referred to above (p. 45). The four-line inscription in cuneiform mentions a certain daughter of Sappitu, handmaid of Marduk, who seems to have been concerned prominently with wakes and lamentations (Ottosson 1980: 103-104). While Ottosson and Hennessy (1970: 308-309) use this information to support their human sacrifice interpretation for the site, it would fit even more aptly the mortuary function suggested here.

The bone data, which represent at least two individuals and probably more, would suggest that the site was not dedicated to the funerary remains of one person only, but rather that it was used for funerary services by at least part of a general population. Other evidences for the multiple utilization of the site (scattered burned bones, charred stones in the pyre, the used "incense altar," burned pockets in the foundation fill [burials of cremated remains?] and evidence of tomb furnishings stored within the building probably for future supply) would support a similar conclusion.

Such a function can explain the isolation of the site, since mortuary ceremonies most likely were traditionally carried on outside the settlement and, more specifically, smoke from cremation fires may have been considered just as objectionable to society then as it is today. This function does not, however, explain the *extent* of its isolation. So far, the closest known settlement during the Late Bronze period was Amman, some four or five kilometers distant, where recent LB remains have been found (above). Although such a mortuary may have purposely been placed beyond the agricultural territories contiguous to the settlement, it cannot be assumed that the airport building was constructed solely for the use of the settlement at Amman.

However, from the bone data, it would appear that at least some of the individuals whose bodies were cremated at the site died not too far distant from the site. The identification of the heavily burned bones originating from parts of the head and upper trunk implies articulation of the body during the burning process; disarticulated bones would not display such selected burning. This would indicate that primary burial had not occurred and that the individuals had died sufficiently close to the site for the bodies to be transported there before offensive decay had set in. The site thus served, at least in part, some nearby group, whether sedentary or transhumant. The fortified nature of the construction and the indications that it served as a repository for expensive funerary goods would lean toward a sedentary constituency, since transhumant groups alone would be unlikely to support or use such an institution to an extent that would make it profitable.

Unfortunately, no tombs have as yet been discovered in the vicinity, though the burned bones and ash pockets discussed by Hennessy (1966a: 157; 1968: 357-358; 1970: 307) may not have been dedicatory foundation burials, but cremated burials inhumed during the course of the building's first stage of existence. However, simply because tombs have not yet been found does not mean they did not exist. Recently, several burial caves with Late Bronze Age remains have been found north of Amman in the Beqa valley (McGovern 1979: 10) about 750 m from a group of structures, one of which is very similar architecturally to the Amman airport building. Near the LB I square structure in Area F at Hazor an LB I tomb was found suggesting a possible similar function for that building (Yadin 1972: 96), although perhaps lacking cremation (note its situation *inside* the city). It is possible that tombs associated with the use of the airport mortuary could be found in the hills to the south of the site which border the valley or to the north along the steep banks of the Wadi Zerqa. In any case, a mortuary need not be situated immediately adjacent to its burial ground. The other site commonly compared with the Amman Airport building, Tananir, (G. H. R. Wright 1966; Campbell and Wright 1969), has no known tombs associated with it (Boling 1975), and its function may have been unrelated to funerary rites. Cremated remains, of course, need not be inhumed, but could be scattered to the wind in the vicinity of the site or elsewhere making tombs unnecessary.

Such scattering could explain the distribution of the burned human bones at topsoil level on all sides of the structure while pottery and artifact remains were found only on the north side and to a much lesser extent, the east side.

Cremation was not unknown during antiquity in the Near East. Signs of its practice in the Early Bronze I period have recently been found at Tel Aviv (Kaplan 1979). It seems to have been practiced during the Late Bronze Age by the Hittites (Otten 1958); burial urns with cremated remains have been found associated with neo-Hittites at Hammath, (apparently from the 12th century [Kempinsky 1979: 39]) Azor (apparently from the early Iron I period [Dothan 1975: 147]) and Tell Qasile (Stratum X from the Iron I period [Dothan 1975: 147]). These burials appear to be culturally foreign to Palestine but were frequent in the Hittite empire (Kempinski, 1979: 43). Although the LB IIB period was a time of Hittite presence in Palestine, unfortunately, there are few other specific indications from the Amman airport mortuary that would connect the Hittites with its use. Robert M. Little's conclusion that the bones may indicate the presence of Indo-Europeans at the site is, however, most suggestive. Hennessy has also noted that large, open foundation trenches such as that at the Amman site are better known from Mesopotamia than Palestine. While this does not pinpoint the Hittites, it may indicate a foreign element involved in the construction of the site. One of the cylinder seals found at the site seems to have been Mitannian (Ward 1964: 50); Hennessy also reports a large cylindrical onyx bead (1968: 161; 1970: 307) with a four-line cuneiform inscription from the Kassite period which seems to have originated in Mesopotamia.

The LB II period was, or course, a time of confrontation between the Egyptians and the Hittites. So far we know of this confrontation only in western Palestine; Transjordan has usually been considered an uninhabited backwater given up to roving beduin bands. As more and more LB settlements are discovered in Transjordan, however, a different picture, one involving settlements, is needed to explain the data. Traditionally, foreign control of Transjordan comes from the north, not the south. A model which proposes that, in their confrontation with Egypt, the Hittites secured their eastern flank by establishing a presence in Transjordan thus suggests itself hypothetically. At least the remains from the Amman mortuary which suggests a possible Hittite presence in the area can provide the basis for a hypothesis which future work in the region should keep in mind.

If Hittites were indeed present in Transjordan during this period, the question as to the type of presence is intriguing. Were they members of a military garrison at Amman? Were they budding neo-Hittites being absorbed into the local population? The late 13th century date of the site's *floruit* when the Hittite military presence was no longer as important as it had been earlier would encourage the latter option, as would the use of local pottery and the value placed on imported and antique objects if the Hittites were indeed the only group making use of the site. Interestingly, it is precisely during the late 13th century that others have noted a Hittite migration to the Palestine region (Kempinski 1979; 41-43). This possible foreign connection could also explain the extent of the site's

isolation from contemporary settlements. Foreign funerary rites involving cremation may have offended the local inhabitants forcing the rite to be performed in a well-isolated spot, far from local habitations.

However, I should emphasize that the above is simply speculation based upon a hypothesis which needs further testing. Until more information is available, it is methodologically risky to suggest with certainty that any specific national group was predominantly influential at the site. Moreover, a mortuary could have served society by practicing more than one ethnic or religious mode of corpse disposal; inhumation could have been practiced as well as cremation. If various ethnic groups made up the population of the region (the Biblical accounts could indicate the presence of Amorites, Ammonites, Hittites, and possibly others) the institution could have attempted to serve its constituency in as cosmopolitan a fashion as was necessary.

BIBLIOGRAPHY

Avi-Yonah, M., and Stern, E.
1978   Rabbath-Ammon. Pp. 989-990 in vol. 4 of *Encyclopedia of Archaeological Excavations in the Holy Land*, ed. M. Avi-Yonah and E. Stern. Jerusalem: Massada Press.

Ben-Arieh, S.
1968   The Late Bronze Age Temple at Amman. *Qadmoniot*: 98-99 (Hebrew).

Bennett, C.-M.
1978   Excavations at the Citadel (El Qal'ah), Amman. *Levant* 10: 1-9.

Biran, A.
1974   Tel Dan. *Biblical Archaeologist* 37: 26-51.

Boling, R. G.
1969   Bronze Age Buildings at the Shechem High Place: ASOR Excavations at Tananir. *Biblical Archaeologist* 32: 82-103.
1975   Excavations at Tananir, 1968. Pp. 24-84 in *Report on Archaeological Work at Suwwānet eth-Thanīya, Tananir, and Khirbet Minḥa (Munhata)*, ed. G. M. Landes. Missoula, Montana: Scholars Press for the American Schools of Oriental Research.

Brady, N. C.
1974   *The Nature and Properties of Soils*. New York: MacMillan Publishing Co.

Campbell, E. F., and Wright, G. E.
1969   Tribal League Shrines in Amman and Schechem. *Biblical Archaeologist* 32: 104-116.

Dajani, R.
1970   A Late Bronze-Iron Age Tomb at Sahab, 1968. *Annual of the Department of Antiquities of Jordan* 15: 29-34.

Dever, W. G. et al.
1970   *Gezer I. Annual of the Hebrew Union College Biblical Archaeological School in Jerusalem*. Jerusalem: Keter Publishing Co.

Dothan, M.
1975   Azor. Pp. 144-147 in vol. 1 of *Encyclopedia of Archaeological Excavations in the Holy Land*, ed. M. Avi-Yonah. Jerusalem: Massada Press.

Dothan, T.
1979   *Excavations at the Cemetery of Deir el-Balah*. Qedem 6. Jerusalem: Hebrew University.

Fritz, V.
1971   Erwägungen zu dem spätbronzezeitlichen Quadratbau bei Amman. *Zeitschrift des deutschen Palästina-Vereins* 87: 140-152.

Gadegaard, N. H.
1978   On the So-Called Burnt Offering Altar in the Old Testament. *Palestine Exploration Quarterly* 110: 35-45.

Green, A. R. W.
1975   *The Role of Human Sacrifice in the Ancient Near East*. Missoula, Montana: Scholars Press for the American Schools of Oriental Research.

Guy, P. L. O., and Engberg, R.
1938   *Megiddo Tombs*. Oriental Institute Publications 33. Chicago: University of Chicago.

Hankey, V.
1974a   A Late Bronze Age Temple at Amman: I. The Aegean Pottery. *Levant* 6: 131-159.
1974b   A Late Bronze Age Temple at Amman: II. Vases and Objects Made of Stone. *Levant* 6: 160-178.

Harding, G. L.
1956   Excavations in Jordan. *Annual of the Department of Antiquities of Jordan* 3: 80.
1958   Recent Discoveries in Jordan. *Palestine Exploration Quarterly* 90: 7-18.

1967   *The Antiquities of Jordan.* Amman: Jordan Distribution Agency.

Hennessy, J. B.
1966a   Excavation of a Late Bronze Age Temple at Amman. *Palestine Exploration Quarterly* 98: 155-162.
1966b   Supplementary Note. *Zeitschrift für die altestestimentliche Wissenschaft* 78: 357-359.
1970   A Temple of Human Sacrifice at Amman. *The Gazette* Nov.: 307-309.

Herr, L. G.
1976   The Amman Airport Excavations, 1976. *Annual of the Department of Antiquities of Jordan* 21: 109-111.
1977   The Amman Airport "Temple"—1976. *Newsletter of the American Schools of Oriental Research* Aug.: 1-4.

Kaplan, H. R.
1979   Tel Aviv, A Burial Cave in the Qirya. Notes and News. *Israel Exploration Journal* 29: 241.

Kempinski, A.
1979   Hittites in the Bible. *Biblical Archaeology Review* 5, no. 5: 20-45.

Kenyon, K. M.
1960   *Jericho I.* London: British School of Archaeology in Jerusalem.
1965   *Jericho II.* London: British School of Archaeology in Jerusalem.

Leonard, A.
1979   Kataret Es-Samra: A Late Bronze Age Cemetery in Transjordan. *Bulletin of the American Schools of Oriental Research* 234: 53-65.

McGovern, P.
1979   Beq'a Valley, Jordan 1977. *Newsletter of the American Schools of Oriental Research* Jan.: 9-11.

Merrillees, R. S.
1968   *The Cypriot Bronze Age Pottery Found in Egypt.* Lund: P. Åstrom.

Miller, J. M.
1979   Archaeological Survey of Central Moab: 1978. *Bulletin of the American Schools of Oriental Research* 234: 43-52.

Nock, A. D.
1942   Cremation and Burial in the Roman Empire. *Harvard Theological Review* 25: 321-359.

Oren, E.
1958   *The Northern Cemetery of Beth Shan.* Leiden: Brill.

Otten, H.
1958   *Hethitische Totenrituale.* Berlin: Akademic-Verlag.

Ottosson, M.
1980   *Temples and Cult Places in Palestine.* Acta Universitatis Uppsaliensis, Boreas. Uppsala Studies in Ancient Mediterranean and Near Eastern Civilizations, 12.

Tufnell, O.
1958   *Lachish IV: The Bronze Age.* London: Oxford.
1962   The Courtyard Cemetery at Tell el-'Ajjul, Palestine. *University of London, Bulletin of the Institute of Archaeology* 3: 1-46.

Ucko, P. J.
1969   Ethnography and Archaeological Interpretation of Funerary Remains. *World Archaeology* 1: 262-280.

Ward, W. A.
1964   Cylinders and Scarabs from a Late Bronze Age Temple at Amman. *Annual of the Department of Antiquities of Jordan* 8-9: 47-55.

Wright, G. H. R.
1966   The Bronze Age Temple at Amman. *Zeitschrift für die altestestimentliche Wissenschaft* 78: 350-357.
1968   Temples at Shechem. *Zeitschrift des deutschen Palästina-Vereins* 84: 9.

Yadin, Y.
1972   *Hazor.* London: Oxford.

Chapter 3
The Local Pottery

ZEIDAN KAFAFI

The local ceramic assemblage from the 1976 excavations at the Amman Airport represented a rather limited repertoire of basic forms. However, a fair amount of variety was found to exist within the most frequently attested forms (bowls and jugs). Because the excavations yielded only 17 very small, undiagnostic sherds of imported wares (14 probable Mycenean, 1 milk bowl and 3 probable base-ring examples), nothing can be added to previous studies (Hankey 1974). The present report thus deals only with the much more frequent local pottery. Due to the one-period nature of the site, finds from all loci including topsoil are considered valid for study. All examples seem to have been wheel made.

Bowls (nos. 1-59)

All but one of the large deep bowls (nos. 1-7) have flaring walls. Three rim forms may be found among these bowls: 1. Simple rims (nos. 1, 2); the latter is a slightly closed form. 2. Everted rims: no. 3 is strongly everted, no. 4 is less everted and no. 5 is just slightly everted; since all three of these bowls are from carinated forms (nos. 3 and 4 show a high carination, but no. 5 was probably carinated lower in the profile than our extant sherd indicated in the typical MB/LB style), everted rims on non-carinated, large deep bowls are not witnessed. 3. Interior thickened rim (nos. 6 and 7); on the latter the thickened rim is flattened.

All large shallow bowls (nos. 8-28) have flaring walls. Although these bowls are more frequent than the large deep forms, they witness the same rim types, but with sub-variations: 1. Simple rims (nos. 8-16); five are squared (nos. 9, 12, 13, 14, 16)

and four are narrowed-and-rounded (nos. 8, 10, 11, 15); the effect of the narrowing on the narrowed-and-rounded bowls tends toward the appearance of very slight eversion, except on the case of no. 15 where the narrowing only occurs on the exterior; interior flattening seems to occur on no. 11. 2. Everted rims (nos. 17-24); except for no. 24 the rims evert very delicately when high carination is not a factor; note again the tendency to flatten the rim interior (nos. 18, 19, 20); no. 21 is the only clean outset rim of the corpus; no. 24, almost a "hammer" rim, is likewise unique to the corpus with its interior thickened rim and downward eversion. 3. Interior thickened rims (nos. 22, 24-28); nos. 22 and 24 are also everted; nos. 25 and 26 illustrate a thickening of the wall toward the rim while nos. 27 and 28 have slight but true thickened rims, almost rolled; no. 25 displays the tendency to flatten the inner rim.

Small bowls with flaring walls (nos. 29-49) have rims reminiscent of the large bowl forms. 1. Simple rims (nos. 29-36); similar sub-types exist here as in the large shallow bowls: squared rims (nos. 30, 34) are relatively few, perhaps due to the difficulty of squaring rims on small forms; narrowed-and-rounded rims are more frequent (nos. 32, 35, 36); rounded rims also occur (nos. 29, 31, 33), though nos. 29 and 31 tend to be flat on the top. 2. Everted rims (nos. 37-45); as with the large bowls, the eversion is delicate except for the carinated forms (nos. 42-45) where it is bold; in nos. 37-39 the rim everts near the top while nos. 40 and 41 evert farther down the wall. 3. Interior thickened rims (nos. 31, 46, 47); the thickening here is very slight and a weak tendency to flatten the tops seems to be present; the thickening on no. 31 is accented by the interior wheel marks just below the rim. 4. Exterior thickened rims (nos. 48, 49); this form does not occur on the large bowls; the thickening is very slight and occurs at the rim on one example (no. 48) and slightly below the rim on the other (no. 49).

Some small bowls had vertical walls near the rim which probably curved into relatively flat bottoms (nos. 50-57). 1. Simple rims dominate this form (nos. 50-54, 56); here again are the three rim sub-types: squared (no. 50), narrowed-and-rounded (nos. 51-54) and rounded (no. 56); no. 51 is a slightly closed form, which, like the large bowls, is rare in this assemblage; no. 56 is slightly carinated and may have been fairly deep. 2. Thickened rim (no. 55); most of the thickening seems to be on the interior; note the squared profile. 3. Slightly everted rim (no. 57); this sherd is similar to no. 56 but its slightly everted rim has accentuated its carination; note again the squared top.

Since carinated bowls represent a discreet group within the corpus, a few specific observations on them are in order. Most of the carinated bowls have a high carination, unlike the common MB/LB carinated bowls, but which may have developed from those forms. Both large and small carinated bowls with high carination display three profiles, related to the degree of carination: 1. "S"-shape (nos. 3, 42, 43, 44, 45); 2. Slight "S"-shape (nos. 4, 57); 3. Slight carination (no. 56). One sherd probably exhibited a lower carination similar to the MB/LB tradition (no. 5); one should note the rarity of this form in the corpus.

Two examples of pedestal bowls or chalices were found (nos. 58, 59) without, however, either rim or base termination. Of note is the appearance together of a very thick-bottomed form (no. 58) with a thin-bottomed form (no. 59).

Most of the bowls were slipped with a white, pink or pinkish white slip and none was burnished. Most examples were also poorly fired displaying prominent cores. Comments on bowl bases will be given below. To be especially noted is the absence, in spite of the large number of bowls found, of painted forms. Only one sherd displayed any paint at all (no. 30). Applied on the top of the rim only, its uniqueness serves only to accent the overall lack of paint.

Jugs (nos. 61-91)

All jug forms have flaring walls except some of those with everted rims where the walls tend to be vertical. By far the majority of the rim sherds come from relatively wide-mouthed jugs.

There are several rim forms on the wide mouthed jugs: 1. Simple flaring rims (nos. 61-66); all rims are rounded except no. 66 which is somewhat pointed and no. 63 which is thickened and slightly squared. 2. Everted rims (nos. 67-70); the rims evert sharply (except no. 70) from vertical necks; very little thickening is apparent; a suggestion that some of these could be small, delicate kraters cannot be disproved. 3. Triangular rim (no. 71); such a rim, reminiscent of cooking pot forms, is surprisingly rare in our corpus; it is possible that no. 141 is a jug though its large diameter makes it unlikely. 4. Thickened rims (nos. 73, 74); both sherds have only slightly flaring walls and are thickened both internally and externally only lightly; no. 73 has a somewhat squared profile. 5. Slightly inverted rim (no. 75); the slight inversion is accentuated by the small groove just beneath the squared top. 6. Exterior thickened rim (no. 76); this is basically a flaring rim, but the rim is thickened in such a way that it coincidently resembles a typical "Hellenistic" profile.

Narrow-mouthed jugs tend to have simple flaring rims (nos. 77-79); whereas nos. 77 and 78 evert from a vertical wall, no. 79 does not evert beyond the slight flare of its wall. No. 80 with its upturned rim would appear to be a narrow-mouthed jug, and may have had an overall form something like no. 78.

Several handles were found which probably belonged to jugs (nos. 81-91) though they may also have belonged to small kraters. Oval sections predominate (nos. 81-87) though flattened sections also occur (nos 88-91).

Most of the jugs carried a white to pink slip and were not burnished. Like the bowls they were badly fired. No jug rims were painted. Jug bases are commented upon below.

Bowl and Jug Bases (nos. 92-130)

Because it is difficult to establish whether the following bases belonged specifically either to bowls or jugs, they are being included together here. The assemblage displays the four main types of bases found in other Late Bronze Age corpora: 1. Low pedestal bases (nos. 92-104); they occur both with simple (nos. 92-99) and everted termi-nations (nos. 100-104), the last may be a high ring base on a small bowl with a vestigial eversion. 2.

Ring bases (nos. 105-124) are the majority of the forms. 3. Disc bases (nos. 125, 126) probably are to be associated with large deep bowls; note that the present examples tend toward ring bases. 4. Flat bases (nos. 127-130) are common on large medium and deep bowls with simple rims on flaring walls throughout the Late Bronze Age.

It is, of course, possible that some of these bases belonged originally to kraters, but they should be as rare as are krater rims in our corpus. Generally, the same slips and ware colors that characterized the bowl and jug rims also describe the bases. Of note are the generally thick profiles of the bases and their variety of size, reflecting the variety of sizes among the bowl and jug rims.

Possible Kraters (nos. 60, 72, 131-139)

The large diameter of no. 60 precludes a jug and the rim profile would be strange with carinated bowl forms. The flaring, inverted rim (moving toward a "hammer"?) curving out to a possible shoulder and the presence of paint points toward a krater. Although the relatively small diameter of no. 72 is more like that of a jug, its thick profile and closed form is more akin to a krater. Note the everted, thickened rim. Nos. 131-136 all display externally thickened, everted rims. It is possible that some of these sherds (especially nos. 132, 133, 136) could have belonged to jars, but the closed forms of nos. 131, 134, and 135, the relatively wide mouths, the complete lack of jar bases in the corpus and the fact that most of these sherds are slipped should point toward rather narrow-mouthed kraters in spite of the lack of "hammer" rims. The profile of no. 131 is squared; on no. 132 the external thickening is rather flanged. The other rims tend toward round, thickened rims. Three of the handles which were found are large enough to be krater handles (nos. 137-139); all are oval in section.

If these sherds were from kraters, the lack of paint should be noted (except no. 60). Otherwise most of the vessels were slipped with colors ranging from white to pink; there was no burnishing. All were poorly fired with prominent cores.

Possible Jars

Though no jar bases whatsoever were found, suggesting a lack of this form in our assemblage, it is possible that nos. 132, 133 and 136 along with some handles (nos. 137-139) were from jars. However, the slip on nos. 133, 136, 138 and 139 would virtually preclude them, leaving only nos. 132 and 137 as possible jars. These forms have been discussed with the kraters above.

Cooking Pots (nos. 140, 141)

It is somewhat surprising that, out of 163 sherds in the corpus, only one certain and one possible cooking pot were discovered. Both rims are triangular in profile but possible cooking pot no. 141 everts more strongly than no. 140. No. 141 with its pinkish white slip and light gray ware may not be a cooking pot, but a jug or, because of its large diameter, a krater with a relatively thin ware. The ware of no. 140, however, is clearly that of a cooking pot.

Saucer Lamps (nos. 142-158)

Three basic types of lamp rims are found in this corpus. 1. Simple rims (nos. 142-146); two of these rims are actually thickened slightly (nos. 142 and 146). 2. Slightly flaring rims (nos. 147-154); some of these rims are simple with only a slight bend to indicate the tendency toward the typical lamp edge; nos. 147 and 148 have outset and slightly thickened rims and nos. 150 and 152 have internally thickened rims which evoke the flare of the typical lamp edge. 3. Flaring rims (nos. 155-158); no. 155 is outset and slightly thickened and no. 158 is especially strong in its flare.

Most of the lamps are slipped with white to pink slips and were poorly fired. Their basic form is a continuation of MBII lamps.

Painted Sherds (nos. 159-163)

Painted sherds which definitely were not imported were comparatively rare. All five such sherds display geometric patterns well attested on Late Bronze Age pottery. Some of the sherds may be local Mycenean imitations, especially those with light cores (nos. 161 and 162). All painted sherds were well fired and often lack observable inclusions (nos. 160, 161, 162).

Parallels to the Corpus

At Megiddo parallels to the Amman airport pottery were found in Stratum VIIB which is generally dated to the LB IIB period with some material possibly from Iron I (compare Loud 1948a and 1948b with Wright 1961: 111-114).

Parallels from Lachish were found in Tombs 501, 532 and 564. Tomb 501 contained a scarab with the name of Amenhotep III (1405-1367 B.C.) (Tufnell et al. 1958a: 236); Tomb 532 seems to have been contemporary with the end of Fosse Temple Structure III at the end of the LB IIB period; Tufnell dates Tomb 564 to a period from LB I to LB II, but does not mention the specific dating evidence (Tufnell et al. 1958a: 247). Other parallels were found in Structures II and III of the Fosse Temple. In Structure II a group of tombs was found which yielded scarabs attributed to Tutmose III, Amenhotep II, and Amenhotep III, dating from late LB I through the middle of LB IIA. In structure III, tombs 4011 and 4013 produced many scarabs attributed to the reigns of Ay, Horemhab, and Ramses II, or basically LB IIB (Tufnell et al. 1958a: 66; Wright 1961: 111-114).

Tell Beit Mirsim also yielded a few parallels from Stratum C, the Late Bronze Age (Albright 1932: pl.47).

At Gezer Stratum 5 in Field I (General Strata XIV and XV) produced one vessel similar to one from the Amman Airport. This stratum has been dated to the 13th century B.C. (Dever et al 1970: 10, 22), and is further divided into three phases; of note is Phase 5A which is said to date to the LB II/Iron I period (Dever et al. 1971: 132). Other general parallels may be found in Strata 12 and 13 of Field II (General Strata XIV) dating to the late LB IIB period (Dever et al. 1974: 48-52).

Hazor Stratum 1A (LB IIB) of Area C produced parallels to the Amman airport corpus. Other parallels were found in cisterns 9017 and 9024 in Area D attributed simply to Stratum 1, the LB II period (Yadin et al. 1958: 118, 133-134). In Area F, parallels were found in tomb 8144-8145. Five hundred pottery vessels came from this tomb which belongs to Stratum 1B and dates to the LB IIA period. Imported pottery vessels were found associated with local wares in this tomb (Yadin et al. 1960: 145, Pls. CXXXVI, CXXXVII).

This discussion of the parallels should indicate that the Amman airport corpus is best dated to the LB II period, more specifically to the LB IIB period.

Introduction to the Figure Descriptions

On the Figure Description pages information is contained in 10 columns. Column 1 contains the serial number of the sherds corresponding with the figures. The Identification in column 2 contains archeological provenance information: Area (upper case letter), Square (Arabic numeral), locus (Arabic numeral separated by a colon) and the sherd registry number (preceded by the symbol #). Column 3 contains the basic typological designation of the vessel form to which the sherd originally belonged.

The surface treatment of the sherd is described in two columns: Column 4 designates any applied or other decoration on the sherd in abbreviated fashion: B: burnish; P: paint; S: slip; horizontal lines indicate no observable traces. Column 5 contains the color designation of the applied decoration utilizing the Munsell soil color code and verbal description.

The ware of the sherd is described in the next four columns: Column 6 gives the color of the ware at its well-fired, outer ceramic matrix; the next column attempts a loose designation of the core (inner ceramic matrix) color: d: dark; m: medium. Column 8 gives a general description of the size and color of the inclusions (grits) within the ceramic matrix: B: black; Br: brown; G: gray; M: medium; R: red; S: small; Y: yellowish. Column 9 is a very general description of the hardness of the ceramic matrix: h: hard; m: medium; s: soft.

In the column of parallels the publication designations are abbreviations for the following publications: Hazor I (Yadin et al. 1958); Hazor II (Yadin et al. 1960); TBM (Albright 1932); Megiddo II (Loud 1948b); Lachish (Tufnell et al. 1958b); Gezer I (Dever et al. 1970).

POTTERY DESCRIPTION

No.	Identification	Form	Surface Treatment			Ware					Parallels
			Decoration	Color		Color		Core	Inclusion	Hard-ness	
1	A.4:1 #125	Bowl	—	—	7.5YR8/2	pinkish white		m	SB	m	Hazor I, Pl.CXXV:6
2	A.3:2 #59	Bowl	—	—	7.5YR7/4	pink		d	SMB	m	Hazor I, Pl.CXXV:8; Megiddo II, Pl.68:12
3	A.4:2 #278	Bowl	S	7.5YR8/2 pinkish white	7.5YR5/2	brown		m	SW	m	TBM, Pl.47:7; Lachish, Pl.XLB:88; Megiddo II, Pl.68:20
4	A.4:1 #229	Bowl	S	2.5YR8/2 white	10YR6/2	light brownish gray		m	SWB	m	Hazor I, Pl.LXXXVII:7; Lachish, Pl.71:620; Megiddo II, Pl.68:18
5	A.2:3 #331	Bowl	S	10YR8/2 white	5YR7/4	pink		—	SMBR	m	—
6	A.2:1 #319	Bowl	S	10YR8/2 white	7.5YR8/4	pink		d	SBW	m	Hazor I, Pl.CXXV:20
7	C.1:2 #16	Bowl	—	—	7.5YR8/4	pink		m	SW	h	Hazor II, Pl.CXXVIII:23
8	C.1:1 #174	Bowl	S	7.5YR8/1 white	10YR8/4	very pale brown		m	SB	m	Hazor I, Pl.CXXV:2; Lachish, Pl.XLB:91
9	A.4:1 #377	Bowl	S	7.5YR8/4 pink	7.5YR7/4	pink		m	SBW	m	Hazor I, Pl.CXXV:7
10	A.4:2 #365	Bowl	S	10YR8/2 white	5YR7/4	pink		—	SBW	m	Hazor I, Pl.CXXV:2
11	C.1:1 #42	Bowl	S	10YR8/2 white	7.5YR8/4	pink		—	SB	m	Hazor II, Pl.CXXVIII:12
12	A.4:1 #373	Bowl	S	7.5YR8/4 pink	2.5YR5/4	reddish brown		—	SBW	m	Hazor II, Pl.XCI:6
13	A.4:1 #228	Bowl	S	5YR7/4 pink	7.5YR8/2	pinkish white		d	—	m	Hazor I, Pl.CXXV:17; Lachish, Pl.XXXVIIB:29
14	C.1:1 #33	Bowl	S	7.5YR8/2 pinkish white	7.5YR7/2	pinkish gray		—	SBW	m	Hazor I, Pl.CXXV:17; Gezer I, Pl.28:14
15	A.4:5 #139	Bowl	S	10YR8/1 white	10YR8/3	very pale brown		—	SBW	h	Hazor I, Pl.CXXV:14
16	A.1:1 #85	Bowl	S	5YR8/2 pinkish white	10YR8/1	white		—	SBW	m	—
17	A.2:3 #410	Bowl	S	10YR8/1 white	10YR5/1	gray		m	SW	m	Lachish, Pl.XXXVIIB:8, XLB:90
18	A.2:2 #69	Bowl	S	7.5YR8/2 pinkish white	5YR7/4	pink		m	SBW	m	Hazor I, Pl.CXXV:2; Lachish, Pl.XLB:93
19	A.2:2 #71	Bowl	S	5YR8/1 white	7.5YR7/2	pinkish gray		d	SW	m	Lachish, Pl.XLB:92; Megiddo II, Pl.69:3
20	A.2:2 #299	Bowl	—	—	5YR7/4	pink		m	SBW	m	Hazor I, Pl.CXI:3; Lachish, Pl.XLB:92
21	C.1:1 #136	Bowl	S	5YR8/2 pinkish white	5YR6/2	pinkish gray		m	SW	m	Lachish, Pl.XLB:93
22	A.4:1	Bowl	S	10YR8/2 white	5YR7/6	reddish yellow		—	SB	h	Hazor II, Pl.CXXVIII:16
23	A.1:3 #144	Bowl	S	7.5YR8/2 pinkish white	5YR6/4	light reddish brown		—	—	h	Hazor II, Pl.CXXVIII:19
24	A.2:1 #177	Bowl	—	—	7.5YR8/4	pink		m	SBW	m	Lachish, Pl.XXXVIIB:53
25	C.1:2 #32	Bowl	S	7.5YR8/2 pinkish white	5YR7/6	reddish yellow		m	SBW	h	Hazor II, Pl.CXXVIII:23
26	A.2:1 #3	Bowl	S	7.5YR8/2 pinkish white	5YR7/4	pink		m	SBW	m	Hazor II, Pl.CXXVIII:20
27	C.1:1 #44	Bowl	S	10YR8/1 white	5YR7/6	reddish yellow		m	—	m	Hazor II, Pl.CXXVIII:21

POTTERY DESCRIPTION

No.	Identification	Form	Surface Treatment				Ware				Parallels
			Decoration		Color		Color	Core	Inclu-sion	Hard-ness	
28	C.1:1 #46	Bowl	S	5YR8/1	white	5YR8/4	pink	m	SBW	m	Hazor II, Pl.CXXVIII:21
29	A.2:2 #312	Bowl	S	10YR8/1	white	10YR8/4	very pale brown	—	SW	m	Hazor II, Pl.CXXVIII:22
30	A.2:1 #115a	Bowl	S p(rim)	10YR8/2 2.5YR4/2	white weak red	7.5YR7/0	light gray	—	SB	m	Hazor II, Pl.CXXVIII:22
31	A.2:2 #72	Bowl	S	7.5YR8/2	pinkish white	7.5YR8/4	pink	—	SB	m	—
32	A.4:4 #270	Bowl	—		—	10YR8/1	white	—	SW	h	—
33	A.2:1 #200	Bowl	S	7.5YR8/2	pinkish white	7.5YR4/0	dark gray	—	G	m	Hazor II, Pl.CXXVIII:9
34	A.2:2 #95	Bowl	S	5YR8/2	pinkish white	5YR7/6	reddish yellow	—	—	m	—
35	A.4:6 #157	Bowl	S	10YR8/2	white	7.5YR8/4	pink	—	SBW	m	Hazor II, Pl.CXXVIII:17
36	D.1:1 #240	Bowl	S(ext)	10YR8/1	white	5YR7/6	reddish yellow	—	SB	m	Lachish, Pl.XCLI:119
37	A.4:4 #384	Bowl	—		—	5YR7/6	reddish yellow	—	SBW	h	—
38	A.4:4 #265	Bowl	S	7.5YR8/2	pinkish white	7.5YR8/4	pink	—	S	m	—
39	A.1:1 #226	Bowl	S	10YR8/2	white	5YR7/3	pink	m	SBW	m	Hazor II, Pl.CXXVIII:19
40	A.4:2 #280	Bowl	S	5YR8/2	pinkish white	5YR7/1	light gray	—	SMBW	m	Hazor II, Pl.CXXVIII:19; Lachish, Pl.71:621
41	A.4:4 #267	Bowl	—		—	7.5YR4/0	dark gray	—	SB	m	Hazor II, Pl.CXXVIII:19
42	A.4:2 #282	Bowl	S	5YR8/2	pinkish white	7.5YR5/2	brown	m	SW	m	TBM, Pl.47:7
43	A.4:2 #272	Bowl	S	5YR8/2	pinkish white	7.5YR5/2	brown	m	SW	m	TBM, Pl.47:7; Megiddo II, Pl.68:20
44	A.4:2 #279	Bowl	S	10YR8/2	white	5YR6/4	light reddish brown	m	SBW	m	TBM, Pl.47:7; Lachish, Pl.XLB:88
45	A.4:2	Bowl	S	5YR8/2	pinkish white	7.5YR5/2	brown	m	SW	m	TBM, Pl.47:7; Lachish, Pl.XLB:88; Megiddo II, Pl.68:18,20
46	A.1:1 #202	Bowl	—		—	7.5YR8/4	pink	m	SBW	m	—
47	A.2:2 #301	Bowl	S	7.5YR8/2	pinkish white	7.5YR7/4	pink	—	SBW	m	Hazor I, Pl.XCI:20
48	C.1:2 #27	Bowl	5	10YR8/2	white	10YR6/2	light brownish gray	m	SBW	h	—
49	A.4:1 #182	Bowl	S	7.5YR8/2	pinkish gray	10YR5/1	gray	m	SBW	h	Hazor II, Pl.CXXVIII:19
50	A.4:1 #178	Bowl	S	7.5YR8/2	pinkish white	7.5YR2.5/0	black	d	SW	m	—
51	A.2:1 #119	Bowl	S	7.5YR8/4	pink	5YR7/1	light gray	m	SB	m	—
52	A.4:4 #252	Bowl	S	10YR8/2	white	2.5YR5/4	reddish brown	d	SBW	m	Hazor II, Pl.CXXVIII:15
53	A.4:4 #269	Bowl	S	10YR8/2	white	5YR5/4	reddish brown	d	SBW	m	Hazor II, Pl.CXXVIII:15
54	A.4:6 #157	Bowl	S	10YR8/2	white	10YR6/1	gray	d	SW	m	Hazor II, Pl.CXXVIII:14
55	D.1:1 #239	Bowl	S	7.5YR8/4	pink	5YR7/6	reddish yellow	—	SB	h	Hazor II, Pl.CXXVIII:18
56	A.4:4 #264	Bowl	—		—	5YR7/4	pink	—	SB	m	Hazor I, Pl.CXXVI:27; Lachish, Pl.XLB:86
57	A.2:2 #93	Bowl Pedestal	S	5YR6/3	light reddish brown	7.5YR8/4	pink	d	SBW	m	—

Fig. 20. Local Pottery.

POTTERY DESCRIPTION

No.	Identification	Form	Surface Treatment				Ware				Parallels
			Decoration	Color			Color	Core	Inclusion	Hardness	
58		Bowl Pedestal									
59		Bowl									
60	A.2:1 #205	Krater?	P	5YR3/2	dark reddish brown	7.5YR8/4	pink	d	SBW	m	—
61	A.4:4 #383	Jug	—		—	10YR8/2	white	—	SBW	m	Hazor II, Pl.CXXXIII:1; Megiddo II, Pl.71:6,7
62	C.1:1 #47	Jug	S	10YR8/2	white	10YR7/1	light gray	m	SB	m	—
63	C.1:1 #55	Jug	—		—	10YR8/1	white	—	—	h	Hazor II, Pl.CXXXIII:1
64	D.1:1 #392	Jug	S	7.5YR8/2	pinkish white	2.5YR6/6	light red	m	SMBW	m	Hazor I, Pl.CVIII:6
65	A.2:1 #109	Jug	S	7.5YR8/2	pinkish white	5YR7/4	pink	—	SBW	m	Hazor I, Pl.CVIII:7
66	A.1:1 #225	Jug	S	7.5YR8/2	pinkish white	10YR6/2	light brownish gray	—	SBW	m	Hazor I, Pl.CVIII:10
67	A.4:4 #248	Jug	—		—	10YR6/1	gray	—	—	m	—
68	A.4:4 #246	Jug	S	7.5YR8/2	pinkish white	5YR7/4	pink	m	SBW	m	—
69	A.4:4 #265	Jug	S	7.5YR8/2	pinkish white	10YR4/1	dark gray	—	—	m	—
70	A.2:3 #400	Jug	S	10YR8/2	white	7.5YR7/4	pink	—	SBW	m	—
71	A.2:12 #321	Jug	S	10YR8/2	white	10YR7/3	very pale brown	—	SBW	m	Hazor II, Pl.CXXXIII:6
72	A.4:1 #177	Krater?	S	10YR8/1	white	5YR6/4	light reddish brown	—	SMBW	m	—
73	A.2:1 #211	Jug	S	7.5YR8/4	pink	7.5YR6.0	gray	—	SW	m	Hazor I, Pl.CVII:2; Megiddo II, Pl.69:14
74	A.1:2 #11	Jug	S	7.5YR8/2	pinkish white	7.5YR8/4	pink	—	SBW	m	Hazor I, Pl.CVIII:5
75	A.2:1 #128	Jug	—		—	10YR8/1	white	m	SB	m	—
76	C.1:1 #41	Jug	S	10YR8/2	white	5YR7/6	reddish yellow	—	SBW	m	—
77	A.2:1 #4	Jug	S	7.5YR8/2	pinkish white	5YR8/3	pink	—	SB	m	Hazor II, Pl.CXXXVIII:10
78		Jug									—
79		Jug									Hazor II, Pl.CXXIV:18
80	D.1:1 #338	Jug	—		—	5YR8/3	pink	—	SBW	m	Hazor II, Pl.CXXXI:22
81	A.4:2 #359	Jug	S	7.5YR8/2	pinkish white	10YR7/6	yellow	d	SBW	m	—
82	A.2:1	Jug	S	5YR8/1	white	10YR7/3	very pale brown	d	SW	m	—
83	A.1:1 #83	Jug	S	5YR8/2	pinkish white	5YR6/4	light reddish brown	—	SBW	h	—
84	C.1:2 #29	Jug	—		—	10YR8/2	white	—	SB	m	—
85	C.1:1 #133	Jug	—		—	7.5YR7/1	light gray	m	—	h	—
86	A.4:4 #259	Jug	S	2.5YR5/6	red	10YR8/2	white	m	—	h	—
87	A.2:1 #206	Jug	S	7.5YR8/2	pinkish white	7.5YR8/4	pink	—	SW	h	—
88	A.1:4 #165	Jug	—		—	5YR7/4	pink	d	SMBW	m	—
89	A.2:3 #396	Jug	S	8YR8/2	white	7.5YR7/4	pink	d	SBW	m	—

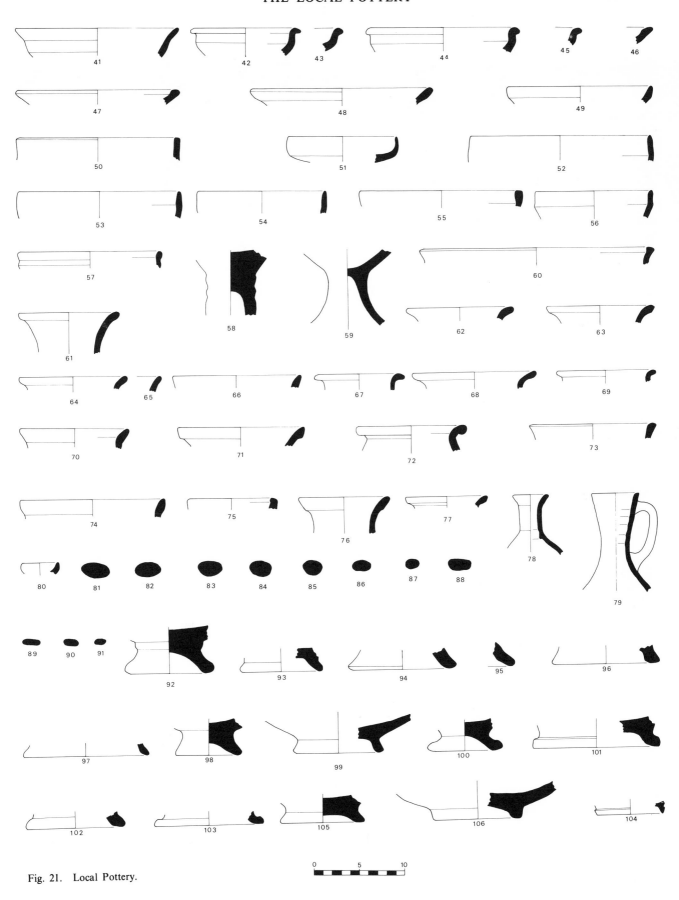

Fig. 21. Local Pottery.

POTTERY DESCRIPTION

No.	Identification	Form	Decoration	Color		Color		Core	Inclusion	Hardness	Parallels
					Surface Treatment		Ware				
90	A.1:4 #169	Jug	—	—		5YR7/4	pink	—	SBW	h	—
91	A.4:2 #347	Jug	—	—		10YR8/4	very pale brown	—	—	h	—
92	A.2:3 #15	Bowl/Jug	—	—		5YR8/2	white	—	SB	m	—
93	A.2:2 #78	Bowl/Jug	S	10YR8/1	white	10YR7/2	light gray	—	SMBW	m	—
94	A.2:2 #76	Bowl/Jug	S	10YR8/2	white	10YR7/3	very pale brown	m	SBW	m	—
95	A.2:2 #77	Bowl/Jug	S	7.5YR8/2	pinkish white	5YR8/4	pink	m	SBW	m	—
96	A.2:2 #101	Bowl/Jug	S	5YR8/1	white	7.5YR8/4	pink	—	SBW	m	—
97	D.1:1 #342	Bowl/Jug	—	—		5YR7/4	pink	m	SBW	m	—
98	C.1:1 #23	Bowl/Jug	S	7.5YR8/2	pinkish white	7.5YR8/4	pink	—	SBW	m	—
99	A.2:1 #301	Bowl/Jug	S	10YR8/2	white	5YR7/4	pink	m	SB	h	—
100	A.2:2 #159	Bowl/Jug	S	10YR8/1	white	7.5YR7/4	pink	m	SBW	m	—
101	A.4:4 #271	Bowl/Jug	S	7.5YR8/2	pinkish white	10YR6/1	gray	d	SBW	m	—
102	A.4:4 #232	Bowl/Jug	—	—		10YR7/1	light gray	d	SW	m	—
1		Bowl/Jug									
103	C.1:1 #61	Bowl/Jug	S	7.5YR8/1	white	7.5YR8/2	pinkish gray	m	SBW	m	—
104	A.4:? #180	Bowl/Jug	S	10YR8/2	white	5YR7/4	pink	—	SB	h	—
105	A.4:1 #222	Bowl/Jug	S	10YR8/1	white	10YR7/1	light gray	d	SBW	m	—
106	A.4:2 #353	Bowl/Jug	S	7.5YR8/2	pinkish white	5YR7/6	reddish yellow	d	SBW	m	Lachish, Pl.XXXVIIB:52
107	A.4:5	Bowl/Jug	S	7.5YR8/2	pinkish white	10YR7/4	very pale brown	d	SB	m	Lachish, Pl.XXXVIIB:30
108	D.1:1 #343	Bowl/Jug	S	10YR8/1	white	10YR7/2	light gray	d	SBW	m	Lachish, Pl.XXXVIIB:31
109	C.1:1 #34	Bowl/Jug	S	10YR8/1	white	10YR7/1	light gray	m	SBBr	m	Lachish, Pl.XXXVIIB:54
110	A.4:4 #378	Bowl/Jug	S	10YR8/2	white	10YR7/1	light gray	—	SBW	m	—
111	A.4:1 #36	Bowl/Jug	S	10YR8/2	white	10YR7/1	light gray	—	SBW	m	—
112	C.1:1 #35	Bowl/Jug	S	7.5YR8/2	pinkish white	5YR5/1	gray	d	SW	m	—
113	A.2:1	Bowl/Jug	—	—		5YR7/4	pink	d	SBW	m	—
114	A.4:4 #258	Bowl/Jug	S	10YR8/1	white	10YR7/3	very pale brown	d	SW	m	—
115	A.4:2 #358	Bowl/Jug	S?	7.5YR8/2	pinkish white	7.5YR7/4	pink	d	SMBW	m	—
116	A.4:2 #281	Bowl/Jug	S	7.5YR7/4	pink	7.5YR6/1	gray	m	SW	m	—
117	A.1:5 #162	Bowl/Jug	S	7.5YR8/2	pinkish white	7.5YR6/4	light brown	d	SBW	h	—
118	A.2:3 #395	Bowl/Jug	S	10YR8/4	white	10YR8/3	very pale brown	d	SBW	m	—
119	A.2:1 #310	Bowl/Jug	—	—		10YR8/3	very pale brown	d	SW	m	—
120	A.2:2 #73	Bowl/Jug	S	7.5YR8/2	pinkish white	2.5Y7/2	light gray	d	SB	m	Hazor II, Pl.CXXXII:3
121	D.1:1 #393	Bowl/Jug	—	—		10YR8/2	white	—	—	h	Hazor II, Pl.CXXXIII:5
122	A.4:2 #350	Bowl/Jug	B(hard) —	—		10YR7/1	light gray	y	—	h	—
123	A.2:10 #317	Bowl/Jug	S	7.5YR8/2	pinkish white	7.5YR6/4	light brown	—	—	m	—
124	C.1:1 #50	Bowl/Jug	—	—		7.5YR6/4	light brown	d	—	h	—

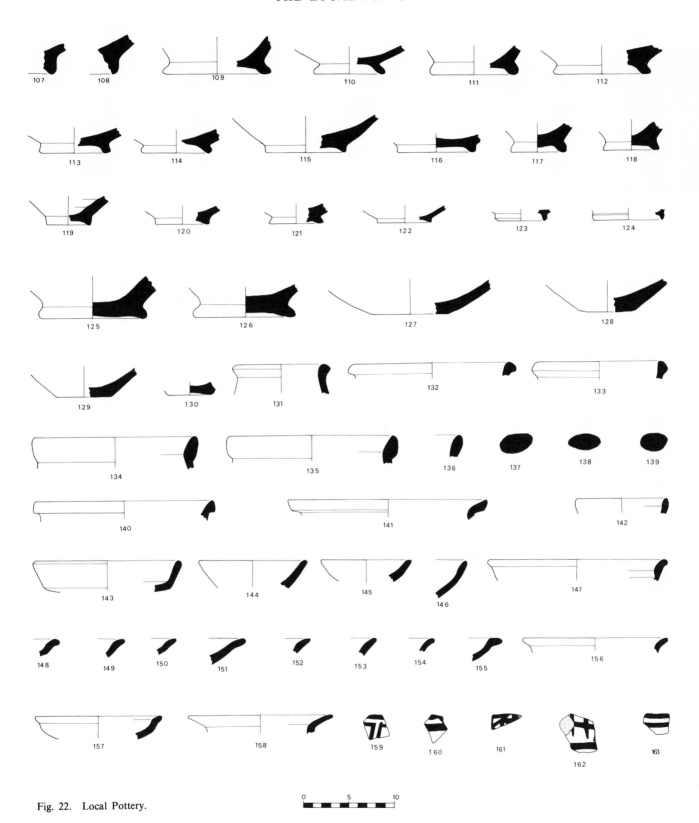

Fig. 22. Local Pottery.

POTTERY DESCRIPTION

No.	Identification	Form	Decoration	Color		Color	Core	Inclusion	Hardness	Parallels
			Surface Treatment			**Ware**				
125	A.2:1 #213	Bowl/Jug	—		—	10YR7/3 very pale brown	d	MBW	m	Hazor I, Pl.XCI:6
126	A.2:3 #405	Bowl/Jug	—		—	10YR8/3 very pale brown	m	MBW	m	Lachish, Pl.XXXVII:29
127	A.2:3 #408	Bowl/Jug	S	10YR8/2 white		5YR7/4 pink	d	SBW	m	Hazor I, Pl.CXXIX:3; Lachish, Pl.LVIIB:390
128	A.3:2 #56	Bowl/Jug	—		—	7.5YR7/4 pink	d	SBW	m	Hazor I, Pl.CXXIX:3; Lachish, Pl.LVIIB:390
129	A.2:3 #409	Bowl/Jug	S	10YR8/1 white		7.5YR8/4 pink	m	BW	m	Hazor I, Pl.CXXIX:3; Lachish, Pl.LVIIB:390
130	A.4:4 #261	Bowl/Jug	—		—	2.5YR8/2 white	—	SMBr	m	—
131	A.2:2 #90	Krater?	S	7.5YR8/4 pink		7.5YR7/4 pink	d	SW	m	Hazor I, Pl.LXXXVIII:19
132	C.1:2 #31	Krater?	—		—	5Y8/2 white	—	—	h	Lachish, Pl.87:1017
133	C.1:2 #17	Krater?	S	7.5YR8/2 pinkish white		10YR6/1 gray	d	SBW	m	Hazor I, Pl.CIX:1; Lachish, Pl.87:1019
134	A.4:1 #231	Krater?	S	5YR8/2 pinkish white		5YR7/6 reddish yellow	—	SB	h	Hazor I, Pl.CXXX:2; Lachish, Pl.87:1021
135	A.3:1 #60	Krater?	S	7.5YR8/2 pinkish white		5YR7/4 pink	m	SB	h	Hazor I, Pl.LXXXVIII:15; Pl.CXXX:2
136	C.1:1 #54	Krater?	S	7.5YR8/2 pinkish white		5YR7/4 pink	m	SBW	m	Hazor I, Pl.CXXX:4
137	A.4:4 #387	Krater?	—		—	10YR8/4 very pale brown	—	SBW	h	—
138	A.2:2 #68	Krater?	S	7.5YR8/1 white		7.5YR7/4 pink	m	MBW	m	—
139	A.3:1 #62	Krater?	S	7.5YR8/2 pinkish white		5YR7/2 pinkish white	m	SBW	h	—
140	A.4:4 #384	Cooking Pot	—	7.5YR8/2 pinkish white		2.5YR5/6 red	—	SBW	m	Hazor I, Pl.CXXVII:2; Pl.LXXXVIII:1; Lachish, Pl.LVI:365
141	C.1:1 #48	Cooking Pot?	S	7.5YR8/2 pinkish white		5YR7/1 light gray	m	SB	m	Hazor I, Pl.CXXVIII:1,3
142	A.2:3 #404	Lamp	S	7.5YR8/2 pinkish white		2.5YR5/4 reddish brown	—	SW	s	—
143	A.4:1 #26	Lamp	S	10YR8/2 white		5YR6/2 pinkish gray	—	SB	m	—
144	A.4:1 #237	Lamp	S	7.5YR8/4 pink		10YR4/1 dark gray	—	SBW	m	Hazor I, Pl.CXXV:25
145	A.2:2 #70	Lamp	S	7.5YR8/2 pinkish white		7.5YR6/2 pinkish gray	d	SBW	m	Hazor I, Pl.LXXXVIII:16; Pl.CXXV:23
146	A.2:1 #116	Lamp	—		—	2.5Y8/2 white	—	SB	m	Hazor II, Pl.CXXXV:7
147	A.2:1 #208	Lamp	S	10YR8/2 white		5YR7/3 pink	d	SBW	m	Lachish, Pl.XLVB:204
148	A.3:1 #56	Lamp	S	10YR8/1 white		10YR5/1 gray	d	SBW	m	—
149	A.2:3 #396	Lamp	S	10YR8/2 white		2.5YR6/4 light reddish brown	—	—	m	Hazor II, Pl.CXXXV:8
150	A.2:2 #96	Lamp	S	5YR8/2 pinkish white		5YR8/4 pink	m	—	h	Hazor I, Pl.CXXB:25
151	A.4:2 #34	Lamp	S	5YR8/2 pinkish white		7.5YR6/2 pinkish gray	—	SBW	m	Hazor II, Pl.CXXXV:4
152	A.7:6 #158	Lamp	—		—	5YR8/3 pink	d	SBW	m	Hazor II, Pl.CXXXV:8
153	A.4:2 #285	Lamp	S	5YR8/2 pinkish white		5YR7/1 light gray	—	SBW	m	Hazor II, Pl.CXXXV:15

No.	Locus	#	Type									Reference
154	A.2:1	#5	Lamp	S	7.5YR8/2	pinkish white	5YR7/4	pink	—	SB	m	—
155	A.4:4	#255	Lamp	S	10YR8/2	white	5YR7/4	pink	m	SBW	m	Hazor II, Pl.CXXXV:12
156	A.4:7	#216	Lamp	—		—	10YR8/1	white	—	SB	m	Hazor II, Pl.CXXXV:12
157	A.4:4	#380	Lamp	S?	7.5YR8/4	pink	10YR6/1	gray	—	SW	m	Hazor II, Pl.CXXXV:8
158	C.1:1	#40	Lamp	S	5YR8/1	white	5YR7/4	pink	—	SBW	m	Hazor II, Pl.CXXXV:8; Megiddo II, Pl.72:6
159	A.3:1	#65	?	S	5YR8/3	pink	10YR5/6	red	—	SW	m	—
				P	2.5YR3/2	dusky red						
160	A.1:1	#88	?	P	2.5YR3/5	dark reddish brown		?	—	—	h	—
161	C.1:1	#49	?	S	5YR8/1	white	7.5YR8/4	pink	—	—	m	—
				P	2.5YR4/4	reddish brown						
162	A.1:1	#106	?	P	2.5YR4/4	reddish brown	10YR8/1	white	—	—	m	—
163	A.2:1	#127	?	P	10R3/2	dusk red	5YR5/4	reddish brown	—	SBW	m	—

BIBLIOGRAPHY

Albright, W. F.
1932   *The Excavations of Tell Beit Mirsim I, the Pottery of the First Three Campaigns. The Annual of the American Schools of Oriental Research* 12 (1930-1931). New Haven: American Schools of Oriental Research.

Dever, W. G. et al.
1970   *Gezer I. Annual of the Hebrew Union College Biblical and Archaeological School in Jerusalem.* Jerusalem: Keter Publishing Company.
1971   Further Excavations at Gezer, 1967-70. *Biblical Archaeologist* 24:4: 94-132.
1974   *Gezer II. Annual of the Hebrew Union College/ Nelson Glueck School of Biblical Archaeology.* Jerusalem: Keter Press.

Hankey, V.
1974   A Late Bronze Age Temple at Amman: I. The Aegean Pottery. II. Vases and Objects Made of Stone. *Levant* 6: 131-179.

Harding, G. L.
1956   Excavations in Jordan. *Annual of the Department of Antiquities of Jordan* 3: 74-88.
1958   Recent Discoveries in Jordan. *Palestine Exploration Quarterly*: 10-12.

Hennessy, J. B.
1966   Excavation of a Late Bronze Age Temple at Amman. *Palestine Exploration Quarterly*: 155-163.

Loud, G.
1948a   *Megiddo II, Seasons of 1935-39, Text.* Chicago: The University of Chicago.

1948b   *Megiddo II, Seasons of 1935-39, Plates.* Chicago: The University of Chicago.

Tufnell, O.; Inge, H. and Harding, G. L.
1940   *Lachish II (Tell ed-Duweir), The Fosse Temple.* London: Oxford University Press.

Tufnell, O. et al.
1958a   *Lachish IV (Tell ed-Duweir), The Bronze Age, Text.* London: Oxford University Press.
1958b   *Lachish IV (Tell ed-Duweir), The Bronze Age, Plates.* London: Oxford University Press.

Ward, W. A.
1964   Cylinders and Scarabs from a Late Bronze Temple at Amman. *Annual of the Department of Antiquities of Jordan* 8-9: 46-55.

Wright, G. E.
1961   The Archaeology of Palestine. Pp. 85-139 in *The Bible and the Ancient Near East: Essays in Honor of William Foxwell Albright*, ed. G. Ernest Wright. Garden City, NY: Doubleday.

Yadin, Y. et al.
1958   *Hazor I, an Account of the First Season of Excavations, 1955.* Jerusalem: The Magnes Press.
1960   *Hazor II, an Account of the Second Season of Excavations, 1956.* Jerusalem: The Magnes Press.
1961   *Hazor III-IV, an Account of the Third and Fourth Seasons of Excavations, 1957-1958.* Jerusalem: The Magnes Press.

Chapter 4

Human Bone Fragment Analysis

ROBERT M. LITTLE

Introduction

This material presents an interesting challenge to laboratory analysis primarily because of the degree of fragmentation (all 1,127 fragments weighed just over 2 kg.).[1] Also, because of the random, scattered provenance of the individual fragments, no data was available enabling the reconstruction of the original relative associations of the fragments.

The animal material had been looked at quickly in Amman (Herr 1976). A number of fragments indicate *ovis-capra* while several additional fragments found in earlier excavations at the site, because of their lightness and thin wall, must be bird (Hankey 1974: 131).

The presence of bone material on a temple site raises many questions. The analysis will be limited to considering the following questions. How many individuals were involved? What was the sex of the individuals? What was the age at time of death? Clues leading to pathological conditions and ob-servations about the appearance of the individuals would also be of interest.

Table 1: Color of Bone Fragments*

The 1,127 bone fragments were first washed and sorted into trays by the color of the bone. (The assigned colors are admittedly somewhat arbitrary since a variety of hues and tones occur with each color. Table 1 is designed simply to give an indication of carbonization.) The expected tan color represented the largest percentage (71%). A heavy dark brown color represented 5% (which may have come from the soil they were buried in or may have been related to the density of the bone). Well carbonized fragments represented 19% (black). Blue, gray and white represented 5%. About 25% of the total showed evidence of fire. The variety of colors may correspond to the intensity of, or time of exposure to, the fire. It would appear that, if all the individuals represented by our bones were burned, the intensity of the fire was relatively low.

Table 1: Color of Bone Fragments*

	white	black	brown	tan	blue	gray	total
Fragments	17	211	53	802	26	18	1127
Percent	1.5	19	5	71	2	1.5	100

[1]Donald Ortner, curator of the Department of Anthropology at the National Museum of Natural History of the Smithsonian Institution, looked at the bone fragments and graciously offered several suggestions on specific items.

*Abbreviations used in the tables are the following: 1. For columns marked "End": P: proximal; D: distal. 2. For columns marked "Position": R: right; L: left. 3. For columns marked "Color": T: tan; B: black; W: white; Br: brown; Bl: blue; G: gray. 4. For columns marked "Age": A: adult; J: juvenile. 5. For columns marked "Type": H: human; A: animal. 6. For columns marked "Preservation": C: complete; F: fragment. The bones themselves are now housed in the Siegfried H. Horn Archaeological Museum at Andrews University, Berrien Springs, Michigan.

Morphological Analysis

The first question to be answered is the number of individuals represented in this collection. Some 93 fragments were recognized as human skull and mandible fragments. There were at least two and possibly three medium point mandible fragments (nos. 15, 16 and 17) that seem to be adult or possibly adolescent. This would give a count of two or possibly three individuals.

Table 2: Parietal Skull Fragments

Fragments	Position	Color	Age
1	R	B	A
1	L	B	?
6	?	B	A
8 (very thin, old? female?)	?	B	A
7	?	Bl	A

Skull fragments that can be identified can also help determine the number of individuals. In Table 2 there is evidence for only one individual. Since most of the fragments are black, this might indicate all of the parietal fragments as coming from one individual (but see conclusion). The eight thin fragments could indicate a female or an individual at an advanced age at time of death. They do not seem to be from a young individual.

Four fragments found were probably frontal bone fragments. They were also black. A fragment 24 × 13 mm from the occipital showed a completely closed suture which would indicate a 40+ year age at time of death. Also the thin wall of these fragments might further indicate age or female.

Table 3: Humerus Fragments

Fragments	End	Position	Color	Age
1	D	L	T	A
5	?	?	T	A
1	D	?	B	A
1	P	?	B	A

Fragments from the humerus (upper arm) were examined. The data presented in Table 3 need not indicate more than one individual.

Table 4: Ulna Fragments

Fragments	End	Position	Color	Age
1	D	R	T	A
45	?	?	T	A
1	P	R	T	A
1	P	?	Br	A
1 (Curved arm)	?	?	T	A
2 (animal)	?	?	T	A

The next group of fragments to be considered involve the ulna and the radius, the lower arm bones. There are only two fragments that could be identified as coming from the right ulna, but one is a distal fragment and one is a proximal fragment so they could still be from one individual. However there is one other proximal fragment and it is dark brown in color. Moreover, there are 48 possible human ulna fragments. This would indicate a good probability that there is at least more than one individual involved. In addition, there are three small ulna fragments that were either juvenile or animal. From the total evidence it would seem that they were animal.

Table 5: Radius Fragments

Fragments	Position	Color	Age
1	?	T	A
1	?	B	A
8 (small-animal or juvenile)	?	B,Br,T	
1	L	T	A

Again with only one left radius that could be clearly identified, the indications here necessitate no more than one adult. The eight small fragments that are burnt may be juvenile, but are probably animal.

Table 6: Scapula Fragments

Fragments	End	Position	Color	Age
1	P	R	T	A
1 (coracoid process)		L	Br	A
1 (superior border)		L	Br	A
1	?	R	B	A
1 (glenoid fossa)	?	R	T	A
5	?	?	T	A
1	?	?	B	A

Fragments of the scapula or shoulder blade are good indicators. This evidence indicates at least two individuals with a right fragment tan in color and another right fragment black in color; both fragments do not seem to come from the same individual due to the relative size in diameter of the two fragments. This is reasonable evidence for at least two individuals, both adult.

Table 7: Femur Fragments

Fragments	Position	Color	Age
1 (head)	?	Br	A
5	?	Br	A
1	?	T	A
1 (head) female?	?	Br	A
5 (head)	?	T	A
5 (head)	?	B	A
1 (shaft) robust-male? ?		B	A

Nothing was found regarding the femur, the upper leg bone, that could indicate right or left With three colors present and with slight indicators for one male and one female due to robust and gracial characteristics of the bone fragments, the evidence seems to indicate at least two individuals. The blackening due to burning in the center of the mass of the body relative to the extremities would also be expected. However in at least one individual the head was also well-burned.

Only one right patella or knee cap fragment was recovered.

Table 8: Fibula and Tibia Fragments

Fibula Fragments	End	Position	Color	Age
10	?	?	T	A
1	?	R	T	A
1	tip	?	T	A
Tibia Fragments				
1	P	?	T	A
1	P (small-? female?)		T	A

Fragments of the lower leg bones, the fibula and tibia, were recognizable. There is one indicator for a possible female, but overall, not more than one individual could be counted.

The data on fingers and toes (nos. 4, 5, 6, 194, 243 and 251) do not necessarily indicate more than one individual, but the total count of 10 fragments could represent the possibility of at least two individuals. Fragment no. 251 may be a metacarpal with the epiphysis exposed (cap missing) which would indicate an approximate age of 15 years at time of death.

Interpretations

Number of Individuals

There appears to be evidence for at least two or three individuals. The two or three median mandible (jaw) fragments support this conclusion. Also there were two thoracic vertebrae fragments that definitely did not come from the same person. With the extreme fragmentation of the bones, however, it is impossible to know how many individuals were involved beyond the minimum of two.

Sex

The sex indicators are weak. The robusticity of the one femur fragment might indicate male as would the sternum fragment (no. 183). The measurement on one fragmented femur head was difficult, but could indicate female. The fragment from the occipital (back of the head) was the right area of the bone but did not show any protuberance and therefore could be female. An os coxae (hip) fragment also had female characteristics. All data considered could allow at least one male and one female. It must be noted here that no single characteristic is absolute proof. All females have male characteristics and vice versa, but as the indicators are counted a pattern seems to develop.

Age at time of death

Again the evidence for age at time of death is weak. The thin skull fragments indicate age and the closed sutures, where visible on skull fragments, likewise indicate age. One fragment from the occipital area (the back of the head) had sutures that were closed indicating an age of around 40+ years at time of death. There are two pieces of evidence indicating a young age. No. 216 is a very small fragment of a long bone, possibly near the proximal end, with the cap missing, therefore the epiphysis is open. If this is a humerus then the age at time of death would be around 20 years. If the fragment is a fibula, then the age at time of death would be 16-18 years. No. 251 is a possible finger bone, probably a metacarpus with the epiphysis exposed. If this is so, then the age at time of death would be approximately 15 years.

Evidence for the presence of animals

It can be said with certainty that nos. 24, 186, 244 and 250 are probably all teeth from ovis-capra (sheep-goat). With good probability some skull fragments (nos. 9, 10, 11, 12, 13, 14, 141, 178 and 190) are animals, probably *ovis-capra*, or possibly, as in the case of no. 178, a sub-adult human. Their curvature in relation to the wall thickness would seem to discourage their identification as human. The largest sheep still has a smaller skull than the smallest child. Two mandible fragments (nos. 23 and 189) are also probably *ovis-capra*. No real attempt was made to consider how many animals, but no more than one is a possibility. While none of the above mentioned bone fragments showed any sign of burning, all of the fragments were from an extremity, i.e. the head and might have been away from the center of the fire (see below).

Evidence for the presence of small children

Of the 93 skull and mandible fragments, there were 8 pieces of very small parietal (side of the head) fragments that were quite thin. Their thinness could represent old age, or possibly juvenility. However, all sutures observable were adult. There were no "lacy", open sutures such as would be seen with a small child. As previously mentioned, there was one fragment (no. 216) of a long bone probably from the humerus with what appears to be evidence for an open epiphysis. If this is a diaphysis (shaft) fragment of the humerus, then the age at time of death would be around 20 years of age. If it is from the fibula, then the age at time of death would be 16-18 years.

A caution must also be noted here. Where animals such as *ovis-capra* are butchered for food, they are almost always young enough so that the epiphysis is not closed on most of the long bones and many such bones are found with the caps separated from the shaft. Unfortunately, this collection is in a condition of extreme fragmentation.

Among the ulna-radius collection there was a small, strongly curved fragment that did not look human. There were also two apparent ulna fragments that were small, but the accumulated evidence would seem to be animal. In addition there were 8 well-burned fragments that had very small diameters. They were classified as radius under Table 5, but it would also be tempting to designate them very short segments of rib. Without any additional supporting evidence, these were also considered animal.

In the tibia-fibula collection there is only one fragment out of 14 that has a small diameter. It is thus possible that bones from pre-adolescents are present, but the evidence is by no means clear.

Method of burning

To be noted is the tendency for the bones of the upper trunk and head to show heavier signs of burning than the bones from the rest of the body, especially the extremities. This would indicate a relatively small fire, incapable of consuming the whole body equally.

Summary

It would seem from the evidence of the 1,127 very small, fragmented and burned bone pieces that at least two individuals and possibly one animal were represented. Although any detailed conclusions drawn from such fragmentary evidence are somewhat speculative, these pieces may represent the partial remains of an older woman over 40 years of age, and the remains of a young man in his late teens, both possible Indo-Europeans (from median points of their rather projecting chins). At least one sheep or goat, or alternatively one juvenile, may have also been involved.

Table 9: Laboratory Bone Analysis

No.		Description	Type	Position	End	Color	Age	Preservation
1	1	Humerus	H	L	D	T	A	F
2	1	Scapula	H	R	P	T	A	F
3	1	Ulna	H	R	D	T	A	F
4	1	Phalange, 1st metatarsal	H	L	P	T	A	C
5	1	2nd or 4th metacarpal	H		D	B	J?	F
6	1	4th Phalange metatarsal	H	L	P	T	J?	F
7	1	Long bone	H			T		F
8	1	Long bone	H			T		F

9	1	Skull	A		T	A	F
10	1	Skull	A		T	A	F
11	1	Skull	A		T	A	F
12	1	Skull	A		T	A	F
13	1	Skull	A		T	J?	F
14	1	Skull	A		T	J?	F
15	1	Mandible—median point	H		T	A??	F
16	1	Mandible—median point	H		T	A??	F
17	1	Mandible	H		T	A??	F
18	1	Mandible—1st molar cavity	H		T	A??	F
19	1	Unidentified	H		T		F
20	1	Unidentified	H		T		F
21	1	Unidentified	H		T		F
22	1	Bird bone	A		T		F
23	1	Mandible (*ovis-capra*?)	A		T		F
24	1	Tooth	A		T		F
25-50	25	Long bones—thick wall	H		T	A	F
51-52	2	Humeri	H		T	A	F
53-83	31	Ulnae—radius?	H		T	A	F
84-96	13	Unidentified			T	A	F
97-100	4	Skulls (*ovis-capra*?)	A?		T		F
101-120	20	Long bones—thin wall	A?			J?	F
121	1	Skull	A?		T		F
122	1	Unidentified	A?		T		F
123	1	Femur head	H		Br	A	F
124	1	Scapula—coracoid	H	L	Br	A	F
125	1	Scapula—superior border?	H	L	Br	A	F
126-128	3	Innominates	H		Br	A	F
129-132	4	Femora	H		Br	A	F
133	1	Petella	H	R	Br	A	F
134	1	Skull—temporal	H		Br	A	F
135-136	2	Skulls	H		Br	A	F
137	1	Skull with sutures—coronal?	H		Br	A	F
138-140	3	Long bones—humerus?	H		Br	A	F
141	1	Skull	A		Br	A	F
142	1	Mandibular cavity—left	H		B	A	F
143	1	2nd Thoracic vertebra—lipping	H		T	A	F
144	1	Parietal skull or coronal suture	H	R	B	A	F
145	1	Parietal skull or temporal sphenoidal suture	H	L	B	A	F
146	3	Parietal fragments	H		B	A	F
147	3	Parietal or coronal suture fragments	H		B	A	F
148	8	Parietal fragments (3 very thin)	H		B	A	F
149	1	Parietal—mastoid	H	L	B	A	F

Table 9: Laboratory Bone Analysis

No.	Description	Type	Position	End	Color	Age	Preservation
150	4 Skulls—frontal?	H			B	A	F
151	2 Skulls	H			Br	A	F
152	7 Skulls—parietal?	H			Bl	A	F
153	18 Long bones	H			Gr	A	F
154	1 Femur	H			T	A	F
155	1 Ulna—deformed?	A?	L		T	A	F
156	4 Unidentifieds	A?			T	J?	F
157	4 Long bones	H			T	A	F
158	1 Bird or juvenile	A?			W	J?	F
159	1 Femur	H			W	A	F
160	7 Fibulae	H			T	A	F
161	7 Ulnae	H			T	A	F
162	1 Radius	H			T	A	F
163	2 Humera	H			T	A	F
164	2 Ulnae—small	A?			T	J?	F
165	1 Radius	H			B	A	F
166	1 Radius—small	A?			B	J?	F
167	5 Radii—small	A?			Br	J?	F
168	3 Radii—small	A?			T	J?	F
169	1 Rib	H			B	A	F
170	9 Ribs	H			Br	A	F
171	1 Rib	A			T	A	F
172	1 Scapula	H	L		B	A	F
173	2 Tooth roots—incisor and canine? green tinge on canine	H				A	F
174	6 Fibers (weed stalks)						
175	3 Potsherds						
176	5 Rocks						
177	2 Skulls	H			T	A	F
178	1 Skull	A?			W	J?	F
179	1 Long bone	A?				J?	F
180	2 Unidentifieds	H			T		F
181	1 Long bone—femur?	H			Br	A	F
182	1 Femur head (ca. 25% extant)— not involved with the fovea; smaller than usual male size— possibly female	H			B	A	F
183	1 Manubrium (sternum); robust— possibly male	H			T		F
184	1 Os coxae of the superior ramus of the pubis plus part of the acetabular fossa; smaller than adult male—probably female	H			T	A	F

No.	Description						
185	1 Spinous process of 7th cervical vertebra	H			T	A	F
186	1 Tooth—probably *ovis-capra*	A			T		F
187	11 Skulls	H			T	A	F
188	1 Skull—24×13 mm.; probably occipital area with suture completely closed; i.e., older than 42 years; thin wall possibly female	H			T	A	F
189	3 Mandibles—*ovis-capra*	A			T	A	F
190	13 Skulls	A			T	A	F
191	3 Rocks						
192	2 Vertebrae	H			T		F
193	1 Tooth root	H			W	A	F
194	2 Metacarpals and 3 phalanges—possibly from the left hand	H			T	A	F
195	6 Unidentifieds						F
196	3 Ribs	A?					F
197	4 Long bones—small with thick walls	H			T	A	F
198	1 Rib	A?			T		F
199	2 Unidentifieds—thin walls	H			T		F
200	1 Fibula	H	R		T	A	F
201	55 Thick spongy pieces—probably *os coxae*	H			T	A	F
202	1 Maxilla—parts of 3 tooth cavities	H	R		T	A	F
203	1 Scapula—glenoid fossa	H	R		T	A	F
204	1 Ulna—near proximal end	H	R		T	A	F
205	3 Ilia	H			T	A	F
206	10 Skulls with closed sutures	H			T	A	F
207	16 Skulls	H			Bl	A	F
208	14 Skulls	H			W	A	F
209	3 Skulls	H			Br	A	F
210	5 Scapulae	H			T	A	F
211	1 Skull?	H			B	A	F
212	4 Vertebrae	H			T	A	F
213	1 Scapula	H			T		F
214	1 Fibula	H		D	T	A	F
215	1 Ulna	H		P	Br	A	F
216	1 Long bone (with cap off?); epiphysis open? (diaphysis shaft); if humerus = 20 years; if fibula = 16-18 years	H		P?	Br		F
217	1 Tibia	H		P	T	A	F
218	1 Calcaneus	H			T	A	F
219	1 Rib	H		D	T	A	F
220	1 Rib	H			T	A	F
221	1 Vertebra—thoracic; no lipping—young adult?	H			T	A	F

Table 9: Laboratory Bone Analysis

No.	Description	Type	Position	End	Color	Age	Preservation
222	5 Femur heads	H			T	A	F
223	3 Os coxae—acetabular area	H			Bl	A	F
224	9 Unidentifieds	H			T		F
225	1 Tibia—near proximal end; small —female?	H			T	A	F
226	1 Iliac crest; large, heavy—male?	H	L		B	A	F
227	1 Humerus	H		D	B	A	F
228	1 Scapula	H			B	A	F
229	1 Rib	H			B	A	F
230	1 Humerus—near proximal end	H			B	A	F
231	1 Rib	H			B	A	F
232	2 Long bones	H			B	A	F
233	5 Femur heads	H			B	A	F
234	1 Skull	H			Br	A	F
235	1 Vertebra	H			Br	A	F
236	21 Unidentifieds—possibly os coxae	H			B	A	F
237	1 Femur shaft; very robust—male?	H			B	A	F
238	67 Long bones—thick wall	H			B	A	F
239	2 Ulna shafts; robust—male?	H			B	A	F
240	119 Long bones—mostly light wall	H			T	A	F
241	10 Long bones—heavy wall	H			Br	A	F
242	1 Rib	H			T	A	F
243	1 Phalange	H			T	A	F
244	2 Teeth—very long	A				A	F
245	4 Ulnae?	H			T	A	F
246	1 Os coxae—acetabular area	H			T	A	F
247	1 Unidentified	A?					
248	270 Long bones—thin wall	H			T		F
249	4 Skulls—very small	H			T	A	F
250	2 Teeth	A			T		F
251	1 Metacarpus?—with epiphysial cap off? if so age = 15 years; medial clavicle? if so age = 6-adult	H			T	A?	F
252	76 Long bones	H			B	A	F
253	1 Vertebra	H			B	A	F
254	1 Skull	H			B	A	F
255	102 Long bones—mostly thick wall	H			T	A	F
256	1 Humerus	H			T	A	F
257	5 Ribs	H			T	A	F
258	1 Radius	H	L		T	A	F
259	3 Ulnae	H			T	A	F
260	1 Tooth root	H			W	A	F

261	3 Fibulae	H		T	A	F
262	1 Rib	H		T	A	F
263	1 Rock					
264	1 Long bone	H		T	A	F

BIBLIOGRAPHY

Hankey, V.
1974   A Late Bronze Age Temple at Amman: I. The Aegean Pottery. *Levant* 6, 131-159.

Herr, L. G.
1976   The Amman Airport Excavations. *Annual of the Department of Antiquities of Jordan* 21, 109-111.

Chapter 5
Non-Ceramic Artifacts

LARRY G. HERR

By far the majority of non-ceramic artifacts found at the Amman Airport in 1976 were stone vessels. These will thus be described first followed by a brief catalogue of the other, miscellaneous objects.

Stone Vessels

Fragments of stone vessels were relatively frequent near and within the rocks of the pyre. Apparently, most of the stone vessels found in the 1966 excavation were also found outside the structure in the neighborhood of the pyre (Hankey 1974: 177).

Since the 1976 corpus of stone vessels is rather limited and because it serves only to augment Hankey's publication (1974) of the 1955 and 1966 finds the 1976 catalogue is presented as a continuation of that catalogue. The numbers of the pieces begin with the letter "S" to conform with Hankey's system, but the numbers begin with 301 since it is possible that the remaining 220-230 pieces excavated during 1955 and 1966 and left unpublished by Hankey (1974: 161) will, in the future, be published completely.

All the stone vessels of the catalogue were examined by geologist Frank Koucky of the College of Wooster who gave the petrological designations listed in the catalogue. For those comparing this study with Hankey's it is probable that Hankey's "calcite" is Koucky's "travertine" and that Hankey's "coarse-grained basalt" is Koucky's "gabbro" and "diorite."

Few of our pieces can be securely dated. S 329 would appear to be the only piece probably dated to a period prior to the Late Bronze Age. Its flat base is similar to jars (Hankey 1974: 169:S 2) made during the Predynastic or Protodynastic periods in Egypt and imported into Syro/Palestine at some later date (Hankey 1974: 166).

S 332, probably a jug stand, was most likely made in Egypt during the 18th Dynasty, as was S 323, a small tazza. The rest of the pieces, especially the platters, mortars and bowls made of magmatic rock cannot be meaningfully dated.

The range of stone vessel types found in 1976 was much more limited than that from the earlier excavations. However, out of 62 published objects from 1955 and 1966 only five, or 8%, were platters or mortars made of magmatic stone (basalt, gabbro or diorite [Hankey 1974: 175]) whereas in 1976 19 out of 32, or 59%, were platters, mortars or bowls made from magmatic stone. It is thus interesting to note that, in 1966, when the excavations cleared only a small part of the structured rock pile and, for the most part, stayed away from that region, 92% were stone vessels other than magmatic platters, mortars and bowls, while the 1976 excavation of the complete pyre found only 41% of its stone vessels to be other than magmatic platters, mortars and bowls. It is, however, possible that most of the unpublished stone vessels from 1966 (Hankey 1974: 161) were made of magmatic stone. As noted above in the conclusions to the stratigraphic discussion, it is possible that the proximity of these vessels to the pyre and the fact that many of them showed signs of heavy burning (S 330 and many of those found in 1955 and 1966) might suggest that the stone vessels were used in some way in connection with the ceremony of cremation. Heating would cause them to crack and thus they would be found in relatively high numbers within the pyre debris itself. Interestingly enough, however, no vessels were completely reconstructable showing that the pyre was kept relatively clean of the broken pieces, or, if Hennessy is correct in proposing two phases of use for the structure, the pyre could be associated with the second phase; the stone vessels would then probably have been simply part of the rock debris from which the pyre was constructed, the source of which would have been an occupational zone, probably the structure itself.

In the catalogue which follows (and the Miscellaneous Artifacts catalogue below) the catalogue number appears first. It is followed by the usual designations for Area, Square and Locus with the original object number given in parentheses.

Catalogue of Stone Vessels

S 301. A.2:2(7); two rim fragments of a platter or mortar; diorite; diameter: .20 m; thickness at rim: .009 m; color: 7.5YRN4/ dark gray; figs. 23, 24.

S 302. A.2:1(8); rim fragment of a platter or bowl; diorite; diameter: ?; thickness at rim: .008 m; color: 7.5YRN5/ gray.

S 303. A.2:1(11); body fragment of a platter or mortar; diorite; length: .05 m; width: .03 m; thickness: .015 m; color: 7.5YRN5/ gray.

S 304. A.2:1(18); rim fragment of a platter or mortar; diorite; diameter: .24 m; thickness at rim: .011 m; color: 7.5YRN4/ dark gray; figs. 23, 24.

S 305. A.2:1(21); two rim fragments of a palette or small bowl; very badly preserved; diorite; diameter: ?; color: 10YR5/1 gray; figs. 23, 24.

S 306. A.1:6(31); body fragment of a bowl; very poorly preserved; diorite; greatest thickness: .015 m; color: 7.5YRN4/ dark gray.

S 307. A.4:1(35); rim and base fragment of a bowl; diorite; diameter: .105 m; thickness at base: .019 m; color: 7.5YRN5/ gray; figs. 23, 24.

S 308. A.4:1(38); rim fragment of a bowl; diorite; diameter: .185 m; color: 7.5YRN5/ gray; figs. 23, 24.

S 309. A.4:2(40); four rim, base and body fragments of a platter or mortar; diorite with sulphide minerals; diameter: .235 m; color: 7.5YRN5/ gray and 7.5YR6/8 reddish yellow; figs. 23, 24.

S 310. A.2:3(58); rim and base fragment of a bowl; diorite with sulphide minerals; diameter: .175 m; thickness at center of base: .032 m; color: 7.5YRN4/ dark gray; figs. 23, 24.

S 311. A.2:1(19); rim fragment of a platter or mortar; gabbro; diameter: .29 m; thickness of rim: .017 m; color: 7.5YRN5/ gray.

S 312. A.4:1(36); grinder; gabbro; diameters: .044 and .033 m; color: 10YR5/1 gray.

S 313. A.4:4(52); ring base fragment of a squared platter or mortar; probable gabbro; no diameter; thickness of vessel wall: .022 m; color: 7.5YRN4/ dark gray; figs. 23, 24.

S 314. A.4:4(53); rim fragment of a bowl; probable gabbro; diameter: .14 m; thickness of rim: .010 m; thickness of body: .027 m; color: 2.5Y5/0 gray.

S 315. A.4:4(59); one rim and one base fragment of a platter or mortar; interior is much smoother than exterior; gabbro; diameter: .29 m; thickness at center of base: .011 m; color: 7.5YRN4/ dark gray; figs. 23, 24.

S 316. A.4:4(60); body fragment of an undistinguishable form; gabbro; thickness: .015 m; color: 7.5YRN4/ gray.

S 317. A.4:4(61); rim fragment of a platter or mortar; gabbro; diameter: .24 m; thickness: .016 m; color: 7.5YRN5/ gray; figs. 23, 24.

S 318. C.1:1(2); rim fragment possibly of a jug or cup; travertine; diameter: ?; thickness: .004 m; color: 10YR8/2 white.

S 319. A.4:1(14); body fragment of an undistinguishable form; travertine; length: .037 m; width: .014 m; thickness: .005 m; color: 10YR8/2 white.

S 320. A.4:7(22); two handle fragments, of an undistinguishable form; travertine; diameter: .018 m; color: 10YR8/2 white.

S 321. A.4:4(29); body fragment of a possible bowl or large jug (compare Hankey 1974: S 15 and 17, the former is possibly travertine); travertine; thickness: .013-.019 m; color: 10YR8/3 very pale brown.

S 322. A.4:4(51); body fragment of an undistinguishable form; probably travertine; blackened on the interior; length: .065 m; width: .028 m; thickness: .013 m; color: 10YR8/3 very pale brown.

S 323. A.4:5(65); rim fragment of a tazza; probable travertine; diameter: ?; thickness: .005 m; color: 7.5YR7/2 pinkish gray; compare with Hankey 1974: S 41 and S 42; though listed as "calcite" they could be our "travertine."

S 324. A.3:1(12); rim fragment of a bowl; basalt; diameter: .145 m; thickness of rim: .012 m; color: 7.5YRN5/ gray.

S 325. A.4:1(13); body fragment of an undistinguishable form; black limestone (the blackness originated from organic debris in the parent material); length: .031 m; width: .025 m; thickness: .008 m; color: 7.5YRN2/ black.

S 326. A.4:4(63); body fragment of a possible jar or jug (compare Hankey 1974: S 15-18); black limestone; thickness: .011 m; color: 7.5YR2/0 black; figs. 23, 24.

S 327. A.4:4(62); rim and base fragment of a platter; dark limestone; diameter: .185 m; thickness: .025 m; color: 7.5YRN4/ dark gray; figs. 23, 24.

S 328. A.4:4(64); rim and base fragment of a tripod-footed bowl or palette; gray limestone; no diameter, most likely triangular; thickness: .023 m; color: 10YR5/1 gray.

S 329. A.2:3(46); base fragment of a large vessel; limestone; solution marks on interior were due to an acidic liquid (or even hot water) which etched away the work marks (no such solution marks were on the exterior); diameter: .16 m; thickness at top: .015 m; color: 5YR8/1 white; figs. 23, 24; possibly an Egyptian Predynastic form (compare Hankey 1974: 52).

S 330. A.4:2=3(47); body fragment of an undistinguishable form; probably limestone; very charred on one side; length: .052 m; width: .048 m; thickness: .022 m; color: 5Y6/1 gray.

S 331. A.2:3(28); body fragment of an uncertain form, possibly a jar; fine grained marble, almost translucent; thickness: .011 .018 m; color: light green.

S 332. Area A surface (43); base fragment possibly of a small carinated jar but more likely of a jug stand; serpentine; diameter at base: .052 m.; color: 5Y4/2 olive gray; photo: 10; compare with Hankey 1974: S 37 (jar) and S 7 (jug stand), the latter is also made of serpentine.

Miscellaneous Artifacts

Very few objects beside the stone vessels were found in 1976. There were only seven items in metal, one bead, a ceramic disk and a stone spindle whorl. Five of the metal items are so fragmentary and indistinguishable that they cannot be catalogued and one more is a modern washer. The remaining items are catalogued below. The catalogue numbers are preceded by the letter "O" to separate them from the stone objects above; however, the numbers are consecutive.

O 333. A.4:2(54); bronze arrowhead; length: .106 m.; blade form: lanceolate (Cross and Milik 1956: 17); blade length: .076 m.; width of blade: .017 m.; thickness of blade at rib: .003 m.; there seems to be at least a rudimentary stem; stem length: .008 m.; there is no cut; the rib is low and rounded but only appears on one side; tang form: rhomboidal (Cross and Milik: 18); tang length: .022 m.; there is no thickening at the blade point; based on the typology worked out by Cross and Milik this arrowhead fits very well the LB IIB date given to the pottery; the photograph pictures it in its uncleaned state; figs. 23, 24.

O 334. A.2:1(34); carved, fluted bead, probably made of lapis (very fine-grained); diameters: .008 and .006 m.; color: light blue; figs. 23, 24.

O 335. A.1:7(44); ceramic disk; edges were worn by use into a patina, though its original purpose is unknown; diameter: .044 m.; thickness: .013 m.; color: 10YR7/4 very pale brown; figs. 23, 24.

O 336. A.4:4(57); spindle whorl; very soft gray limestone; diameter: .051 m.; thickness: .007 m.; color: 7.5YR7/2 pinkish gray; figs. 23, 24.

Fig. 23. Photographs of the non-ceramic artifacts.

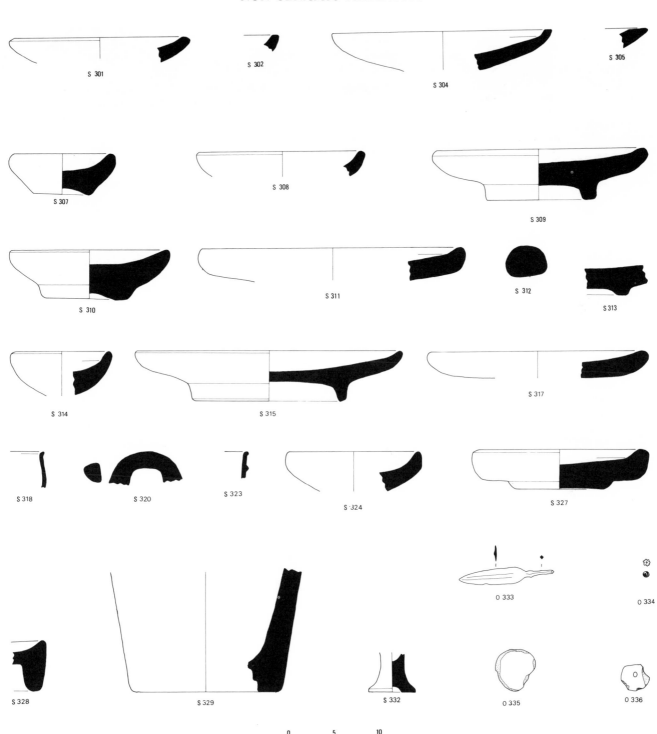

Fig. 24. Drawings of the non-ceramic artifacts.

BIBLIOGRAPHY

Cross, F. M. and Milik, J. T.
  1956   A Typological Study of the El Khadr Javelin and
           Arrowheads. *Annual of the Department of Antiq-
           uities of Jordan* 3: 15-23.
Hankey, V.
  1974   A Late Bronze Age Temple at Amman: II. Vases
           and Objects Made of Stone. *Levant* 6: 160-178.

Tubb, J. N.
  1980   A Bronze Arrowhead with Engraved Mark from
           Gezer in the British Museum Collection. *Palestine
           Exploration Quarterly* 112: 2-9.

Chapter 6
The Flints

ROBERT MILLER

The flints excavated in the 1976 Amman Airport excavation were largely waste flakes from the process of tool manufacture and maintenance rather than tools. Most of these flints were probably in secondary rather than primary context, to judge from the heavily altered surface condition.

Many flints are covered with a light patina and calcium carbonate deposits which could have developed during sub-soil weathering. Exposure to surface weathering conditions is indicated on a number of pieces (e.g. nos. 4 and 7), where the flint surface is covered with wind gloss and a well-developed dark brown patina such as that found on the rocks of the *hamada* flint desert, suggesting a relatively long interval, perhaps on the order of one or more millennia, between the flintknapping and the eventual burial of the flints.

Few of the flake edges are in fresh condition. They are largely chipped and sometimes heavily battered in more than one episode, as the retouch scars along the edges are covered with patinas at different stages of development ranging from the dark brown *hamada* color to very fresh chipping. Although this edge damage can approximate the characteristics of relatively regular continuous chipping, sometimes taken as evidence of "utilization" or even deliberate tool shaping, microscopic examination of flakes treated with hydrochloric acid and sodium hydroxide (to clean organic and inorganic residues from the surface), and using high magnifications and techniques developed by Keeley (1977, 1980), failed to show any trace of use-polished surfaces. It seems more likely that, although these flakes are by-products of human tool-making, they were not themselves used as tools. The range of forms taken by the secondary edge flaking is well within the range of forms produced by environmental disturbance during activities such as trampling, ploughing, construction or even recent archaeological excavation. Even though an atypical endscraper (no. 10), a notch (no. 8) and a denticulate (no. 22) could be isolated on typological grounds, these are most similar to pseudo-tools described in analogous disturbed contexts by Warren (1905, 1914), Pei (1936) and Bordes (1961: 45-46).

However even though the flakes from the 1976 Amman Airport excavations cannot be said to be intentionally retouched or definitely used, some tentative conclusions can be drawn from the chronological range of the flintworking styles represented, which are probably to be dated sometime between the late 6th millennium B.C. and the late 3rd millennium B.C., without ruling out the possibility of later episodes of flint working also being present.

Most flints from this group are waste flakes and flake fragments which could have been produced from local flint pebbles without difficulty at any period.

Some flakes show evidence of more specialized and skillful techniques of production which do have possible chronological significance. Three thinning flakes with faceted butts or evidence of centripetal flaking were found (nos. 1, 16 and 10). Waste flakes with these characteristics are common by-products associated with the manufacture and re-sharpening of bifacial tools such as hoes, axes and foliate projectile points.

Centripetal flaking, together with discoidal cores and even a revival of the Levallois technique, is characteristic of late Neolithic flint industries (Cauvin 1968) and continued in use down to the end of the 3rd millennium B.C. in some instances

(Miller 1978, 1980). A similar time range is probable for the small blade and blade butts at the site (nos. 22, 20, 19). The relatively thick butts, well-developed bulbs of percussion and minimal striking platform preparation on these would argue against a date any earlier than the late Neolithic.[1]

While the earliest possible date for the flints seems to be sometime in the late 6th millennium B.C., what is the possible range of flintworking in the Near East generally and on Syro-Palestinian sites specifically with which these flints could be associated? Here the relative thoroughness with which the flints were recovered at the Amman Airport excavations in 1976 is one problem for comparative study; the lack until recently of comparable complete collections of tools, waste flakes and evidence of flaking technology is another; the latter inhibits the drawing of parallels to a few general observations.

Flintworking, on a casual basis, continued until very recently in the Near East, largely for strike-a-light and casual cutting edges to be discarded immediately after use. The state of the art of flintworking before the first World War was still flourishing, as described by Woolley and Lawrence (1915: 19-20):

> Today throughout all Syria flint instruments are freely used. The teeth of chaff-cutting instruments are always small pointed flakes of flint properly struck from a core. Oval "scrapers" are used by shepherd boys to shear the sheep, ousting, in many cases, the iron shears to which European commerce gave a brief vogue, and straight heavy knives, often a foot or more in length, are made in any emergency for hacking to pieces a dead animal. Zeyd, Mr. Holland's guide, knapped a flint when he wanted to trim his toe nails, and sometimes a flint razor is still used for shaving the head. In all cases the implement is used upon the one occasion and then thrown away. To date such castaways is difficult . . . Any man at any period may knap and use a flint, especially when there is such a profusion of raw material, and one cannot from the casual product of his industry argue a Stone Age in the exclusive sense of the term.

The significance of Near Eastern flint industries continuing after the introduction of metal tools was raised in passing over a century ago by John Evans (1872). The contemporaneity of stone and metal tools has been widely recognized in the study of late Neolithic and Chalcolithic flaked stone industries and has been lucidly discussed by Cauvin (1968). Later evidence of flintworking has been less studied until recently, due to a joint neglect by prehistorians choosing an arbitrary cut-off point for the discussion of lithic technology with the introduction of metals, pottery or texts and by historic archaeologists unacquainted with the methods of analysis needed for lithic technology.

However the continuation of important and widely distributed evidence of flintworking down to the end of the 3rd millennium B.C. was underlined half a century ago by Neuville (1930) and a number of reports on flintworking from Syro-Palestinian Early Bronze sites have appeared in subsequent excavation reports from Jericho (Crowfoot 1935, 1937), Judaidah (Crowfoot Payne 1960), Beth Shan (Fitzgerald 1934: 129), Hama (Fugman 1958: fig. 103), Megiddo (Garrod 1934: 78), Arad (Schick 1978), Bethel (Swauger 1968) and Lachish (Waechter 1958). Evidence of continuing flintworking traditions on a smaller scale (often only a handful of blades and sickle blade elements per site) is found from the Middle Bronze Age, the Late Bronze Age and the Iron Age at Jericho (Crowfoot 1937), Beth Shan (Fitzgerald 1934: 127), Bethel (Kelso 1968: 84-92, 117), Jemmeh (Petrie 1928: pl. xvi) and Lachish (Waechter 1958: 325-27). But most of this evidence relates only to sickle blades and blade sections. One is left with the impression that, apart from sickle blades or clearly thinned and shaped tool forms such as projectile points, most post-prehistoric flaked stone would tend to get discarded as "unworked" by overworked finds processors who share the common view that flintworking effectively ceased with the Stone Age, and who would discard casually flaked pieces without recognizing their potential for technological reconstruction.[2]

Although the conclusions that can be drawn from the flints excavated in 1976 at the Amman Airport are quite limited, relating mainly to the evidence of extensive secondary disturbance in the areas excavated and the broad chronological and technological horizon into which they fit, the possibility of late Neolithic, Bronze Age and even

---

[1] I would like to thank Mrs. Lorraine Copeland for examining the 1976 Amman Airport flints and suggesting this as the probable earliest limit for dating the flints.

[2] The list of flintworking reports is not meant to be exhaustive and fuller documentation can be found in the bibliography of Schick (1978). At the time of writing I have not been able to consult recent studies on flintworking at Bab edh-Dhra, Tell Hesi and Tel Halif; the report on the Tel Halif industry by a practising flintknapper, Warburton, should be especially valuable.

modern flintworking being represented raises questions which future work on the lithic industries of Jordan may one day, with the aid of more and larger assemblages, be able to resolve. Certainly the potential for the study of the widely distributed and incompletely reported flint industry from late periods could shed much light on the potential for understanding the economic and cultural value of maintaining simple craft traditions in complex urban societies.

BIBLIOGRAPHY

Bordes, F.
1961 *Typologie du paléolithique ancien et moyen.* Bordeaux: Delmas.

Cauvin, J.
1968 *Les outillages néolithiques de Byblos et du littoral libanais. Fouilles de Byblos* IV. Paris: Maisonneuve.

Crowfoot, J.
1935 Notes on the Flint Implements of Jericho, 1935. I. Cananean. *Annals of Archaeology and Anthropology, Liverpool* 22: 174-76.

1937 Notes on the Flint Implements of Jericho, 1936. *Annals of Archaeology and Anthropology, Liverpool* 24: 35-49.

Evans, J.
1872 Note on the Implements from Bethlehem. *Journal of the Anthropological Institute* 1: 342-44.

Fitzgerald, G. M.
1934 Excavations at Beth Shan in 1933. *Palestine Exploration Fund Quarterly Statement* 66: 123-134.

Fugmann, E.
1958 *Hama II: 1. l'architecture des périodes préhellénistiques.* Copenhagen: National Museum.

Garrod, D. A. E.
1934 Notes on the Flint Implements. Pp. 78-91 in *Notes on the Chalcolithic and Early Bronze Pottery of Megiddo,* ed. R. M. Engberg and G. M. Shipton. Chicago: University of Chicago.

Keeley, L. H.
1977 The Functions of Paleolithic Flint Tools. *Scientific American* 8/5: 108-26.

1980 *Experimental Determination of Stone Tool Uses and Microwear Analysis.* Chicago: Aldine.

Kelso, J. L.
1968 The Excavation of Bethel. *Annual of the American Schools of Oriental Research* 39. Cambridge: American Schools of Oriental Research.

Miller, R.
1978 A Flint-knapper's Workshop at Tell Hadidi, Syria. Paper submitted to Xth International Congress of Anthropological and Ethnological Science, New Delhi.

1980 *Flintworking in the Upper Euphrates Valley, Syria in the Third Millennium* B.C. Unpublished Ph.D. Thesis, Institute of Archaeology, University of London.

Neuville, R.
1930 Notes de préhistoire palestinienne: III. les industries lithiques de l'age du bronze. *Journal of the Palestine Oriental Society* 10: 199-210.

Payne, J. Crowfoot
1960 Flint Implements from Tell el-Judaidah. Pp. 525-539 in *Excavations in the Plain of Antioch I,* ed. R. J. Braidwood and L. S. Braidwood. Chicago: University of Chicago.

Pei, W. C.
1936 Le rôle des phénoménes naturels dans l'éclatement et le façonnement des roches dures utilisées par l'homme préhistorique. *Revue de Géographie Physique et de Géologie Dynamique* 9: fasc. 4: 1-61.

Petrie, W. M. F.
1928 *Gerar.* London: Quaritch.

Schick, T.
1978 Flint Implements, Strata V-I. Pp. 58-63 in *Early Arad,* ed. R. Amiran. Jerusalem: Israel Exploration Society.

Swauger, J. L.
1968 Bethel Flints from Early Canaanite High Place and MB I Temple above it. Pp. 93-95 in *The Excavation of Bethel,* J. L. Kelso.

Waechter, J.
1958 Flint Implements. *Lachish IV: the Bronze Age,* ed. O. Tufnell. London: Oxford University.

Warren, S. H.
1905 On the Origin of Eoliths. *Man.* 1905 No. 103.

1914 The Experimental Investigation of Flint Fracture and its Application to Problems of Human Implements. *Journal of the Royal Anthropological Institute* 44: 412-450.

Woolley, C. L. and Lawrence, T. E.
1936 *The Wilderness of Zin* (1st edition 1915). London: Palestine Fund.

FLINT CATALOGUE

The first number which appears with the discussion of each flint in the catalogue is the serial number of the flints. Provenance is listed by Area (capital letter), Square (Arabic number) and Locus (Arabic number with colon). The phase of excavation to which the locus belonged is given so that easy reference may be had to the stratigraphic discussion. These data are followed by the description of the flint.

1. A.1:5 #10; Phase 5; 4.87 × 4.37 cm; cortical flake, older flake surface and cortex still visible.
2. A.1:7 #24; Phase 6; 4.00 × 3.99 × .67 cm; very fresh flaking bulb fracture from proximal to distal end.
3. A.1:7 #25; Phase 6; 4.28 × 2.25 × .86 cm; core-preparation flake with older patina still visible.
4. A.1:3 #32; Phase 5; 5.41 × 3.64 × 1.27 cm; batter flake, not artificial, batter retouch along edges.
5. A.4:4 #55; Phase 4; 5.42 × 4.23 × 1.12 cm; batter flake, very fresh fracture.
6. A.4:2=3 #48; Phase 3; 3.23 × 1.78 × .44 cm.
7. A.4:2=3 #49; Phase 3; 2.52 × 2.02 × .59 cm.
8. A.4:2=3 #50; Phase 3; 2.82 × 2.09 × .81 cm; pseudo-end-scraper, traces of earlier patina are visible.
9. A.2:3 #45; Phase 4; 3.46 × 4.13 × .79 cm; shatter-fracture from striking against an object.
10. A.4:2=3 #39; Phase 3; 2.47 × 1.80 × .45 cm; batter retouch along edges.
11. A.2:2 #9; Phase 3; 4.73 × 3.01 × .84 cm; battered flake, old patina over most of surface except for more recent batter retouch along edges.
12. A.1:3 #26; Phase 5; 4.14 × 3.77 × 1.01 cm; battered flake.
13. A.1:3 #27; Phase 5; 2.67 × 2.54 × .84 cm; battered flake.
14. A.1:5 #16; Phase 5; 4.18 × 2.13 × .81 cm; battered flake; cortex showing.
15. A.1:5 #15; Phase 5; 4.37 × 3.73 × .81 cm; cortex flake, very fresh appearance but limestone encrustation on surface.
16. A.1:3 #17; Phase 5; 1.60 × .85 × .23 cm; aborted bladelet, fresh appearance.
17. A.1:3 #23; Phase 5; 4.13 × 1.75 × .97 cm; battered flake, not artificial, three patinas visible.
18. C.1:1 #30; Phase 1; 3.44 × .36 cm.
19. A.1:3 #33; Phase 5; 1.91 × 1.73 × .63 cm; small blade butt, cortex remaining on one side.
20. A.1:3 #20; Phase 5; 4.15 × 2.36 × .83 cm; blade butt, batter retouch with younger patina than blade.
21. A.4:4 #56; Phase 4; 4.20 × 5.49 × .64 cm; flake with older patina scarred by bulb of percussion.
22. A.3:1 #1; Phase 1; 3.50 × 1.60 cm; small concave, denticulate blade, older patina on one edge.

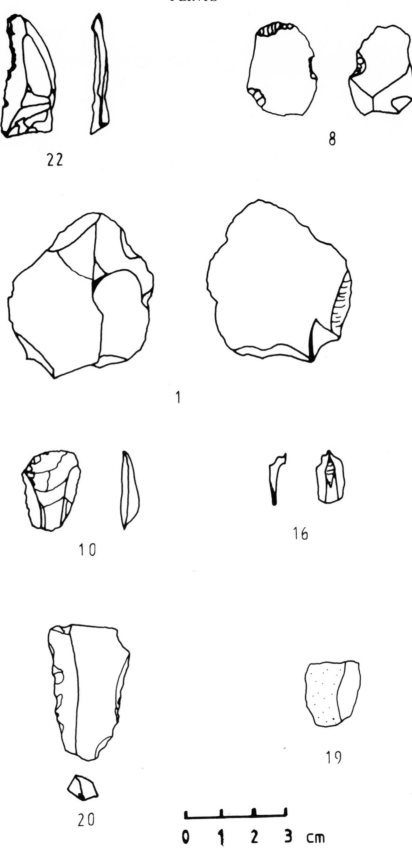

Fig. 25. Selected flints.

Chapter 7

List of Loci

LARRY G. HERR

The list of loci is organized in numerical order of loci by Square and Area. The locus numbers themselves are made up of the Area designation (upper case letter), the Square number (Arabic numeral) and the locus number (Arabic numeral preceded by a colon). Immediately following the locus number is the stratigraphic phase to which the locus belongs. Beneath the phase number are references to illustrations (sections, plans, and photos) in the publication and the page where the locus is discussed in the text.

The locus descriptions themselves are organized similarly for each locus. First is a general interpretive description followed by a more detailed description including color (using the Munsell soil color designations), texture, consistence, inclusions, slope, and location. Stratigraphic information is next; the description ends with a detailed list of levels.

The material culture finds are listed beneath the description. The pottery pails for each locus appear by number (each Square had its own sequence) in a vertical column with the registered sherd numbers included alongside. All other artifacts are listed by Artifact Number with a brief description of each artifact.

A.1:1	Phase 1	Topsoil. 7.5YR7/6 (reddish-yellow); silt (loess); some gravel at bottom; no
	Fig. 10	slope except where it sloped over the lines of an excavated pit in NE quad-
	P. 17	rant. Over: A.1:2, A.1:4; equals: A.2:1; seals against: A.1:8 (previously excavated structure). Levels: at south balk: top: 99.73, bottom: 99.70; 2.00 m from south balk: top: 99.80, bottom: 99.70; at north balk: top: 99.70, bottom: 99.57.

Pottery pails: 1 #83-89
                9 #102-106
               16 #223-227

Other Artifacts: #4 worked calcite fragment
                  #37 yellow ochre

A.1:2	Phase 4	Surface contemporary with structure on north exterior. 10YR7/4 (very pale
	Figs. 10, 11,12	brown) silt with coarse sand and small pebbles; no slope; extended north only 2.10 m from Wall A.1:8.
	Pp. 11,12, 13,14,15	Under: A.1:1, A.1:4; over: A.1:5; seals against: A.1:8; cut by: A.1:4?. Levels: at south balk: top: 99.70, bottom: 99.69; 2.00 m from south balk: top: 99.70, bottom: 99.64.

Pottery pail: 2 #10-15

Other Artifacts: Stone disc fragment

A.1:3	Phase 5	Fill in Foundation Trench A.1:9 (for Wall A.1:8). 7.5YR7/6 (reddish yel-
	Fig. 10	low); silt with very few pebbles except near bottom where pebbles and cob-
	Pp. 12,13	bles appeared with a few boulders; some ash lenses; extended north only 1.80 m from Wall A.1:8. Under: A.1:5; over: A.1:7; cut by?: A.1:5 in sector next to Wall A.1:8. Levels: at south balk: top: 99.49, bottom: 99.40; 1.00 m from south balk: top: 99.66, bottom: 99.40.

Pottery pails: 4 #8-9
               11 #144
               12 #192-194
               15 #371-372

Other Artifacts: #17, 20, 23, 26, 27, 32, 33 flint flakes

A.1:4	Phase 3	Post-abandonment debris. 7.5YR6/4 (light brown); silt with cobbles; sloped

Figs. 10, 16 · Pp. 13,15 down to north 3°; began 1.40 m from Wall A.1:8; appears only along west balk. Under: A.1:1; over: A.1:2, A.1:7; cuts?: A.1:2; cut by: excavated pit in NE quadrant; equals: A.2:2. Levels: 1.50 m from south balk: top: 99.74, bottom: 99.68; at north balk: top: 99.57, bottom: 99.47.

Pottery pails: 3 No registered sherds
8 #164-169

Other Artifacts: #3 pierced metal disc (modern)

A.1:5 · Phase 5 · Fig. 10 · Pp. 12,13 Fill in Foundation Trench A.1:9 (for Wall A.1:8). 7.5YR6/6 (reddish yellow); silt with small pebble-sized chips of nari; extended 1.80 m from Wall A.1:8 to north; no slope. Under: A.1:2; over: A.1:3; cuts?: A.1:3. Levels: at south balk: top: 99.69, bottom: 99.49; 1.50 m from south balk: top: 99.72, bottom: 99.60.

Pottery pails: 5 #161-163
7 #188-191

Other Artifacts: #10, 15, 16 flint flakes

A.1:6 · Phase 5 · Fig. 10 · Pp. 12,13 Fill in Foundation Trench A.1:9 (for Wall A.1:8). 7.5YR5/2 (brown); very fine silt with a few pebbles; from .65 m. to 1.40 m north of Wall A.1:8; very patchy; no slope. Under: A.1:5; over: A.1:3. Levels: top: 99.55, bottom: 99.45.

Pottery pail: 6 #141-143

Other Artifacts: #31 diorite bowl fragment

A.1:7 · Phase 6 · Fig. 10 · Pp. 11,12, 13 Virgin Soil. 7.5YR7/6 (reddish yellow); some pottery at very top; tightly packed silt and clay with some pebbles; sloped down to north 3° outside Foundation Trench A.1:9. Under: A.1:3, A.1:4; Cut by: A.1:9; equals: A.2:4. Levels: at south balk: 99.69; at north balk: 99.47.

Pottery pails: 10 #148-152
13 no pottery
14 #368-370

Other Artifacts: #24 flint flake
#44 ceramic disc fragment

A.1:8 · Phase 5-4 · Figs. 6,10 North wall of previously excavated structure. The outside line of the structure's north wall was used as the south balk of A.1; the wall itself was not excavated.

A.1:9 · Phase 5 · Fig. 10 · P. 9 Foundation trench for Wall A.1:8. Shallow pit with irregular, outer line 1.50 m north of Wall A.1:8 at west balk and 2.20 m north of Wall A.1:8 at the east balk; bottom sloped down to the south 5°. Under: A.1:3, over: A.1:7; cuts: A.1:7; dug from: A.1:7. Level: top: 99.68, bottom: 99.40.

A.2:1 · Phase 1 · Fig. 10 · Pp. 14,17 Topsoil. 7.5YR7/6 (reddish yellow); silt (loess) with some pebbles and cobbles; few pockets of modern gravel 7.5YRN/8 (white); sloped down to north 3°. Over: A.2:2, A.2:3; equals: A.1:1, A.3:1, A.4:1. Levels: NW corner: top: 99.34, bottom: 99.23; NE corner: top: 99.21, bottom: 99.18; SW corner: top: 99.63, bottom: 99.50; SE corner: top: 99.28, bottom: 99.15.

Pottery pails: 1 #80-82
2 no registered pottery
3 #1-7
6 #107-122
7 #90-101
8 #127-132
9 #195-214
10 #286-298
11 #299-314
13 #315-327

Other Artifacts: #8 diorite bowl rim
#11 diorite vessel fragment
#18 diorite platter rim
#19 gabbro platter rim
#21 two diorite bowl fragments
#34 blue bead

A.2:2 · Phase 3 · Figs. 10,16 · Pp. 15,16 Post-abandonment debris. 5YR6/6 (reddish yellow); hard-packed silt with many cobbles from Structured Rock Pile A.2:3 beneath; sloped down to north 3°. Under: A.2:1; over: A.2:4; equals: A.1:4, A.3:2; seals against: A.2:3. Levels: SW corner: top: 99.50, bottom: 99.33; SE corner: top: 99.15, bottom: 99.12; NE corner: top: 99.18, bottom: 99.04.

Pottery pails: 4 #68-78
5 #159-160

Other Artifacts: #5 limestone fossil
#6 limestone fossil
#7 diorite handle fragment
#9 flint

A.2:3   Phase 4   Structured rock pile. Mass of cobbles
                    and small boulders, some burnt on
         Figs. 10,11 one side; structured by semi-hewn
                    boulders on the east and in A.4
         Photos 7, (A.4:4); located in NW quadrant;
         10   sloped down to north 2°. Under:
                    A.2:1; over: A.2:4; sealed against by:
         Pp. 13,14 A.2:2; equals: A.4:4. Levels: southern-
                    most structuring boulder: top: 99.38,
                    bottom: 99.12; NW corner: top: 99.22,
                    bottom: 99.09.

                    Pottery pails: 12 #328-332
                                   14 #394-415

                    Other Artifacts: #28 marble vessel
                                        fragment
                                     #45 flint
                                     #46 limestone bowl
                                        fragment
                                     #58 diorite bowl
                                        fragment

A.2:4   Phase 6   Virgin soil. 7.5YR7/6 (reddish yellow);
                    tightly packed silt and clay with some
         Fig. 10   pebbles; sloped down to north 3°.
                    Under: A.2:2, A.2:3; equals: A.1:7,
         P. 11   A.3:3, A.4:7. Levels: NW corner:
                    99.22; NE corner: 99.04; SE corner:
                    99.33; SE corner: 99.12.

A.3:1   Phase 1   Topsoil. 10YR6/4 (light yellowish
                    brown); silt (loess) with pebbles and
         Fig. 10   cobbles; more artifacts in south than
                    north, very few in north; several pieces
         P. 17   of modern glass; sloped down to north
                    3°. Over: A.3:2; equals: A.2:1. Levels:
                    at south balk: top: 99.35, bottom:
                    99.21; at north balk: top: 99.10, bot-
                    tom: 99.08.

                    Pottery pail: 1 #60-67

                    Other Artifacts: #1 flint

A.3:2   Phase 3   Post-abandonment debris. 5YR5/6
                    (yellowish red); friable, packed silt
         Figs. 10,16 (much looser in south) with cobbles
                    and pebbles at bottom; very few arti-
         Pp. 15,16 facts; only a few body sherds found in
                    south, nothing in north; sloped down
                    to north 3° on top, no slope at
                    bottom. Under: A.3:1; over: A.3:3.
                    Levels: at south balk: top: 99.21, bot-
                    tom: 98.90; at north balk: top: 99.08,
                    bottom: 98.90.

                    Pottery pails: 2 #56-59
                                   3 #79
                                   4 #145-147

                    Other Artifacts: #12 basalt rim
                                        fragment

A.3:3   Phase 6   Virgin soil. 7.5YR7/6 (reddish yellow);
                    fine silt and clay with a layer of very
         Fig. 10   small pebble-sized nari chips near bot-
                    tom which may have resulted from
         P. 11   human activity; no artifacts; no slope.
                    Under: A.3:2; equals: A.2:4. Levels: at
                    south balk: 98.90; 2.00 m from south
                    balk: 98.93. Note: a similar layer to
                    the nari chip layer was found in the
                    "Long Trench" below virgin soil de-
                    posits ca. 10 m to the east.

A.4:1   Phase 1   Topsoil. 7.5YR6/6 (reddish yellow);
                    loose silt (loess) with small pebbles
         Fig. 18   and a few cobbles; few flint flakes; no
                    pottery near north balk; sloped down
         Pp. 14,17 to north 3°. Over: A.4:2=3, A.4:4,
                    A.4:6, A.4:7; equals: A.2:1. Levels:
                    NE corner: top: 99.30, bottom: 99.18;
                    NW corner: top: 99.22, bottom: 99.15;
                    SE corner: top: 99.60, bottom: 99.45;
                    SW corner: top: 99.39, bottom: 99.31.

                    Pottery pails: 1 #176-187
                                    2 #123-126
                                    6 #219-222
                                    8 #373-377
                                   10 #228-238

                    Other Artifacts: #13 black limestone
                                        vessel frag-
                                        ment
                                     #14 travertine ves-
                                        sel fragment
                                     #35 diorite bowl
                                        fragment
                                     #36 gabbro grinder
                                     #38 diorite bowl
                                        rim

A.4:2=3 Phase 3   Post-abandonment debris. 5YR5/6
                    (yellowish red); hard-packed silt with
         Figs. 14,16 NS line of random cobbles (formed by
                    edge of previous excavation trench
         Pp. 14,15, A.4:9 on the west); several stones were
         16   burned (heavily charred) on one side;
                    located in NW quadrant; sloped down
                    to north 3°. Under: A.4:1; over: A.4:7;
                    cut by: A.4:9, A.4:10, A.4:11. Levels:
                    at north balk: top: 99.23, bottom:
                    98.99.

                    Pottery pails: 11 #275-285
                                   12 #344-367

                    Other Artifacts: #39 flint flake
                                     #40 diorite platter
                                        (four pieces)
                                     #47 limestone ves-
                                        sel fragment
                                     #48 flint flake
                                     #49 flint flake
                                     #50 flint flake
                                     #54 bronze dagger

A.4:4 Phase 4 Structured rock pile. Line of medium-sized boulders with mass of cobbles and small boulders to the east; many stones had signs of burning on one side; soil: 5YR5/6 (yellowish red); silt firmly packed between stones with some concentrations of sand and fine pebbles; high ash content in southern part of the rock pile, 5YR3/2 (dark reddish brown) to 5YR4/3 (reddish brown); high frequency of pottery and other artifacts; located in NE quadrant; sloped down to north 3°. Under: A.4:1, over: A.4:7; sealed against by: A.4:2=3; equals: A.2:3. Levels: northernmost boulder in line: top: 99.47, bottom: 99.02; second from end boulder at south of line: top: 99.54, bottom: 99.19; cobbles in NE corner: top: 99.24, bottom: 99.03.

Figs. 11, 14,15

Pp. 13,14

Pottery pails: 13 #244-274
               14 #378-387

Other Artifacts: #29 travertine vessel fragment
                 #41 metal pin fragment
                 #42 undistinguishable bronze fragments
                 #51 travertine vessel fragment
                 #52 gabbro vessel base
                 #53 gabbro platter rim
                 #55 flint flake
                 #56 flint flake
                 #57 spindle whorl
                 #59 gabbro platter fragment
                 #60 gabbro vessel fragment
                 #61 gabbro vessel fragment
                 #62 dark limestone vessel fragment
                 #63 black limestone vessel fragment
                 #64 gray limestone vessel fragment

A.4:5 Phase 2 Backfill in probe from previous excavation (1966). 7.5YR6/6 (reddish yellow); very loosely packed silt with pebbles, cobbles and flat boulders; contained modern glass, plastic and aluminum foil; located in north central part of Square. Under: A.4:1; over: A.4:7; filled: A.4:9; cut: A.4:7. Levels: top: 99.30, bottom: 98.85.

Figs. 1, 6,17

Pottery pails: 4 #139-140
               5 #333-334
               9 no registered sherds

A.4:6 Phase 2 Small lens of previous excavation dump. 7.5YR5/6 (strong brown); loose silt with some pebbles and cobbles (some burnt on one side); located in SE quadrant; sloped down to west 2°; few modern glass fragments. Under: A.4:1; over: A.4:7; lensed out before it reached A.4:4. Levels: top: 99.50, bottom: 99.40.

Fig. 18

P. 16

Pottery pail: 3 #153-158

A.4:7 Phase 6 Virgin soil (some pottery at very top). 7.5YR8/6 (reddish yellow); firmly packed clay and silt with pebbles, cobbles and small boulders; some ash pockets on top; no slope. Under: A.4:1, A.4:4, A.4:6; cut by: A.4:9, A.4:10, A.4:11. Levels: SW corner: 99.31; SE corner: 99.31; NW corner: 99.08; NE corner: 99.02.

Fig. 18

P. 11

Pottery pail: 7 #215-218

Other Artifacts: #22 travertine vessel handle

A.4:8 Phase 2 Backfill in probe from previous excavation (1966). Flat, slab-stones from floor of structure found below the soil filling the 1966 excavation probe A.4:9; the stones were originally flaked from the limestone quarry along joint lines in the rock; largest stones measured 40 × 50 × 10 cm; very loose soil similar to A.4:5 above was between the stones; plastic bags and modern rubbish found at bottom; located in north central part of Square. Under: A.4:5; over: bottom of A.4:9; filled: A.4:9. Levels: top: 99.30, bottom: 98.98.

Figs. 1,6

P. 16

A.4:9 Phase 2 Probe from previous excavation (1966). Ca. 1 m (EW) × 2 m (NS) in north central part of Square. Under: A.4:1; over: A.4:7; cuts: A.4:2=3; filled by: A.4:5, A.4:8. Levels: top: 99.30, bottom: 98.98.

Figs. 1,6

P. 16,17, 19

A.4:10 Phase 2 Probe from previous excavation (1966). Ca. 1.50 m (EW) × 1.75 m (NS) in south central part of Square. Under: A.4:1; over: A.4:7; cuts:

Figs. 1,6

P. 16   A.4:2=3. Levels: top: 99.28, bottom: 99.15.

A.4:11   Phase 2   Probe from previous excavation (1966). Ca. 1 m (EW) × 2.50 m (NS) in NW quadrant. Under: A.4:1; over: A.4:7; cuts: A.4:2=3. Levels: top: 99.28, bottom: 98.99.

Figs. 1,6

P. 16

A.4:12   Phase 3   Post-abandonment debris. 7.5YR7/6 (reddish yellow); loosely packed silt between cobbles and small boulders outside of structured rock pile; excavated as part of A.4:4; located along the eastern half of the north balk; no slope. Under: A.4:1; over: A.4:7; seals against: A.4:4. Levels: at NE corner: top: 99.20, bottom: 99.05.

Figs. 14,16

Pp. 15,16

C.1:1   Phase 1   Topsoil. 7.5YR6/6 (reddish yellow); loose silt (loess) with few pebbles; artifacts found in west, none in east; no slope in west but sloped down to east 4° at east end. Over: C.1:2; sealed against: C.1:3. Levels: at west balk: top: 100.81, bottom: 100.70; 4.00 m from west balk: top: 101.26, bottom: 100.99; 8.00 m from west balk: top: 100.96, bottom: 100.85; 11.90 m from west balk: top: 100.90, bottom: 100.79.

P. 17

Pottery pails: 1 #33-55
               3 #170-175
               4 #133-138
               5 no registered sherds

Other Artifacts: #2 travertine rim fragment
                  #30 flint flake

C.1:2   Phase 6/3   Post-abandonment debris and virgin soil. 5YR3/3 (dark reddish brown); very firm silt and clay with few pebbles and cobbles; no artifacts found beyond 4.00 m from the west balk; transition from occupation debris to virgin soil was very difficult to observe. Under: C.1:1. Levels: at west balk: top: 100.70, bottom: 100.56;

4.00 m from west balk: top: 100.99, bottom: 100.75; 11.90 m from the west balk: top: 100.79, bottom: 100.59.

Pottery pail: 2 #10-15

C.1:3   Phase 5/4   East wall of previously excavated structure. The outside line of the structure's east wall was used as the west balk of C.1: the wall itself was not excavated.

Figs. 1,6

D.1:1   Phase 1   Topsoil. 7.5YR6/6 (reddish yellow); loose silt (loess) with a few pebbles; no artifacts; no slope except for sharp slope in south, 10° down to south. Levels: at north balk: top: 101.06, bottom: 100.98; 4.00 m from north balk: top: 101.03, bottom: 100.84; 8.00 m from north balk: top: 100.60, bottom: 100.50.

P. 17

D.1:2   Phase 6   Virgin soil. 5YR3/3 (dark reddish brown); very firm silt and clay with few pebbles and cobbles; no artifacts; no slope until sharp slope of 10° in southernmost 2.00 m. Under: D.1:1; cut by: D.1:5. Levels: at north balk: 100.98; 4.00 m from north balk: 100.84; 8.00 m from north balk: 100.50.

P. 11

D.1:3   Phase 5/4   South wall of previously excavated structure. The outside line of the structure's south wall was used as the north balk of D.1; the wall itself was not excavated.

D.1:4   Phase 1?   Modern trench. Ran EW; .15 m deep and .25 m wide; 4.00 m from north balk. Over: D.1:2; cuts: D.1:1. Levels: top: 101.03, bottom: 100.84.

P. 17

D.1:5   Phase 1?   Modern trench. Ran EW; .95 m wide; 6.00 m from north balk; not excavated to bottom. Cuts: D.1:1, D.1:2. Levels: top: 101.02, bottom of excavation: 100.55.

P. 17